Lecture Notes in Computer Science 12295

Kent Milfeld · Bronis R. de Supinski ·
Lars Koesterke · Jannis Klinkenberg (Eds.)

OpenMP: Portable Multi-Level Parallelism on Modern Systems

16th International Workshop on OpenMP, IWOMP 2020
Austin, TX, USA, September 22–24, 2020
Proceedings

 Springer

Editors
Kent Milfeld (ID)
Texas Advanced Computing Center (TACC)
Austin, TX, USA

Bronis R. de Supinski (ID)
Lawrence Livermore National Laboratory
Livermore, CA, USA

Lars Koesterke (ID)
Texas Advanced Computing Center (TACC)
Austin, TX, USA

Jannis Klinkenberg (ID)
RWTH Aachen University
Aachen, Germany

ISSN 0302-9743   ISSN 1611-3349   (electronic)
Lecture Notes in Computer Science
ISBN 978-3-030-58143-5   ISBN 978-3-030-58144-2   (eBook)
https://doi.org/10.1007/978-3-030-58144-2

LNCS Sublibrary: SL2 – Programming and Software Engineering

This Springer imprint is published by the registered company Springer Nature Switzerland AG
The registered company address is: Gewerbestrasse 11, 6330 Cham, Switzerland

Preface

OpenMP is a widely used application programming interface (API) for high-level parallel programming in Fortran, C, and C++. OpenMP has been supported in most high-performance compilers and by hardware vendors since it was introduced in 1997. Under the guidance of the OpenMP Architecture Review Board (ARB) and the diligent work of the OpenMP Language Committee, the OpenMP specification has evolved up to version 5.0, with version 5.1 soon to be released. It extends parallelism at several levels: offloading in heterogeneous systems; task-based processing across processors; and vectorization in SIMD units. It also goes beyond parallel computing by including and enhancing memory operations, management, and affinity policy; matching directives and functions to computing environments; and processor affinity.

These advances are realized by the major 5.0 features: context selectors and the declare variant construct and metadirectives that use them; the requires directive; memory allocators and support for deep copy of pointer-based data structures; acquire and release semantics; task (memory) affinity; the descriptive loop construct; reverse offloading; affinity display; and first and third-party tool interfaces. OpenMP 5.0 also significantly enhanced many existing features, such as implicit declare target semantics, support for task reductions, discontiguous array shaping in target updates, and imperfectly nested loop collapsing.

The latest proposed additions, which are found in OpenMP Technical Report 9 (TR9), are expected to be included in OpenMP 5.1 when the ARB releases it later this year. The base languages C11, C18, C++18, C++11, C+14, C++17, and Fortran 2008 are fully supported. Initial support of C++20 and Fortran 2018 will be provided. Directives can now be specified as C++ attributes, facilitating and simplifying template creation. The new directive features in OpenMP 5.1 include: tile and unroll transforms; interop and API routines for portable interactions with non-OpenMP device execution contexts (e.g., CUDA streams and OpenCL queues); the assume directive for specifying OpenMP invariants to enable more effective compiler optimization; support for compare-and-swap and min/max atomics; a scope construct that enables reductions outside of loops; and an error directive that supports compile-time and runtime error/warning messages and actions.

The advancements, big and small, reflect the use cases that come from our OpenMP user, vendor, and research communities. The OpenMP Language Committee carefully evaluates and incorporates community needs into the OpenMP specification, a multi-language high-level parallel paradigm that is performant, productive, and portable for the entire hardware spectrum from embedded and accelerator devices to manycore shared-memory systems.

OpenMP is important both as a stand-alone parallel programming model and as part of a hybrid programming model for massively parallel, distributed memory systems consisting of homogeneous manycore nodes and heterogeneous node architectures, as found in leading supercomputers. As much of the increased parallelism in the exascale systems is expected to be within a node, OpenMP will become even more widely used in top-end systems. Importantly, the features in OpenMP 5.0 and 5.1 support applications on such systems in addition to facilitating portable exploitation of specific system attributes.

The community of OpenMP, researchers, and developers are united under the cOMPunity organization. This organization has held workshops on OpenMP around the world since 1999: the European Workshop on OpenMP (EWOMP), the North American Workshop on OpenMP Applications and Tools (WOMPAT), and the Asian Workshop on OpenMP Experiences and Implementation (WOMPEI) attracted annual audiences from academia and industry. The International Workshop on OpenMP (IWOMP) consolidated these three workshop series into a single annual international event that rotates across Europe, Asia-Pacific, and the Americas. The first IWOMP workshop was organized under the auspices of cOMPunity. Since that workshop, the IWOMP Steering Committee has organized these events and guided development of the series. The first IWOMP meeting was held in 2005, in Eugene, Oregon, USA. Since then, meetings have been held each year, in Reims, France; Beijing, China; West Lafayette, USA; Dresden, Germany; Tsukuba, Japan; Chicago, USA; Rome, Italy; Canberra, Australia; Salvador, Brazil; Aachen, Germany; Nara, Japan; Stony Brook, USA; Barcelona, Spain; and Auckland, New Zealand. Each workshop draws participants from research, program developer groups, and industry throughout the world. In 2020, IWOMP continued the series with technical papers and tutorials presented through a virtual conference, due to the COVID-19 pandemic. We thank the generous support of sponsors that help make these meetings successful; they are cited on the conference pages (present and archived) at the iwomp.org website.

The evolution of the specification would be impossible without active research in OpenMP compilers, runtime systems, tools, and environments. The many additions in OpenMP 5.0 and 5.1 reflect a vibrant and dedicated research community, committed to OpenMP support. As we move beyond the present needs, and adapt and evolve OpenMP to the expanding parallelism in new architectures, the OpenMP research community will continue to play a vital role. The papers in this volume demonstrate the adaption of new features found in OpenMP 5.0 and show how the OpenMP feature set can significantly enhance user experiences on a wide range of systems. These papers also demonstrate the forward thinking of the research community, and potential OpenMP directions and further improvements for systems on the horizon.

The IWOMP website (www.iwomp.org) has the latest workshop information, as well as links to archived events. This publication contains proceedings of the 16th edition of the conference series (IWOMP 2020). The workshop program included 21 technical papers, 3 keynote talks, and a tutorial on OpenMP. All technical papers were peer reviewed by at least four different members of the Program Committee. The work evidenced by these authors and the committee demonstrates that OpenMP will remain a key technology well into the future.

September 2020

Kent Milfeld
Bronis R. de Supinski
Lars Koesterke
Jannis Klinkenberg

Organization

General Chair

Kent Milfeld   Texas Advanced Computing Center, USA

Program Committee Co-chairs

Bronis R. de Supinski   Lawrence Livermore National Laboratory, USA
Lars Koesterke   Texas Advanced Computing Center, USA

Publication Chair

Jannis Klinkenberg   RWTH Aachen University, Germany

Tutorial Chairs

Yun (Helen) He   National Energy Research Scientific Computing Center
                                (NERSC), USA
Chris Ramos   Texas Advanced Computing Center, USA

Sponsorship Chair

Melyssa Fratkin   Texas Advanced Computing Center, USA

Program Committee

Alex Duran   Intel Iberia, Spain
Amit Ruhela   Texas Advanced Computing Center, USA
Chunhua Liao   Lawrence Livermore National Laboratory, USA
Deepak Eachempati   Hewlett Packard Enterprise, USA
Eduard Ayguade   BSC, Universitat Politècnica de Catalunya, Spain
Florina Ciorba   University of Basel, Switzerland
Gaurav Mitra   Texas Instruments, Inc., USA
James Beyer   NVIDIA, USA
Jannis Klinkenberg   RWTH Aachen University, Germany
Jini Susan George   AMD, Inc., USA
Joachim Protze   RWTH Aachen University, Germany
Johannes Doerfert   Argonne National Laboratory, USA
Kelvin Li   IBM, Canada
Larry Meadows   Intel, USA
Mark Bull   The University of Edinburgh, UK
Michael Kruse   Argonne National Laboratory, USA

Mitsuhisa Sato	RIKEN Center for Computational Science (R-CCS), Japan
Oliver Sinnen	The University of Auckland, New Zealand
Oscar Hernandez	Oak Ridge National Laboratory, USA
Stephen Olivier	Sandia National Laboratories, USA
Terry Wilmarth	Intel, USA
Thomas Scogland	Lawrence Livermore National Laboratory, USA

Website

Tim Lewis	Croftedge Marketing Limited, USA

IWOMP Steering Committee

Steering Committee Chair

Matthias S. Müller	RWTH Aachen University, Germany

Steering Committee

Dieter an Mey	RWTH Aachen University, Germany
Eduard Ayguadé	BSC, Universitat Politècnica de Catalunya, Spain
Mark Bull	EPCC, The University of Edinburgh, UK
Barbara Chapman	Stony Brook University, USA
Bronis R. de Supinski	Lawrence Livermore National Laboratory, USA
Rudolf Eigenmann	University of Delaware, USA
William Gropp	University of Illinois, USA
Michael Klemm	Intel, Germany
Kalyan Kumaran	Argonne National Laboratory, USA
Lawrence Meadows	Intel, USA
Stephen L. Olivier	Sandia National Laboratories, USA
Ruud van der Pas	Oracle, USA
Alistair Rendell	Flinders University, Australia
Mitsuhisa Sato	RIKEN Center for Computational Science (R-CCS), Japan
Sanjiv Shah	Intel, USA
Oliver Sinnen	The University of Auckland, New Zealand
Josemar Rodrigues de Souza	SENAI Unidade CIMATEC, Brazil
Christian Terboven	RWTH Aachen University, Germany
Matthijs van Waveren	OpenMP ARB & CS Group, France

Contents

Memory

Performance Methodologies

FAROS: A Framework to Analyze OpenMP Compilation Through Benchmarking and Compiler Optimization Analysis

Giorgis Georgakoudis[1]([⊠]) [iD], Johannes Doerfert[2] [iD], Ignacio Laguna[1] [iD], and Thomas R. W. Scogland[1] [iD]

[1] Lawrence Livermore National Laboratory, Livermore, CA 94550, USA
{georgakoudis1,lagunaperalt1,scogland1}@llnl.gov
[2] Argonne National Laboratory, Lemont, IL 60439, USA
jdoerfert@anl.gov

Abstract. Compilers optimize OpenMP programs differently than their serial elision. Early outlining of parallel regions and invocation of parallel code via OpenMP runtime functions are two of the most profound differences. Understanding the interplay between compiler optimizations, OpenMP compilation, and application performance is hard and usually requires specialized benchmarks and compilation analysis tools.

To this end, we present FAROS, an extensible framework to automate and structure the analysis of compiler optimization of OpenMP programs. FAROS provides a generic configuration interface to profile and analyze OpenMP applications with their native build configurations. Using FAROS on a set of 39 OpenMP programs, including HPC applications and kernels, we show that OpenMP compilation hinders optimization for the majority of programs. Comparing single-threaded OpenMP execution to its sequential counterpart, we observed slowdowns as much as 135.23%. In some cases, however, OpenMP compilation speeds up execution as much as 25.48% when OpenMP semantics help compiler optimization. Following analysis on compiler optimization reports enables us to pinpoint the reasons without in-depth knowledge of the compiler. The information can be used to improve compilers and also to bring performance on par through manual code refactoring.

Keywords: Compilation analysis · OpenMP performance · Benchmarking and profiling

1 Introduction

Compiling OpenMP code introduces non-trivial complexity in the compiler and its optimization pipeline. The state-of-the-art approach is *outlining* [3]. The compiler transforms an annotated parallel region to a closure, encapsulating the region as a function with its context of operating variables. Outlined region

© Springer Nature Switzerland AG 2020
K. Milfeld et al. (Eds.): IWOMP 2020, LNCS 12295, pp. 3–17, 2020.
https://doi.org/10.1007/978-3-030-58144-2_1

closures are passed as callbacks to runtime functions that implement parallel execution. The context variables of a closure follow the data sharing specifications of the region to either copy variables in the calling environment, if those have *private* semantics, or become pointers to them, if those are *shared*.

Implementing parallel execution via outlining and runtime function calls has significant impact on how compilers optimize parallel OpenMP code. Prior work [9,10] has shown that OpenMP compilation hinders optimizations that would otherwise apply to the serial elision of a program, that is compiling the program without enabling OpenMP to ignore OpenMP directives. Executing an OpenMP program single-threaded can be more than 2× slower than its sequentially compiled and executed counterpart, solely due to missing compiler optimizations. Improving OpenMP compilation is an active field of research [10,11] and better understanding performance differences is crucial to guide and accelerate this research.

Although there are numerous benchmark suites [4–7,13,17,18,23] that include OpenMP programs, there are none designed to perform analysis on the compilation of OpenMP itself and analyze its implications for performance. Understanding the implications of OpenMP compilation is important to both compiler developers, seeking to improve optimization on OpenMP code, and application developers for interpreting their application's performance and refactoring their codes to help compiler optimization. Lack of such tools motivates this work, which aims to evaluate OpenMP compilation and especially how it affects compiler optimization and application performance.

In particular, we present FAROS[1], a framework to analyze OpenMP compilation. The contributions of this work are:

- The extensible framework FAROS that integrates OpenMP applications to benchmark their execution and performed compiler optimizations. FAROS takes as input a configuration file that specifies build and execution options of applications under test, to generate compilation reports by leveraging compiler optimization remarks and profile execution.
- We provide FAROS open-source[2] integrating an initial collection of 39 programs, including HPC proxy apps, NAS and Rodinia kernels, and GROMACS, a large real-world scientific application. FAROS interfaces with the Clang/LLVM compiler for compiler optimization analysis. Commercial compilers that leverage Clang should be able to provide the same interface.
- We present new results and insight using FAROS to investigate missing compiler optimizations when compiling OpenMP programs contrasted with their serial elision. Results show that, for most programs, OpenMP compilation slows down execution ranging from 8.25% to 135.23%. In a small number of cases, OpenMP compilation speeds up execution up to 25.48% due to OpenMP semantics enabling additional compiler optimization. For both types of results, we complement the analysis with methods to bring on par the performance between sequential and OpenMP compilation.

---

[1] Faros is a transliteration of the greek word $\varphi\acute{\alpha}\rho o\varsigma$, which means lighthouse or beacon, in an analogy to our framework set to guide the analysis of OpenMP compilation.
[2] https://github.com/ggeorgakoudis/FAROS.

Section 2 details the methodology, design, and implementation of FAROS. Sect. 3 presents new results and insight using FAROS to evaluate OpenMP compilation. Section 4 discusses related work, and Sect. 5 concludes the paper and discusses future work.

2 FAROS: Design and Implementation

Figure 1 presents an overview of the workflow in FAROS. FAROS includes a *harness* script driven by a YAML configuration file. The configuration includes information on fetching, building, and running test applications. FAROS leverages compilation remarks when building an application to generate a set of compilation reports that highlight the differences in compiler optimization between different build options. Further, FAROS executes different executables, corresponding to the different build options, to collect performance timing information and aggregate those results. The following sections provide more details on the components of FAROS and their operation.

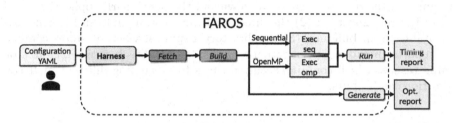

Fig. 1. Workflow of FAROS

2.1 Harness and Configuration

The harness script in python, named `harness.py`, takes as input a YAML configuration file and a set of options to build and run programs described in that configuration. Fig. 2 shows the help output of the script. The configuration file is set with the `-i`, `--input` argument. There are three different actions the harness performs: (1) *fetch*, with the option `-f`, `--fetch`, fetches the program sources from the specified repositories; (2) *build*, with the option `-b`, `--build`, builds the selected program using specified compilation options in the configuration, also fetching if needed; (3) *generate*, with the option `-g`, `--generate`, generates compilation reports by combining optimization remarks for different compilation configurations, creating remark *diff* files between them, from all the sources of an application to a single file; (4) *run*, with the option `-r`, `--run` and a following argument on how many repetitions to perform, that runs the executable with the specified input. The flags can be individually set or combined to perform multiple actions in a single harness run – fetching takes precedence over building, building over generating reports and running. Also, the harness has

```
usage: benchmark.py [-h] -i INPUT [-f] [-b] [-r RUN] [-g] -p PROGRAMS
                    [PROGRAMS ...] [-s] [-d]

Harness for benchmarking a set of programs and compilation options

optional arguments:
  -h, --help            show this help message and exit
  -i INPUT, --input INPUT
                        configuration YAML input file for programs
  -p PROGRAMS [PROGRAMS ...], --programs PROGRAMS [PROGRAMS ...]
                        selected programs from the config
  -f, --fetch           fetch program repos (without building)
  -b, --build           build programs (will fetch too)
  -g, --generate        generate compilation reports
  -r RUN, --run RUN     run <repetitions>
  -d, --dry-run         enable dry run
```

Fig. 2. The help output for harness.py

a dry run option, -d, --dry-run, that prints what actions would be performed without actually performing them.

The harness creates four extra directories for its operation when building and running: (1) the directory repos to download the benchmark application specified in the configuration; (2) the directory bins to store and run the generated executables from building; (3) the directory reports, where it stores compilation reports, including optimization remarks; (4) the directory results to store timing results, which contain execution times from running different built configurations and inputs.

```
LULESH:
  fetch: 'git clone -q https://github.com/LLNL/LULESH.git'
  build_dir: 'LULESH'
  build: {
    seq: 'make CXX=clang++ CXXFLAGS="-g -O3 -march=native
          -I. -Wall -DUSE_MPI=0 -fsave-optimization-record
          -save-stats"',
    omp: 'make CXX=clang++
          CXXFLAGS="-g -fopenmp -O3 -march=native -I. -Wall
          -DUSE_MPI=0 -fsave-optimization-record -save-stats"'
  }
  copy: [ 'lulesh2.0' ]
  run: 'env OMP_NUM_THREADS=1 OMP_PROC_BIND=true ./lulesh2.0'
  input: '-i 500'
  measure : 'Grind time.* (\d+\.\d+) .*overall'
  clean : 'git clean -fx'
```

Fig. 3. An example YAML configuration

Figure 3 shows the format of the YAML configuration, exemplified through specifying the application LULESH. Configuring an application is a hierarchy of keys that prescribe actions for the harness script. The root of the hierarchy is a user-chosen, descriptive name of the application, LULESH in this example. The harness creates a sub-directory matching the name of the root key under **bins** to store executables, so this directory is **bins/LULESH** in this case. The key **fetch** contains the command to fetch the application code, which is specified as cloning from a GitHub repo in the case of LULESH. Note that the fetching command can also include patching, if needed, provided by the user. For example, for some programs in our benchmark suite, we apply a patch to guard calls to OpenMP runtime functions using the standard approach of enabling those calls within **#ifdef _OPENMP ... #endif** preprocessor directives.

Regarding building, the key **build_dir** specifies the directory to build the application, so harness changes to this directory to execute the build commands specified under the key **build**. There is a different sub-key for each building specification. In this example, the key **seq** specifies building LULESH without OpenMP to produce an executable for sequential execution, whereas, the key **omp** specifies building LULESH with OpenMP enabled. The harness creates different sub-directories under **bins/LULESH** for each different compilation configuration. In the example, it creates directories **bins/LULESH/seq** and **bins/LULESH/omp**. The key **copy** specifies a list of files or directories that the harness copies out to those sub-directories. The list contains the executable file and possibly any input files needed for execution, if the user desires to have **bins** self-contained by avoiding referring to input files in the directory **repos**, which is useful for relocating **bins** without copying over **repos**.

Further, the key **run** specifies the command to execute, which is typically the executable binary of the application, prepended with any environment variables. In the example YAML file, the **run** command sets OpenMP environments variables **OMP_NUM_THREADS = 1** and **OMP_PROC_BIND = true** to contrast sequential vs. single-threaded OpenMP execution and to bind OpenMP threads for reducing variability and best performance – note those environment variables have no effect on the sequential binary, hence sequential execution is not pinned though without discernible difference in performance by our experiments. Moreover, the key **input** specifies the input arguments for the application in the run command. The key **measure** specifies a regular expression, conforming to Python's regular expression syntax, to match in the application's executable output. This makes possible to capture an application-specific measure of performance, such as execution time of a region of interest or some other Figure of Merit (FoM). If the value of the key **measure** is empty, the harness measures end-to-end, wall clock execution time of the application, using python's *time* module. Specifically, it invokes **time.perf_counter()** before launching and after application execution ends to calculate the duration of execution as the difference of those two timestamps. Lastly, the key **clean** specifies the commands that harness executes to clean the repo for building a different compilation configuration.

Note that this YAML design provides significant flexibility. Keys that specify the actions **fetch**, **build**, **run**, and **clean** contain commands to execute in the command-line shell, thus they can include any executable command or program available to the shell. For example, the *build* action can include *cmake* target generation for building, or the action *run* can execute a generated executable through a job scheduler. Also, this YAML configuration is flexible to extend with more keys or to enhance the semantics of existing ones. For example, it is possible to extend the `run` with a sub-dictionary of keys that correspond to the different build configurations to customize the run command, or to make the value of the key `input` a list of different input configurations to run. We are working in extensions like those for the harness in our open-source implementation.

There is an initial effort to create this YAML configuration file that requires understanding the directory structure, building environment, and execution configurations of the included applications. However, this format is flexible to implement building and testing any application, buildable through the command line. Once a harness configuration is created, it is straightforward to extend it for different compilation or execution configurations. Moreover, this configuration is shareable with other users to enable reproducible testing for different compilation and execution options.

2.2   Analyzing Compiler Optimization and Performance

FAROS generates compiler optimization reports that highlight compilation differences to contrast the specified build configurations. To do that, FAROS leverages LLVM optimization remarks[3] generated during compilation. Optimization remarks present a line-by-line record of applied or missed compiler optimizations, or of analysis results related to compiler optimization, for each source file built. LLVM stores this information in a file, serialized in a YAML format. Also, FAROS makes use of two tools provided by LLVM for analyzing optimization remarks: the tool `opt-diff`, which generates the *diff* YAML file given as input different YAML files of optimization remarks, and the tool `opt-viewer`, which takes as input a YAML file of optimizations remarks (or a *diff* file) to generate an easy-to-read, HTML output. FAROS extends `opt-diff` with a *filter* input argument to filter output by selecting a single class of optimization remark type for generating the *diff* to ease analysis: either missed, or passed optimizations, or analysis information. For example, that makes easy to contrast what optimizations applied for a sequential build but not for an OpenMP build, and vice versa, by observing only the *diff* output of passed optimizations. FAROS generates reports for all combinations of build options and optimization remarks types, in both YAML and HTML formats. We show excerpts of the report output later, in the evaluation (Sect. 3), when discussing results.

Analyzing performance is done experimentally. FAROS runs the program executable, compiled with the different build options specified in the configuration file, to collect performance results. Specifically, the user executes the harness and provides the argument `-r,--run` with input the number of repetitions to execute each configuration's executable, for collecting a statistically significant number of performance samples. As explained in Sect. 2.1, FAROS collects measurements of either the end-to-end execution time of the program or the user-specified performance figure corresponding to the regular expression in

---

[3] https://llvm.org/docs/Remarks.html.

the `measure` field of the configuration YAML file. It outputs those performance measurements in the directory `results`, creating a different YAML output file for each program, named `results-<program name>.yaml`. The format of this result output is a 2-level dictionary, where the first level key is the program name, and the second level consists of a key for each build configuration containing a list of the measured performance value of each run repetition.

3   Evaluation

Table 1 presents programs integrated in FAROS so far, including HPC applications, NAS and Rodinia kernels, along with inputs used for evaluation. We use Clang/LLVM version 10.0.0 for compilation and generation of optimization remarks. Experiments run on an Intel Xeon E5-2695v4. For each build option, sequential or OpenMP, we do 30 independent runs per program and calculate 95% confidence intervals using the t-distribution to avoid assumptions on the sampled population.

Figure 4 shows results contrasting execution time of sequential vs. single-threaded OpenMP execution with the percentage slowdown of OpenMP execution highlighted with a label (negative results signify speedup). We downselect the number of programs shown for presentation, selecting programs that have either discernible slowdown (more than 5%) due to OpenMP compilation or the few cases that OpenMP compilation results in better performance.

Discussing results, 17 out of 21 programs slow down when compiled with OpenMP enabled and executing single-threaded compared to sequential compilation and execution. Interestingly, 4 of them speedup. Slowdown ranges from 8.25%, for the program *MG*, to 135.23%, for *srad*. Infrequent speedup from OpenMP compilation ranges from 7.01% for *gromacs-2019.5* to 25.48% for *hotspot*.

We focus on *srad* and *hotspot* and explain their results through compilation remarks. Figure 5 shows excerpts of the compilation report output for *srad*, using our extensions. Figure 5a show only applied optimizations, while Fig. 5b shows analyses output. Both plots highlight the *diff* between sequential and OpenMP compilation. Sequential compilation successfully vectorizes the loop at line 130, whereas OpenMP fails – the same happens to a later loop, not shown for brevity. In OpenMP, the vectorizer cannot statically determine accessed array ranges within the loop due to the extra pointer indirection emitted for accesses to shared pointers. Hence, it fails to deduct accesses are alias-free, or to generate a sufficient runtime alias check for vectorization. We verified our analysis of compilation remarks in two ways. First, we manually inserted a `#pragma omp simd` directive to explicitly vectorize the loop. Second, we run experimental inter-procedural optimization [9,10] that performs value propagation through OpenMP runtime functions to remove one level of indirection. Either of those changes rendered the single-threaded OpenMP execution on par with sequential.

Regarding *hotspot*, Fig. 6 shows the passed optimization *diff* between sequential and OpenMP compilation. The first thing to notice is that OpenMP

Table 1. List of programs integrated in FAROS with inputs tested

Application	Input
HPC proxy/mini/large	
AMG [25]	-problem 1 -n 128 128 128
CoMD [22]	-e -i 1 -j 1 -k 1 -x 20 -y 20 -z 20
CoSP2 [8]	–hmatName hmatrix.1024.mtx –N 12288 –M 256
Kripke [20]	(default)
LULESH [19]	-i 500
Quicksilver [26]	–nSteps 1
RSBench [28]	-t 1 -s small
SimpleMOC [15]	-s -t 1
XSBench [29]	-t 1 -k 1 -s small
miniAMR [16]	–num_refine 4 –max_blocks 6000 –init_x 1 –init_y 1 –init_z 1 –npx 1 –npy 1 –npz 1 –nx 8 –ny 8 –nz 8 –num_objects 1 –object 2 0 -0.01 -0.01 -0.01 0.0 0.0 0.0 0.0 0.0 0.0 0.0009 0.0009 0.0009 –num_tsteps 100 –comm_vars 2
miniAero [30]	(default)
miniFE [16]	-nx 64
hpcg [12]	128 128 128
gromacs-2019.5 [1]	mdrun -ntmpi 1 -s ion_channel.tpr -maxh 0.50 -resethway -noconfout -nsteps 1000
NAS	[17]
BT	A
CG	B
EP	A
FT	A
IS	B
LU	A
MG	B
SP	A
Rodinia	[7]
b+tree	cores 1 file mil.txt command command.txt
backprop	16777216
bfs	1 graph1MW_6.txt
cfd	fvcorr.domn.097K
heartwall	test.avi 20 1
hotspot	1024 1024 1000 1 temp_1024 power_1024 output.out
hotspot3D	512 8 1000 power_512x8 temp_512x8 output.out
kmeans	-n 1 -i kdd_cup
lavaMD	-cores 1 -boxes1d 16
leukocyte	5 1 testfile.avi
lud	-n 1 -s 8000
nn	filelist 10000 30 90
nw	32000 10 1
particlefilter	-x 128 -y 128 -z 10 -np 100000
pathfinder	1000000 100
srad	2048 2048 0 127 0 127 1 0.5 100
streamcluster	10 20 256 65536 65536 1000 none output.txt 1

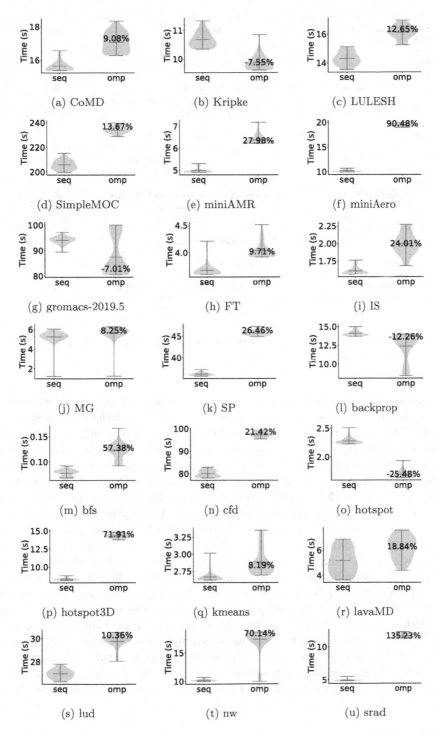

Fig. 4. Execution time violin plots of sequential vs. OpenMP single-threaded execution. Percentage labels show slowdown of OpenMP single-threaded execution

Line	Optimization	Source	Inline Contex
124			
125		`#ifdef OPEN`	
126		`omp_set_num_threads(nthreads);`	
127		`#pragma omp parallel for shared(J, dN, dS, d`	
	+licm	sinking getelementptr	main
	+inline	.omp_outlined._debug__ inlined into .omp_ou...	.omp_outl...
	+licm	hoisting getelementptr	main
128		`#endif`	
129		`for (int i = 0 ; i < rows ; i++) {`	
	-licm	hoisting icmp	main
	-licm	hoisting zext	main
	-licm	sinking zext	main
130		`for (int j = 0; j < cols; j++) {`	
	-loop-vectorize	vectorized loop (vectorization width: 8, interleaved ...	main
	-licm	sinking zext	main
	-licm	hoisting zext	main

(a) *diff* on passed optimizations

130		`for (int j = 0; j < cols; j++) {`	
	+loop-vectorize	loop not vectorized: cannot identify array bounds	.omp_outl...

(b) *diff* on analysis output

Fig. 5. Optimization remarks *diff* between sequential (remarks signed −) and OpenMP compilation (remarks signed +) for *srad*

compilation applied unrolling after the vectorization, which sequential misses. This is an important optimization as the loop has 16 iterations in total (given `BLOCK_SIZE_C` is a preprocessor constant equal to 16), 8 of which are part of one vector iteration, thus only two iterations are left after vectorization. To verify that the directive `simd` directive causes the performance difference, we remove it and observe that indeed sequential and single-threaded OpenMP performance is on par, though performance is worse overall by disabling this hint. Following, to bring performance on par and include the unrolling optimization, we try the `clang loop unroll(full)` pragma. However, this fails too due to an artifact in the loop trip count computation, which we reported to LLVM developers, that prevented the compiler from determining a static constant iteration count. The OpenMP compilation benefits from the fact that it directly emits the loop in a normalized form because of the canonical loop restrictions of OpenMP. We manually made the loop trip count obvious to the compiler via refactoring. Although, this enables unrolling in sequential compilation too, sequential execution performance still lags compared to single-threaded OpenMP. To bring performance on par, we additionally declare the pointers `result`, `temp`, `power` as `restrict`, which roughly signifies that they point to distinct objects. This is an approximation of the `simd` semantics that imply accesses are dependence free[4].

---

[4] Simplified for the sake of brevity.

Declaring the pointers as `restrict` is a common way to unlock further optimization, in this case vectorization without a runtime alias check and respective fallback code.

4   Related Work

Benchmark Suites. There are numerous benchmark suites [4–7,13,17,18,23] that include a collection of OpenMP programs with a fixed build configuration per program. Their main purpose is to evaluate the performance of parallel execution on the particular hardware to run. As such, they do not offer an automated way to evaluate different build configurations or produce any output to analyze compiler optimization. By contrast, FAROS targets analysis of the impact of compiler optimization on OpenMP execution. It is flexible to include programs from different benchmark suites or other OpenMP applications and define different build configurations, through its generic configuration file format. Also, FAROS provides an automated way to extract information from compilation remarks into reports to help the analysis of how different build configurations change compiler optimization on source code.

```
136                     for ( r = r_start; r < r_start + BLOCK_SIZE_R; ++r ) {
137            #pragma omp simd
      +loop-unroll completely unrolled loop with 2 iterations                    .omp_ou...
      +loop-vectorize vectorized loop (vectorization width: 8, interleaved count: 1)   .omp_ou...
138                     for ( c = c_start; c < c_start + BLOCK_SIZE_C; ++c
           -licm            hoisting icmp                                         single_it...
           -licm                              sinking trunc                       single_it...
      -loop-vectorize       vectorized loop (vectorization width: 8, interleaved co...  single_it...
           +licm                                                          ...    .omp_ou...
           -licm            hoisting shufflevector                                single_it...
           -licm            hoisting insertelement                                single_it...
           -licm            hoisting add                                          single_it...
           -licm            hoisting and                                          single_it...
139                     /* Update Temperatures */
140                     result[r*col+c] =temp[r*col+c]+
           +licm                                  hoisting load                   .omp_ou...
           +licm            hoisting load                                         .omp_ou...
141                     ( Cap_1 * (power[r*col+c] +
           +licm                                  hoisting load                   .omp_ou...
142                     (temp[(r+1)*col+c] + temp[(r-1)*col+c] - 2
143                     (temp[r*col+c+1] + temp[r*col+c-1] - 2.f*t
144                     (amb_temp - temp[r*col+c]) * Rz_1));
145                 }
146             }
```

Fig. 6. Optimization remarks *diff* between sequential (remarks signed −) and OpenMP compilation (remarks signed +) for *hotspot*

Profiling Tools. Profiling tools [2,14,21,24,27] for parallel programs target performance and bottleneck analysis in program execution to guide optimization.

They profile a program, compiled with a particular set of options, through instrumentation and sampling to find hotspots, where most of the execution time is spent, to target further analysis. Further, they collect hardware-oriented performance metrics, such as cache misses, instructions-per-cycle and other hardware performance counters, to correlate with execution for manual analysis or for automatic analysis through an abstract performance model, such as the roofline model [21]. In its current implementation, FAROS profiles execution time, or some other performance metric reported in the output of the application, for different configured build options. Extra profiling information from those tools is complementary to the compilation analysis of FAROS to focus inspection and analysis of compiler optimization reporting on hotspots and quantify the performance difference in more detail. Nevertheless, we consider extending FAROS to integrate execution performance analysis offered by those tools to provide profiling information alongside compiler optimization remarks in a unified report.

Compiler Test Suites. Compiler test suites, such as those in LLVM[5] and GCC[6], evaluate the correctness of compilation and the performance of the compilation process itself. They typically provide a set of micro-benchmarks and expected outputs, to debug the operation of the compiler and uncover any performance problems in to help compiler developers. FAROS complements those test suites by analyzing the performance and compiler optimization on generated code of larger programs, focusing on OpenMP compilation in this use case. However, FAROS is expandable to other use cases by changing its configuration input to different build options, for example enabling or disabling distinct sets of compiler optimizations to evaluate their effectiveness and performance improvement.

5   Conclusion and Future Work

We have presented FAROS, an extensible framework for integrating benchmark applications, to contrast and analyze different compilation options and how they affect compiler optimization and application performance. In FAROS, we have already integrated a diverse set of 39 programs, including HPC proxy/mini applications, NAS and Rodinia kernels, and the large application GROMACS. Using FAROS, we analyzed the compilation and performance of OpenMP programs versus their serial elision. This analysis provided new insight on understanding and quantifying sub-optimal OpenMP compilation that hinders optimization found in its sequential counterpart, and interestingly revealing also few cases where OpenMP semantics enable additional compiler optimization.

For future work, we plan to expand the analysis of compilation remarks to present more informative visual output, for example including IR code besides source code and hotspot information, and also provide recommendations to

---

[5] https://llvm.org/docs/TestingGuide.html.
[6] https://gcc.gnu.org/onlinedocs/gccint/Testsuites.html.

developers for enabling optimization. Further, we intend to expand FAROS to more compilers, besides Clang/LLVM, by integrating their own compilation reporting.

Acknowledgments. The authors would like to thank the anonymous referees for their valuable comments and helpful suggestions. This work was performed under the auspices of the U.S. Department of Energy by Lawrence Livermore National Laboratory under contract DEAC52-07NA27344 (LLNL-CONF-810797) and also partially supported by the Exascale Computing Project (17-SC-20-SC), a collaborative effort of two U.S. Department of Energy organizations (Office of Science and the National Nuclear Security Administration) responsible for the planning and preparation of a capable exascale ecosystem, including software, applications, hardware, advanced system engineering, and early testbed platforms, in support of the nation's exascale computing imperative.

References

1. Abraham, M.J., et al.: GROMACS: high performance molecular simulations through multi-level parallelism from laptops to supercomputers. SoftwareX **1–2**, 19–25 (2015). https://doi.org/10.1016/j.softx.2015.06.001. http://www.sciencedirect.com/science/article/pii/S2352711015000059
2. Adhianto, L., et al.: HPCToolkit: tools for performance analysis of optimized parallel programs. Concurr. Comput.: Pract. Exp. **22**(6), 685–701 (2010)
3. Bataev, A., Bokhanko, A., Cownie, J.: Towards OpenMP support in LLVM. In: 2013 European LLVM Conference (2013)
4. Bienia, C., Kumar, S., Singh, J.P., Li, K.: The PARSEC benchmark suite: characterization and architectural implications. In: Proceedings of the 17th International Conference on Parallel Architectures and Compilation Techniques, PACT 2008, pp. 72–81. Association for Computing Machinery, New York (2008). https://doi.org/10.1145/1454115.1454128
5. Bronevetsky, G., Gyllenhaal, J., de Supinski, B.R.: CLOMP: accurately characterizing OpenMP application overheads. In: Eigenmann, R., de Supinski, B.R. (eds.) IWOMP 2008. LNCS, vol. 5004, pp. 13–25. Springer, Heidelberg (2008). https://doi.org/10.1007/978-3-540-79561-2_2
6. Bull, J.M., Enright, J.P., Guo, X., Maynard, C., Reid, F.: Performance evaluation of mixed-mode OpenMP/MPI implementations. Int. J. Parallel Program. **38**, 396–417 (2010). https://doi.org/10.1007/s10766-010-0137-2
7. Che, S., et al.: Rodinia: a benchmark suite for heterogeneous computing. In: Proceedings of the 2009 IEEE International Symposium on Workload Characterization (IISWC), IISWC 2009, pp. 44–54. IEEE Computer Society, USA (2009). https://doi.org/10.1109/IISWC.2009.5306797
8. Cook, J., Finkel, H., Junghams, C., McCorquodale, P., Pavel, R., Richards, D.F.: Proxy app prospectus for ECP application development projects. Office of Scientific and Technical Information (OSTI), October 2017. https://doi.org/10.2172/1477829
9. Doerfert, J., Diaz, J.M.M., Finkel, H.: The TRegion interface and compiler optimizations for OPENMP target regions. In: Fan, X., de Supinski, B.R., Sinnen, O., Giacaman, N. (eds.) IWOMP 2019. LNCS, vol. 11718, pp. 153–167. Springer, Cham (2019). https://doi.org/10.1007/978-3-030-28596-8_11

10. Doerfert, J., Finkel, H.: Compiler optimizations for OpenMP. In: de Supinski, B.R., Valero-Lara, P., Martorell, X., Mateo Bellido, S., Labarta, J. (eds.) IWOMP 2018. LNCS, vol. 11128, pp. 113–127. Springer, Cham (2018). https://doi.org/10.1007/978-3-319-98521-3_8
11. Doerfert, J., Finkel, H.: Compiler optimizations for parallel programs. In: Hall, M., Sundar, H. (eds.) LCPC 2018. LNCS, vol. 11882, pp. 112–119. Springer, Cham (2019). https://doi.org/10.1007/978-3-030-34627-0_9
12. Dongarra, J., Heroux, M.A., Luszczek, P.: High-performance conjugate-gradient benchmark: a new metric for ranking high-performance computing systems. Int. J. High Perform. Comput. Appl. **30**(1), 3–10 (2016). https://doi.org/10.1177/1094342015593158
13. Duran, A., Teruel, X., Ferrer, R., Martorell, X., Ayguade, E.: Barcelona OpenMP tasks suite: a set of benchmarks targeting the exploitation of task parallelism in OpenMP. In: 2009 International Conference on Parallel Processing, pp. 124–131 (2009)
14. Geimer, M., Wolf, F., Wylie, B.J., Ábrahám, E., Becker, D., Mohr, B.: The Scalasca performance toolset architecture. Concurr. Comput.: Pract. Exp. **22**(6), 702–719 (2010)
15. Gunow, G., Tramm, J., Forget, B., Smith, K., He, T.: SimpleMOC - a performance abstraction for 3D MOC (2015)
16. Heroux, M.A., et al.: Improving performance via mini-applications. Sandia National Laboratories, Technical Report SAND2009-5574 3 (2009)
17. Jin, H., Frumkin, M.A., Yan, J.M.: The OpenMP Implementation of NAS Parallel Benchmarks and Its Performance (1999)
18. Juckeland, G., et al.: SPEC ACCEL: a standard application suite for measuring hardware accelerator performance. In: Jarvis, S.A., Wright, S.A., Hammond, S.D. (eds.) PMBS 2014. LNCS, vol. 8966, pp. 46–67. Springer, Cham (2015). https://doi.org/10.1007/978-3-319-17248-4_3
19. Karlin, I., et al.: Exploring traditional and emerging parallel programming models using a proxy application. In: 2013 IEEE 27th International Symposium on Parallel and Distributed Processing, pp. 919–932 (2013)
20. Kunen, A.J., Bailey, T.S., Brown, P.N.: KRIPKE - a massively parallel transport mini-app. Office of Scientific and Technical Information (OSTI), June 2015
21. Marques, D., et al.: Performance analysis with cache-aware roofline model in intel advisor. In: 2017 International Conference on High Performance Computing Simulation (HPCS), pp. 898–907 (2017)
22. Mohd-Yusof, J., Swaminarayan, S., Germann, T.C.: Co-design for molecular dynamics: an exascale proxy application. Technical report LA-UR 13-20839 (2013)
23. Müller, M.S., et al.: SPEC OMP2012—An application benchmark suite for parallel systems using OpenMP. In: Chapman, B.M., Massaioli, F., Müller, M.S., Rorro, M. (eds.) IWOMP 2012. LNCS, vol. 7312, pp. 223–236. Springer, Heidelberg (2012). https://doi.org/10.1007/978-3-642-30961-8_17
24. Niethammer, C., Gracia, J., Knüpfer, A., Resch, M.M., Nagel, W.E. (eds.): Tools for High Performance Computing 2014. Springer, Cham (2015). https://doi.org/10.1007/978-3-319-16012-2
25. Park, J., Smelyanskiy, M., Yang, U.M., Mudigere, D., Dubey, P.: High-performance algebraic multigrid solver optimized for multi-core based distributed parallel systems. In: SC 2015: Proceedings of the International Conference for High Performance Computing, Networking, Storage and Analysis, pp. 1–12 (2015)

26. Richards, D.F., Bleile, R.C., Brantley, P.S., Dawson, S.A., McKinley, M.S., O'Brien, M.J.: Quicksilver: A Proxy App for the Monte Carlo Transport Code Mercury. Office of Scientific and Technical Information (OSTI), July 2017
27. Shende, S.S., Malony, A.D.: The TAU parallel performance system. Int. J. High Perform. Comput. Appl. **20**(2), 287–311 (2006). https://doi.org/10.1177/1094342006064482
28. Tramm, J.R., Siegel, A.R., Forget, B., Josey, C.: Performance analysis of a reduced data movement algorithm for neutron cross section data in Monte Carlo simulations. In: Markidis, S., Laure, E. (eds.) EASC 2014. LNCS, vol. 8759, pp. 39–56. Springer, Cham (2015). https://doi.org/10.1007/978-3-319-15976-8_3
29. Tramm, J.R., Siegel, A.R., Islam, T., Schulz, M.: XSBench - the development and verification of a performance abstraction for Monte Carlo reactor analysis. In: PHYSOR 2014 - The Role of Reactor Physics toward a Sustainable Future. Kyoto (2014). https://www.mcs.anl.gov/papers/P5064-0114.pdf
30. Trott, C.R., et al.: ASC Trilab L2 Codesign Milestone 2015. Office of Scientific and Technical Information (OSTI), September 2015. https://doi.org/10.2172/1221176

Evaluating the Efficiency of OpenMP Tasking for Unbalanced Computation on Diverse CPU Architectures

Stephen L. Olivier[✉][iD]

Center for Computing Research, Sandia National Laboratories,
Albuquerque, NM, USA
slolivi@sandia.gov

Abstract. In the decade since support for task parallelism was incorporated into OpenMP, its use has remained limited in part due to concerns about its performance and scalability. This paper revisits a study from the early days of OpenMP tasking that used the Unbalanced Tree Search (UTS) benchmark as a stress test to gauge implementation efficiency. The present UTS study includes both Clang/LLVM and vendor OpenMP implementations on four different architectures. We measure parallel efficiency to examine each implementation's performance in response to varying task granularity. We find that most implementations achieve over 90% efficiency using all available cores for tasks of $O(100k)$ instructions, and the best even manage tasks of $O(10k)$ instructions well.

Keywords: OpenMP Tasks · Unbalanced Tree Search · Load balancing

1 Introduction

The introduction of asynchronous task parallelism was the primary focus of version 3.0 of the OpenMP® API specification published in 2008 [24]. Subsequent versions of the specification up to and including version 5.0 [25] have added numerous enhancements to the OpenMP tasking model. Tasking has carved out an important role in OpenMP as the mechanism for asynchronous device offload, but its use remains somewhat limited in CPU-only OpenMP programs. Common concerns include finding the optimal task granularity to amortize the overhead costs of task creation, scheduling, and synchronization while at the same time exposing sufficient application parallelism.

Shortly after the first OpenMP 3.0 implementations appeared, the Unbalanced Tree Search Benchmark (UTS) [20] was ported to the OpenMP tasking model as a stress test [21]. The OpenMP tasking version of UTS was initially compared against an OpenMP version that handled load balancing at user level and a Cilk [10] version. An expanded study [22] included comparisons to Cilk++ [15] (forerunner of Intel® Cilk™ Plus) and Threading Building Blocks

© Springer Nature Switzerland AG 2020
K. Milfeld et al. (Eds.): IWOMP 2020, LNCS 12295, pp. 18–33, 2020.
https://doi.org/10.1007/978-3-030-58144-2_2

(TBB) [26]. The results shed light on the ability of runtime systems of the time to cope with large numbers of tasks generated in an unpredictable manner. UTS was later added to the Barcelona OpenMP Tasks Suite (BOTS)[1].

At the time of this writing, the UTS OpenMP tasking studies are just over a decade old. They were carried out on a board comprised of eight dual-core "Santa Rosa" Opteron processors manufactured in a 90 nm feature size. In contrast, Intel and AMD are currently transitioning down from 14 nm to smaller feature sizes, and processors with up to 72 cores per chip have been deployed in high performance computing (HPC) systems. Arm systems capable of 64-bit server-class computing were not even available until recently. Compilers and runtime systems have evolved in the intervening years as well. Many are now based on the LLVM project [14], and its permissively licensed open-source code base has enabled cooperation among vendors and researchers while still allowing vendors to maintain custom versions with proprietary optimizations for added value. In addition, the evolution of the OpenMP tasking model since its inception has required some changes to the data structures and algorithms used in implementations. In light of these developments in hardware and software, the time is ripe to reprise the UTS stress testing evaluation of OpenMP tasking.

We do not attempt to reproduce exactly the earlier UTS OpenMP tasking studies. The problem size used then is much too small for current systems, and only one machine was used. The present study explores the following dimensions:

- Diversity of architectures (IBM POWER9, Arm Thunder X2, Intel Xeon Skylake, and Intel Xeon Phi Knights Landing);
- Comparison of Clang/LLVM and vendor implementations;
- Measuring parallel efficiency as a function of task granularity;
- Quantifying load balancing operations per thread per unit time.

This effort aims to offer insights into the present state of OpenMP tasking efficiency for the benefit of OpenMP users and implementors.

2   UTS: The Benchmark and Its Implementation

The UTS benchmark is a traversal of a dynamically generated tree. The end result is a count of all the tree nodes. Since the computation of the result does not require storage of tree nodes already explored, it is possible to generate and process massive problems on even a small system. A variety of tree types are specified in the original UTS paper [20], but this study is confined to the "binomial" tree type, which is particularly challenging to load balance due to its unpredictability. In particular, simply distributing nodes near the root of the tree across threads is not sufficient, because some of those nodes produce very few descendants and the size of the subtree rooted at any node in the tree is not known *a priori*. Rather, continuous dynamic load balancing is required.

---

[1] https://github.com/bsc-pm/bots.

Though the benchmark itself is synthetic, it is representative of applications that perform an exhaustive search of a large irregular state space.

The key benchmark parameters are the root branching factor (b_0), the non-root branching factor (m), and the probability of generating children (q). At the start of the benchmark only the root node of the tree exists. After the b_0 child nodes of the root are generated, each of those nodes and each of their descendants determine the number of children to generate by sampling a binomial probability distribution. Each non-root node has m children with probability q and no children with probability $1 - q$. Each node is identified by a 20-byte descriptor. The generation of a child executes a SHA-1 cryptographic hash [9] on the combination of the parent's descriptor and its child index. Thus, successful completion of the benchmark on an n-node tree requires n SHA-1 evaluations.

An additional parameter is useful for the present study, compute granularity (g). This parameter specifies the number of times to repeat the SHA-1 hash at each node and it defaults to 1. Repeating the hash does not change the result of the computation, but it changes the amount of work done at each node. The effect of increasing the compute granularity is to coarsen the tasks.

The version of UTS used in this study is based on the implementation in the Barcelona OpenMP Tasks Suite (BOTS). The code for the recursive function that performs the tree traversal is shown in Fig. 1. The code in the figure includes some minor simplifications, but it also shows one substantive change from the BOTS version that has been made to the actual code run in the experiments. That change is the **if** statement that ensures recursive calls are only made in the case where a child node itself has children.[2] This change aids analysis of the benchmark by ensuring that all tasks do the same number of SHA-1 hash operations (including only those performed within that task itself, not its descendants). Recall that each node has m children with probability q and no children with probability $1 - q$. Thus, each task performs exactly $m \times g$ hash operations, where g is the compute granularity parameter specifying the number of repetitions of the hash operation for each node. In the original BOTS version, the **if** statement was not present, and tasks were created for child nodes that themselves produced no children and thus did no SHA-1 hash operations.[3]

3   Test Problem

The problem input used in the study is tree "T3S", found in the small.input file in the inputs/uts subdirectory of the BOTS distribution. The root node of the tree has $b_0 = 2000$ child nodes. Each non-root nodes has $m = 5$ children with probability $q = 0.200014$ and no children with probability $(1 - q) = 0.799986$.

---

[2]   An **if** clause on the **task** construct would still create a task, though it would be undeferred. The combination of **final** and **mergeable** clauses would allow but not require that child tasks be merged, and it would require additional look-ahead since the parent task must also be final to enable merging of the child tasks.

[3]   The version used in the 2009 UTS OpenMP tasking study [21] also had uniform work per task, but with each task performing the SHA-1 hash for only a single node.

```
unsigned long long search(Node *parent, int numChildren)
{
  Node n[numChildren], *nodePtr;
  int i, j;
  unsigned long long subtreesize = 1, partialCount[numChildren];

  // Recurse on the children of Node
  for (i = 0; i < numChildren; i++) {
    nodePtr = &n[i];

    // The following line is the work (one or more SHA-1 ops)
    for (j = 0; j < granularity; j++) {
      sha1_rng(parent->state.state, nodePtr->state.state, i);
    }

    // Sample a binomial distribution to determine the number of children of child i
    nodePtr->numChildren = uts_numChildren(nodePtr);

    if (nodePtr->numChildren > 0) {
      // Traverse the subtree rooted at child i to get subtree size
      #pragma omp task untied firstprivate(i, nodePtr) shared(partialCount)
        partialCount[i] = search(nodePtr, nodePtr->numChildren);
    }
    else
      partialCount[i] = 1;
  }

  // Wait for all subtree traversals
  #pragma omp taskwait

  // Combine subtree counts from children to get total size of subtree rooted at Node
  for (i = 0; i < numChildren; i++) {
    subtreesize += partialCount[i];
  }

  return subtreesize;
}
```

Fig. 1. UTS code

The resulting tree has 111 345 631 nodes and with a maximum depth of 17 844 nodes. Only 22 268 727 nodes (19.99964% of the total nodes) have children, while the remaining 89 076 904 nodes (80.00036% of the total nodes) have no children. These numbers match closely the expected number of nodes with no children based on the parameterized bias of the probability distribution given by q and $(1-q)$. Since the parallel code used in the experiments is structured to create one task per child-producing node, 22 268 727 is also the number of OpenMP tasks.

The compute granularity is varied in the experiments, but where not specified explicitly it is only one SHA-1 hash operation per tree node.

Each experiment consisted of ten trials. Perhaps due in part to effective load balancing, percent standard deviation was no more than 2% and in most cases a fraction of a percent. Hence, error bars are omitted from the graphs.

4   Experimental Setup

The present study spans four different architectures and 2–3 OpenMP implementations per architecture:

- **Xeon SKL:** Intel® Xeon® "Skylake" Platinum 8160 Processors, dual socket with 24 cores per socket (48 cores total), 2 hardware threads per core, 2.1 GHz, 192 GB DDR4 memory, Red Hat® Enterprise Linux® 7.1. *Compilers:* Intel® C/C++ Compiler 19.0.5 using "-fopenmp -O3 -xHost"; Clang LLVM 9.0.1 using "-fopenmp -O3 -march=native" with LLVM OpenMP Runtime.
- **IBM P9:** IBM® POWER9™ 8335-GTW Processors, dual socket with 22 cores per socket (44 cores total), 4 hardware threads per core, 2.3 GHz, 256 GB DDR4 memory, Red Hat® Enterprise Linux® 7.6. *Compilers:* PGI® Compiler 20.1 using "-mp -O3 -tp=pwr9"; Clang LLVM 9.0.1 using "-fopenmp -O3 -mcpu=pwr9" with LLVM OpenMP Runtime.
- **Arm TX2:** Marvell® ThunderX2® CN9975-2000 Arm® v8 Processors, dual socket with 28 cores per socket (56 cores total), 2 hardware threads per core[4], 2.0 GHz, 128 GB DDR4 memory, Tri-Lab Operating System Stack (TOSS) based on Red Hat® Enterprise Linux® 7.6. *Compilers:* Arm® Compiler 20.0 ("armclang") using "-fopenmp -O3 -mcpu=native"; Clang LLVM 9.0.1 using "-fopenmp -O3 -mcpu=native" with LLVM OpenMP Runtime.
- **Xeon Phi:** Intel® Xeon Phi™ "Knights Landing" 7250 Processor, single socket with 68 cores, 1.4 GHz, 4 hardware threads per core, 16 GB Multi-Channel MCDRAM on-package memory, 96 GB DDR4 memory, Cray Linux® Environment (CLE) based on SUSE Linux® Enterprise Server. *Compilers:* Intel® C/C++ Compiler 19.0.4 using "-fopenmp -O3 -xMIC-AVX512"; Cray® Compiling Environment (CCE) "Cray clang" 9.1.2 using "-fopenmp -O3 -h cpu=mic-knl"; Clang LLVM 9.0.1 using "-fopenmp -O3 -mcpu=knl" with LLVM OpenMP Runtime.

Clock speeds quoted above are as reported by **/proc/cpuinfo**, but processors may operate at higher "turbo" speeds given sufficient thermal headroom. To enable the large stack sizes required by the recursion (and recursive parallelism) in UTS, the system stack limit is set to "unlimited" via the **ulimit** command and the **OMP_STACKSIZE** environment variable is set to 100 MB. For the Intel TBB version of UTS, per-thread stack size is provided as an argument at TBB runtime initialization. Intel Cilk Plus limits maximum spawn depth to 1024 tasks, rendering it unable to run our test problem regardless of stack size.

---

[4] Each core has 4, but the BIOS configuration on the test system only has 2 enabled.

Two major OpenMP implementations not included in the study are IBM XL and GCC. Unfortunately, the executable generated by the XL 20.1 compiler encounters a segmentation fault each time, regardless of stack size. This issue has been reproduced by an IBM compiler engineer. GCC 9.2 correctly executes UTS, but the task parallel OpenMP program does not scale at all: Even 2-thread executions run no faster than the sequential program. Code inspection reveals that GCC continues to employ a centralized queue for OpenMP tasks, while most other implementations use scalable distributed work-stealing schedulers.

While task reductions would be useful for the expression of the UTS tree traversal code, they are not used in the version tested in this study. Of the few compilers that so far claim support for this OpenMP 5.0 feature, only GCC successfully compiled a UTS version adapted to use task reductions. The others reject the use of the **in_reduction** clause on orphaned tasks. Bug reports have been filed for clang and LLVM, with fixes expected to be available in the 11.0 release and subsequently in derivative vendor implementations.

5 Results

The primary independent variable in this study is task granularity. Recall that the granularity of each task is the product $m \times g$ where m is the non-root branching factor and g is the number of repeated SHA-1 hash operations per tree node. Since each non-leaf node in the tree, excluding the root node, has 5 children, the lowest granularity of 5 hash operations per task represents only one SHA-1 hash operation per child node in the tree. Coarser granularities are obtained by repeating the hash operations.

The number of SHA-1 hash operations per tree node is a metric particular to the UTS benchmark, but Tables 1 and 2 present task granularity in terms of execution time and instructions, respectively. This data is taken from sequential executions, representing lower bounds since the time to do the calculations in each task may increase in parallel executions. This "work-time inflation" can result, e.g., from cache and NUMA effects [23]. Moreover, the integer-heavy instruction mix of SHA-1 means that these numbers may not be universally applied to other programs. In spite of these differences, our results provide some rough guidance for acceptable granularity of OpenMP tasks.

The time required to perform one SHA-1 hash operation (the first column of numbers in Table 1) varies widely across the four systems, roughly 3× slower on Xeon Phi compared to Xeon Skylake. Differences in clock speed and in core and memory subsystem design contribute to these different computation rates. Using different compilers on the same system mostly results in similar SHA-1 execution rates, with some differences attributable to optimization choices and vectorization capability. The number of instructions required to perform one SHA-1 hash operation (the first column of numbers in Table 2) is a much narrower range (1.39–1.74 kilo-instructions) across systems than the time per operation. This observation suggests that generalizations of task granularity trends across systems may be more meaningful when expressed in terms of instructions per task rather than time per task.

Table 1. Translating task granularity from SHA-1 operations/task to time/task

Architecture and implementation	Time (μs) per op.	Time (μs) per recursive call at granularity					
		5 ops.	10 ops.	20 ops.	40 ops.	80 ops.	160 ops.
Xeon SKL - ICC	0.22	1.12	2.23	4.47	8.94	17.9	35.7
Xeon SKL - Clang	0.18	0.89	1.78	3.55	7.10	14.2	28.4
IBM P9 - PGI	0.31	1.53	3.06	6.13	12.2	24.5	49.0
IBM P9 - Clang	0.29	1.45	2.90	5.80	11.6	23.2	46.4
Arm TX2 - Armclang	0.32	1.61	3.22	6.43	12.9	25.7	51.4
Arm TX2 - Clang	0.34	1.73	3.45	6.90	13.8	27.6	55.2
Xeon Phi - ICC	0.64	3.21	6.42	12.8	25.7	51.4	103
Xeon Phi - Clang	0.74	3.68	7.36	14.7	29.4	58.9	118
Xeon Phi - CCE	0.63	3.14	6.29	12.6	25.2	50.3	101

Table 2. Translating task granularity from SHA-1 operations/task to machine instructions/task

Architecture and implementation	Kilo instr. per op.	Kilo instr. per recursive call at granularity					
		5 ops.	10 ops.	20 ops.	40 ops.	80 ops.	160 ops.
Xeon SKL - ICC	1.74	8.72	17.4	34.9	69.7	139	279
Xeon SKL - Clang	1.70	8.51	17.0	34.0	68.1	136	272
IBM P9 - PGI	1.65	8.26	16.5	33.1	66.1	132	264
IBM P9 - Clang	1.67	8.35	16.7	33.4	66.8	133	267
Arm TX2 - Armclang	1.39	6.97	13.9	27.9	55.7	111	223
Arm TX2 - Clang	1.51	7.59	15.2	30.4	60.7	121	243
Xeon Phi - ICC	1.70	8.51	17.0	34.0	68.1	136	272
Xeon Phi - Clang	1.71	8.57	17.1	34.3	68.6	137	274
Xeon Phi - CCE	1.63	8.15	16.3	32.6	65.2	130	261

5.1 Comparing Parallel Efficiency

The ability to compare across platforms with different architectures and core counts makes *percent parallel efficiency* an ideal metric. It is calculated by the formula $\frac{speedup}{number\_of\_threads} \times 100$, where *speedup* is $\frac{sequential\_excution\_time}{parallel\_execution\_time}$. Ideal speedup is a speedup equal to the number of threads, yielding a percent parallel efficiency of 100%.

Figures 2 and 3 show percent parallel efficiency for the UTS benchmark across architectures and OpenMP implementations (and TBB on the Intel Skylake platform). The vertical axis indicates percent parallel efficiency. The horizontal axis indicates the task granularity on a logarithmic scale, in thousands of instructions, derived from the data in Table 2. For each platform, the number of OpenMP threads is equal to the number of available cores on the machine, and each thread is bound to a single core.

ICC on Intel Skylake and PGI on IBM POWER9 are the top performers among OpenMP implementations, bested only by TBB (compiled with ICC). Even at the lowest granularity all three exceed 65% efficiency, and at a granularity of 67–70 kilo-instructions per task, they exceed 90% efficiency. On Intel Skylake, IBM POWER9, and Arm ThunderX2, the Clang/LLVM implementation achieves 43.0–47.7% efficiency at the lowest granularity and above 80% with tasks of 61–68 kilo-instruction granularity. While the efficiency of the Arm implementation is similar to clang on ThunderX2 at low granularity, it achieves better efficiency at the coarser granularities. The Intel Xeon Phi exhibits the

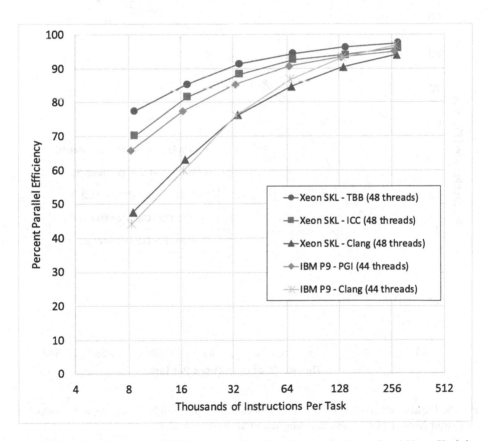

Fig. 2. Parallel efficiency of UTS as a function of task granularity on Intel Xeon Skylake and IBM POWER9 using various compilers

lowest efficiency of all architectures at the lowest granularity, but ICC fares much better than Clang or CCE. At a granularity of 65–68 kilo-instructions per task, CCE and ICC reach 80% efficiency while Clang lags behind at 72.3%.

Several trends emerge from the data. At the finest task granularity, the range of parallel efficiency is wide (16.8–77.5%). However, at the coarsest granularity it is much narrower (89.7–96.9%). Better performance at fine task granularity requires low overheads on the part of the OpenMP runtime implementations. Vendor implementations exhibit the best results on each architecture among those tested: ICC on Skylake and Xeon Phi, PGI on IBM, and armclang on ThunderX2. However, Clang/LLVM reaches reasonable efficiency at the coarser granularities on all architectures. Xeon Phi appears be the most challenging architecture for implementations to target efficiently, but it also has the most cores.

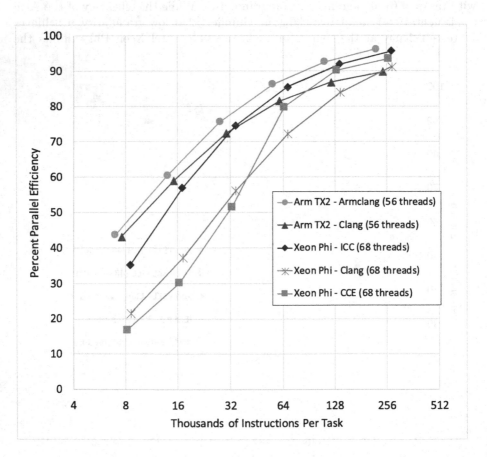

Fig. 3. Parallel efficiency of UTS as a function of task granularity on Arm ThunderX2 and Intel Xeon Phi Knights Landing using various compilers

The best implementations are successfully processing tasks consisting of $O(10k)$ instructions, but most implementations need a task granularity of $O(100k)$ instructions to reach high efficiency. Due to lack of space, the results in terms of execution time per task are not shown. However, Tables 1 and 2 can help to translate the results: In terms of execution time, the best implementations can manage tasks with only a few microseconds of work, but most require tasks to have at least tens of microseconds of work.

5.2 Thread Scalability and Simultaneous Multithreading

All platforms used in this study support multiple hardware threads per core, sometimes referred to as simultaneous multithreading (SMT). To assess the benefits of SMT, we compared the speedup of executions using only one OpenMP thread per core and executions using a number of OpenMP threads equal to

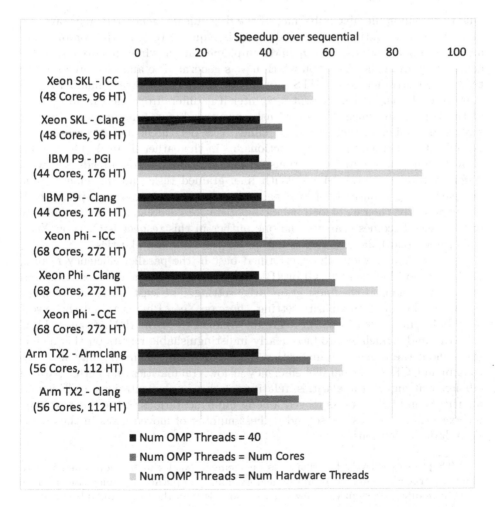

Fig. 4. Speedup at the coarsest granularity, varying thread count

the number of available hardware threads. Figure 4 shows the results across the various architectures with the maximum task granularity from the earlier experiments (223–279 kilo-instructions per task). Also included are results using 40 threads, which allows comparison of speedup for the same thread count across the architectures. All implementations achieve over 37X speedup using 40 threads, and speedup continues to improve as more threads are added from 40 threads to the number of threads equal to the number of cores on each architecture.[5] POWER9 exhibits the best improvement from SMT, with its 4 hardware threads more than doubling the performance compared to using a single thread per core. The Arm ThunderX2 system shows a more modest benefit from SMT. On Skylake (2-way SMT), ICC delivers a performance improvement with SMT while Clang sees none. The reverse occurs on Xeon Phi, with its 4-way SMT.

5.3 Quantifying Load Balancing Operations

Due to the unpredictable imbalance of the dynamically generated tree traversed in UTS, nearly continuous load balancing is required to scale the computation across available threads. The OpenMP implementation is free to move any unexecuted task from the thread on which it was generated to another thread in the team. We instrumented the UTS source code to check the thread number at the start of each task and increment a counter if it differs from the thread number of the thread on which its parent task executed. Figure 5 reports on a log-log scale the number of these "moved" child tasks per thread per second at each granularity (in thousands of instructions, as in the earlier figures). This metric allows comparison across executions on different numbers of threads and with different total execution times. With finer-grained tasks, all implementations are performing thousands of load balancing operations per second per thread. Unsurprisingly, the rate of load balancing operations decreases as the granularity of the tasks becomes coarser. The one outlier in this respect is CCE on Xeon Phi, whose load balancing rate is flat across the finer granularities.

The implementations that performed best in the parallel efficiency results, ICC on Xeon Skylake and PGI on IBM POWER9, carry out the most load balancing operations at the finest granularity setting. The least efficient implementations at the finest granularity setting, those on Xeon Phi, carry out the fewest load balancing operations. As a group, Clang/LLVM on IBM, Clang/LLVM on Arm, and Armclang produce nearly indistinguishable results on this metric throughout the range of granularities. The load balancing metric may also help to explain CCE's poor parallel efficiency at low granularities and better parallel efficiency at higher granularities, relative to other implementations: CCE is tied for the second-fewest tasks moved among implementations in the fine granularity executions but has the second-highest number of moved tasks in the coarse granularity executions.

---

[5] UTS places relatively low demands on memory, so it can be more amenable to adding threads compared to more memory-hungry applications, which can saturate the memory subsystem with fewer active threads than the total available cores.

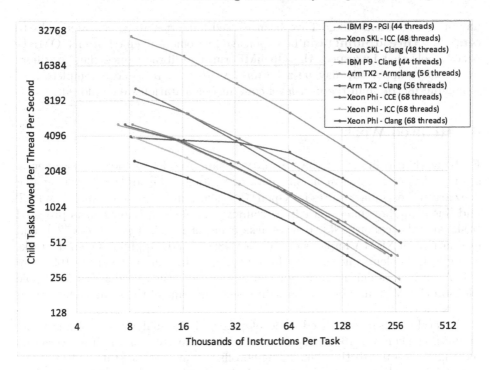

Fig. 5. Load balancing: Number of child tasks executing on different threads than their parent tasks, per thread, per second (log-log scale)

Table 3. Pearson correlation between speedup and number of moved child tasks per second per thread

SHA-1 ops. per task	5	10	20	40	80	160
Pearson correlation	0.69	0.59	0.42	0.42	0.38	0.12

Table 3 shows the Pearson correlation between speedup and the number of moved child tasks per second per thread, calculated across implementations at each granularity. A correlation coefficient near 1.0 or −1.0 indicates high positive or negative correlation, respectively, and a correlation coefficient near 0.0 indicates low correlation. Observe from the table that the finer the granularity of tasks, the more correlated are speedup and the number of load balancing operations. This data suggests that carrying out large numbers of load balancing operations per unit time becomes more important to the performance of OpenMP implementations as task granularity becomes finer.

Our moved child tasks metric is actually only a lower bound on the number of load balancing operations since we use untied tasks. Implementations can move untied tasks between threads during execution at any task scheduling points, such as at child task creation and when waiting in a **taskwait** region. Since we did not check the thread number after each task scheduling point, any such operations would have been missed. Unfortunately, repeated calls to **omp_get_thread_num()** can be expensive for some implementations. OMPT-based tools that introspect the OpenMP runtime library, once they are more universally supported, may be a better way to capture a more complete load balancing metric than the user-level code instrumentation we employed.

6   Related Work

Early work pertaining to the OpenMP tasking model included experimental studies [4,7] and a treatment on the design rationale [3]. BOTS [8] was among the earliest benchmark suites for OpenMP tasking and included kernels like FFT and linear algebra, many based on recursive parallelism. Later efforts provided basic microbenchmarks [5], benchmarks exercising task dependences [29], and evaluations of NUMA impacts on tasking [28]. A study applying OpenMP tasks to a graph problem is noteworthy for its scale, having run on an entire 1024-core SGI Altix UV system [1]. A more recent application study used a Fast Multipole Method (FMM) mini-application with results on some of the same architectures that we used [2].

Several efforts have focused on developing tools for analysis of programs using OpenMP tasking [11,16–18,27]. Previous work to analyze and reduce overheads has taken several directions, including cutoffs (adaptive [6] or static [13]) to limit parallelism. Others studied task granularity through profiling [12] or dynamic adjustment of granularity [19]. The unpredictable parallelism of UTS makes it a challenging target for the use of cutoffs or aggregation techniques.

7   Conclusions

The UTS benchmark is an extreme stress test, resulting in thousands of load balancing operations per second per thread. The study's focus on parallel efficiency allows comparison across diverse architectures and OpenMP implementations. The results illustrate that all implementations tested, except GCC, can efficiently manage tasks of $O(100k)$ instructions per task using all available cores, and the best implementations perform well with tasks of even $O(10k)$ instructions per task. The adequate efficiency of OpenMP tasking in Clang/LLVM as demonstrated in this study is particularly important for the OpenMP community due to its free availability under a permissive license and its role as a base for vendors to build upon. Still, we find that vendor OpenMP implementations, many of which are LLVM-based, do perform best. The overarching conclusion is that OpenMP tasking can be very efficient for unbalanced computation on a variety of architectures.

Acknowledgment. This work used advanced architecture testbed systems provided by the National Nuclear Security Administration's Advanced Simulation and Computing Program. Sandia National Laboratories is a multimission laboratory managed and operated by National Technology and Engineering Solutions of Sandia, LLC., a wholly owned subsidiary of Honeywell International, Inc., for the U.S. Department of Energy's National Nuclear Security Administration under contract DE-NA-0003525.

References

1. Adcock, A.B., Sullivan, B.D., Hernandez, O.R., Mahoney, M.W.: Evaluating OpenMP tasking at scale for the computation of graph hyperbolicity. In: Rendell, A.P., Chapman, B.M., Müller, M.S. (eds.) IWOMP 2013. LNCS, vol. 8122, pp. 71–83. Springer, Heidelberg (2013). https://doi.org/10.1007/978-3-642-40698-0_6

2. Atkinson, P., McIntosh-Smith, S.: On the performance of parallel tasking runtimes for an irregular fast multipole method application. In: de Supinski, B.R., Olivier, S.L., Terboven, C., Chapman, B.M., Müller, M.S. (eds.) IWOMP 2017. LNCS, vol. 10468, pp. 92–106. Springer, Cham (2017). https://doi.org/10.1007/978-3-319-65578-9_7

3. Ayguadé, E., et al.: The design of OpenMP tasks. IEEE Trans. Parallel Distrib. Syst. **20**, 404–418 (2009)

4. Ayguadé, E., Duran, A., Hoeflinger, J., Massaioli, F., Teruel, X.: An experimental evaluation of the new OpenMP tasking model. In: Adve, V., Garzarán, M.J., Petersen, P. (eds.) LCPC 2007. LNCS, vol. 5234, pp. 63–77. Springer, Heidelberg (2008). https://doi.org/10.1007/978-3-540-85261-2_5

5. Bull, J.M., Reid, F., McDonnell, N.: A microbenchmark suite for OpenMP tasks. In: Chapman, B.M., Massaioli, F., Müller, M.S., Rorro, M. (eds.) IWOMP 2012. LNCS, vol. 7312, pp. 271–274. Springer, Heidelberg (2012). https://doi.org/10.1007/978-3-642-30961-8_24

6. Duran, A., Corbalán, J., Ayguadé, E.: An adaptive cut-off for task parallelism. In: SC 2008: ACM/IEEE Supercomputing 2008, pp. 1–11. IEEE (2008)

7. Duran, A., Corbalán, J., Ayguadé, E.: Evaluation of OpenMP task scheduling strategies. In: Eigenmann, R., de Supinski, B.R. (eds.) IWOMP 2008. LNCS, vol. 5004, pp. 100–110. Springer, Heidelberg (2008). https://doi.org/10.1007/978-3-540-79561-2_9

8. Duran, A., Teruel, X., Ferrer, R., Martorell, X., Ayguadé, E.: Barcelona OpenMP tasks suite: a set of benchmarks targeting the exploitation of task parallelism in OpenMP. In: ICPP 2009: Proceedings of the 38th International Conference on Parallel Processing, pp. 124–131. IEEE, September 2009

9. Eastlake, D., Jones, P.: US Secure Hash Algorithm 1 (SHA-1). RFC 3174, Internet Engineering Task Force, September 2001. http://www.rfc-editor.org/rfc/rfc3174.txt

10. Frigo, M., Leiserson, C.E., Randall, K.H.: The implementation of the Cilk-5 multithreaded language. In: PLDI 1998: Proc. ACM SIGPLAN 1998 Conference on Programming Language Design and Implementation, PLDI 1998, pp. 212–223. Association for Computing Machinery, New York (1998)

11. Fürlinger, K., Skinner, D.: Performance profiling for OpenMP tasks. In: Müller, M.S., de Supinski, B.R., Chapman, B.M. (eds.) IWOMP 2009. LNCS, vol. 5568, pp. 132–139. Springer, Heidelberg (2009). https://doi.org/10.1007/978-3-642-02303-3_11

12. Gautier, T., Perez, C., Richard, J.: On the impact of OpenMP task granularity. In: de Supinski, B.R., Valero-Lara, P., Martorell, X., Mateo Bellido, S., Labarta, J. (eds.) IWOMP 2018. LNCS, vol. 11128, pp. 205–221. Springer, Cham (2018). https://doi.org/10.1007/978-3-319-98521-3_14

13. Iwasaki, S., Taura, K.: A static cut-off for task parallel programs. In: PACT 2016: International Conference on Parallel Architecture and Compilation Techniques, pp. 139–150, September 2016
14. Lattner, C., Adve, V.: LLVM: a compilation framework for lifelong program analysis and transformation. In: CGO 2004: International Symposium on Code Generation and Optimization, San Jose, CA, USA, pp. 75–88, March 2004
15. Leiserson, C.E.: The Cilk++ concurrency platform. J. Supercomput. **51**(3), 244–257 (2010)
16. Lin, Y., Mazurov, O.: Providing observability for OpenMP 3.0 applications. In: Müller, M.S., de Supinski, B.R., Chapman, B.M. (eds.) IWOMP 2009. LNCS, vol. 5568, pp. 104–117. Springer, Heidelberg (2009). https://doi.org/10.1007/978-3-642-02303-3_9
17. Lorenz, D., Mohr, B., Rössel, C., Schmidl, D., Wolf, F.: How to reconcile event-based performance analysis with tasking in OpenMP. In: Sato, M., Hanawa, T., Müller, M.S., Chapman, B.M., de Supinski, B.R. (eds.) IWOMP 2010. LNCS, vol. 6132, pp. 109–121. Springer, Heidelberg (2010). https://doi.org/10.1007/978-3-642-13217-9_9
18. Lorenz, D., Philippen, P., Schmidl, D., Wolf, F.: Profiling of OpenMP tasks with score-P. In: ICPPW 2012: 41st International Conference on Parallel Processing Workshops, pp. 444–453. IEEE Computer Society (2012)
19. Navarro, A., Mateo, S., Perez, J.M., Beltran, V., Ayguadé, E.: Adaptive and architecture-independent task granularity for recursive applications. In: de Supinski, B.R., Olivier, S.L., Terboven, C., Chapman, B.M., Müller, M.S. (eds.) IWOMP 2017. LNCS, vol. 10468, pp. 169–182. Springer, Cham (2017). https://doi.org/10.1007/978-3-319-65578-9_12
20. Olivier, S., et al.: UTS: an unbalanced tree search benchmark. In: Almási, G., Caşcaval, C., Wu, P. (eds.) LCPC 2006. LNCS, vol. 4382, pp. 235–250. Springer, Heidelberg (2007). https://doi.org/10.1007/978-3-540-72521-3_18
21. Olivier, S.L., Prins, J.F.: Evaluating OpenMP 3.0 run time systems on unbalanced task graphs. In: Müller, M.S., de Supinski, B.R., Chapman, B.M. (eds.) IWOMP 2009. LNCS, vol. 5568, pp. 63–78. Springer, Heidelberg (2009). https://doi.org/10.1007/978-3-642-02303-3_6
22. Olivier, S.L., Prins, J.F.: Comparison of OpenMP 3.0 and other task parallel frameworks on unbalanced task graphs. Int. J. Parallel Program. **38**(5–6), 341–360 (2010)
23. Olivier, S.L., de Supinski, B.R., Schulz, M., Prins, J.F.: Characterizing and mitigating work time inflation in task parallel programs. In: SC 2012: Proceedings of the International Conference on High Performance Computing, Networking, Storage and Analysis, pp. 65:1–65:12. IEEE Computer Society Press (2012)
24. OpenMP Architecture Review Board: OpenMP application programming interface, version 3.0, May 2008. https://www.openmp.org/wp-content/uploads/spec30.pdf
25. OpenMP Architecture Review Board: OpenMP application programming interface, version 5.0, November 2018. https://www.openmp.org/wp-content/uploads/OpenMP-API-Specification-5.0.pdf
26. Reinders, J.: Intel Threading Building Blocks: Outfitting C++ For Multi-Core Processor Parallelism. O'Reilly, Beijing (2007)
27. Schmidl, D., et al.: Performance analysis techniques for task-based OpenMP applications. In: Chapman, B.M., Massaioli, F., Müller, M.S., Rorro, M. (eds.) IWOMP 2012. LNCS, vol. 7312, pp. 196–209. Springer, Heidelberg (2012). https://doi.org/10.1007/978-3-642-30961-8_15

28. Terboven, C., Schmidl, D., Cramer, T., an Mey, D.: Assessing OpenMP task-ing implementations on NUMA architectures. In: Chapman, B.M., Massaioli, F., Müller, M.S., Rorro, M. (eds.) IWOMP 2012. LNCS, vol. 7312, pp. 182–195. Springer, Heidelberg (2012). https://doi.org/10.1007/978-3-642-30961-8_14
29. Virouleau, P., et al.: Evaluation of OpenMP dependent tasks with the KASTORS benchmark suite. In: DeRose, L., de Supinski, B.R., Olivier, S.L., Chapman, B.M., Müller, M.S. (eds.) IWOMP 2014. LNCS, vol. 8766, pp. 16–29. Springer, Cham (2014). https://doi.org/10.1007/978-3-319-11454-5_2

Applications

A Case Study of Porting HPGMG
from CUDA to OpenMP Target Offload

Christopher Daley$^{(\boxtimes)}$, Hadia Ahmed, Samuel Williams, and Nicholas Wright

Lawrence Berkeley National Laboratory (LBNL),
1 Cyclotron Road, Berkeley, CA 94720, USA
{csdaley,hahmed,SWWilliams,NJWright}@lbl.gov

Abstract. The HPGMG benchmark is a non-trivial Multigrid benchmark used to evaluate system performance. We ported this benchmark from CUDA to OpenMP target offload and added the capability to use explicit data management rather than managed memory. Our optimized OpenMP target offload implementation obtains a performance of 0.73x and 2.04x versus the baseline CUDA version on two different node architectures with NVIDIA Volta GPUs. We explain how we successfully used OpenMP target offload, including the code refactoring required, and how we improved upon our initial performance with LLVM/Clang by 97x.

Keywords: HPGMG · Managed memory · CUDA · OpenMP target offload · NVIDIA · Volta · V100 · GPU

1 Introduction

The systems deployed at supercomputing centers increasingly consist of heterogeneous node architectures with both CPUs and GPUs. At the present time this includes the Summit supercomputer at ORNL and the Sierra supercomputer at LLNL. However, there are also many planned deployments which will use GPU accelerators from NVIDIA, AMD or Intel. It is important that user applications can run efficiently on a variety of accelerators. Non-portable programming approaches are not practical for a large number of application code teams because of lack of resources, no detailed knowledge of specific accelerators, or code maintainability concerns. OpenMP target offload is one approach to enable users to portably offload computation to accelerators using directives [29].

There are case studies of user experiences of OpenMP target offload and even an entire benchmark suite to evaluate OpenMP target offload performance (SPEC ACCEL [16]). However, the case studies often consider relatively simple micro-benchmarks or mini-apps. There is generally a gap between OpenMP target offload case studies and the complexity of full applications run at supercomputing centers. It is thus important to assess the ease and success of using OpenMP target offload in non-trivial applications. This can find gaps in the OpenMP specification, assist with developing best practices for other users to follow, and identify bugs and performance issues in OpenMP compilers.

© Springer Nature Switzerland AG 2020
K. Milfeld et al. (Eds.): IWOMP 2020, LNCS 12295, pp. 37–51, 2020.
https://doi.org/10.1007/978-3-030-58144-2_3

In this work, we ported a non-trivial application named HPGMG [1,32] from CUDA to OpenMP target offload and extended the code to use explicit data management rather than managed memory. Managed memory is a capability enabling the CPU and GPU to transparently access the same data. It is used in many non-trivial applications [3], however it is not portable to all systems with GPUs and has potential performance issues [31]. We explain the code modifications required to use explicit data management as well as situations where a detailed understanding of the OpenMP specification is needed to correctly and efficiently manage data. We show performance of both code versions with multiple OpenMP compilers against the baseline CUDA performance. Our contributions include:

- We created an optimized OpenMP target offload implementation of HPGMG which achieves a performance of 0.73x and 2.04x versus the baseline CUDA version on two different node architectures with NVIDIA Volta GPUs.
- We describe how we successfully ported the managed memory CUDA version of HPGMG to OpenMP target offload and how we added explicit data management. This includes details about the refactoring required and the issues we encountered when mapping complicated data structures to the device.
- We compare the performance of 3 OpenMP offload compilers and detail a major bottleneck in the open-source LLVM/Clang compiler related to the size of the OpenMP present table. We describe our code changes to workaround LLVM/Clang compiler limitations and how we improved upon the initial LLVM/Clang performance by 97x.

The remainder of the paper is organized as follows. Section 2 discusses related work. Section 3 introduces the HPGMG application and discusses how we ported it to OpenMP target offload and added explicit data management. Section 4 introduces the systems and compilers used as well as the benchmarked HPGMG configuration. Section 5 shows the performance of the managed memory and explicit data management versions of HPGMG, and explains our progressive code optimizations for more efficient execution with the LLVM/Clang compiler. Section 6 discusses lessons learned. Section 7 concludes the paper.

2   Related Work

There are many examples of using OpenMP target offload to execute applications on platforms with GPUs, e.g. Nekbone [14], Lulesh [6,17], miniMD [30], Neutral [22] and other UK mini-apps [21,23]. The performance analysis in these papers mostly focuses on how well a compiler optimizes compute kernels for GPUs. User guidelines exist for achieving high performance with OpenMP target offload on CPU and GPU targets, e.g. using combined `teams distribute parallel for` OpenMP constructs and avoiding the use of explicit OpenMP schedules [15,24]. Similar guidelines were followed to port the entire SPEC ACCEL benchmark suite from OpenACC to OpenMP target offload [16]. Compiler optimization research exists that explores how to accelerate a broader range of OpenMP target regions on GPUs, specifically when user code appears between `target` and `parallel` constructs [5,11,15,34]. There has been some initial work done on identifying sources of overheads in OpenMP runtimes [26]. In this publication, we evaluate GPU compute performance with 3 OpenMP compilers and identify a significant LLVM/Clang OpenMP runtime overhead not previously reported.

There are fewer publications detailing data management challenges. The challenge of mapping structs containing pointers to the device is described in [22]. Here, the authors suggest a user code transformation of adding a new pointer variable that points to a struct pointer, and then mapping and operating on the new pointer variable. Cleaner methods to map structs containing pointers are explained in [12]. In a follow on paper, the authors show how managed memory allocations via `cudaMallocManaged` simplifies the use of C++ objects and enables `std::vector` to be used in OpenMP target offload applications [13]. There has been a successful study modifying OpenMP target offload applications and the LLVM/Clang compiler to use managed memory allocations [25]. However, managed memory is not available on all CPU/GPU systems and there have been several studies reporting higher than expected overheads when using managed memory [25,31]. One method to successfully use explicit data management is to create data management abstractions using OpenMP runtime API calls only, e.g. RAJA OpenMP target offload backend [4], and GenAsis [7]. The use of data management directives can be problematic because of lack of compiler support [35]. In this publication, we explain how we successfully used OpenMP data management directives to map a complicated nested data structure to the GPU.

3 The HPGMG Mini Application

HPGMG is a finite-volume geometric Multigrid HPC benchmark [1]. It is written in C99 and has been parallelized using MPI and optionally OpenMP. The benchmark creates a Multigrid grid hierarchy once and repeats the same Multigrid solve operation a user-specified number of times. The benchmark performance metric is a throughput metric of Degrees of Freedom per second (DOF/s). The metric does not include the time to build the Multigrid grid hierarchy.

A Multigrid solver is an iterative linear solver which achieves fast convergence by solving an $Ax = B$ equation at different resolutions. Multigrid solvers often use a V-cycle computational pattern. The fine-to-coarse part of the V-cycle consists of a smoothing operation on the finest structured grid, the calculation of a residual, and restriction of this data to the next coarsest grid. A direct solver is used on the coarsest level. The coarse-to-fine part of the V-cycle consists of interpolation of data to finer grids followed by a smoothing operation. An alternative to a V-cycle computational pattern is an F-cycle computational pattern which consists of multiple V-cycles using progressively more levels.

The coarsest level in the Multigrid hierarchy consists of a level with 2^3 grid points. Each successive finer level of the hierarchy has 4^3, 8^3, 16^3, ... grid points. The level data is divided into blocks of variable size up to a user-specified maximum size, typically 32^3 or 64^3 grid points. These blocks are distributed between

MPI ranks to balance computational load and memory footprint. HPGMG uses a nested data structure named `level_type` to hold all block data, communication buffers, and block neighbor metadata for a single level.

3.1 HPGMG-CUDA

HPGMG-CUDA is a CUDA port of HPGMG [32]. It depends on CUDA managed memory allocations using `cudaMallocManaged` to enable the same data to be accessed by CPU and GPU. A single execution of HPGMG-CUDA uses 14 different CUDA kernels. HPGMG-CUDA includes an optimization where operations for coarse levels are run on the CPU and operations for fine levels are run on the GPU.

3.2 Porting HPGMG-CUDA to OpenMP Target Offload

The approach we took to port HPGMG-CUDA to OpenMP target offload involved mixing the original CUDA memory allocation API calls with newly-created OpenMP target offload regions. In HPGMG-CUDA, the CUDA kernels access block data through a `level` structure variable of type `level_type` which is passed by value as part of the CUDA kernel launch. This data structure contains many scalar and pointer variables, where pointer variables accessed by CPU and GPU point to memory allocated using `cudaMallocManaged`. This makes OpenMP data management as simple as adding `map(to:level)` to the OpenMP target region because the targets of the pointer variables can be accessed by the CPU and the GPU.

Our OpenMP target offload code regions look nearly identical to the original CUDA kernels. The only difference is that the CUDA launch configuration is replaced with loops inside the OpenMP target region. There is a repeating pattern in our OpenMP target regions of a coarse-grained loop over blocks, followed by extraction of block data, followed by a fine-grained loop over grid points in a block. We parallelized and work-shared these loops using the `teams distribute` combined construct on the outer loop and the `parallel for` combined construct on the inner loop.

We implemented an incremental porting approach by creating a wrapper layer that dispatched to the original CUDA kernel or our newly-created function containing an OpenMP target region. This allowed us to test the correctness of one OpenMP function at a time. If the numerical results are not identical then we know we made a mistake in the OpenMP function or there is a compiler bug. This methodology requires compiling all code without fused-multiply-adds and fast math in order to expect a numerically identical solution.

3.3 Adding Explicit Data Management to HPGMG

Efficient explicit data management requires minimizing the number of data transfers between host and device. Our approach involved creating the `level` structure variable once on the device at program initialization. Most fields in the device version of **level** never need to be accessed by the host. The exception is the raw block data which must be transferred to the host every solution step because some HPGMG functions do not have GPU implementations. In order to use this approach, we had to refactor the code so that our modified OpenMP target regions access level data through a pointer to the device version of **level**. The code transformation is shown in Fig. 1.

Example initial code using managed memory

```
void smooth(level_type level, ...) {
// Map "level" to the device. All pointer variables in "level" point to
// data allocated with cudaMallocManaged. These addresses are thus valid
// on host and device
#pragma omp target teams distribute map(to:level)
   for (int blk=0; blk < level.num_my_blocks; blk++) {
```

Example refactored code using explicit data management

```
void smooth(level_type *level, ...) {
// Map zero-length array section of "level". This attaches the "level"
// pointer in the target region to the device copy of "level" which
// is already present on the device
#pragma omp target teams distribute map(to:level[:0])
   for (int blk=0; blk < level->num_my_blocks; blk++) {
```

Fig. 1. The code transformation used to efficiently implement explicit data movement in HPGMG.

The **level** structure variable contains a small number of data buffers for the entire level. This enables the data buffers to be copied efficiently between CPU and GPU in bulk data transfers. However, it has a software consequence that the blocks for each level must contain multiple pointers to different offsets within the larger data buffers. This necessitates additional OpenMP data management to ensure that the pointers point to the appropriate device data buffer and not the original host data buffer. The way we attached the appropriate device address to the device block pointers used the [:0] syntax and is shown in Fig. 2. This syntax has an additional effect of creating an association between the host and device address in the OpenMP runtime.

We implemented two techniques to ensure correctness of the explicit data management version of HPGMG. The first technique involved adding a print statement in the wrapper layer to enable tracing of the executed GPU functions in both managed memory and explicit data management versions. This allowed us to find a case where a missing **target update** construct caused the BiCGStab iterative solver to terminate early. Our second technique involved creating functions that calculated mean and L1 norm summary statistics of the level data in the location that owns the level, i.e. fine levels are owned by the GPU and coarse levels are owned by the CPU. We called these functions after each function and compared results against the managed memory version.

Attaching a device address to a device pointer

```
for (shape=0; shape<STENCIL_MAX_SHAPES; shape++) {
  for (block=0; block<3; ++block) {
    for (b=0; b<level->exchange_ghosts[shape].num_blocks[block]; ++b) {

#pragma omp target enter data \
  map(alloc:level->exchange_ghosts[shape].blocks[block][b].read.ptr[:0])

    }
  }
}
```

Fig. 2. OpenMP target offload [:0] syntax to make device pointers point to device addresses and not host addresses.

4   Experimental Methodology

4.1   Hardware and Software Environment

We used the Summit supercomputer at OLCF [18] and the Cori-GPU testbed at NERSC [27]. The characteristics of the two systems which are most relevant for this study are shown in Table 1.

Table 1. Overview of the Cori-GPU and Summit systems.

	Cori-GPU	Summit
Node architecture	Cray CS-Storm 500NX	IBM AC922
Node CPUs	2 × Intel Skylake	2 × IBM Power 9
Available cores per CPU	20 @ 2.40 GHz	21 @ 3.07 GHz
Node GPUs	8 x 16 GB NVIDIA V100	6 x 16 GB NVIDIA V100
CPU-GPU interconnect	PCIe 3.0 switch	NVLink 2.0

We evaluated multiple compilers on both systems to assess the OpenMP offload performance of HPGMG. We compared performance against the original CUDA version and also an OpenACC version which was ported to the GPU in an identical way as the OpenMP offload version. The OpenACC version was included to provide additional performance results for directive-based GPU offload. The benefit of including OpenACC in our study is that the PGI compiler provides mature OpenACC support and is available on both systems. The full list of compilers is shown in Table 2.

The Cori-GPU MPI stack was always OpenMPI-4.0.3, except for the CCE compiler which was limited to using MPICH-3.3.2. The OpenMPI library was built with UCX support enabling CUDA-aware MPI communication, but not GPUDirect support which would have enabled direct peer-to-peer data transfers between GPUs. The Summit MPI stack was always IBM Spectrum MPI 10.3.1.2-20200121. Our Summit job launch scripts always specified --smpiargs="-gpu"

Table 2. Compilers and GPU offload methods evaluated on the Cori-GPU and Summit systems.

Compiler	GPU offload	Cori-GPU version	Summit version
GCC + NVCC	CUDA	7.3.0 + 10.1.243	7.4.0 + 10.1.243
NVIDIA/PGI	OpenACC	20.4	20.1
Cray CCE	OpenMP	9.1.0 (LLVM version)	–
IBM XL	OpenMP	–	16.1.1-5
LLVM/Clang	OpenMP	11.0.0-git (#17d8334)	11.0.0-git (#17d8334)

to enable the use of CUDA-aware MPI with GPUDirect. We used the NVIDIA nvprof profiler on both platforms to measure the time spent in GPU kernels and data movement operations between CPU and GPU. nvprof was active for all results shown in this study. We used the ECP-funded HPCToolkit profiler [2] on Cori-GPU to identify bottlenecks in the LLVM/Clang OpenMP runtime.

4.2   Application Configuration

We configured the HPGMG benchmark to use the out-of-place Gauss Seidel Red Black (GSRB) smoother, 4th order boundary conditions, and a Multigrid F-Cycle. A single run executes 3 different problem sizes with a grid spacing of h, $2\,h$, and $4\,h$. In this work we only consider the performance of the largest problem: that is the problem with a grid spacing of h. Our chosen problem has a grid spacing of $h = \frac{1}{512}$, a maximum box size of 32^3, and is executed between 3 and 100 steps depending on the throughput of the benchmark for each compiler. This problem has a memory footprint of approximately 38 GB and thus exceeds the memory capacity of the 16 GB GPUs in both our test platforms. In our tests we choose to use a single CPU socket and optionally 3 GPUs. The CPU-only configurations are executed with 1 MPI rank per core, and the CPU+GPU configurations are executed with 1 MPI rank per GPU.

5   Performance Evaluation

5.1   Performance When Using Managed Memory

Figure 3 shows the performance of the managed memory versions of HPGMG. The GPU versions of HPGMG generally performed better on Summit than Cori-GPU because of higher data transfer bandwidth between CPU and GPU (NVLink-2.0 versus PCIe 3.0), fewer GPU page faults, and less data movement between CPU and GPU. The system-level reasons for the differences are out of scope for this paper. Our performance evaluation will thus only compare compilers on the same system and not between systems. Figure 3a shows that the CCE and LLVM/Clang OpenMP compilers were not competitive with CUDA on Cori-GPU. CCE performed poorly because the code needed to be compiled at -O0 to workaround a compiler bug [10] (upstream issue at [19]). LLVM/Clang performed poorly because of significant time spent in `cuMemAlloc` and `cuMemFree` functions which are used to allocate and free device memory. These functions were called when mapping the `level` structure variable to the device. Figure 3b shows that the XL OpenMP compiler achieved 0.70x of CUDA performance on Summit. The PGI OpenACC compiler achieved 0.76x and 0.89x of CUDA performance on Cori-GPU and Summit, respectively, indicating that directive-based programming can deliver performance competitive with CUDA.

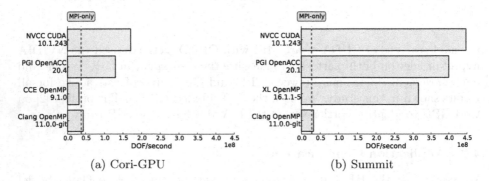

(a) Cori-GPU   (b) Summit

Fig. 3. HPGMG throughput for the managed memory version of HPGMG on Cori-GPU and Summit (higher is better). All configurations used 1 CPU socket and 3 GPUs. The dashed line shows the best MPI-only performance out of all available compilers when using 1 CPU socket.

5.2   Performance When Using Explicit Data Management

The performance results for the explicit data management version of HPGMG are limited because of various compiler issues: the XL compiler failed to correctly create the HPGMG device data structures [28] and the CCE 9.1.0 compiler does not support the OpenMP-5.0 pointer attachment rules required by HPGMG (the recently released CCE-10.0.0 compiler should provide this capability [9]). Henceforth, all performance results are obtained using the LLVM/Clang compiler. The initial results were disappointing compared to the OpenMP managed memory version: 12.0x slower on Cori-GPU and 5.7x slower on Summit.

The HPCToolkit profiler showed that most of the runtime was spent executing a `target update` construct used to copy data from GPU to CPU. The bottleneck was not data movement but instead time spent in a library function provided by `libstdc++` named `std::_Rb_tree_increment`. Our hypothesis is that this function is used by the LLVM/Clang OpenMP runtime to find out which host pointer corresponds to which device pointer before copying data between memories. OpenMP runtimes maintain an association between host and device pointers in a present table; it is expected to be efficient even when it contains many entries [8,14,36]. We describe our optimizations to workaround this LLVM/Clang bottleneck and other bottlenecks below. The impact of the individual optimizations are shown in Fig. 4 and explained below.

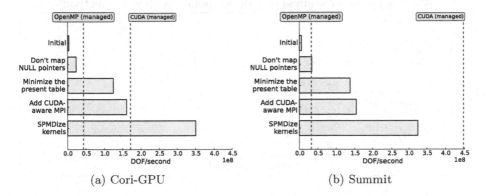

(a) Cori-GPU   (b) Summit

Fig. 4. HPGMG throughput for the explicit data management version of HPGMG on Cori-GPU and Summit using the LLVM/Clang compiler (higher is better). All configurations used 1 CPU socket and 3 GPUs. Optimizations apply additively, e.g. the code changes associated with the 4th bar down includes the code changes associated with the 2nd and 3rd bars. The dashed lines show the performance of the managed memory version of HPGMG when using OpenMP target offload and CUDA (values obtained from Fig. 3).

Don't Map NULL Pointers: Many HPGMG block pointers point to NULL for the duration of the application. These pointer addresses can safely be kept out of the OpenMP runtime present table. We added an `if` statement around the `target enter data` directive in Fig. 2 to only map data when it is not NULL. This improved the solve performance by 6.5x on Cori-GPU. It also reduced the initialization time from 392 s to 40 s on Cori-GPU. This is primarily because of less exclusive time in the OpenMP runtime but also because of significantly fewer CUDA HtoD memcpy transfers of 8 bytes. Here, an 8 byte transfer corresponds to setting a pointer in the device environment to a new device address.

Minimize the Present Table: The HPGMG block pointers are simply a convenience in the device kernels. Therefore, there is no need for the OpenMP runtime to maintain an association between block pointer host and device addresses. This is because all data transfers between CPU and GPU involve the larger `level` data buffers pointed to by the block pointers. We avoid creating an association by manually updating the device pointers in the device environment instead of using the `[:0]` syntax shown earlier (Fig. 2). Our function to do this is named `omp_attach` and is shown in Fig. 5. It performs the same task as the OpenACC runtime API function named `acc_attach`. This improved the performance by 5.3x on Cori-GPU and reduced initialization time to 9.3 s. The nvprof profiler shows that we called the OpenMP target region in `omp_attach` 103,644 times.

This implies that LLVM/Clang present table lookup time slows down significantly when the present table has O(100K) entries.

Attaching a device address to a device pointer - alternate method

```
void omp_attach(void **ptr)
{
   void *dptr = *ptr;
   if (dptr) {
#pragma omp target data use_device_ptr(dptr)
      {
#pragma omp target is_device_ptr(dptr)
         {
            *ptr = dptr;
         }
      }
   }
}
omp_attach((void**)&level->exchange_ghosts[shape].
                         blocks[block][b].read.ptr);
```

Fig. 5. The function `omp_attach()` attaches a device address to a device pointer without creating an entry in the present table of the OpenMP runtime. The function assumes it is passed the address of a pointer variable which is pointing to the host address of a mapped variable. We use the `use_device_ptr` clause to obtain the device address of the mapped variable. We then use an OpenMP target region to set the device pointer to the device address of the mapped variable.

Add CUDA-Aware MPI: The expensive `target update` code path can be avoided by exchanging GPU data between processes using CUDA-aware MPI communication. CUDA-aware MPI simplifies the OpenMP source code because it only involves adding a `target data` region with a `use_device_ptr` clause to pass the device address of a data buffer to a MPI communication call. The use of CUDA-aware MPI improved performance by 1.3x on Cori-GPU. However, CUDA-aware MPI is a capability that is not available in all MPI libraries.

SPMDize Kernels: The LLVM/Clang OpenMP compiler is known to perform poorly when there is user code in between `target` and `parallel` OpenMP directives [33]. As mentioned in Sect. 3.2, this code pattern happens frequently in HPGMG. It is possible to use the faster LLVM/Clang "SPMD" code generation scheme by creating all parallelism upfront to ensure that all threads execute the same code. It is impractical for us to use a combined `teams distribute parallel for` construct in the HPGMG OpenMP target regions because this would omit worksharing of the fine-grained loop over threads. Therefore we used strictly nested `teams` and `parallel` constructs with a manual distribution of the coarse-grained loop over teams based on the team ID. This was done because the OpenMP specification does not provide a combined `teams distribute parallel` construct and specifies that the `distribute` construct must be strictly nested inside a teams region. The SPMD code transformation improved LLVM/Clang performance by 2.2x on Cori-GPU. There was no benefit to the XL compiler because this compiler already implements interprocedural static compiler analysis to determine when all threads execute the same code [34].

6   Discussion

In this section we discuss whether the abstractions provided by the OpenMP specification were sufficient for our coding exercise as well as OpenMP compiler maturity and performance.

6.1   Assessment of OpenMP Abstractions

The directives and runtime API functions provided by the OpenMP specification enabled us to translate CUDA kernels into OpenMP target offload regions. They also enabled us to successfully implement explicit data management in a code that uses nested data structures with many pointer fields. We are concerned that only a small minority of users will be able to explicitly manage data movement in CPU/GPU systems in similarly complicated codes, however, this is no fault of the OpenMP specification. The barrier to entry is significantly lowered by relying on managed memory. We demonstrated that today's compilers correctly interoperate with CUDA managed memory and we are looking forward to compilers eventually supporting `requires unified_shared_memory` OpenMP directive to eliminate the need to mix OpenMP with lower-level non-portable APIs.

The only abstractions that could benefit similar coding efforts are related to performance. We found that a manual implementation of `acc_attach` in OpenMP enabled us to create a complicated data structure on the device in less time and assisted the LLVM/Clang OpenMP runtime to more quickly find the association between host and device addresses. However, this API function was only necessary because of a significant bottleneck in the LLVM/Clang present table implementation. We found that a manual implementation of a `teams distribute parallel` combined construct enabled us to use a faster LLVM/Clang code generation scheme for most of the HPGMG functions containing OpenMP target offload, however, it was detrimental to the performance of XL generated compute kernels.

6.2   Assessment of Compiler Maturity and Performance

We encountered issues with XL and CCE compilers which limited the OpenMP target offload results in Sect. 5. The only compiler which successfully compiled and executed the explicit data management version of HPGMG was LLVM/Clang (versions prior to LLVM/Clang-11.0.0 also had issues [19]). We found that the XL-compiled managed memory version of HPGMG achieved 0.70x of HPGMG-CUDA performance. This is encouraging because we made no specific optimizations to achieve high performance with the managed memory version of the code. The LLVM/Clang compiler performed poorly with the managed memory code version and abysmally with the initial explicit data management code version on both computing platforms.

We optimized the initial explicit data management code to achieve higher performance with the LLVM/Clang compiler: 2.04x of HPGMG-CUDA performance on Cori-GPU and 0.73x of HPGMG-CUDA performance on Summit. It should be mentioned that this is not the fairest of comparisons because HPGMG-CUDA does not include explicit data management to enable efficient bulk data transfers between CPU and GPU. One concern we have about our optimizations for LLVM/Clang are that they are unintuitive to the average OpenMP programmer and should instead be performed by a tuned OpenMP compiler and runtime. The runtime overheads in LLVM/Clang included excessive time spent in device memory management functions and a slow present table implementation (we have reported this issue [20]). Neither the CCE or XL compiler use device memory management functions as frequently as the LLVM/Clang compiler. We have not been able to test whether the same present table bottleneck exists in the CCE or XL compilers yet. The LLVM/Clang compiler also generated relatively slow device code without our manual SPMD code transformation. This hopefully will not be needed for much longer, since a prototype exists to use the faster code generation scheme in LLVM/Clang [11].

7   Conclusion

This paper describes how we ported HPGMG from CUDA to OpenMP target offload, added explicit data management, measured performance with multiple OpenMP compiler and runtimes on two different node architectures, and finally optimized HPGMG performance when using LLVM/Clang. Our work shows that OpenMP target offload compiler and runtimes still need to fix compiler bugs, implement more complete OpenMP 5.0 feature support, efficiently compile a broader range of application usage of OpenMP directives, and fix overheads in OpenMP runtimes. However, there were positive performance results compared to HPGMG-CUDA (managed memory CUDA implementation of HPGMG): the XL-compiled managed memory version of HPGMG achieved 0.70x of HPGMG-CUDA performance on Summit, and the LLVM/Clang-compiled explicit data management version of HPGMG achieved 2.04x of HPGMG-CUDA performance on Cori-GPU and 0.73x of HPGMG-CUDA performance on Summit.

Acknowledgments. This research used resources of the National Energy Research Scientific Computing Center (NERSC), a U.S. Department of Energy Office of Science User Facility operated under Contract No. DE-AC02-05CH11231. This research also used resources of the Oak Ridge Leadership Computing Facility, which is a DOE Office of Science User Facility supported under Contract DE-AC05-00OR22725. The authors would like to thank Mat Colgrove of NVIDIA for the initial development of an explicit data management version of HPGMG using OpenACC. The authors would also like to thank Brian Friesen of LBNL for installing CUDA-aware versions of OpenMPI for several different compiler stacks.

References

1. Adams, M., Brown, J., Shalf, J., Van Straalen, B., Strohmaier, E., Williams, S.: HPGMG (2020). https://bitbucket.org/hpgmg/hpgmg
2. Adhianto, L., et al.: HPCTOOLKIT: tools for performance analysis of optimized parallel programs. Concurr. Comput.: Pract. Exp. **22**(6), 685–701 (2010). https://doi.org/10.1002/cpe.1553
3. Almgren, A.S., Bell, J.B., Lijewski, M.J., Lukić, Z., Van Andel, E.: Nyx: a massively parallel AMR code for computational cosmology. Astrophys. J. **765**, 39 (2013). https://doi.org/10.1088/0004-637X/765/1/39
4. Beckingsale, D.A., et al.: RAJA: portable performance for large-scale scientific applications. In: 2019 IEEE/ACM International Workshop on Performance, Portability and Productivity in HPC (P3HPC), pp. 71–81, November 2019. https://doi.org/10.1109/P3HPC49587.2019.00012
5. Bercea, G.T., Bataev, A., Eichenberger, A.E., Bertolli, C., O'Brien, J.K.: An open-source solution to performance portability for Summit and Sierra supercomputers. IBM J. Res. Dev. **64**(3/4), 12:1–12:23 (2020)
6. Bercea, G.T., et al.: Performance analysis of OpenMP on a GPU using a CORAL proxy application. In: Proceedings of the 6th International Workshop on Performance Modeling, Benchmarking, and Simulation of High Performance Computing Systems, PMBS 2015. Association for Computing Machinery, New York (2015). https://doi.org/10.1145/2832087.2832089
7. Budiardja, R.D., Cardall, C.Y.: Targeting GPUs with OpenMP directives on summit: a simple and effective Fortran experience. Parallel Comput. **88**, 102544 (2019)
8. Colgrove, M., Wolfe, M.: Personal Communication, May 2020
9. Crayport: Case 247291 - Cray CCE-9.0.0 has OpenMP offload bugs when mapping structs (2020). https://portal.cray.com
10. Crayport: Case 256571 - Test program must be compiled at -O0 when using CCE/9.1.0 (2020). https://portal.cray.com
11. Doerfert, J., Diaz, J.M.M., Finkel, H.: The TRegion interface and compiler optimizations for OPENMP target regions. In: Fan, X., de Supinski, B.R., Sinnen, O., Giacaman, N. (eds.) IWOMP 2019. LNCS, vol. 11718, pp. 153–167. Springer, Cham (2019). https://doi.org/10.1007/978-3-030-28596-8_11
12. Grinberg, L., Bertolli, C., Haque, R.: Hands on with OpenMP4.5 and unified memory: developing applications for IBM's Hybrid CPU + GPU systems (part I). In: de Supinski, B.R., Olivier, S.L., Terboven, C., Chapman, B.M., Müller, M.S. (eds.) IWOMP 2017. LNCS, vol. 10468, pp. 3–16. Springer, Cham (2017). https://doi.org/10.1007/978-3-319-65578-9_1
13. Grinberg, L., Bertolli, C., Haque, R.: Hands on with OpenMP4.5 and unified memory: developing applications for IBM's hybrid CPU + GPU systems (part II). In: de Supinski, B.R., Olivier, S.L., Terboven, C., Chapman, B.M., Müller, M.S. (eds.) IWOMP 2017. LNCS, vol. 10468, pp. 17–29. Springer, Cham (2017). https://doi.org/10.1007/978-3-319-65578-9_2
14. Hart, A.: First experiences porting a parallel application to a hybrid supercomputer with OpenMP4.0 device constructs. In: Terboven, C., de Supinski, B.R., Reble, P., Chapman, B.M., Müller, M.S. (eds.) IWOMP 2015. LNCS, vol. 9342, pp. 73–85. Springer, Cham (2015). https://doi.org/10.1007/978-3-319-24595-9_6
15. Hayashi, A., Shirako, J., Tiotto, E., Ho, R., Sarkar, V.: Performance evaluation of OpenMP's target construct on GPUS - exploring compiler optimisations. Int. J. High Perform. Comput. Network. **13**(1), 54–69 (2019). https://doi.org/10.1504/IJHPCN.2019.097051

16. Juckeland, G., et al.: From describing to prescribing parallelism: translating the SPEC ACCEL OpenACC suite to OpenMP target directives. In: Taufer, M., Mohr, B., Kunkel, J.M. (eds.) ISC High Performance 2016. LNCS, vol. 9945, pp. 470–488. Springer, Cham (2016). https://doi.org/10.1007/978-3-319-46079-6_33

17. Karlin, I., et al.: Early experiences porting three applications to OpenMP 4.5. In: Maruyama, N., de Supinski, B.R., Wahib, M. (eds.) IWOMP 2016. LNCS, vol. 9903, pp. 281–292. Springer, Cham (2016). https://doi.org/10.1007/978-3-319-45550-1_20

18. Vergara Larrea, V.G., et al.: Scaling the summit: deploying the world's fastest supercomputer. In: Weiland, M., Juckeland, G., Alam, S., Jagode, H. (eds.) ISC High Performance 2019. LNCS, vol. 11887, pp. 330–351. Springer, Cham (2019). https://doi.org/10.1007/978-3-030-34356-9_26

19. LLVM Bugzilla: Bug 44390 - Incorrect OpenMP target offload code at > -O0 optimization (2020). https://bugs.llvm.org

20. LLVM Bugzilla: Bug 46107 - Poor present table performance (2020). https://bugs.llvm.org

21. Martineau, M., McIntosh-Smith, S., Gaudin, W.: Evaluating OpenMP 4.0's effectiveness as a heterogeneous parallel programming model. In: 2016 IEEE International Parallel and Distributed Processing Symposium Workshops (IPDPSW), pp. 338–347 (2016)

22. Martineau, M., McIntosh-Smith, S.: The productivity, portability and performance of OpenMP 4.5 for scientific applications targeting Intel CPUs, IBM CPUs, and NVIDIA GPUs. In: de Supinski, B.R., Olivier, S.L., Terboven, C., Chapman, B.M., Müller, M.S. (eds.) IWOMP 2017. LNCS, vol. 10468, pp. 185–200. Springer, Cham (2017). https://doi.org/10.1007/978-3-319-65578-9_13

23. Martineau, M., et al.: Performance analysis and optimization of Clang's OpenMP 4.5 GPU support. In: Proceedings of the 7th International Workshop on Performance Modeling, Benchmarking and Simulation of High Performance Computing Systems, PMBS 2016, pp. 54–64. IEEE Press (2016)

24. Martineau, M., Price, J., McIntosh-Smith, S., Gaudin, W.: Pragmatic performance portability with OpenMP 4.x. In: Maruyama, N., de Supinski, B.R., Wahib, M. (eds.) IWOMP 2016. LNCS, vol. 9903, pp. 253–267. Springer, Cham (2016). https://doi.org/10.1007/978-3-319-45550-1_18

25. Mishra, A., Li, L., Kong, M., Finkel, H., Chapman, B.: Benchmarking and evaluating unified memory for OpenMP GPU offloading. In: Proceedings of the Fourth Workshop on the LLVM Compiler Infrastructure in HPC. LLVM-HPC 2017. Association for Computing Machinery, New York (2017). https://doi.org/10.1145/3148173.3148184

26. Monsalve Diaz, J.M., Friedline, K., Pophale, S., Hernandez, O., Bernholdt, D., Chandrasekaran, S.: Analysis of OpenMP 4.5 offloading in implementations: correctness and overhead. Parallel Comput. **89**, 102546 (2019). https://doi.org/10.1016/j.parco.2019.102546

27. NERSC: Cori GPU Nodes (2020). https://docs-dev.nersc.gov/cgpu/

28. OLCF Support: IBM ticket TS003552272 - IBM compiler OpenMP target offload data management bug (2020)

29. OpenMP Architecture Review Board: OpenMP application programming interface version 5.0, November 2018. https://www.openmp.org/wp-content/uploads/OpenMP-API-Specification-5.0.pdf

30. Pennycook, S.J., Sewall, J.D., Hammond, J.R.: Evaluating the impact of proposed OpenMP 5.0 features on performance, portability and productivity. In: 2018 IEEE/ACM International Workshop on Performance, Portability and Productivity in HPC (P3HPC), pp. 37–46 (2018)
31. Rabbi, F., Daley, C.S., Aktulga, H.M., Wright, N.J.: Evaluation of directive-based GPU programming models on a block eigensolver with consideration of large sparse matrices. In: Wienke, S., Bhalachandra, S. (eds.) WACCPD 2019. LNCS, vol. 12017, pp. 66–88. Springer, Cham (2020). https://doi.org/10.1007/978-3-030-49943-3_4
32. Sakharnykh, N., Wang, P., Williams, S.: HPGMG-CUDA (2020). https://bitbucket.org/nsakharnykh/hpgmg-cuda
33. The Clang Team: Clang 11 Documentation, OpenMP Support (2020). https://clang.llvm.org/docs/OpenMPSupport.html
34. Tiotto, E., Mahjour, B., Tsang, W., Xue, X., Islam, T., Chen, W.: OpenMP 4.5 compiler optimization for GPU offloading. IBM J. Res. Dev. **64**(3/4), 14:1–14:11 (2020)
35. Vergara Larrea, V.G., Budiardja, R.D., Gayatri, R., Daley, C., Hernandez, O., Joubert, W.: Experiences in porting mini-applications to OpenACC and OpenMP on heterogeneous systems. Concurr. Comput.: Pract. Exp. e5780 (2020). https://doi.org/10.1002/cpe.5780. https://onlinelibrary.wiley.com/doi/abs/10.1002/cpe.5780. [Published online ahead of print (24 April 2020)]
36. Wolfe, M., Lee, S., Kim, J., Tian, X., Xu, R., Chandrasekaran, S., Chapman, B.: Implementing the OpenACC data model. In: 2017 IEEE International Parallel and Distributed Processing Symposium Workshops (IPDPSW), pp. 662–672, May 2017. https://doi.org/10.1109/IPDPSW.2017.85

P-Aevol: An OpenMP Parallelization of a Biological Evolution Simulator, Through Decomposition in Multiple Loops

Laurent Turpin[1,2]([⊠]), Thierry Gautier[1], Jonathan Rouzaud-Cornabas[2], and Christian Perez[1]

[1] Univ. Lyon, Inria, CNRS, EnsL, UCBL, LIP, Lyon, France
{laurent.turpin,christian.perez}@inria.fr, thierry.gautier@inrialpes.fr
[2] Univ. Lyon, INSA Lyon, Inria, CNRS, UCBL, LIRIS, Lyon, France
jonathan.rouzaud-cornabas@inria.fr

Abstract. This paper presents how we have achieved the paralleliza-tion of Aevol, a biological evolution simulator, on multi-core architecture using the OpenMP standard. While it looks like a simple for-loop prob-lem with independent iterations, the stochastic nature of Aevol makes the duration of the iterations unpredictable and it conveys a high irregular-ity. Classical scheduling algorithms of OpenMP runtimes turn out to be inefficient. By analysing the origin of this irregularity, this paper present how to transform the highly irregular Aevol for-loop to a sequence com-posed by a small duration irregular for-loop followed by work intensive for-loop easy to schedule using classical LPT algorithm. This method leads to a gain up to 27% from the best OpenMP loop schedule.

Keywords: Loop scheduling · Irregular iterations · Multi-core · OpenMP · *in-silico* simulation

1 Introduction

Scientific applications made the development of High Performance Computing more and more relevant. Frequently, these applications are based on independent iterations loops. Aevol is an example of such application. The purpose of Aevol is to simulate millions of generations of an evolving population of micro-organisms. Each generation consists of a for loop iterating over the population. For each individual, the model simulates their evolution through stochastic selection and mutations that consist on random modifications of their structures. Our goal is to parallelize with OpenMP the evolutionary loop of Aevol, that is, at first glance, a simple for-loop with independent iterations.

The OpenMP API standard proposes 3 loop schedulers: static, dynamic and guided. Due to the Aevol stochastic model, the irregularity of the application requires a dynamic scheduler, like other scientific applications [1,18], in order to well balance the workload between the threads of the parallel region.

© Springer Nature Switzerland AG 2020
K. Milfeld et al. (Eds.): IWOMP 2020, LNCS 12295, pp. 52–66, 2020.
https://doi.org/10.1007/978-3-030-58144-2_4

We, as most of HPC developers, are concerned with the following questions. Can better schedule be computed for our application? What would be the gains? How to implement it? The underlying problem was at first glance a list scheduling problem with unknown duration of tasks. Thanks to an analysis of the application structured as compositions of functions, we refine the problem by decomposing the loop in two sub-loops: the first one being a loop scheduling problem with unknown durations that permits to estimate the iteration's duration of the second loop. By doing so, it becomes possible to use a clairvoyant list scheduling algorithm. Using a method inspired by LPT scheduling [11] for the second loop, and thanks to a well balanced first loop and a limited impact of sorting tasks, we gain up to 27% more performance than the OpenMP dynamic.

The remainder of this paper is organized as follows: Sect. 2 introduces the Aevol software, how its computation is structured and how it is characterized. Sect. 3 explains the methodology developed to split the loop and how we use the application data to design a new scheduling method and some practical implementations done with OpenMP. Sect. 4 deals with the experimental evaluations of these implementations. Related work is discussed in Sect. 5. Last, Sect. 6 concludes the paper and opens up some future work.

2 Aevol, An Irregular Stochastic Program

This section presents Aevol, a computational biology software. It describes its computational model and characterizes the underlying main loop to parallelize.

2.1 Aevol: A Simulation of Darwinian Evolution

Biologists run *in-vitro* experiments in Petri dishes to observe the growth and evolution of simple organisms [3]. Aevol[1] proposes to run the same kind of experiments but *in-silico* [13]. Aevol is a C++ implementation of the biological model presented in [15]. It makes use of a stochastic model that puts uni-cellular organisms in a well defined environment and lets them evolve. Each organism, or individual, encloses genetic code in the form of a sequence of characters representing its DNA. The information contained in the genetic code is treated and eventually forms the phenotype of the individual, *i.e.*, its macroscopic behaviour or appearance. The phenotype is compared to an environmental target that models the environment where the micro-organisms leave. The difference tells how well the individual fits the environment. In Aevol, the *fitness* is represented as a scalar. For each generation, the whole population follows the three evolution steps:

1. **Selection:** the fitness of each individual is computed. The higher the fitness of an individual, the higher its probability of reproduction.
2. **Reproduction:** the survivors have the opportunity to pass their genetic code to their offspring. It is the principle of heredity.

---

[1] http://www.aevol.fr/.

3. Mutation: the new-born individuals may get random variations on the genetic code that may modify their phenotype and their fitness.

The world in which individuals evolve is a 2D toric grid. In each cell of the grid lies one and only one individual. For each cell, competition is made among the 9 individuals of its neighborhood and only one of these 9 individuals is selected as the reproducer for this cell. That means that a single individual can reproduce multiple times within its neighborhood. After selecting all the reproducers for the entire grid, the population is wiped out and the reproducers are copied in the cells where they reproduce. Then mutation may occur randomly, depending on a mutation rate parameter defined by the user, on the DNA of the new population. Their new phenotype and fitness are computed.

At runtime, the computation time of a generation is very short *i.e.*, around 10 ms, thanks to a simple model and a small population. For instance in [16], the population size was 1024 individuals for a 32×32 square grid with different mutation rates (10^{-4}, 10^{-5} and 10^{-6}). But they computed for a total of 81 millions of generations demanding weeks of computations. Improving the performance of one generation becomes essential especially since Aevol is evolving toward a more complex model [17].

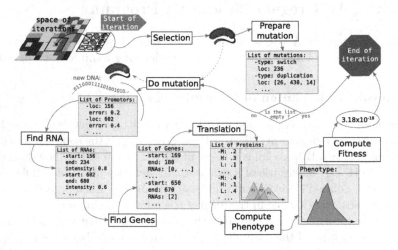

Fig. 1. Workflow followed by each cell for one generation. The data (orange boxes) pass through the different functions (white boxes). The output is the *fitness* value. (Color figure online)

2.2 Computational Workflow of Aevol

As mentioned previously, Aevol runs forward generation by generation. For each generation n, the population of generation $n-1$ is known. The evolutionary loop iterates on each cell. The *selection* step is a *stencil* computation. Each cell clones the selected individual (DNA, phenotype and *fitness*) from neighborhood cells from generation $n - 1$. In that way, all cell computations are independent and can be computed in any order. At the end of the generation, individuals have to wait for their neighbors to start the new generation. However, a global barrier is used to simplify the synchronization at the end of each generation.

Once the selection is done, the remaining computation of an iteration can be viewed as a sequential workflow, as shown in Fig. 1. An individual has a probability to mutate depending on the size of its DNA and the mutation rate specified as an user parameter. There are several kinds of mutation such as a one bit modification of the genetic code or duplication of the entire genetic code or even more. If an individual does not change, then all its information is known by its parent. For the others, so called mutants, their new DNA must be processed to compute their new fitness. It consists mainly on reading and recognizing sequences of characters. These functions are mostly memory-intensive computation.

2.3 Dynamic Characterization of the Computation

The time to process an individual (*i.e.*, a single iteration of a generation) strongly depends on its data (DNA) and if it is a mutant or not. The computation loop over the individuals is said to be *irregular* and it requires dedicated scheduling as discussed hereafter.

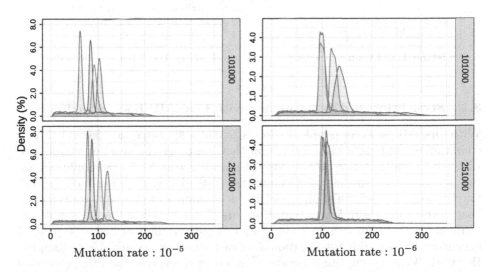

Fig. 2. Density in function of the time to process mutants (in μs). The colors correspond to distinct experiments. Top (bottom) plots are extracted at generation 101 000 (resp 251 000). Time scale is cut at 350 μs as very few (0.01%) individuals last longer. (Color figure online)

The first origin of irregularity comes from the distinction between mutants and non-mutants which do not follow the same process. Non-mutants are significantly faster to compute *i.e.*, around 1% of the total runtime of a generation.

This proportion depends on the mutation rate which influences the number of mutants. Nevertheless, mutants always count for the large majority (99%) of the computation time. Besides, even among the mutants, we observe a large irregularity. As shown in Fig. 2, a high density of individuals takes a similar amount of time to be processed, but there are still some individuals that can last up to 10 times longer than the others. In addition the distribution of these iterations varies depending on the generation and experimental parameters specified by the user. It is especially true for the mutation rate that can be strongly linked to size of the DNA [8]. Last, because the evolutionary model is stochastic, it is not possible to know which and how individual will mutate before its computation. The duration of each individual is therefore *a priori* unpredictable.

3   Parallelization of the Evolutionary Loop

To accelerate the simulation time, it is necessary to parallelize the evolutionary loop. The main issue is a loop scheduling issue, with time per iteration at fine grain. We limit our presentation to multi-core architecture for which OpenMP is an acceptable parallel environment with good performance.

```
1  /* original pattern in
      Aevol */
2  for i = 1..N do
3    fitness[i] = compute(indiv[i])
```

Listing 1.1. Evolutionary loop.

```
1  #pragma omp parallel loop \
2    schedule(<arguments>)
3  for i = 1..N do
4    fitness[i] = compute(indiv[i])
```

Listing 1.2. First parallelisation.

3.1   Straightforward Performance with OpenMP Loop Schedulers

With OpenMP, a direct parallelization is to add a `#pragma omp parallel for` construct around the evolutionary loop that computes the new generation (see Listings 1.1 and 1.2). However, due to the irregular work load, one should not use the default *static* scheduler and should use instead *dynamic* or *guided*. Indeed, for our case *static* scheduler only performs a speedup up to 16 on 32 cores for the best configuration with lowest mutation rate. Table 1 reports the measured performance of this approach on a 16, 32 and 64-core machine against a sequential execution. By summing the duration d_i of each iteration, we are able to compute the work W of a complete generation[2] in order to express the *idle proportion* $I = 1 - \frac{W}{p \times T_p}$ where the p cores stay idle during the time T_p of the for-loop execution, with no iteration left to distribute and wait for others to finish their work. There are two important remarks. First, the work is inflated when running on parallel NUMA architecture [19]. That explains the poor efficiency with respect to a lower idle proportion. Second, the efficiency is not that good. It is important to realise that the number of iterations (the population size) is not that large in respect with the number of cores. Moreover, there are even fewer iterations

---

[2] Iterations only perform computation.

Table 1. Performance of Aevol with several mutation rates using *dynamic* and *guided* schedulers. Environment: gcc8.3, libGOMP on 4 SkyLake Xeon Gold 6130.

# cores	Mutation rate	SpeedUp		Efficiency		Idle proportion	
		Dynamic	Guided	Dynamic	Guided	Dynamic	Guided
16	10^{-4}	11.2	10.9	70%	68.1%	4.1%	7.5%
	10^{-5}	11.2	10.1	70%	63.1%	5.0%	14.6%
	10^{-6}	10.2	8.6	63.8%	53.8%	11.2%	27.0%
32	10^{-4}	20.3	19.5	63.4%	60.9%	9.2%	15.3%
	10^{-5}	20.0	17.0	62.5%	53.1%	11.1%	26.3%
	10^{-6}	16.5	13.1	51.6%	40.9%	21.4%	41.7%
64	10^{-4}	34.4	32.8	53.8%	51.3%	18.2%	27.0%
	10^{-5}	33.1	26.2	51.7%	40.9%	22.1%	41.1%
	10^{-6}	23.9	18.2	37.3%	28.4%	36.6%	56.5%

that represent the treatment of mutants: Function `compute` of listing 1.2 is very fast for non-mutants. This kind of irregularity makes the *guided* scheduler ineffective [18]. For the case of the *dynamic* scheduler, even with 64 cores, speed-up is only around 33. The idle proportion of the cores varies from 9% to 36%. This reveals work imbalance due to not so good schedule. The population size is a very important parameter for a biological point of view [2]. Doing experiments with small, medium or large population will not produce the same results and cannot be interpreted the same way. Thus, we cannot blindly increase the size of population to convey more parallelism because the experiments will not be the same.

3.2 Scheduling Iterations Based on Their Data

A finer inspection of the evolution loop of Aevol shows that it iterates over a *composition of functions* $f_n \circ ... f_2 \circ f_1$ applied to each individual (see Listing 1.3). The classical list-scheduling algorithms [10] such as implemented in OpenMP runtimes delivers medium level of performance with parallel efficiency ranging from 37% to 63% as shown in the previous section. To increase performance of the loop scheduler, we need extra information to schedule loop with a better clairvoyance. For instance, LPT [11] requires the knowledge of execution time for a better competitive ratio.

```
1   for i = 1..N do
2     fitness[i] = fn ∘ ...f2 ∘ f1(indiv[i])
```

Listing 1.3. Initial evolutionary loop.

```
1   for i = 1..N do
2     r[i] = fk ∘ ...f2 ∘ f1(indiv[i])
3   for i = 1..N do
4     fitness[i] = fn ∘ ...fk+2 ∘ fk+1(r[i])
```

Listing 1.4. Our loop decomposition.

Our approach is to look whether the data generated during the execution of a function f_k may give clues on the remaining computation of this iteration. Accordingly, our methodology is to split the functions into two groups and to specialize the scheduling algorithm for each part: i) let schedule the first k function calls $f_k \circ ...f_2 \circ f_1$ with a non-clairvoyant scheduling algorithm, and ii) let use the data produced after this step to gain in information to better schedule the remaining function calls $f_n \circ ... \circ f_{k+1}$ by a clairvoyant scheduling algorithm.

Listing 1.4 illustrates the resulting loops after having split the loop in two. The remaining questions are: Why not to split in more than two the composition? Which kind of clairvoyant loop scheduling algorithm? and finally: How to find the right separator k to split the composition of functions? The first question is related to the structure of the computation and we show *a posteriori* that splitting the loop in two is enough. Moreover, each loop decomposition implies a synchronization and we have found that a good trade-off for this application is two.

Because the computation is at fine grain, we have decided to select an existing loop scheduler with low overhead at runtime. Our final choice was to base our second loop scheduler on the original LPT algorithm [11] where individuals are sorted according to the size of their DNA after mutation. This information strongly correlates to the execution time of a mutant and the next sections focus on it.

3.3   Predicting the Execution Time

A deep analysis of the Aevol code and, more precisely, the underlying computational biological model, leading to the creation of the Fig. 1, was necessary. Knowing, for instance, that the `Translation` function take as input the list of all the genes of an individual, we could induce the time of this function with the number of genes *i.e.*, thanks to the output of the `Find_Genes` function. Going backward again, as genes are segments of characters inside RNA (which is also a segment of characters inside the total DNA), the more RNA will be found in the function `Find_RNA`, the more time function `Find_Genes` will take.

Finally, keeping the same logic, Fig. 3 illustrates that the size of the DNA after mutation linearly correlates with the execution time of the iterations of the loop $f_n \circ ...f_2(r[i])$, where f_1 applies the mutations on one individual. The parameter of the linear model changes over the generations, but the linearity between size of DNA and execution time permits us to schedule loop with the LPT algorithm where individuals are sorted accordingly to their DNA sizes.

Simulation of LDNA Schedule. To test our hypothesis, we collect the execution time of each function f_i call on all the individuals and we simulate our scheduler called LDNA: as for LPT individuals are sorted decreasingly with their DNA size after mutation. We compare our LDNA with respect to LPT thanks to the postmortem simulation with known execution times. Figure 4 displays the simulated efficiency for 100 generations with the *dynamic* scheduler of OpenMP (Dyn), LPT, and LDNA on a 64 cores machine. We see that LDNA almost

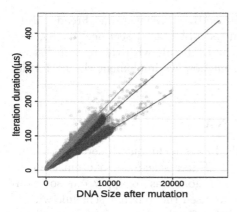

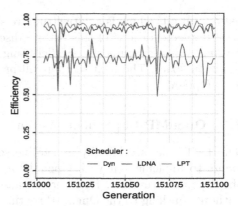

Fig. 3. Scatter plot with duration of iterations vs the size of DNA after mutation. The different color represent different point in time of the execution. (Color figure online)

Fig. 4. Simulation of a posteriori schedules of generation of Aevol on 64 cores with different scheduler

```
1   #pragma omp parallel for schedule(static)
2   for (auto i = 0; i<N; ++i) {
3       indiv[i] = prepare_mutation o selection(cell[i])
4       if has_mutate(indiv[i])
5           mutant_list.push_back(i) // Concurrent access to the list
6   }
7   << synchronize_sort(mutant_list) >>
8   #pragma omp parallel for schedule(monotonic: dynamic(1))
9   for (auto i: mutant_list)
10      fitness[i] = do_fitness o ... o do_mutation(indiv[i])
```

Listing 1.5. General structure of the code to compute a generation with LDNA. Sections of the code depend on the way sort is implemented, see Sect. 3.5

achieves the performance of LPT which is almost optimal most of the time. Next sections present how to build LDNA for the evolution loop.

3.4 LDNA, A Scheduling Algorithm for Aevol

Listing 1.5 describes the new organization of the computation of Aevol with two parallel loops following our loop decomposition. The first loop computes in parallel the selection and prepares the mutations and give us the new DNA size of the mutants. It also discriminates the mutants inside a shared data structure. Because the duration of the iterations of this loop are small and with less irregularity than the initial problem, we can apply a static scheduling. At this point, the computation for the non-mutants is finished and we only have to deal with mutants. As previously, we applied the simplicity of LPT schedule with the DNA size of the mutant. Iterations are sorted with this data by `synchronize_sort()` as shown in the Listing 1.5. This function hides the complexity of managing the list of mutants which is a data structure shared by all the working threads. Multiple implementations of this list are discussed in the next section. Finally, the second loop is executed in parallel using the LPT rule with the mutant list as iteration space. The next section will present how we implement the LPT rule with OpenMP.

3.5   OpenMP Implementation of LDNA

The LPT rule is originally an off-line scheduling technique. Therefore, if one wants to implement it with OpenMP as an off-line scheduler, one must touch the OpenMP runtime. However, because our goal was to apply our solution without touching to the OpenMP runtime, we used the dynamic schedule with 1 iteration per chunks using an already sorted list for the iteration space as shown in Listing 1.5. This configuration will complete an LPT schedule if we assure that an idle thread will pick the next iteration on the logical order, *i.e.*, the longest available iteration. Fortunately, OpenMP4.5 [20] introduces the *monotonic* modifier to be added to the scheduler (as shown on the second loop): it ensures that chunks are assigned in the increasing logical iteration order.

An other issue was the management of the list of mutants shared between all threads and subject to concurrent accesses. Because of fine grain operation, the best implementation is a compromise between an algorithmic variant and the overhead at runtime. We have followed a pragmatic experimental evaluation of several variants that relies on different OpenMP features to manage it.

Our two promising implementations distribute the list where each thread keeps a local sorted list, then `synchronization_sort` (Line 7) merges all the data. In our first implementation, the merge operation is be done in two ways: i) using the `reduction` construct of OpenMP4.0 or ii) do it ourselves. The first implementation views concurrent list insertion as reduction operation between lists. It relies on the declaration of reduction operator, called by the OpenMP runtime, in charge of merge two lists. We call this implementation `LDNA_Omp_Redux`.

In our second implementation, all the local lists are merged by our program using a binary merge tree. This is `LDNA_Par_Tree`. Parallel merge may be of interest but it depends on the size of the list. A first attempt has shown that parallelism variant does not outperform sequential binary merge with useful data size for our problem. So we call this implementation `LDNA_Seq_Tree`.

omp for vs taskloop. The OpenMP standard propose another way of parallelism using tasks. The *taskloop* construct allows to execute and schedule chunks of iterations as tasks. One could even turn each sub function of an iteration in a new task and the program could convey more parallelism. However, the current implementations of OpenMP have tremendous overhead at the creation of tasks[9] prohibiting their use in the case of lots of small tasks. This is why we only use the *omp for* construct for our implementation waiting for evolution in the tasks management by the OpenMP runtimes.

4   Experimental Results

This section deals with the evaluation of LDNA against the *dynamic* schedule
of OpenMP. For the experimentation, the program was compiled with GCC
8.3, linked with jemalloc5.2.1 [7] as a memory allocator more suited for parallel
allocations. The OpenMP runtime is libGOMP and the execution was done
on a *yeti* node running on Debian 10 from the Grid5000 platform. A node is
equipped, with 4 Skylake Intel Xeon Gold 6130 processors for a total of 64 cores
(Hyper-Threading was not used) and 768 GiB of memory on 4 NUMA sockets.
The memory allocation policy is the *first-touch* policy. As the computation of
a mutant asks the thread to copy (meaning memory allocation) the ancestor
and then work on the copy a thread will then work on his local NUMA node
to process a mutant. We select the libGOMP runtime because other runtimes
(from LLVM or Intel), did not show significant difference in performance.

4.1   Protocol of Experimentation

All the experiments were populated with 1024 individuals (see reason in
Sect. 2.1). Three mutation rates are used: 10^{-4}, 10^{-5} and 10^{-6}. For each mutation rate, we did 4 repetitions with different seeds for the random generator.
For each experiment, we selected 6 starting generations separated by 50 000 generations from Generation 1000 to Generation 251 000. For each the 72 starting
generations, the protocol of execution was the following: for doubling numbers
of cores from 4 to 64 (using the least NUMA nodes possible thanks to *numactl*),
we computed 100 generations in which we timestamped the beginning and the
end of each iteration. During our preliminary study of Aevol, we observed that
the behavior of the computation only changes on large scale of generations. This
explains why we take this few contiguous generations but spread on 251 000
generations.

4.2   Results

The following figures summarize data averaged on all the executions. We
observed that the first 3 generations had a strange behavior certainly due to
a warming up effect and they are not counted in these means. Fig. 5 compares
the proportion of the time taken by the `synchronization_sort` step during
one generation. `LDNA_Seq_Tree` shows itself the best option over the two solutions. For the case of `LDNA_Omp_Redux`, the results were surprising and further
analysis shows that all the operations of reduction occur sequentially with lots
of time spent in the OpenMP runtime. We chose to continue experiments with
`LDNA_Seq_Tree` as our LDNA scheduler.

Figure 6 compares the speedup of our LDNA scheduler with the reference
dynamic scheduler of OpenMP (Dyn). It is clear that LDNA outperforms Dyn.
For 64 cores the LDNA scheduler is on average 19%, 21% and 27% faster for
respectively 10^{-4}, 10^{-5} and 10^{-6} mutation rates. In Fig. 7, an example of the
execution of one generation with mutation rate 10^{-5} is given. It shows how LDNA

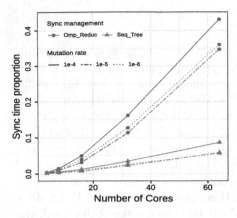
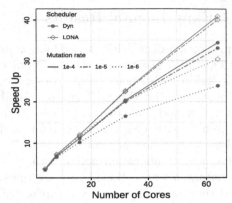

Fig. 5. Average proportion of time used for synchronization with the different implementations depending on mutation rate

Fig. 6. Average speed up of Dyn and LDNA depending on the mutation rate

(bottom) succeeds to compact the computation compared to Dyn (top). With the latter, the mutants (blue) and non-mutants (red) are treated in a random order, explaining why large mutants are computed only at the and. For LDNA, non-mutants are all treated in the first part which is scheduled statically. This reduces the schedule overhead that the non-mutants induce compared to the Dyn scheduling. The second part only computes what remains for the mutant in a specific order that permits to compact all the iteration. The blank part corresponds to the sort and merge of the list of mutants. For this example, it takes about 0.03 ms which represents 5% of the computation time (On average for a mutation rate at 10^{-5}, it is 5.8%, Fig. 5).

For 10^{-4} and 10^{-5} mutation rates, the idle time proportion, without counting synchronization and sort, dropped to a maximum of 7%. In the case of 10^{-6} mutation rate, we can see that it scales less than the others, and the idle time is more difficult to reduce. In fact, the mutation rate is so low that the number of mutants reaches is about 60 individuals. Therefore, the number of iterations is very close to the number of cores and sometimes less. The program lacks of parallelism and a solution would be to parallelize at the sub-functions grain. As seen in Sect. 3.5 this could be easily done with task parallelism but will suffer the large overhead due to the current OpenMP runtime.

4.3 Evaluation on Larger Populations

If the size of the population is 10 times larger than in previous experiments, and future use of Aevol could use this for biological interests, the parallelism would be greater. As the number of iterations rises, a simple dynamic schedule could be enough and LDNA could suffer from the overhead from the management of the mutant list. Nevertheless, LDNA succeeds to scale up the population better

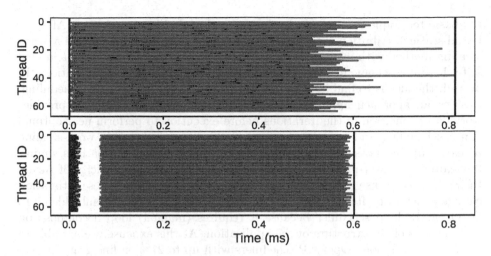

Fig. 7. Example of the execution of one generation with two scheduler. Blue rectangles correspond to mutants and red to non-mutants. At the top `Dyn`, where iteration executes at random order, and at the bottom `LDNA`, where the few step of evolution are performed with a *static* scheduler, then the mutant list is merged and sorted (blank part) and then only mutants are evaluated to find their fitness. (Color figure online)

than `Dyn`. Larger experiments with 9.216 individuals on 64 cores show that our scheduling stay better but not as much. The difference is around 12% with mutation rate at 10^{-6} and 2% at 10^{-4}. With the smaller mutation rate, mutants are enough so that `Dyn` suffers from the irregularity. At the end, a larger population would mean that any scheduling algorithm would approach optimal result but simulations with small population will still be used in the future. However, to avoid prohibitive computation times, in the case of a larger population, we will have to use a larger number of cores and thus return to a similar scheduling problem that the one with 1.024 individuals on 64 cores. Still, LDNA could do better because we observe that NUMA effects became important and it is clear that the cores wait because of communication latency during the first loop. Taking NUMA into account would certainly improve LDNA scalability.

5 Related Work

Our scheduling problem is largely studied since at least 50 years. In [12], the $P \parallel C_{max}$ problem is presented as NP-complete. Two approaches exist to deal with this problem: whether the duration of iteration is known in advance or not. [14] is certainly the best off-line algorithm but LPT [11] is a well known heuristic with great performance [5] and simplicity and an even better version has been developed by Cheng et al. [4].

When the information about the iterations is unknown before execution, the *list-scheduling* algorithm described by Graham [10] is the upper-bound limit and the basic technique for most of the dynamic scheduler developed since. After an initial static distribution of the iterations, Durand et al. [6] implemented a work-stealing method with memory location awareness. Lucco [18] presented a guided self-scheduling scheme improved with statistics computed on early iterations. In overall, the idea is to find information during execution to refine the scheduling. Besides an approach applied in [21, 22] consists on letting the user provides workload estimation of the iterations before execution to perform near-optimal static scheduling and balance the final workload with dynamic work-stealing to catch up the possible mistakes of the estimation. Our approach is similar but cannot use user-provided estimation because of the stochasticity of Aevol. Instead, it has to use estimation from the application itself and these estimation change generation after generation. Our method cannot be easily embedded into an OpenMP loop scheduler because it requires (manual) loop decomposition and analysis of the structure of the application. At this expense, we are able to improve existing loop OpenMP schedulers with up to 27% on fine grain loop.

6   Conclusion and Future Work

In this paper, we present a new methodology to schedule irregular independent iterations of an application structured as a composition of functions. Mixing non-clairvoyant and clairvoyant techniques, we show that splitting the execution of the loop in several loops is a valid approach if the data gathered in the first loop help the scheduling of the next one. Applying our method to Aevol, a computational biology software, we implemented the algorithm LDNA to schedule the computation of evolving uni-cellular organisms. Experimental evaluations on a multi-core architecture computer show that our scheduler improves by about 27% the performance of the dynamic scheduler of OpenMP often used for irregular applications. We discuss on the implementation of the method and how to manage the synchronization to optimize the execution of our solution.

As other work [22] that uses workload-aware scheduler, we think that allowing the user to inform the runtime through the OpenMP standard would help this kind of method. The standard could accept an estimation function or even a way to pass a scheduler to be used by the runtime.

The management of the list of mutants brought to use a binary merge tree that we kept sequential. However, this part take up to 10% of the total computing and more work could certainly find a way to parallelize efficiently this part.

Finally, it would be on interest to evaluate if the methodology used to find where to split the evolutionary loop could be generalized and automated to other parallel applications.

Acknowledgement. Experiments presented in this paper were carried out using the Grid'5000 testbed, supported by a scientific interest group hosted by Inria and including CNRS, RENATER and several Universities as well as other organizations (see https:// www.grid5000.fr).

References

1. Banicescu, I., Velusamy, V.: Load balancing highly irregular computations with the adaptive factoring. In: Proceedings 16th International Parallel and Distributed Processing Symposium, p. 12, April 2002
2. Caballero, A.: Developments in the prediction of effective population size. Heredity **73**(6), 657–679 (1994)
3. Card, K.J., LaBar, T., Gomez, J.B., Lenski, R.E.: Historical contingency in the evolution of antibiotic resistance after decades of relaxed selection. PLoS Biol. **17**(10), 1–18 (2019)
4. Cheng, T.C.E., Kellerer, H., Kotov, V.: Algorithms better than LPT for semi-online scheduling with decreasing processing times. Oper. Res. Lett. **40**(5), 349–352 (2012)
5. Coffman, Jr., E.G., Sethi, R.: A generalized bound on LPT sequencing. In: Proceedings of the 1976 ACM SIGMETRICS Conference on Computer Performance Modeling Measurement and Evaluation, pp. 306–310. ACM (1976)
6. Durand, M., Broquedis, F., Gautier, T., Raffin, B.: An efficient OpenMP loop scheduler for irregular applications on large-scale NUMA machines. In: Rendell, A.P., Chapman, B.M., Müller, M.S. (eds.) IWOMP 2013. LNCS, vol. 8122, pp. 141–155. Springer, Heidelberg (2013). https://doi.org/10.1007/978-3-642-40698-0_11
7. Evans, J.: A Scalable Concurrent malloc(3) Implementation for FreeBSD, p. 14, April 2006
8. Fischer, S., Bernard, S., Beslon, G., Knibbe, C.: A model for genome size evolution. Bull. Math. Biol. **76**(9), 2249–2291 (2014)
9. Gautier, T., Perez, C., Richard, J.: On the impact of OpenMP task granularity. In: de Supinski, B.R., Valero-Lara, P., Martorell, X., Mateo Bellido, S., Labarta, J. (eds.) IWOMP 2018. LNCS, vol. 11128, pp. 205–221. Springer, Cham (2018). https://doi.org/10.1007/978-3-319-98521-3_14
10. Graham, R.L.: Bounds for certain multiprocessing anomalies. Bell Syst. Tech. J. **45**(9), 1563–1581 (1966)
11. Graham, R.L.: Bounds on multiprocessing timing anomalies. SIAM J. Appl. Math. **17**(2), 416–429 (1969)
12. Graham, R.L., Lawler, E.L., Lenstra, J.K., Kan, A.H.G.R.: Optimization and approximation in deterministic sequencing and scheduling: a survey. In: Hammer, P.L., Johnson, E.L., Korte, B.H. (eds.) Annals of Discrete Mathematics, vol. 5, pp. 287–326. Elsevier, January 1979
13. Hindré, T., Knibbe, C., Beslon, G., Schneider, D.: New insights into bacterial adaptation through in vivo and in silico experimental evolution. Nat. Rev. Microbiol. **10**(5), 352–365 (2012)
14. Hochbaum, D.S., Shmoys, D.B.: Using dual approximation algorithms for scheduling problems theoretical and practical results. J. ACM **34**(1), 144–162 (1987)
15. Knibbe, C.: Structuration des génomes par sélection indirecte de la variabilité mutationnelle: une approche de modélisation et de simulation. thesis, Lyon, INSA, January 2006
16. Liard, V., Parsons, D., Rouzaud-Cornabas, J., Beslon, G.: The complexity Ratchet: stronger than selection, weaker than robustness. Artif. Life Conf. Proc. **30**, 250–257 (2018)

17. Liard, V., Rouzaud-Cornabas, J., Comte, N., Beslon, G.: A 4-base model for the aevol in-silico experimental evolution platform. In: Knibbe, C., et al. (eds.) Proceedings of the Fourteenth European Conference Artificial Life, ECAL 2017, Lyon, France, 4–8 September 2017, pp. 265–266. MIT Press (2017)
18. Lucco, S.: A dynamic scheduling method for irregular parallel programs. In: Proceedings of the ACM SIGPLAN 1992 Conference on Programming Language Design and Implementation, pp. 200–211. Association for Computing Machinery, San Francisco, July 1992
19. Olivier, S., Supinski, B., Schulz, M., Prins, J.: Characterizing and mitigating work time inflation in task parallel programs. Sci. Program. **21**, 1–12 (2012)
20. OpenMP Architecture Review Board: OpenMP Application Program Interface. Specification (2015). https://www.openmp.org/wp-content/uploads/openmp-4.5.pdf
21. Penna, P.H., Castro, M., Freitas, H.C., Broquedis, F., Méhaut, J.F.: Design methodology for workload-aware loop scheduling strategies based on genetic algorithm and simulation. Concurr. Comput.: Pract. Exp. **29**(22), e3933 (2017)
22. Penna, P.H.: A comprehensive performance evaluation of the BinLPT workload-aware loop scheduler. Concurr. Comput.: Pract. Exp. **31**(18), e5170 (2019)

Evaluating Performance of OpenMP Tasks in a Seismic Stencil Application

Eric Raut[1]([✉]) [iD], Jie Meng[2], Mauricio Araya-Polo[2], and Barbara Chapman[1]

[1] Stony Brook University, Stony Brook, NY 11794, USA
{eric.raut,barbara.chapman}@stonybrook.edu
[2] Total EP R&T, Houston, TX 77002, USA

Abstract. Simulations based on stencil computations (widely used in geosciences) have been dominated by the MPI+OpenMP programming model paradigm. Little effort has been devoted to experimenting with task-based parallelism in this context. We address this by introducing OpenMP task parallelism into the kernel of an industrial seismic modeling code, Minimod. We observe that even for these highly regular stencil computations, taskified kernels are competitive with traditional OpenMP-augmented loops, and in some experiments tasks even outperform loop parallelism.

This promising result sets the stage for more complex computational patterns. Simulations involve more than just the stencil calculation: a collection of kernels is often needed to accomplish the scientific objective (e.g., I/O, boundary conditions). These kernels can often be computed simultaneously; however, implementing this simultaneous computation with traditional programming models is not trivial. The presented approach will be extended to cover simultaneous execution of several kernels, where we expect to fully exploit the benefits of task-based programming.

Keywords: OpenMP · Task parallelism · Stencil computation · Loop scheduling

1 Introduction

Many industrial and scientific applications use stencil computation for solving PDEs discretized with Finite Difference (FD) or Finite Volume (FV) methods. These can range from geophysics to weather forecasting models [32]. Improving performance is of utmost interest since this facilitates faster decision making as well as more opportunities to explore further scientific questions. Optimization of stencil computation has been addressed in the past aplenty (see Sect. 2) from many different angles, e.g. low-level optimization, parallelism at different levels, and DSLs.

In this work, we create OpenMP task-based versions of an industrial stencil-based seismic modeling code and compare performance of the task-based versions to traditional loop-parallelized versions of the code. The motivation of this

© Springer Nature Switzerland AG 2020
K. Milfeld et al. (Eds.): IWOMP 2020, LNCS 12295, pp. 67–81, 2020.
https://doi.org/10.1007/978-3-030-58144-2_5

work is to explore how task-based programming models and task parallelism can support the stencil computation pattern in practice.

OpenMP [26] is the de-facto standard programming model for shared-memory parallelism. OpenMP introduced tasks in version 3.0. OpenMP 4.0 added automatic dependency analysis to tasks, such that the compiler can automatically determine the order of task execution based on user-supplied data dependences.

In task-based OpenMP programming, an application is written as a set of units of work called *tasks*. Each task is executed sequentially, but multiple tasks can be run simultaneously subject to the availability of resources and dependencies between the tasks. The set of tasks and dependencies between them can be represented as a directed acyclic graph (DAG).

Our main contributions are the following: (1) we introduce task parallelism to a stencil code in a proxy for an industrial application; (2) we test our task-based stencil code on several architectures and compilers; and (3) we analyze its behavior and compare results of the task-based stencil with several variants written using parallel loops.

The paper is organized as follows: Sect. 2 describes relevant literature works and contributions. Section 3 describes the target application. Section 4 details the application code structure and how it was ported to task parallelism. In Sect. 5, the experimental environment and results are presented. Section 6 and 7 provide discussion and conclusions.

2   Related Work

A great amount of research effort has been devoted to optimizing stencil computations to achieve higher performance. For example, Nguyen et al. [24] introduced higher dimension cache optimizations, and de la Cruz et al. proposed the semi-stencil algorithm [8] which offers an improved memory access pattern and efficiently reuses accessed data by dividing the computation into several updates. In 2012, Ghosh et al. [13] analyzed the performance and programmability of three high-level directive-based GPU programming models (PGI, CAPS, and OpenACC) on an NVIDIA GPU against isotropic and tilted transversely isotropic finite difference kernels in reverse time migration (RTM), which is a widely used method in exploration geophysics. In 2017, Qawasmeh et al. [28] implemented an MPI + OpenACC approach for seismic modeling and RTM. Also, from a programming language perspective, domain-specific languages (DSLs) for stencils have been proposed (e.g., [19]). Even performance models have been developed for this computing pattern (see [9]).

In recent years, task-based parallel programming has been recognized as a promising approach to improve performance in scientific applications such as stencil-based algorithms. For example, in [22], Moustafa et al. illustrated the design and implementation of a FD method-based seismic wave propagation simulator using PaRSEC.

Researchers have been working on exploring the advantages of tasking in OpenMP since tasks were introduced in version 3.0. Right after its release,

Virouleau et al. [34] evaluated OpenMP tasks and dependencies with the KAS-TORS benchmark suite. Duran et al. [12] evaluated different OpenMP task scheduling strategies with several applications. Rico et al. [30] provided insights on the benefits of tasking over the work-sharing loop model by introducing tasking to an adaptive mesh refinement proxy application. Atkinson et al. [2] optimized the performance of an irregular algorithm for the fast multipole method with the use of tasks in OpenMP. Vidal et al. [33] evaluated the task features of OpenMP 4.0 extensions with the OmpSs programming model.

Several programming systems supporting tasks have been proposed, some of which (e.g., OpenMP) focus on shared-memory systems. Cilk [6] is an early programming API supporting tasks using **spawn** keyword. Intel Thread Building Blocks [29] also supports shared-memory task parallelism. StarSs [27] is a task-based framework for multi/many-core systems using a pragma syntax. OmpSs [11] is an attempt to extend OpenMP with tasking features using StarSs runtime.

Distributed-memory task-based systems have been explored as well, in which the runtime automatically schedules tasks among the available nodes and takes care of communication and data transfer. Charm++ [1] is a C++ framework supporting distributed task parallelism. Legion [4], and its DSL, Regent [31], are data-centric task-based programming systems developed at Stanford. PaRSEC [7] enables an application to be expressed as a "parameterized task graph" which is problem-size-independent and therefore highly scalable. HPX [15] is a task-based framework which uses a global address space to distribute computations across nodes. XcalableMP [18] is a PGAS language with elementary support for task parallelism. YML [10,14] allows the user to specify a computation as a graph of large-scale tasks; it can be combined with XcalableMP. StarPU [3] supports OpenMP-style pragmas and provides a runtime for distributed execution. Klinkenberg et al. [16] propose a framework for distributing tasks across MPI ranks in MPI+OpenMP hybrid applications.

3 Minimod Description

Minimod is a proxy application that simulates the propagation of waves through the Earth models, by solving a Finite Difference (FD) discretized form of the wave equation. It is designed and developed by Total Exploration and Production Research and Technologies [21]. Minimod is self-contained and designed to be portable across multiple compilers. The application suite provides both non-optimized and optimized versions of computational kernels for targeted platforms. The main purpose is benchmarking of emerging new hardware and programming technologies. Non-optimized versions are provided to allow analysis of pure compiler-based optimizations. Minimod is currently not publicly available; however, the plan is to eventually make it available to the community as open-source software.

In this work, we study one of the kernels contained in Minimod, the isotropic propagator in a constant-density domain [28]. For this propagator, the wave equation PDE has the following form:

$$\frac{1}{\mathbf{V}^2} \frac{\partial^2 \mathbf{u}}{\partial t^2} - \nabla^2 \mathbf{u} = \mathbf{f}, \tag{1}$$

where $\mathbf{u} = \mathbf{u}(x, y, z)$ is the wavefield, $\mathbf{V}$ is the Earth model (with velocity as rock property), and $\mathbf{f}$ is the source perturbation. The equation is discretized in time using a second-order centered stencil, resulting in the semi-discretized equation:

$$\mathbf{u}^{n+1} - \mathbf{Q}\mathbf{u}^n + \mathbf{u}^{n-1} = \left(\Delta t^2\right) \mathbf{V}^2 \mathbf{f}^n, \text{ with } \mathbf{Q} = 2 + \Delta t^2 \mathbf{V}^2 \nabla^2. \tag{2}$$

Finally, the equation is discretized in space using a 25-point stencil in 3D space, with four points in each direction as well as the centre point:

$$\nabla^2 \mathbf{u}(x, y, z) \approx \sum_{m=0}^{4} c_{xm} \left[\mathbf{u}(i + m, j, k) + \mathbf{u}(i - m, j, k) \right]$$
$$+ c_{ym} \left[\mathbf{u}(i, j + m, k) + \mathbf{u}(i, j - m, k) \right]$$
$$+ c_{zm} \left[\mathbf{u}(i, j, k + m) + \mathbf{u}(i, j, k - m) \right]$$

where c_{xm}, c_{ym}, c_{zm} are discretization parameters.

A simulation in Minimod consists of solving the wave equation at each timestep for some number of timesteps. Pseudocode of the algorithm is shown in Algorithm 1. We apply a Perfectly Matched Layer (PML) [5] boundary condition to the boundary regions. The resulting domain consists of an "inner" region where Eq. 2 is applied, and the outer "boundary" region where a PML calculation is applied, as shown in Fig. 1.

Data: $\mathbf{f}$: source
Result: $\mathbf{u}^n$: wavefield at timestep n, for $n \leftarrow 1$ **to** T
1 $\mathbf{u}^0 := 0$;
2 **for** $n \leftarrow 1$ **to** T **do**
3   **for** *each point in wavefield* $\mathbf{u}^n$ **do**
4 | Solve Eq. 2 (left hand side) for wavefield $\mathbf{u}^n$;
5   **end**
6       $\mathbf{u}^n = \mathbf{u}^n + \mathbf{f}^n$ (Eq. 2 right hand side);
7 **end**

Algorithm 1: Minimod high-level description

We note that the stencil does not have a uniform computational intensity across the domain: the PML regions require more calculations than the inner regions. This suggests an inherent load imbalance that may be amenable to improvement with tasks. Furthermore, a full simulation includes additional kernels, such as I/O and compression. These additional kernels are not evaluated in this study but will be added in the future.

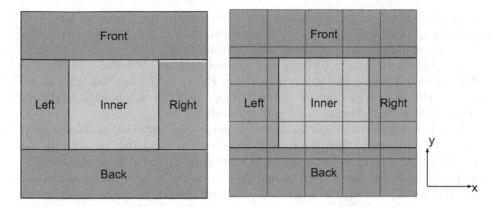

Fig. 1. (left) x-y plane view of domain; (right) xy blocking scheme.

4 Code Structure and Taskification of Minimod

In this section, we describe the code structure of Minimod and explain how it has been ported to a version that makes use of OpenMP tasks. The most computationally expensive component of Minimod (Algorithm 1) is the computation of the wavefield for each point. The (original) serial version of the code has the structure shown in Algorithm 2.

Data: u^{n-1}, u^{n-2}: wavefields at previous two timsteps
Result: u^n: wavefield at current timestep
```
1  for i ← xmin to xmax do
2      if i ≥ x3 and i ≤ x4 then
3          for j ← ymin to ymax do
4              if j ≥ y3 and j ≤ y4 then
5                  // Bottom Damping (i, j, z1...z2)
6                  // Inner Computation (i, j, z3...z4)
7                  // Top Damping (i, j, z5...z6)
8              else
9                  // Back and Front Damping (i, j, zmin...zmax)
10             end
11         end
12     else
13         // Left and Right Damping (i, ymin...ymax, zmin...zmax)
14     end
15 end
```

Algorithm 2: Wavefield solution step

We evaluate several different configurations for the parallelization of this code, using both OpenMP parallel loops and tasks. In the *x-loop* versions, we simply apply an `omp parallel for` directive to the x-loop on line 1 of Algorithm 2. The OpenMP schedule is selected at runtime; we test the static, dynamic, and guided OpenMP schedules in this study.

In addition to simply looping over the x-dimension, we also evaluate the effect of loop blocking in the x-y plane. See Fig. 1. In the blocked version, we apply OpenMP loop parallelism to the 2-D loop nest over x-y blocks. Again, we evaluate the static, dynamic, and guided schedules.

In the task-based configurations, we insert a `omp parallel master` region surrounding the entire timestep loop (before line 2 in Algorithm 1). Then, in the wavefield solution step we generate tasks representing parallel units of work. The OpenMP `depend` clause is used to manage dependencies between timesteps. In this stencil computation, the computation of each block depends on its neighbors from the previous timestep.

The OpenMP depend clause does not support overlapping array sections as dependencies. The most natural way to express dependencies between the regions is to list, in array section form, the specific array elements that each block depends on. However, this would result in overlapping dependency regions and is therefore not supported. Instead, in our implementation we simply choose one element of each neighboring block to include in the dependency list. This workaround, however, is limited to simple dependence patterns. For example, it is not possible to use more blocks (smaller block size) in the PML regions than in the inner region, because each inner block would depend on multiple PML blocks. OpenMP 5.0 supports using iterators in the depend clause, which provides some additional flexibility; however, iterators are not supported in any compilers we tested.

We evaluate the following configurations in this paper:

- *Loop x static/dynamic/guided*: an OpenMP parallel for loop is applied to the x loop in line 1 of Algorithm 2. A static/dynamic/guided schedule is used.
- *Loop xy static/dynamic/guided*: Uses blocking in the x and y dimensions. A OpenMP parallel for loop is applied to the 2-D loop nest over x-y blocks. (A `collapse(2)` is used to combine the two loops). A static/dynamic/guided schedule is used. Several different block sizes are evaluated.
- *Tasks xy*: Each x-y block is a task. OpenMP's `depend` clause is used to manage dependencies between timesteps.
- *Tasks xy nodep*: Same as above, but OpenMP dependencies are not used. In order to prevent a race condition, an explicit task synchronization point (`taskwait`) is added at the end of the timestep (i.e., before line 7 of Algorithm 1).

An alternative approach, not evaluated here, would be to apply a `taskloop` construct to the loops, generating one task for each chunk of iterations (with configurable size). Currently, the `taskloop` construct does not support dependencies, so an explicit task synchronization would be required, as in *Tasks xy nodep*.

Our application is not currently NUMA-aware, which hurts performance on NUMA architectures, including the nodes used in this study. The conventional

NUMA awareness for OpenMP tasks can be achieved with the `affinity` clause of OpenMP 5.0 [17]; however, to the best of our knowledge, this clause is not supported on any publicly available compilers as of the time of writing. (In [17], an LLVM runtime with preliminary support of task affinity is implemented. We are currently evaluating our application with this runtime.) In our application, all data is allocated and initialized by a single thread and so will likely reside on a single NUMA domain.

5 Evaluation

The different versions of Minimod are evaluated on Summit (a supercomputer with IBM POWER9 architecture) and Cori and SeaWulf (supercomputers with an Intel architecture).

5.1 Experimental Setup

Table 1. Hardware and software configuration of the experimental platforms.

Computer	Hardware		Software
Summit	CPUs	2x IBM Power9	LLVM 9.0
	CPU cores	44 (22 per CPU)	
	Memory	512 GB	
	L3	10 MB (per two cores)	
	L2	512 KB (per two cores)	
	L1	32+32 KB	
	Device fabrication	14 nm	
Cori	CPUs	2x Intel Xeon E5-2698v3	LLVM 10.0
	CPU cores	32 (16 per CPU)	
	Memory	128 GB	
	L3	40 MB (per socket)	
	L2	256 KB	
	L1	32+32 KB	
	Device fabrication	22 nm	
SeaWulf	CPUs	2x Intel Xeon Gold 6148	LLVM 11.0 (git 3cd13c4)
	CPU cores	40 (20 per CPU)	
	Memory	192 GB	
	L3	28 MB (per socket)	
	L2	1024 KB	
	L1	32+32 KB	
	Device fabrication	14 nm	

Summit [25] is a computing system at the Oak Ridge Leadership Computing Facility (see Table 1 top panel). Each node also has 6 NVIDIA V100 GPUs;

however, we do not use GPUs in this study. We use 42 OpenMP threads in all experiments with each thread bound to a physical core.

Cori [23] is a computing system at the National Energy Research Scientific Computing Center (NERSC) (see Table 1 middle panel). We perform experiments on *Haswell* nodes of Cori. 32 OpenMP threads on the Haswell nodes were used, each thread bound to a physical core (using `OMP_PLACES=cores` and `OMP_PROC_BIND=true`).

SeaWulf is a computing system at Stony Brook University. Details are given in Table 1 (bottom panel). In each run, we use 40 OpenMP threads (one per physical core) with each thread bound to a physical core.

Each simulation is run with grid sizes between 64^3 (64 in each of the three dimensions) and 1024^3. Sizes 512^3 and 1024^3 are reported in this paper. Results with the LLVM compiler on each computer are reported in this paper. Cache statistics were collected using the Perf and HPCToolkit [20] profilers. Execution times are averaged over three trials on Summit and SeaWulf. We were unable to compute a three-run average on Cori due to lack of availability; however, the application shows little variation in run time on the other machines, so it likely would make little difference.

5.2 Results

Execution times for each configuration from Sect. 4 on all three platforms are shown in Fig. 2. For each of the xy-blocked configurations, the time shown is for the block size that gives the lowest execution time for each configuration. On Cori, poor performance is seen from "Loop x static" as compared to other configurations. Performance among the xy-blocked configurations are generally quite similar.

To understand the relative performance and how it relates to the architecture used, we gathered cache use statistics for each configuration. Table 2 shows the

Table 2. L3 miss rate [%] on each computer for each configuration.

	Grid size 512^3			Grid size 1024^3		
	Summit	Cori	SeaWulf	Summit	Cori	Seawulf
Loop x static	16	19	49	12	16	50
Loop x dynamic	42	10	27	35	9	28
Loop x guided	45	15	41	36	15	47
Loop xy static	9	11	47	7	12	43
Loop xy dynamic	26	11	45	27	11	43
Loop xy guided	26	12	47	22	12	44
Tasks xy	27	12	45	27	11	43
Tasks xy nodep	27	11	45	26	11	43
Average	27.3	12.6	43.3	24.0	12.1	42.6

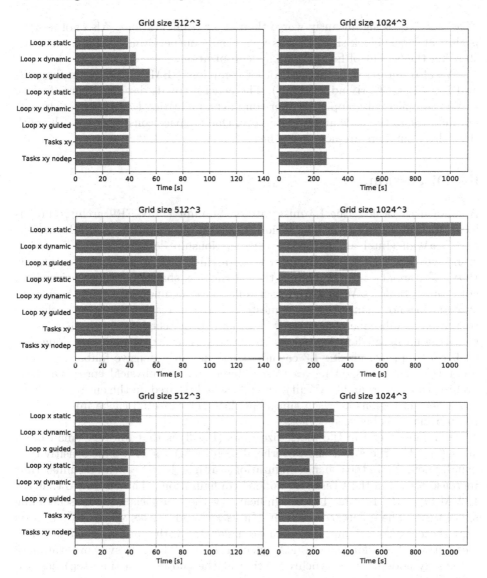

Fig. 2. Execution time (in seconds), top panel Summit, mid panel Cori and bottom panel SeaWulf.

L3 miss rate for each configuration on Summit, Cori, and SeaWulf, respectively. On Summit, the miss rate is significantly lower for static configurations than for the other configurations. On Cori and SeaWulf, the L3 miss rate is highest for "Loop x static", and relatively similar among all xy-blocked configurations.

Figure 3 shows the effect of block size on execution time for each of the xy-blocked configurations. The given block size is the size of both the x and y dimensions of each block/task. We frequently see that at a small block size of 4^2,

"Tasks xy" does significantly worse than other configurations. Also noteworthy is that at larger block sizes, "Tasks xy" usually outperforms "Tasks xy nodep", showing the benefit of fine-grained synchronization.

We also ran experiments with other compilers (IBM XL 16.1.1 on Summit, and Intel 19 on Cori and SeaWulf). The general trends discussed here (for the LLVM compiler) also apply to other compilers, indicating that these conclusions are intrinsic to the code and architecture. Due to space constraints, results with the other compilers are not shown here.

6   Discussion

As shown in Table 2, the L3 miss rate on Summit (POWER9 architecture) is lower for static-schedule configurations than other configurations, while for Cori and SeaWulf (Intel architectures) this relationship does not hold. To understand why, we must examine the cache hierarchies of these architectures. On the POWER9 architecture (Summit), the L3 cache is shared between each pair of cores only (Table 1). With a static schedule, the assignment of domain regions to threads does not change between timesteps, and data resident in the L3 cache will be reused at subsequent timesteps. With non-static schedules (including tasks), the assignment of domain regions to threads is arbitrary and can change at each timestep, introducing L3 cache misses (and an expensive fallback to main memory) when a region moves to a different pair of physical cores. On Intel architectures (Cori and SeaWulf), the L3 cache is shared on the entire socket, so movement of regions between timesteps does not cause L3 cache misses unless the movement is between sockets.

A notable trend in the block size plots (Fig. 3) is that for very small block sizes (i.e., 4^2), there is a large overhead seen in "Tasks xy". This sensitivity is usually not seen in the other configurations (although on SeaWulf a similar time increase occurs in the "Tasks xy nodep" configuration). This indicates that the LLVM OpenMP runtime has a significant overhead associated with scheduling small tasks. The difference between "Tasks xy" and "Tasks xy nodep" suggests that there is also a significant overhead associated with handling the dependencies between tasks for fine-grained synchronization. The bulk synchronization of "Tasks xy nodep" (task synchronization at the end of each timestep) has less overhead.

Most of the block size experiments in Fig. 3 show that there is a "minimum point", usually around a square block size of 16–32, where the execution time is minimized. In general, there is a trade-off with respect to choosing a block size. Small block sizes expose more parallelism to the runtime, resulting in more opportunities for load balancing. However, as each block is a task that must be scheduled for execution, small block sizes incur increased runtime task scheduling overhead. It is interesting to see that the minimum point for block size is relatively similar across computers in Fig. 3.

Especially at larger block sizes, we see a significant improvement of "Tasks xy" over "Tasks xy nodep". This shows potential for improvement of the

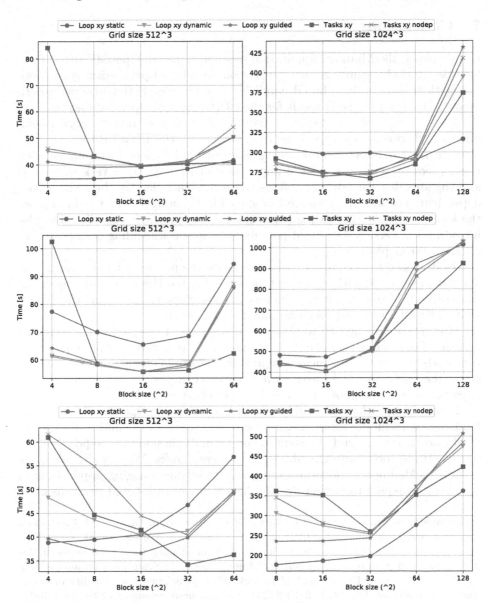

Fig. 3. Effect of block size on execution time using the LLVM compiler on Summit (top), Cori (middle), and SeaWulf (bottom).

fine-grained synchronization provided by task dependencies. However, this improvement is diminished at smaller block sizes. If the overheads of task dependency resolution could be reduced, this approach might also benefit smaller block sizes.

7 Conclusions

In this paper, the Minimod application was ported to use OpenMP tasks. Even for this relatively regular stencil application, task-based parallelism is competitive with traditional loop-based parallelism, and is even better in some experiments. This is a promising result for the effectiveness of OpenMP tasking.

A key finding of this paper is that the movement of domain region computations between timesteps is more expensive on the POWER9 architecture than on Intel architectures due to the difference in L3 cache hierarchy between them (Sect. 6). This stresses the importance of locality-aware task scheduling and suggests that the optimal policies for such a scheduler may be architecture-dependent. The `affinity` clause introduced in OpenMP 5.0 may help improve the locality of tasks, increasing performance. The OpenMP metadirective, also introduced in version 5.0, could potentially help set scheduling parameters for different target platforms.

As discussed in Sect. 6, our results indicate the potential for decreasing the overhead associated with handling task dependencies. However, task dependencies currently also have a lack of expressivity (see Sect. 4). Increasing the expressivity without increasing overhead may prove difficult.

More research is needed to pinpoint the causes of these performance characteristics. For example, we plan to use a profiler to continue to explore OpenMP overheads and barriers for each configuration. We would also like to better understand the extent to which tasks move between threads over the simulation. We hope to see better support for tasks from performance tools.

In future work, this code will be ported to GPUs using OpenMP 4.0+ offloading features, including using tasks to coordinate the work of multiple GPUs. We would also like to extend the code to run on multiple nodes. One possibility is to use MPI to coordinate OpenMP tasks between nodes. We will also add more kernels to Minimod to form a more complete seismic imaging application; in doing so, we expect to further exploit the benefits of task-based parallelism.

Acknowledgements. We would like to thank Total Exploration and Production Research and Technologies for their support of this work. We also thank Vivek Kale at Brookhaven National Laboratory for his help in guiding the experiments in this paper. We used resources of the National Energy Research Scientific Computing Center (NERSC), a U.S. Department of Energy Office of Science User Facility operated under Contract No. DE-AC02-05CH11231. We also used resources of the Oak Ridge Leadership Computing Facility at the Oak Ridge National Laboratory, which is supported by the Office of Science of the U.S. Department of Energy under Contract No. DE-AC05-00OR22725. Furthermore, we would like to thank Stony Brook Research Computing and Cyberinfrastructure, and the Institute for Advanced Computational Science at Stony Brook University for access to the SeaWulf computing system, which was made possible by a 1.4M National Science Foundation grant (#1531492).

References

1. Acun, B., et al.: Parallel programming with migratable objects: Charm++ in practice. In: SC 2014: Proceedings of the International Conference for High Performance Computing, Networking, Storage and Analysis, pp. 647–658 (2014). https://doi.org/10.1109/SC.2014.58
2. Atkinson, P., McIntosh-Smith, S.: On the performance of parallel tasking runtimes for an irregular fast multipole method application. In: de Supinski, B.R., Olivier, S.L., Terboven, C., Chapman, B.M., Müller, M.S. (eds.) IWOMP 2017. LNCS, vol. 10468, pp. 92–106. Springer, Cham (2017). https://doi.org/10.1007/978-3-319-65578-9_7
3. Augonnet, C., Thibault, S., Namyst, R., Wacrenier, P.A.: StarPU: a unified platform for task scheduling on heterogeneous multicore architectures. Concurr. Comput.: Pract. Exp. 23(2), 187–198 (2011). https://doi.org/10.1002/cpe.1631
4. Bauer, M., Treichler, S., Slaughter, E., Aiken, A.: Legion: expressing locality and independence with logical regions. In: SC 2012: Proceedings of the International Conference on High Performance Computing, Networking, Storage and Analysis, pp. 1–11, November 2012. https://doi.org/10.1109/SC.2012.71
5. Berenger, J.P.: A perfectly matched layer for the absorption of electromagnetic waves. J. Comput. Phys. 114(2), 185–200 (1994). https://doi.org/10.1006/jcph.1994.1159
6. Blumofe, R.D., Joerg, C.F., Kuszmaul, B.C., Leiserson, C.E., Randall, K.H., Zhou, Y.: Cilk: an efficient multithreaded runtime system. SIGPLAN Not. 30(8), 207–216 (1995). https://doi.org/10.1145/209937.209958
7. Bosilca, G., Bouteiller, A., Danalis, A., Faverge, M., Herault, T., Dongarra, J.J.: PaRSEC: exploiting heterogeneity to enhance scalability. Comput. Sci. Eng. 15(6), 36–45 (2013). https://doi.org/10.1109/MCSE.2013.98
8. de la Cruz, R., Araya-Polo, M.: Algorithm 942: semi-stencil. ACM Trans. Math. Softw. 40(3) (2014). https://doi.org/10.1145/2591006
9. de la Cruz, R., Araya-Polo, M.: Towards a multi-level cache performance model for 3D stencil computation. Proc. Comput. Sci. 4, 2146 –2155 (2011). https://doi.org/10.1016/j.procs.2011.04.235. Proceedings of the International Conference on Computational Science, ICCS 2011
10. Delannoy, O., Petiton, S.: A peer to peer computing framework: design and performance evaluation of YML. In: Third International Symposium on Parallel and Distributed Computing/Third International Workshop on Algorithms, Models and Tools for Parallel Computing on Heterogeneous Networks, pp. 362–369 (2004). https://doi.org/10.1109/ISPDC.2004.7
11. Duran, A., et al.: OmpSs: a proposal for programming heterogeneous multi-core architectures. Parallel Process. Lett. 21(02), 173–193 (2011). https://doi.org/10.1142/S0129626411000151
12. Duran, A., Corbalán, J., Ayguadé, E.: Evaluation of OpenMP task scheduling strategies. In: Eigenmann, R., de Supinski, B.R. (eds.) IWOMP 2008. LNCS, vol. 5004, pp. 100–110. Springer, Heidelberg (2008). https://doi.org/10.1007/978-3-540-79561-2_9
13. Ghosh, S., Liao, T., Calandra, H., Chapman, B.M.: Experiences with OpenMP, PGI, HMPP and OpenACC directives on ISO/TTI kernels. In: 2012 SC Companion: High Performance Computing, Networking Storage and Analysis, pp. 691–700, November 2012. https://doi.org/10.1109/SC.Companion.2012.95

14. Gurhem, J., Tsuji, M., Petiton, S.G., Sato, M.: Distributed and parallel programming paradigms on the K computer and a cluster. In: Proceedings of the International Conference on High Performance Computing in Asia-Pacific Region, HPC Asia 2019, pp. 9–17. Association for Computing Machinery, New York (2019). https://doi.org/10.1145/3293320.3293330
15. Kaiser, H., Heller, T., Adelstein-Lelbach, B., Serio, A., Fey, D.: HPX: a task based programming model in a global address space. In: Proceedings of the 8th International Conference on Partitioned Global Address Space Programming Models, PGAS 2014. Association for Computing Machinery, New York (2014). https://doi.org/10.1145/2676870.2676883
16. Klinkenberg, J., Samfass, P., Bader, M., Terboven, C., Müller, M.S.: Chameleon: reactive load balancing for hybrid MPI + OpenMP task-parallel applications. J. Parallel Distrib. Comput. **138**, 55–64 (2020). https://doi.org/10.1016/j.jpdc.2019.12.005
17. Klinkenberg, J., et al.: Assessing task-to-data affinity in the LLVM OpenMP runtime. In: de Supinski, B.R., Valero-Lara, P., Martorell, X., Mateo Bellido, S., Labarta, J. (eds.) IWOMP 2018. LNCS, vol. 11128, pp. 236–251. Springer, Cham (2018). https://doi.org/10.1007/978-3-319-98521-3_16
18. Lee, J., Sato, M.: Implementation and performance evaluation of XcalableMP: a parallel programming language for distributed memory systems. In: 2010 39th International Conference on Parallel Processing Workshops, pp. 413–420 (2010). https://doi.org/10.1109/ICPPW.2010.62
19. Louboutin, M., et al.: Devito (v3.1.0): an embedded domain-specific language for finite differences and geophysical exploration. Geosci. Model Dev. **12**(3), 1165–1187 (2019). https://doi.org/10.5194/gmd-12-1165-2019
20. Mellor-Crummey, J., Fowler, R., Whalley, D.: Tools for application-oriented performance tuning. In: Proceedings of the 15th International Conference on Supercomputing, ICS 2001, pp. 154–165. Association for Computing Machinery, New York (2001). https://doi.org/10.1145/377792.377826
21. Meng, J., Atle, A., Calandra, H., Araya-Polo, M.: Minimod: a finite difference solver for seismic modeling. arXiv (2020). https://arxiv.org/abs/2007.06048
22. Moustafa, S., Kirschenmann, W., Dupros, F., Aochi, H.: Task-based programming on emerging parallel architectures for finite-differences seismic numerical kernel. In: Aldinucci, M., Padovani, L., Torquati, M. (eds.) Euro-Par 2018. LNCS, vol. 11014, pp. 764–777. Springer, Cham (2018). https://doi.org/10.1007/978-3-319-96983-1_54
23. NERSC: Cori. https://docs.nersc.gov/systems/cori/
24. Nguyen, A., Satish, N., Chhugani, J., Kim, C., Dubey, P.: 3.5-D blocking optimization for stencil computations on modern CPUs and GPUs. In: SC 2010: Proceedings of the 2010 ACM/IEEE International Conference for High Performance Computing, Networking, Storage and Analysis, pp. 1–13 (2010)
25. Oak Ridge Leadership Computing Facility: Summit. https://www.olcf.ornl.gov/olcf-resources/compute-systems/summit/
26. OpenMP Architecture Review Board: OpenMP Application Programming Interface, November 2018. https://www.openmp.org/wp-content/uploads/OpenMP-API-Specification-5.0.pdf. version 5.0
27. Planas, J., Badia, R.M., Ayguadé, E., Labarta, J.: Hierarchical task-based programming with StarSs. Int. J. High Perform. Comput. Appl. **23**(3), 284–299 (2009). https://doi.org/10.1177/1094342009106195

28. Qawasmeh, A., Hugues, M.R., Calandra, H., Chapman, B.M.: Performance portability in reverse time migration and seismic modelling via OpenACC. Int. J. High Perform. Comput. Appl. **31**(5), 422–440 (2017). https://doi.org/10.1177/1094342016675678
29. Reinders, J.: Intel Threading Building Blocks: Outfitting C++ for Multi-core Processor Parallelism. O'Reilly Media, Beijing (2007)
30. Rico, A., Sánchez Barrera, I., Joao, J.A., Randall, J., Casas, M., Moretó, M.: On the benefits of tasking with OpenMP. In: Fan, X., de Supinski, B.R., Sinnen, O., Giacaman, N. (eds.) IWOMP 2019. LNCS, vol. 11718, pp. 217–230. Springer, Cham (2019). https://doi.org/10.1007/978-3-030-28596-8_15
31. Slaughter, E., Lee, W., Treichler, S., Bauer, M., Aiken, A.: Regent: a high-productivity programming language for HPC with logical regions. In: Proceedings of the International Conference for High Performance Computing, Networking, Storage and Analysis, SC 2015. Association for Computing Machinery, New York (2015). https://doi.org/10.1145/2807591.2807629
32. Thaler, F., et al.: Porting the COSMO weather model to manycore CPUs. In: Proceedings of the Platform for Advanced Scientific Computing Conference, PASC 2019. Association for Computing Machinery, New York (2019). https://doi.org/10.1145/3324989.3325723
33. Vidal, R., et al.: Evaluating the impact of OpenMP 4.0 extensions on relevant parallel workloads. In: Terboven, C., de Supinski, B.R., Reble, P., Chapman, B.M., Müller, M.S. (eds.) IWOMP 2015. LNCS, vol. 9342, pp. 60–72. Springer, Cham (2015). https://doi.org/10.1007/978-3-319-24595-9_5
34. Virouleau, P., et al.: Evaluation of OpenMP dependent tasks with the KASTORS benchmark suite. In: DeRose, L., de Supinski, B.R., Olivier, S.L., Chapman, B.M., Müller, M.S. (eds.) IWOMP 2014. LNCS, vol. 8766, pp. 16–29. Springer, Cham (2014). https://doi.org/10.1007/978-3-319-11454-5_2

OpenMP Extensions

Unified Sequential Optimization Directives in OpenMP

Brandon Neth[1]($\boxtimes$), Thomas R. W. Scogland[2], Michelle Mills Strout[1], and Bronis R. de Supinski[2]

[1] University of Arizona, Tucson, AZ 85721, USA
brandonneth@email.arizona.edu
[2] Lawrence Livermore National Lab, Livermore, CA 94550, USA

Abstract. OpenMP began as a mechanism to support portability of shared-memory, loop-level parallelization via directives. OpenMP has become widely popular due to the high value that users place on portability. Its original motivation has justified additions to its specification to support SIMD parallelism and, as has been adopted for OpenMP 5.1, directives for common loop optimizations such as tiling and unrolling.

In this paper, we explore another opportunity for OpenMP to provide portability to common compiler directives – ones that support sequential optimizations such as inlining or providing information about aliasing. We survey the current support in production compilers for these features. We find that the situation is similar to the one that originally motivated OpenMP's creation. Different compilers have different syntax and sometimes different semantics for the same directives, thus requiring complicated pragma configuration for an application to support the use of multiple compilers. We also find that interaction of these directives with OpenMP further complicates their use. Our performance study demonstrates that these directives can substantially improve the performance of common programming usage by as much as 406%. Overall, we argue that inclusion of similar directives in OpenMP would substantially benefit users and compiler implementers.

1 Introduction

Prior to the specification of OpenMP, a wide range of compilers supported shared-memory, loop-level parallelization via directives. Unfortunately, those diverse directive sets often used different directives for the same functionality and even occasionally supported slightly different semantics with the same directives. This diversity significantly reduced the utility of those directives as users could not reliably use them across architectures; OpenMP has become widely used since the specification of portable directives with consistent semantics greatly increased the utility of such parallel functionality.

This work was performed under the auspices of the U.S. Department of Energy by Lawrence Livermore National Laboratory under Contract DE-AC52-07NA27344. LLNL-CONF-812472.

K. Milfeld et al. (Eds.): IWOMP 2020, LNCS 12295, pp. 85–97, 2020.
https://doi.org/10.1007/978-3-030-58144-2_6

OpenMP support has become ubiquitous among production-grade compilers because of the popularity of consistent, portable semantics among users. OpenMP has fulfilled its original purpose well and has gained support for more and more programming constructs, including task parallelism and accelerator offload, potentially with discrete memories. It has even built on its original purpose through the standardization of directives to support SIMD parallelism and traditional loop optimizations such as tiling.

In contrast to the consistent semantics for parallelization directives that OpenMP provides, sequential optimization directives, such as those for inlining or aliasing, remain fractured. While most compilers support directives for them, the syntax and, once again, the semantics vary. Users would greatly benefit from standardization. While these directives usually do not impact correctness, although mis-applied alias information certainly could, they can significantly improve performance of both parallel and serial codes. Having to use per-compiler versions of optimization directives imposes many of the same costs and issues as using compiler-specific parallelism directives did when OpenMP was first formed. We argue that we need sequential optimization directives with consistent, portable semantics and that OpenMP is the ideal avenue for them.

The contributions of this work are:

- A survey of the sequential optimization directives available in three production C++ compilers: Intel, GCC, and IBM XL;
- An analysis of the interactions between OpenMP and sequential optimization directives;
- A case study of the importance of sequential optimization directives; and
- A proposed concrete syntax for including these directives in OpenMP.

Our case study finds that the appropriate use of inlining directives can improve performance of common programming patterns by up to 406%.

In Sect. 2, we survey existing sequential optimization directives available in GCC, Intel, and IBM compilers and argue that these directives should be standardized. Section 3 describes how sequential optimizations interact in sometimes problematic ways with OpenMP thus supporting standardizing sequential optimization directives in OpenMP. Section 4 demonstrates the significant impact on performance available through inlining directives for applications written in the RAJA parallel library [10]. Section 5 concludes with a summary of possible standardizations for inlining and aliasing in OpenMP.

2   Sequential Optimizations

Many of the common sequential optimization directives of the Intel, IBM, and GCC compilers fall into one of five different categories: aliasing, inlining, optimization control, side effects, and alignment. Due to their semantic variety and usefulness in program optimization, we propose that OpenMP incorporate aliasing, inlining, alignment, and side-effect directives, similarly to the addition of sequential-loop optimizations in OpenMP 5.1.

```
1  void f() {
2    int a[100];
3    int b[100];
4    int * p = a;
5    int * q = b;
6    // p and q do not alias
7    q = a;
8    // p and q alias
9  }
```

Listing 1. Example of Pointer Aliasing

```
1  #pragma omp aliases( list )
2  #pragma omp disjoint( list )
```

Listing 2. Syntax for Aliasing Directives

2.1 Aliasing

Aliasing directives inform the compiler about symbols with possible overlap. Listing 1 shows an example of pointer aliasing. Because pointer aliasing presents a major roadblock to compiler analyses and optimizations, many compilers have directives to restrict the possibility of aliasing. For example, XL has the disjoint pragma, which indicates that the identifiers in the argument list will never alias, specifically that the identifiers do not share physical storage [3]. In the function in Listing 1, appropriate directives include #pragma disjoint(p,b) and #pragma disjoint(a,b) GCC takes a different approach with its alias attribute [1,2]. The alias attribute indicates that a variable or function aliases with another symbol in the program.

OpenMP should incorporate both approaches. The positive information of the alias annotations and the negative information of the disjoint pragmas provide orthogonal information for the compiler. These directives could be incorporated into the existing assume directive introduced in OpenMP 5.1, or introduced as standalone directives. Listing 2 shows concrete syntax for inclusion as standalone directives while Listing 3 shows alternative assume clauses.

2.2 Inlining

Inlining directives instruct the compiler whether it should attempt to inline functions. Listing 4 shows examples of inlining used in all three of the different compilers. While all have inlining directives, the syntax and semantics differ.

IBM's XL compiler has the least support for inlining directives, with the pragmas inline and noinline [5]. The inline pragma can only be used in C source code and indicates that the function in the directive is to be inlined whenever it is called. The noinline pragma can be used in C and C++ code and indicates that the function in the directive should never be inlined.

```
1  aliases( list )
2  disjoint( list )
3  pure
4  const
```

Listing 3. Syntax for `assumes` Clauses to Support Aliasing and Side Effect Information

Intel has three inlining pragmas: `inline`, `noinline`, and `forceinline` [11]. Unlike the XL pragmas, these pragmas are statement-specific: they are applied to functions at their call sites. The `noinline` directive precludes the compiler from inlining the function call, while `inline` is a hint that inlining the call would be beneficial but does not require inlining. The stronger `forceinline` pragma requires that the compiler to inline the function if possible. Both the `inline` and `forceinline` directives allow the optional `recursive` argument, which indicates that as a function call is inlined, the calls made within the inlined code should also be (recursively) inlined. Recursive functions are one example of functions that cannot be inlined.

GCC has three inlining function attributes, `noinline`, `always_inline`, and `flatten` [1]. The `noinline` attribute works like the `noinline` pragma in XL. Similarly, `always_inline` works like XL's `inline`. The `flatten` attribute is analogous to the `inline recursive` pragma in Intel's compiler, but is applied to function definitions. When compiling a function with the `flatten` attribute, GCC tries to inline all calls within the function definition, but will not do so recursively. Flattening a function does not affect whether it will be inlined itself.

We argue that OpenMP should include directives that require inlining. Directives give developers more control over their compilation. The compiler should not ignore those directives; at most the directives should support a clause to indicate that they are hints. A pair of directives, `noinline` and `inline`, completely encompasses existing support if `inline` has a clause to indicate that it should apply recursively. As with the surveyed compilers, the semantics of an inlined function should be the same as if the function were not inlined. Listing 5 shows concrete syntax for inlining directives.

2.3   Optimization Control

All three compilers have directives that support fine-grained control of optimization passes. For optimization level controls, such as O2 or O3, XL has `option_override`, Intel has `optimization_level`, and GCC has `optimize` [1, 7,11]. These directives apply optimization options at the function level. XL and GCC have directives to guide compiler optimization towards more frequently executed code. XL has the `execution_frequency` pragma, which has options for high frequency and low frequency [4]. Similarly, GCC has two attributes, `hot` and `cold` [1]. In contrast to XL's directive, which can be applied at any level of a program, GCC's attributes can only be applied to functions. However, GCC does support the GCC `optimize` pragma for finer levels of optimization control.

```
1  void foo() {printf("foo\n");}
2  void bar() {printf("bar\n");}
3
4  void no_inlining() {
5    foo();
6    bar();
7  }
8
9  void all_inlined() {
10   printf("foo\n");
11   printf("bar\n");
12 }
13
14 void intel_inlined() {
15   #pragma inline
16   foo();
17   #pragma inline
18   bar();
19 }
20
21 __attribute__((flatten))
22 void gcc_inlined() {
23   printf("foo\n");
24   printf("bar\n");
25 }
26
27 #pragma inline(foo)
28 #pragma inline(bar)
29 void xl_inlined() {
30   foo();
31   bar();
32 }
```

Listing 4. Inlining Using Directives for All Three Compilers

```
1  #pragma omp inline [ recursive ]
2  #pragma omp noinline
```

Listing 5. Syntax for Inlining Directives in OpenMP

2.4   Side Effects

Knowledge about the side effects of a function (or more specifically its lack of side effects) allows compilers to optimize more aggressively. XL and GCC support directives to indicate this type of information. In XL, the `isolated_call` pragma indicates that a function makes absolutely no changes to the state of the runtime environment [6]. This pragma corresponds to the GCC attribute `pure`.

```
 1  void neither(double * arr, size_t n) {
 2    for(size_t i = 0; i < n; ++i) {
 3      arr[i] = arr[i] + 1; // cannot modify program state
 4    }
 5  }
 6
 7  #pragma isolated_call
 8  __attribute__ ((pure))
 9  double pure_function(double * arr, size_t n) {
10    double sum = 0.0;
11    for(size_t i = 0; i < n; ++i) {
12      sum = sum + arr[i]; // can read non-volatile memory
13    }
14    return sum;
15  }
16
17  __attribute__ ((const))
18  double * const_function(double * arr, size_t n) {
19    return arr + n; // const functions cannot dereference pointers
20  }
```

Listing 6. Example of pure and const Functions with GCC Attributes

Stronger than these directives is GCC's const attribute [1]. In addition to the restrictions implied by pure, a const function cannot rely on the program state for its result. Listing 6 provides an example of the difference between these attributes. Like aliasing, side effect information can be incorporated as an additional clause to the assume directive, for which Listing 3 shows concrete syntax. Alternatively, Listing 7 shows concrete syntax for standalone directives.

2.5   Alignment

Changing the alignment of variables can shrink memory footprints and improve performance. All three compilers support directives for scoped alignment control and not just for specific variables. GCC's aligned attribute can be applied to functions, variables, or fields, and takes an optional alignment value [1]. The alignment value must be a power of two. Both XL and Intel support GCC's aligned attribute [9,11]. XL also supports the pack pragma [9]. The pack pragma is used to manage the alignment of members of aggregates like structures, unions, and classes [8]. OpenMP should extend its memory management

```
 1  #pragma omp pure
 2  #pragma omp const
```

Listing 7. Syntax for Side Effect Directives in OpenMP

```
1  #pragma omp aligned [( alignment )]
2  #pragma omp begin aligned [( alignment )]
3  #pragma omp end aligned
```

Listing 8. Syntax for Alignment Directives in OpenMP

directives to support scoped alignment control, which is frequently easier to use than having to identify specific variables. Listing 8 shows concrete syntax for inclusion in OpenMP.

3 Directive Interaction

A major reason that OpenMP should adopt sequential optimizations is to clarify their interaction with existing OpenMP directives. For example, outlining is a common technique used in OpenMP implementations. Code regions decorated with **parallel** or **task** pragmas are outlined into their own function and passed to the OpenMP runtime as function pointers. This outlining process occurs at different times in different compilers. In LLVM/Clang, outlining occurs early on as part of the front end, causing LLVM to receive OpenMP code as runtime calls and native functions rather than OpenMP constructs. Other compilers lower OpenMP pragmas to function calls on a spectrum from early to late, sometimes providing OpenMP information to the backend to support construct-aware optimizations. When parallel code regions occur in the presence of sequential optimization directives, problems may arise.

For example, in Listing 9, the flatten attribute inlines all function calls within the body of **foo** if possible. However, nearly all OpenMP implementations outline the loop into a function. When the outlining is combined with the flatten attribute, the result is ambiguous. The flattening could occur first, resulting in a parallel function with inlined calls, which is closer to the desired effect. Alternatively, outlining could occur first, resulting in a parallel function that makes calls to **bar** and **baz**, losing the intent to inline them.

Aliasing directives suffer from a similar ambiguity. Aliasing information such as disjoint, applies to the original variables. When those variables are used in

```
1  __attribute__((flatten))
2  void foo(int N) {
3    #pragma omp parallel for
4    for(int i = 0; i < N; i++) {
5      bar();
6      baz();
7    }
8  }
```

Listing 9. Interaction with Flatten Attribute

an OpenMP region, the aliasing information may not propagate during out-lining. This problem occurs with many compilers even with the C standard `restrict` type qualifier, let alone with implementation-specific directives. Fur-ther, the effect of data-sharing attributes such as `firstprivate` may obscure the aliasing relationships. Finally, OpenMP support for aliasing would allow the specification of relationships between copies created through those data-sharing attributes. OpenMP should make clear statements about its impact on aliasing; the inclusion of aliasing directives would facilitate them.

4   Case Study: Inlining in RAJA

To highlight the need for portable programmer control with respect to serial optimization, we performed a case study using inlining macros in the context of the RAJA Portability Layer and the GCC and Intel compilers. The results show that on the RAJA benchmark suite and the proxy application LULESH, the default compiler inlining decisions sometimes results in improved performance and sometimes does not. Thus providing portable pragmas for specifying such optimizations is important.

4.1   RAJA

The RAJA Performance Portability Layer [10] demonstrates the critical nature of sequential optimization directives. RAJA heavily uses inlining to reduce abstrac-tion costs. Inlining heuristics generally can determine when inlining is profitable. Nonetheless they fail frequently for large applications with complex functions with many variables, as is common for scientific codes that use RAJA. Thus, RAJA extensively uses inlining directives to ensure its use.

As Listing 10 shows, RAJA uses two inlining macros, `RAJA_INLINE` and `RAJA_FORCEINLINE_RECURSIVE` The latter is especially important for perfor-mance due to the function call depth that the RAJA kernel abstraction intro-duces. The `kernel` function takes a policy that represents a nested loop execu-tion DSL as a C++ type, the interpretation of these policies requires non-trivial metaprogramming and at least one level of nesting per level before execution of the user's provided lambda.

Each kernel statement, such as the one in Listing 11, starts with a call to a more general kernel function, `kernel_param`. This function builds a loop data object that represents the current state of the loop's iterators, param-eters and iteration values. It then prepares a statement list that recursively instantiates `StatementListExecutor` instances and invokes their methods to walk the policy's type tree, as Listing 12 shows. Each statement invokes a `StatementExecutor` that creates a wrapper for the nested For statements within the outermost For. A reference to the loop data avoids unnecessary copies. That wrapper is passed to a RAJA `forall` function that implements the loop-level policy. The `forall` executes this wrapper for each value of the first iterator. Similarly, wrapper execution unpacks the loop data and executes the next level

```
 1  RAJA_INLINE void kernel_param(SegmentTuple &&segments,
 2                                ParamTuple &&params,
 3                                Bodies &&... bodies)
 4  {
 5    util::PluginContext context{util::make_context<PolicyType>()};
 6    util::callPreLaunchPlugins(context);
 7
 8    using segment_tuple_t =
 9        typename IterableWrapperTuple<camp::decay<SegmentTuple>>::type;
10    using param_tuple_t = camp::decay<ParamTuple>;
11    using loop_data_t = internal::LoopData<PolicyType,
12                                   segment_tuple_t,
13                                   param_tuple_t,
14                                   camp::decay<Bodies>...>;
15
16    loop_data_t loop_data(make_wrapped_tuple(
17                      std::forward<SegmentTuple>(segments)),
18                      std::forward<ParamTuple>(params),
19                      std::forward<Bodies>(bodies)...);
20
21    // Execute!
22    RAJA_FORCEINLINE_RECURSIVE
23    internal::execute_statement_list<PolicyType>(loop data);
24
25    util::callPostLaunchPlugins(context);
26  }
```

Listing 10. The `RAJA_FORCEINLINE_RECURSIVE` Pragma in Use

of nesting in the statement list, the internal For loop. Eventually, when the `StatementExecutor` specialization for Lambda is reached, the body of the loop executes with the arguments that are collected in the loop data as it passed through the other levels.

Overall, a single loop-nest kernel has nested calls to `execute_statement_list`, `StatementListExecutor::exec`, `StatementExecutor::exec`, `forall_impl`, and body for each nesting level. A three-dimensional loop has 15 levels of function calls that must be inlined to maintain performance, and for moderately complex policies that number can increase significantly. Fortunately, most compilers inline all levels as well as function and method invocations in the lambda. However, compilers sometimes require hints due to the large number of levels that a kernel can generate for a single statement.

The semantics of the inlining directive are critical. Recursive inlining directives are essential since they inline all function call levels. The flatten attribute inlines only the first layer of function calls within the kernel implementation. Our case study demonstrates the necessity of recursive inlining.

```
1  using EXECPOL =
2        RAJA::KernelPolicy<
3          RAJA::statement::For<0, RAJA::loop_exec, // k
4            RAJA::statement::For<1, RAJA::loop_exec, // j
5              RAJA::statement::Lambda<0>
6            >
7          >
8        >;
9
10 RAJA::kernel<EXECPOL>(
11              RAJA::make_tuple( RAJA::RangeSegment(kbeg, kend),
12                                RAJA::RangeSegment(jbeg, jend)),
13            hydro2d_lam1);
```

Listing 11. An Example RAJA Kernel

4.2   Evaluation

We evaluate the impact of inlining directives on RAJA performance using two applications:

- the RAJA Performance Suite of RAJA implementations of streaming, simulation, polyhedral, and scientific kernels
- LULESH, a hydrodynamics proxy application

By modifying the generalized `RAJA_INLINE` and `RAJA_FORCEINLINE_RECURSIVE` macros, we created three versions of the applications for each compiler. The first version uses the inline attribute/pragma. The second version uses the noinline attribute/pragma. The third version uses no attributes or pragmas. We compile the applications with two compilers: GCC version 11.0.0 and Intel version 19.1.1.217. We report the average of three executions for the execution time evaluations.

For the RAJA Performance Suite, the compilers apply inlining successfully with or without the directives. However, the explicit inlining and no inlining versions perform significantly different, as Tables 1 and 2 summarizes. On average, when inlining is removed the suite takes four times as long as when inlining is applied. Most prominently, the slowdown of the polybench category is more than $23\times$ for GCC. The likely cause is the deeper nesting and more structurally complicated kernels within these benchmarks. The performance of this application demonstrates the necessity of inlining as an optimization for performance.

```
1  template <typename StmtList, typename Data>
2  RAJA_INLINE void execute_statement_list(Data &&data) {
3    //creates StatementExecutors for the statements in the loop nest
4    StatementListExecutor<0, camp::size<StmtList>::value, StmtList>::
         exec(std::forward<Data>(data));
5  }
6  template <camp::idx_t ArgumentId, typename ExecPolicy, typename
       EnclosedStmts>
7  struct StatementExecutor<statement::For<ArgumentId, ExecPolicy,
       EnclosedStmts...>> {
8    template <typename Data> static RAJA_INLINE void exec(Data &&data) {
9      // Create a wrapper, in case forall_impl needs to thread_privatize
10     ForWrapper<ArgumentId, Data, EnclosedStmts...> for_wrapper(data);
11     auto len = segment_length<ArgumentId>(data);
12     using len_t = decltype(len);
13     forall_impl(ExecPolicy{}, TypedRangeSegment<len_t>(0, len),
           for_wrapper);
14   }
15 };
16 template <typename Iterable, typename Func>
17 RAJA_INLINE void forall_impl(const seq_exec &, Iterable &&iter, Func
       &&body) {
18   RAJA_EXTRACT_BED_IT(iter);
19   for (decltype(distance_it) i = 0; i < distance_it; ++i) { body(*(
         begin_it + i)); }
20 }
```

Listing 12. Statement Execution

Table 1. Average slowdowns when inlining is removed from RAJA Performance Suite, GCC.

Benchmark Category	Benchmark Count	Average Execution Time with Inlining (s)	Average Execution Time without Inlining (s)	Average Slowdown without Inlining
basic	10	0.45	1.37	3.03x
lcals	11	0.76	1.22	1.59x
polybench	13	0.88	20.46	23.23x
stream	5	1.31	1.62	1.23x
apps	7	1.05	3.12	2.97x
total	46	.79	3.30	4.18x

For LULESH, as Table 3 summarizes, the no directive version performs better than the version with explicit no inlining. In contrast to the performance suite, where inlining directives do not lead to more inlining, LULESH sees performance benefits when inlining is specified directly. The performance of this application demonstrates that compiler heuristics alone do not lead to sufficient inlining.

Table 2. Average slowdowns when inlining is removed from RAJA Performance Suite, Intel.

Benchmark Category	Benchmark Count	Average Execution Time with Inlining (s)	Average Execution Time without Inlining (s)	Average Slowdown without Inlining
basic	10	0.48	1.37	2.85x
lcals	11	0.93	1.64	1.75x
polybench	13	0.96	11.37	11.76x
stream	5	1.04	1.05	1.01x
apps	7	0.83	3.37	4.04x
total	46	0.81	3.24	3.98x

Table 3. Execution Times and Binary Sizes for LULESH Variants

Compiler	Version	Average Execution Time (s)	Binary Size (kb)
GCC	Inlining	112.33	530
	No Directives	117.06	187
	No Inlining	115.14	315
Intel	Inlining	103.39	1490
	No Directives	108.87	732
	No Inlining	109.83	675

5 Conclusion

Regardless of programming language, directives are an important communication mechanism between developers and the compiler. However, directive divergence across compilers significantly hampers developers. OpenMP's history of unifying different directive languages into a *lingua franca* for parallel programming is a key reason for its popularity. Additionally, by supporting multiple source languages, it further unifies parallel programming. However, it has left other crucial types of directives, such as sequential program optimizations, to evolve in disparate directions. We have shown that these directives are critical to performance and that they interact with directives in OpenMP. Thus, users need well-defined semantics for those directive and their interaction with OpenMP. OpenMP 6.0 will be the ideal mechanism to provide those semantics.

References

1. 33.1 common function attributes. https://gcc.gnu.org/onlinedocs/gcc/Common-Function-Attributes.html#Common-Function-Attributes. Accessed 24 May 2020
2. 34.1 common variable attributes. https://gcc.gnu.org/onlinedocs/gcc/Common-Variable-Attributes.html#Common-Variable-Attributes. Accessed 24 May 2020

3. #pragma disjoint. https://www.ibm.com/support/knowledgecenter/SSLTBW_2.
   4.0/com.ibm.zos.v2r4.cbclx01/pragma_disjoint.htm. Accessed 24 May 2020
4. #pragma execution_frequency. https://www.ibm.com/support/knowledgecenter/
   SSLTBW_2.4.0/com.ibm.zos.v2r4.cbclx01/zos_pragma_execution_frequency.htm.
   Accessed 24 May 2020
5. #pragma inline (c only) / noinline. https://www.ibm.com/support/
   knowledgecenter/SSLTBW_2.4.0/com.ibm.zos.v2r4.cbclx01/zos_pragma_inline.
   htm#cplrill. Accessed 24 May 2020
6. #pragma isolated_call. https://www.ibm.com/support/knowledgecenter/
   SSLTBW_2.4.0/com.ibm.zos.v2r4.cbclx01/opt_isolated_call.htm#opt_isolated_
   call. Accessed 24 May 2020
7. #pragma option_override. https://www.ibm.com/support/knowledgecenter/
   SSLTBW_2.4.0/com.ibm.zos.v2r4.cbclx01/pragma_option_override.htm#pragma_
   option_override. Accessed 24 May 2020
8. #pragma pack. https://www.ibm.com/support/knowledgecenter/SSLTBW_2.4.0/
   com.ibm.zos.v2r4.cbclx01/pragma_pack.htm?view=kc#pragma_pack. Accessed 24
   May 2020
9. Using alignment modifiers. https://www.ibm.com/support/knowledgecenter/
   SSGH2K_12.1.0/com.ibm.xlc121.aix.doc/proguide/modificrs.html#modifiers.
   Accessed 24 May 2020
10. Beckingsale, D.A., et al.: Raja: portable performance for large-scale scientific appli-
    cations. In: 2019 IEEE/ACM International Workshop on Performance, Portability
    and Productivity in HPC (P3HPC), pp. 71–81. IEEE (2019)
11. Intel. Intel C++ Compiler 19.0 Developer Guide and Reference, December 2019

Supporting Data Shuffle Between Threads in OpenMP

Anjia Wang, Xinyao Yi, and Yonghong Yan$^{(\boxtimes)}$

University of North Carolina at Charlotte, Charlotte, NC 28262, USA
{awang15,xyi2,yyan7}@uncc.edu

Abstract. Both NVIDIA and AMD GPUs provide shuffle or permutation instructions to enable direct data movement between private registers of different threads. Since it doesn't involve the shared memory or global memory on the device which are slower than direct register access, data shuffling provides opportunities of optimizing data copy to improve computing performance. However, shuffle is low-level primitive(warp- or lane-level for NVIDIA and AMD GPUs) for GPU programming. It requires advanced knowledge and skills to effectively use it. In this paper, we present two approaches of using shuffle in OpenMP, 1) a high performance runtime implementation of reduction clause using shuffle instruction; and 2) proposed **shuffle** extension to OpenMP to let users specify when and how the data should be moved between threads. Using sum reduction and 2D stencil as examples in our experiment, the shuffle implementation always delivers the best performance with up to 2.39x speedup compared with other high performance implementation. Compared with standard OpenMP offloading code for 2D stencil, our shuffle implementation delivers superior performance for as many as 25x better. We also provide study of simulated shuffle using shared memory on NVIDIA GPUs to demonstrate how to support this extension on hardware that has no native shuffle support.

Keywords: OpenMP · CUDA · Shuffle · Reduction · Stencil

1 Introduction

OpenMP has been known for productive shared-memory programming on multi-core, multi-processor and many-core homogeneous systems in which data movement between computing elements such as cores or CPUs are via memory implicitly. The recent specification introduced **target**-family constructs for specifying offloading data and computation to accelerators whose memory are physically separate from the host CPU memory. E.g. the **map** clause can be used to explicitly specify data movement between memories of host and an accelerator GPU. From OpenMP users' perspective, data sharing and movement between parallel threads and tasks must go through the memory system, implicitly or explicitly. This memory model has been both productive for programming and also well

© Springer Nature Switzerland AG 2020
K. Milfeld et al. (Eds.): IWOMP 2020, LNCS 12295, pp. 98–112, 2020.
https://doi.org/10.1007/978-3-030-58144-2_7

abstracting hardware systems of parallel architectures, thus reducing programming efforts significantly for writing performance portable programs.

For manycore accelerators such as GPUs and vector architectures, data can be copied between registers of multiple computing elements such as cores or vector lanes without going through the memory and cache system, using shuffle or permutation operations. For example, NVIDIA introduced shuffle instruction from Kepler architecture to conduct data transfer between registers of different threads in a warp. The feature enables a multi-thread kernel to perform vector-like operations synchronously within a warp. When shared data is small and can reside in register within a warp of threads (32 threads), those threads can access registers from each other. Considering that register access latency could be 10x and 100x smaller than SRAM and DRAM respectively, taking advantage of this data shuffle feature between threads could significantly improve computation performance of worksharing or vector loops.

In this paper, we present two approaches of using shuffle in OpenMP. First, we provide a high performance runtime implementation of reduction clause using shuffle. Then, a new directive and a new clause both named shuffle are introduced for programmers to specify explicit data movement between threads. The shuffle clause is used to specify the data that can be shuffled between threads, and the directive to specify when and how the data are transferred. While the motivation is to support shuffling data between cores or vector lanes via registers on many-core and vector architectures, the support in general is designed to bypass slow memory for data movement between thread via explicit data shuffle operation. We develop a prototype implementation of the proposed support and evaluate it using reduction and stencil algorithm. The shuffle implementation always delivers the best performance with up to 2.39x speedup compared with other high performance implementation. Compared with standard OpenMP offloading code for 2D stencil, our shuffle implementation delivers superior performance for as many as 25x better. We also provide study of simulated shuffle using shared memory on NVIDIA GPUs to demonstrate how to support this extension on hardware that has no native shuffle support.

In the rest of paper, Sect. 2 presents the data shuffle operations in the existing NVIDIA GPUs, AMD GPUs and Intel vector architectures, and motivate our work. Section 3 shows the high performance implementation of reduction using shuffle instruction. Section 4 presents the shuffle extension to OpenMP with syntax details and how to use it for 2D stencil. Then we show the performance evaluation in Sect. 5. At last, we discuss some related work in Sect. 6 and conclude our paper in Sect. 7.

2 Motivation

Manycore architecture such as GPUs and vector architecture excels in delivering high performance and energy efficiency for data parallel computations. These two architectures are more and more widely used in the HPC field because of its highly parallelized architecture. While a CPU has less than a hundred of cores in most cases, a GPU could have thousands of cores and run tens to hundreds of thousands of threads in parallel. In this section, we present the feature of data shuffling between GPU cores and vector lanes available in NVIDIA GPU, AMD GPU and vector architectures.

2.1   CUDA shuffle Instruction for NVIDIA GPUs

Since Kepler architecture, NVIDIA releases the warp shuffle instructions to allow data exchange between registers without touching memory. Before that, exchanging data between threads must go through shared memory (within a block) or global memory. If the operation is not atomic, developers have to insert synchronization calls before and after the data transferring, which introduces overhead and increases the programming complexity. The shuffle instructions introduced in NVIDIA CUDA include __shfl_sync, __shfl_up_sync, __shfl_down_sync, and __shfl_xor_sync. Using those instructions, data in private registers of threads within the same warp could be exchanged directly. They are atomic operations and the synchronization is enforced naturally by the SIMT execution model of the NVIDIA GPU architecture. The shuffle instructions are read-only operations to the threads that provide the data.

Table 1. CUDA shuffle instructions

Instruction	Description	Parameters
__shfl_sync	Direct copy from indexed lane	unsigned mask, T var, int srcLane, int width=warpSize
__shfl_up_sync	Copy from a lane with lower ID relative to caller	unsigned mask, T var, unsigned int delta, int width=warpSize
__shfl_down_sync	Copy from a lane with higher ID relative to caller	unsigned mask, T var, unsigned int delta, int width=warpSize
__shfl_xor_sync	Copy from a lane based on bitwise XOR of own lane ID	unsigned mask, T var, int laneMask, int width=warpSize

The description of the CUDA's shuffle instructions are shown in Table 1. They take four parameters and the last one for warp size is optional. mask is used to indicate which threads are involved. var is the targeting data, which could be integer, float, double and other types. srcLane is an absolute lane ID in the warp while delta represents the relative difference to the lane ID of caller thread. laneMask is used to perform a bitwise operation to the lane ID of caller thread.

We use a sum reduction as example to show how shuffle works. To simplify the case, we assure there are only 8 lanes, which hold their own copy of variable v. Without shuffle, they need to store the value into shared memory so that other threads can access it. Between each iteration of reduction, the intermediate result

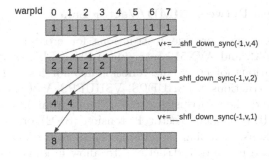

Fig. 1. Shuffle example using NVIDIA GPU instruction [7]

also need to be maintained in the shared memory and the synchronization has to be handled properly to avoid data race. By using shuffle instruction, a thread can directly access the private register of another thread without routing via shared memory. Furthermore, the shuffle operation is atomic and executed in lock step. In Fig. 1 [7], initially the first four threads read v from the last four threads and add it up to their own copy of v. Then the same kind of reduction continued among these four threads and so on. Eventually, the very first thread sets the sum of all eight elements. Through the whole procedure, only registers are used for computing.

2.2   Cross-Lane Operations of AMD GPUs

The AMD GPUs also provide a set of instructions similar to the `shuffle` instructions in CUDA. Wavefront on AMD GPU plays the same role as warp on NVIDIA GPU. Within a wavefront, there are 64 lanes that can execute the same code simultaneously as a SIMD vector.

Table 2. Summary of AMD GPU `shuffle` instruction [9]

Instruction	Description	Parameters
ds_permute_b32	Push `src` data to a lane indicated by `addr`	dest, addr, src [offset:addr_offset]
ds_bpermute_b32	Pull `src` data from a lane indicated by `addr`	dest, addr, src [offset:addr_offset]

There are two instructions related to `shuffle` (Table 2). Unlike the read-only operations in CUDA, AMD allows a thread to push its own data to another thread's private register using `ds_permute_b32`. `ds_bpermute_b32` is used to read data from another thread's private register.

2.3   Shuffle Data Between SIMD/Vector Lanes

Vector architectures also provide instructions for cross-lane operations. For example, Intel AVX2 and AVX512 introduced SHUFFLE, BROADCAST and PERMUTE operations for cross-lane functionality for floating-point and integer operations. Instructions are SHUFPS, VSHUFPS, VPERMI2D, VPERMD, VPERMQ, etc, and their intrinsics can be found from Intel compiler developer guide [5]. ARM Scalable Vector Extension (SVE) provides permutation and shuffle operations, including reductions across vector lanes. RISC-V vector extensions also have permute instructions to allow cross-lane data movement. While OpenMP's simd directive can be used for instruct the compiler to vectorize a loop, advanced operations such for cross-lane data movement have not yet supported in the standard.

3   Using Shuffle to Implement the reduction Clause

In parallel computing, reduction is a very common operation used for aggregating partial results. For multi-thread programming, it repeatedly applies the same operation by multiple threads that have the partial results. The final result resides in one thread. Figure 2 shows the sum reduction using OpenMP. The task is offloaded onto an accelerator that has multiple teams of threads to perform the reduction operation. Within a team, data from all threads are accumulated. Then those partial results are reduced into one final result and can be copied back to host. By default, data and operations are performed off the global memory which is DRAM memory on GPUs. An optimized implementation can takes advantage of shared memory (SRAM) in NVIDIA to accelerate the reduction operations, e.g. the reduction from the official CUDA examples of NVIDIA.

```
1   // prerequisite data declaration and computing
2   #define BLOCK_SIZE 64
3   float src[N] = ...;
4   #pragma omp target teams distribute parallel for map(to: src[0:N]) map(
        from: sum) num_teams(N/BLOCK_SIZE) num_threads(BLOCK_SIZE) reduction
        (+: sum)
5     for (i = 0; i < N; i++)
6       sum += src[i];
```

Fig. 2. Sum reduction using OpenMP

The reduction clause in OpenMP can be implemented in CUDA using shuffle operations, along with other optimization techniques. Such implementation can be done in the runtime system, thus requires minimum compiler transformation. In Fig. 4, we show the implementation that is similar to the one presented in [7]. In this algorithm, it divides the whole input in the global memory to multiple tiles and each block on GPU reads a tile to its shared memory. Using shuffle, threads in the same warp share their partial results directly between private registers as soon as they are available. Only the results from warps will be reduced in the shared memory.

```
1   template <class T>
2   __inline__ __device__ T warpReduceSum(T val) {
3     for (int offset = warpSize/2; offset > 0; offset /= 2)
4       val += __shfl_down_sync((unsigned int)-1, val, offset);
5     return val;
6   }
7   template <class T>
8   __global__ void reduce(T *g_idata, T *g_odata, unsigned int n) {
9     T mySum = ...; // prepare the local partial sum per thread
10    mySum = warpReduceSum<T>(mySum);
11    int lane = threadIdx.x % warpSize;
12    int wid = threadIdx.x / warpSize; // warp id
13    if (lane == 0) sdata[wid] = mySum; // the partial result of a warp
14    ... // rest of reduction
15  }
```

Fig. 3. Reduction implementation using native shuffle

For comparison, the same algorithm can be implemented using CUDA shared memory, and the algorithm can be used for GPUs that has no native shuffle instruction. The implementation is shown in Fig. 4. For each variable that needs to be shuffled, an array of block size is created so that each thread in that block can maintain a copy of the variable in that array. From the user's point of view, the simulated shuffle can still directly access the private data of another thread even though they didn't declare the shuffle variable as shared data. Comparing the two implementation in Fig. 3 and Fig. 4, it is shown that their algorithms are identical, and the only difference is the implementation of shuffle function.

4   Proposing shuffle Clause and Directive for OpenMP

As we discussed in Sect. 1 for the current OpenMP memory model, sharing data between threads must go through the memory system. This is defined based on the fact that most existing multi-core and many-core architectures only allow sharing data between functional units via memory. Shuffle primitives enable direct data movement between threads, hence function units of a system, allowing data sharing by bypassing memory system. For the second contribution of this paper, we experiment high-level language support of data sharing between threads without using any kind or level of memory. We introduce a shuffle clause and a shuffle directive to OpenMP for such experiment.

```
1   template <class T>
2   __inline__ __device__ T warpReduceSum(T val) {
3     T *buffer = SharedMemory<T>();
4     int lane = threadIdx.x % warpSize;
5     int wid = threadIdx.x / warpSize;
6     buffer[threadIdx.x] = val;
7     __syncthreads();
8     for (int offset = warpSize/2; offset > 0; offset /= 2)
9       if (lane + offset < warpSize) {
10          val += buffer[wid*warpSize + lane + offset];
11          buffer[threadIdx.x] = val;
12          __syncthreads();
13      }
14    return val;
15  }
16  template <class T>
17  __global__ void reduce(T *g_idata, T *g_odata, unsigned int n) {
18    T mySum = ...; // prepare the local partial sum per thread
19    mySum = warpReduceSum<T>(mySum);
20    int lane = threadIdx.x % warpSize;
21    int wid = threadIdx.x / warpSize; // warp id
22    if (lane == 0) sdata[wid] = mySum; // the partial result of a warp
23    ... // rest of reduction
24  }
```

Fig. 4. Reduction kernel using simulated shuffle

First, the shuffle clause can be used with parallel and teams directives to declare the shuffling variables. Its syntax is simply as "shuffle (*src-variable-list*)", in which the *src-variable-list* specifies the variables that can be shuffled. Compared with the two similar clauses that are used in OpenMP to specify data sharing attribute, the shared or private clauses, variables that are annotated to be shuffled are read-only shared variables to other threads and access to the variable must use the shuffle directive proposed. The shared clause indicate read-write sharing among all threads while the private clause indicates that the data are only available to the thread itself.

Second, the proposed shuffle directive is an executive directive to specify how exactly the data should be shuffled between registers of different threads. It must used within a parallel or teams region. The syntax is: "shuffle *clause*", and the *clause* must be in the following format:

"sync|up|down(*mask-modifier[,]   src-modifier[,]   dst-variable   [operator], shuffle-variable*)"

The shuffle directive performs operation of moving data of a shuffled variable from a source thread or lane (specified by the *src-modifier*), and then accumulating the data using specified operation (the *operator*) with a variable (the *dst-variable*), and then storing the result in the variable. The *mask-modifier* is a mask to indicate which threads to participate shuffle operation, similar to the

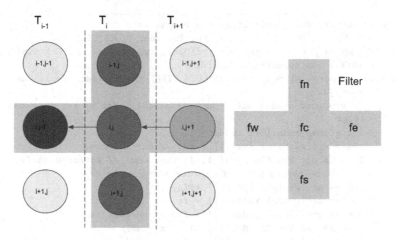

Fig. 5. 2D 5 points stencil using shuffle. Each circle indicates an original pixel. Each thread loads three pixels. Pixels in color are involved with computation of pixel (i,j). Arrow represents the shuffle direction

first parameter in the CUDA's **shuffle** primitives. The *src-modifier* is used to specify the threads or lanes that supply the data. For the **sync** shuffling which is used to specify that all participating threads shuffle data from a single source thread, the *src-modifier* is the absolute warp or lane ID, such as 25 or 31. For **up** and **down** clauses, the *src-modifier* is used to indicate the relative distance between the participating thread and the source thread. *operator* is the operation to be applied to the shuffled data, which could be =, +=, -=, \= and so on. It equals to *dst-variable = dst-variable operator shuffle-variable*. The default operator is = if none is specified. The *shuffle-variable* must be the variable specified by the **shuffle** clause.

Currently, the most usage of **shuffle** operation is for using GPUs because of its availability on NVIDIA and AMD GPUs. On CPU and other platforms, shuffle can be easily implemented using shared memory and performance can be optimized by taking advantage of last level of shared cache. While our proposal is one approach of exposing this features to users, shuffle can be used in other approach such as via runtime function, or used with **metadirective** or **declare variant** for performance optimization. Yet those approaches require knowledge and skills of CUDA and OpenCL programming. One limitation of this proposal is that the use of **shuffle** directive may render incorrect execution of the OpenMP code if OpenMP compilation is turned off since the use of **shuffle** requires parallel SIMD-type of data movement between variables of the same symbol.

4.1 Stencil Example

In stencil, a filter is applied to each pixel and several pixels around it to compute a new value for that pixel. Since a pixel can be involved multiple times during computing, if we can load several pixels to register once in one thread and

```
1   // prerequisite data declaration and computing
2   float src[N], dst[N], fw, fc, fe, fn, fs, sum, BLOCK_SIZE = ...;
3   #pragma omp target teams map(to: src[0:N], fw, fc, fe, fn, fs) map(from:
        dst[0:N]) num_teams(N/BLOCK_SIZE)
4   #pragma omp parallel num_threads(BLOCK_SIZE) shuffle(sum) // declare sum
        for shuffle
5       {  // prepared needed data, such as global index of src item and dst
           item
6           int global_index[3], index = ...;
7           sum = src[global_index[1]] * fe; // partial sum1
8           #pragma omp shuffle down(-1, 1, sum, sum) // thread n shuffles sum
                from thread n+1 and replace its own sum copy
9           sum += src[global_index[0]] * fn;
10          sum += src[global_index[1]] * fc;
11          sum += src[global_index[2]] * fs; // partial sum2
12          #pragma omp shuffle down(-1, 1, sum, sum)
13          sum += src[global_index[1]] * fw; // partial sum3
14          dst[index] = sum; // write the final result to output array dst
15      }
```

Fig. 6. 2D 5 points stencil using shuffle OpenMP extension

```
1   // prerequisite data declaration and computing
2   float src[N], dst[N], fw, fc, fe, fn, fs, sum, BLOCK_SIZE = ...;
3   int N = width*height;
4   #pragma omp target map(to: src[0:N], fc, fn0, fn1, fw1, fw0, fe1, fe0,
        fs1, fs0, height, width) map(from: dst[0:N])
5   #pragma omp teams distribute parallel for num_teams(N/BLOCK_SIZE)
        num_threads(BLOCK_SIZE) collapse(2) schedule(static, 1) shuffle(sum)
6   for (int i = 0; i < height; i++) {
7     for (int j = 0; j < width; j++) {
8       sum = src[i*width+j+1] * fe;
9       #pragma omp shuffle(-1, 1, sum, sum)
10      sum += src[(i-1)*width+j] * fn;
11      sum += src[i*width+j] * fc;
12      sum += src[(i+1)*width+j] * fs;
13      #pragma omp shuffle(-1, 1, sum, sum)
14      sum += src[i*width+j-1] * fw;
15      dst[i*width+j+1] = sum;
16    }
17  }
```

Fig. 7. 2D 5 points stencil using worksharing and shuffle OpenMP extension

complete all the computations, it would be faster than multiple threads all load the pixels from global memory repeatedly. Taking 2D 5 points stencil as example, to compute the pixel (i,j) it needs 4 adjacent pixels and itself. We consider these

```
1   __global__ void stencil(const float* src, float* dst, ...,
2           float fc, float fn, float fw, float fe, float fs) {
3       // prepared needed data, such as global index of src item and dst item
4       int global_index[3], index = ...;
5       sum = src[global_index[1]] * fe; // partial sum1
6       sum = __shfl_down_sync(0xFFFFFFFF, sum, 1);
7       sum += src[global_index[0]] * fn;
8       sum += src[global_index[1]] * fc;
9       sum += src[global_index[2]] * fs; // partial sum2
10      sum = __shfl_down_sync(0xFFFFFFFF, sum, 1);
11      sum += src[global_index[1]] * fw; // partial sum3
12      dst[index] = sum; // save the result back to the output array
13  }
```

Fig. 8. 2D stencil kernel using shuffle instructions

5 pixels as 3 columns handled by 3 threads (Fig. 5). Each thread calculates a partial sum and passes it to the left neighbor. The leftmost thread collects all partial results and gets the final result. In this example, thread T_{i+1} computes $sum1_{i,j} = P_{i,j+1} \times fe$ and passes it to thread T_i. Thread T_i computes $sum2_{i,j} = P_{i-1,j} \times fn + P_{i,j} \times fc + P_{i+1,j} \times fs$ and passes $sum1_{i,j} + sum2_{i,j}$ to thread T_{i-1}. Then thread T_{i-1} computes $sum3_{i,j} = P_{i,j+1} \times fw$. As the last step, thread T_{i-1} stores the final result $sum_{i,j} = sum1_{i,j} + sum2_{i,j} + sum3_{i,j}$ to a proper location.

In Fig. 6, it shows a simplified 2D 5 points stencil using shuffle constructs. As we described above, each thread reads 3 points. It generates two partial results and passes them to neighbours. Two partial sums are retrieved back as well. At last, three partial results corresponding to three columns of filter are combined together as the final result. Figure 7 presents a worksharing version of 2D stencil. The nested loop is flatten by collapse. schedule clause ensures that the threads next to each other process continuous pixels so that they can correctly pass intermediate results.

We create a prototype implementation in CUDA to demonstrate how the compiler would transform the OpenMP code in Fig. 6. It doesn't perform shuffle operation across the whole team. Instead, the operation is mapped to a warp on NVIDIA GPU, which means the shuffle is conducted within a warp. For other platforms, it depends on what native shuffle instruction is available and how it works on the hardware level. The shuffle operations are implemented using both native shuffle instructions and shared memory. In Fig. 8, the intermediate results of a column of pixels are shuffled between adjacent threads at line 6 and 10, which correspond to line 8 and 12 in Fig. 6. Each thread makes the maximum use of the pixels and produces all the possible results from them. Then it exchanges the partial results among private register of neighbours via shuffle to avoid shared memory access. The shuffle instruction can be simulated using shared memory at line 8–14 and 18–24 so that the code will support the devices without native shuffle (Fig. 9). They still share the same kernel function.

```
1   __global__ void stencil(const double* src, double* dst, ...,
2          double fc, double fn, double fw, double fe, double fs) {
3     // prepared needed data, such as global index of src item and dst item
4     int global_index[3], index = ...;
5     // an array shared in a block to exchange sum between threads
6     __shared__ double shared_sum[BLOCK_SIZE];
7     float sum = src[global_index[1]] * fe;
8     shared_sum[thread_id] = sum;
9     __syncwarp();
10    if (lane_id < warpSize) { // lane_id is the thread id within a warp
11      shared_sum[thread_id] = shared_sum[thread_id+1];
12      __syncwarp();
13      sum = shared_sum[sumId];
14    }
15    sum += src[global_index[0]] * fn;
16    sum += src[global_index[1]] * fc;
17    sum += src[global_index[2]] * fs;
18    shared_sum[thread_id] = sum;
19    __syncwarp();
20    if (lane_id < warpSize) {
21      shared_sum[thread_id] = shared_sum[thread_id+1];
22      __syncwarp();
23      sum = shared_sum[thread_id];
24    }
25    sum += src[global_index[1]] * fw;
26    dst[index] = sum; // save the result back to the output array
27  }
```

Fig. 9. 2D Stencil kernel using shuffle simulated by shared memory

5   Experimental Results

The experimental platform used for reduction has a 12 cores Intel Xeon W-2133 CPU, 32 GB DRAM, and one NVIDIA Quadro P400 GPU with 2 GB of memory. The other platform that is used for stencil has two 18 cores Intel Xeon E5-2699 v3 CPUs, 256 GB DRAM, and two NVIDIA Tesla K80 GPUs with 24 GB of memory. Both systems run Ubuntu 18.04 LTS and NVIDIA CUDA SDK 10.2.

As baseline, `omp target teams distribute parallel for` is used to implement reduction and stencil, and then compiled by Clang/LLVM 10.0.1 with -O3 parameter. Thus the baseline performance completely depends on the transformation and optimization by Clang/LLVM compiler. The kernel time on GPU is measured as execution time, the time cost of data transfer is not included. There are four more versions of implementation to be evaluated, including accessing global memory directly, using shared memory as software cache for a tile of loop tiling, using shared memory to simulate shuffle, and using native shuffle. The version of using shared memory as software cache for loop tiling is considered as highly optimized implementation on NVIDIA GPUs [10].

In both tests, the baseline OpenMP version is much slower than the rest four versions. The native shuffle version is about 20x faster than the baseline. Beside the shuffle instruction, the reason could be that the manually transformed CUDA code and the baseline OpenMP code compiled by LLVM have different mechanism of parallelization. It may lead to various memory access behaviors, such as coalesced memory access versus uncoalesced memory access.

5.1   Reduction

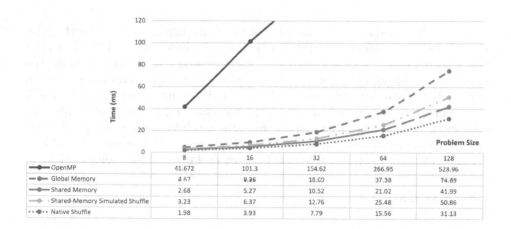

	8	16	32	64	128
OpenMP	41.672	101.3	154.62	266.95	528.96
Global Memory	4.67	9.36	18.60	37.38	74.89
Shared Memory	2.68	5.27	10.52	21.02	41.99
Shared-Memory Simulated Shuffle	3.23	6.37	12.76	25.48	50.86
Native Shuffle	1.98	3.93	7.79	15.56	31.13

Fig. 10. Performance of reduction

The input is an array of given size that filled with randomly generated numbers. We can see the native shuffle version is the fastest as expected since it has the least amount of access to slower memories (Fig. 10). It shows up to 25x better performance than the standard OpenMP version and 2.39x speedup over the global memory version. The version using shared memory to simulate the shuffle instruction is slower than the second version that uses shared memory without shuffle. It's reasonable because the simulated shuffle requires more resources to maintain an array to share data and it performs more synchronizations in the block to make sure atomic data operations.

The memory access of reduction can be modeled in Table 3. $f(x)$ is the amount of memory operations for reducing x numbers, where $f(x) = \sum_{0}^{k} 2^k$ and $k = \log_2 x$. Different versions incurs different amount of memory access to each memory. In the global memory version, all those accesses occur in the global memory. In the shared memory version, the elements are reduced in the shared memory. It reads and writes this memory location $f(B)$ times, respectively. Since there are G blocks, the total number of shared memory access is $2 * G * f(B)$.

For the native shuffle version, within a warp the elements are reduced among registers directly. Then the partial results from all warps in the same block are

Table 3. Memory accesses for reduction.

	Global Memory	Shared Memory	Shared Memory Simulated Shuffle	Native Shuffle
Global memory access	2 * G * B + 2 * G * f(B)	2 * G * B	2 * G * B	2 * G * B
Shared memory access	0	2 * G * f(B)	2 * G * f(B)	2 * G * W
Cross-bock synchronization	2 * G	2 * G	2 * G * (f(B)+1)	2*G

N: problem size = G * B, G: grid size = 32768, B: block size = 256, W: warp size = 32

reduced in the shared memory as usual or via shuffle again. The simulated shuffle shares the same operations. However, it accesses shared memory $2 * G * f(B)$ times to shuffle data. It also requires two more synchronizations to make the operation atomic and prevent data race. Given one shuffle operation per iteration of reduction, the additional amount of cross-block synchronization is $2 * G * f(B)$.

According to the analysis above, the performance improvement of native shuffle over the shared memory version is from the much less access to shared memory. The time overhead of simulated shuffle is caused by excessive cross-block synchronization, which is a trade-off between performance and compatibility.

5.2   2D Stencil

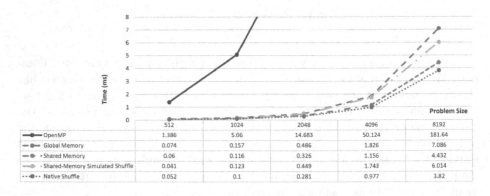

Fig. 11. Performance of 2D 9 points stencil

The input of this test is an automatically generated image by random numbers. The results present a very similar trend between four versions to reduction experiments (Fig. 11). The native shuffle version has the best performance. According to the breakdown of memory accesses, this version has the least amount of slower memory accesses and cross-block synchronizations (Fig. 4). The average speedup of native shuffle over hand-written tiled shared memory

Table 4. Memory accesses for 2D stencil

	Global Memory	Shared Memory	Shared Memory Simulated Shuffle	Native Shuffle
Global memory access	G * B * 4 * 10	G * B * 9	G * B * 9	G * B * 9
Shared memory access	0	G * B * (8 + 4 * 9)	G * B * 4 * 16	0
Cross-bock synchronization	0	1	4 * 4 * 2	0
Shared memory size used	0	B * 8	B	0

N: problem size = 4 * G * B, G: grid size = N/4B, B: block size = 128, W: warp size = 32

version, which has been highly optimized, is 1.11. While sharing the same source code, the simulated shuffle version suffers from the overhead of cross-block synchronization.

6 Related Work

There are several work that have adopted the CUDA `shuffle` instructions in their studies for performance improvement. CUDA `shuffle` instructions can improve the performance of reduction operation by computing on private registers of multiple threads [1,7,8]. Liu and Schmit use warp shuffle functions in a similar way to develop LightSpMV, which is a faster algorithm of sparse matrix-vector multiplication [6]. For a more general linear solver, `shuffle` instructions are able to speed up the computation by exchanging values stored on registers directly as well [1]. Tangram is a high-level programming framework, which provides APIs to perform computation on GPU [2]. It has been extended to use atomic and shuffle functions in the framework [4]. During AST construction, an additional pass is added to determine the opportunity of inserting `shuffle` instruction for loop optimization. With the help of `shuffle` instructions, Chen et al. [3] realize the systolic execution on GPU and demonstrate superior performance for 2D stencil in CUDA than most of state-of-the-art implementations. In comparison, our work proposes high-level interface of using shuffle instruction with OpenMP.

7 Conclusion

Data shuffling between threads or lanes of many-core GPUs allows data copy between threads without involving the memory system. It could be exploited to improve the computing performance when there are large amount of data communication between threads. In this paper, we experiment two approaches of using shuffle in the OpenMP high-level programming model, 1) a high performance runtime implementation of reduction clause; and 2) proposed `shuffle` extension to OpenMP to let users specify when and how the data should be moved between threads. Superior performance improvement has been achieved and demonstrated when using shuffle to implement the reduction and 2D stencil kernels. While the effort of correctly programming using shuffle primitive is significant, our language extension to allow users to use it in high-level programming model can reduce its complexity. These exploration and experiment provide a strong proof of concept that shuffle instructions should be exploited in compiler code generation and application optimization for performance improvement. In the future, we would like to explore the shuffle implementation on CPU by exploiting prefetching and non-temporal accesses, and on other heterogeneous architectures to enable shuffle in more scenarios. We would also like to explore the use of shuffle in OpenMP `SIMD` directive for vector architectures.

Acknowledgment. This work was supported by the National Science Foundation under Grant No. 2015254 and 1409946.

References

1. Bernaschi, M., Carrozzo, M., Franceschini, A., Janna, C.: A dynamic pattern factored sparse approximate inverse preconditioner on graphics processing units. SIAM J. Sci. Comput. **41**(3), C139–C160 (2019)
2. Chang, L.W., El Hajj, I., Rodrigues, C., Gómez-Luna, J., Hwu, W.M.: Efficient kernel synthesis for performance portable programming. In: 2016 49th Annual IEEE/ACM International Symposium on Microarchitecture (MICRO), pp. 1–13. IEEE (2016)
3. Chen, P., Wahib, M., Takizawa, S., Takano, R., Matsuoka, S.: A versatile software systolic execution model for GPU memory-bound kernels. In: Proceedings of the International Conference for High Performance Computing, Networking, Storage and Analysis. pp. 1–81 (2019)
4. Gonzalo, S.G.D., Huang, S., Gómez-Luna, J., Hammond, S., Mutlu, O., Hwu, W.M.: Automatic generation of warp-level primitives and atomic instructions for fast and portable parallel reduction on GPUs. In: 2019 IEEE/ACM International Symposium on Code Generation and Optimization (CGO), pp. 73–84, February 2019
5. Intel: Intel C++ compiler 19.1 developer guide and reference (2019). https://software.intel.com/content/www/us/en/develop/documentation/cpp-compiler-developer-guide-and-reference/
6. Liu, Y., Schmidt, B.: LightSpMV: Faster CSR-based sparse matrix-vector multiplication on CUDA-enabled GPUs. In: 2015 IEEE 26th International Conference on Application-specific Systems, Architectures and Processors (ASAP), pp. 82–89, July 2015
7. Luitjens, J.: Faster parallel reductions on Kepler. Parallel Forall. NVIDIA Corporation. https://devblogs.nvidia.com/parallelforall/faster-parallel-reductions-kepler (2014)
8. NVIDIA: CUDA programming guide (2020). https://docs.nvidia.com/cuda/cuda-c-programming-guide/index.html
9. Sander, B.: AMD GCN assembly: cross-lane operations (2016). https://gpuopen.com/learn/amd-gcn-assembly-cross-lane-operations/
10. Volkov, V., Demmel, J.W.: Benchmarking GPUs to tune dense linear algebra. In: Proceedings of the 2008 ACM/IEEE Conference on Supercomputing, SC 2008, IEEE Press (2008)

Performance Studies

Towards an Auto-Tuned and Task-Based SpMV (LASs Library)

Sandra Catalán[1]([✉]), Tetsuzo Usui[2], Leonel Toledo[3], Xavier Martorell[4], Jesús Labarta[4], and Pedro Valero-Lara[3]

[1] Universidad Complutense de Madrid (UCM), Madrid, Spain
scatalan@ucm.es
[2] Next Generation Technical Computing Unit, Fujitsu Limited, Kawasaki, Japan
[3] Barcelona Supercomputing Center (BSC), Barcelona, Spain
[4] Universitat Politècnica de Catalunya Barcelona, Barcelona, Spain

Abstract. We present a novel approach to parallelize the SpMV kernel included in LASs (Linear Algebra routines on OmpSs) library, after a deep review and analysis of several well-known approaches. LASs is based on OmpSs, a task-based runtime that extends OpenMP directives, providing more flexibility to apply new strategies. Based on tasking and nesting, with the aim of improving the workload imbalance inherent to the SpMV operation, we present a strategy especially useful for highly imbalanced input matrices. In this approach, the number of created tasks is dynamically decided in order to maximize the use of the resources of the platform. Throughout this paper, SpMV behavior depending on the selected strategy (state of the art and proposed strategies) is deeply analyzed, setting in this way the base for a future auto-tunable code that is able to select the most suitable approach depending on the input matrix. The experiments of this work were carried out for a set of 12 matrices from the Suite Sparse Matrix Collection, all of them with different characteristics regarding their sparsity. The experiments of this work were performed on a node of Marenostrum 4 supercomputer (with two sockets Intel Xeon, 24 cores each) and on a node of Dibona cluster (using one ARM ThunderX2 socket with 32 cores). Our tests show that, for Intel Xeon, the best parallelization strategy reduces the execution time of the reference MKL multi-threaded version up to 67%. On ARM ThunderX2, the reduction is up to 56% with respect to the OmpSs parallel reference.

This project has received funding from the Spanish Ministry of Economy and Competitiveness under the project Computación de Altas Prestaciones VII (TIN2015- 65316-P), the Departament d'Innovació, Universitats i Empresa de la Generalitat de Catalunya, under project MPEXPAR: Models de Programació i Entorns d'Execució Parallels (2014-SGR-1051), and the Juan de la Cierva Grant Agreement No IJCI-2017- 33511, and the Spanish Ministry of Science and Innovation under the project Heterogeneidad y especialización en la era post-Moore (RTI2018-093684-B-I00). We also acknowledge the funding provided by Fujitsu under the BSC-Fujitsu joint project: Math Libraries Migration and Optimization.

© Springer Nature Switzerland AG 2020
K. Milfeld et al. (Eds.): IWOMP 2020, LNCS 12295, pp. 115–129, 2020.
https://doi.org/10.1007/978-3-030-58144-2_8

Keywords: SpMV · Parallel programming · Tasking · Auto-tuning · Taskloop · Nesting · LASs · OmpSs.

1   Introduction

Sparse linear algebra is key in many scientific and engineering applications. One of the most representative and used operations is the sparse matrix-vector product (SpMV), defined as

$$y := \alpha Ax + \beta y, \tag{1}$$

where α and β are scalars, x and y are dense vectors and, A is a sparse matrix. The sparse nature of the input matrix makes this operation highly unbalanced, due to the non-uniform pattern when accessing the elements of the matrix. However, several storage formats have been proposed in order to palliate this effect.

The relevance of SpMV kernel is shown in the wide range of vendors and open-source libraries [1,3,6,9], and the large number of applications that make use of it. A few of these reference sparse linear algebra libraries are MUMPS [4], that implements a parallel sparse direct solver, SuperLU [12], a general purpose library for the direct solution of systems of linear equations, MAGMA-Sparse [5], that provides sparse linear algebra solutions for heterogeneous architectures, cuSparse [1], which contains a set of basic sparse linear algebra subroutines developed by Nvidia, PETSC [6], a suite of data structures and routines for the solution of partial differential equations, FenicS [3], an open-source computing platform for solving partial differential equations, or HPCG [9], a benchmark project that aims to create a new metric for ranking HPC systems.

In this work, we focus on the sparse matrix-vector kernel (kdspmv) in LASs[1], a linear algebra library based on OmpSs [2,23,24]. Given that LASs is implemented in OmpSs, the analyzed strategies are implemented with this programming model throughout this work, although other programming models can be used to this end and benefit from those approaches. OmpSs is an open-source programming model [10] that has the following advantages in contrast to other runtimes: i) The model presents efficient management of the threads based on the use of queues, without the need of dealing with the overhead found in others models, such as the fork-join model used in OpenMP. ii) OmpSs is specifically designed for the use of tasks, making it a good choice for the study of task-based approaches. iii) It allows the user to have deeper control of the thread scheduling. iv) It provides us with tighter control and better knowledge about the taskloop implementation necessary to improve the proposed optimizations of the code, especially for nesting. iv) OmpSs is especially well integrated with the tools used for performance evaluation Extrae and Paraver. Extrae [13] is a dynamic instrumentation package to trace programs which generates trace files that can be later visualized with Paraver. Thanks to the its integration with OmpSs more information can be retrieved for those implementations in comparison to other programming models.

---

[1] https://pm.bsc.es/gitlab/pvalero/lass/.

We propose and analyze different strategies in order to parallelize the SpMV kernel included in LASs library [17–19], which implements the general SpMV (see Eq. 1) and operates on an input matrix stored in CSR format [11]. The main challenge we target through the parallelization of this kernel is balancing the computations among the cores in order to attain good performance. Four different parallel approaches based on OmpSs features are proposed and analyzed to tackle sparsity and achieve a balanced workload distribution.

2   State of the Art

Sparse matrices are present in a wide variety of applications used in very different fields such as graph analytics or economics. All these applications require the resolution of large-scale linear systems, usually done through iterative methods, and/or eigenvalue problems, whose most relevant component is the SpMV. For this reason, improving the portability of this kernel and increasing the performance delivered by making good use of the underlying resources is key for the mentioned applications.

Big efforts have been carried out by the scientific community in order to increase SpMV performance. An important part of the optimization of scientific codes consists of using the appropriate format to represent matrices in memory [8,20,21,25]. Following different approaches, cache performance, data locality and, consequently, the overall performance of SpMV, has been proven to be affected substantially. Some of the most common formats for sparse matrices are Coordinate format (COO), Compressed Row Storage (CRS), Compressed Column Storage (CCS) [11] or ELLPACK-R [15]. Among these options, CSR is the most widely used and the de facto standard due to the fact that no assumptions on the sparsity structure of the matrix are made.

There exist several works that target the parallelization of SpMV on multi-core CPU, GPU, and MIC (many integrated cores). In [14] different scheduling strategies for particular matrices are explored for both architectures, multi-core CPU (SPARC64 IXfx and Intel Xeon Ivy Bridge-EP) and MIC (Knights Corner). Following the same type of comparison, but focused on analyzing the impact of using a hybrid MPI/OpenMP approach to make better exploitation of the hardware resources, [26] presents the results on the Knights Corner. Halfway between applying new parallelization algorithms and choosing an appropriate storage format, in [27] the authors propose the Blocked Compressed Common Coordinate (BCCOO) storage format and improve load balancing through a matrix-based segmented sum/scan algorithm on AMD FirePro W8000, GeForce Titan X, and Nvidia Tesla K20.

The analysis of the bibliography regarding SpMV shows that works in this area mostly focus on studying and proposing new storage formats that exploit better the features of specific hardware or application. On the contrary, in this work, we focus on CSR format, the most wide-used format for sparse matrices, and target algorithms that can be easily implemented and tuned on a multi-core CPU.

3 Parallelizing SpMV

Parallelizing SpMV is key to solve nowadays problems in a wide spectrum of engineering and scientific operations. For this reason, we explore four different approaches based on OmpSs, that aim to increase the performance attained by SpMV thanks to making better use of the platform resources. In this section, we present these approaches and provide a small schema and pseudo-code to illustrate each case.

3.1 One Task Per Row

One task per row is a simple and straight-forward approach in which one task per row is created (see the pseudo-code and schema in Fig. 1). Given that each task deals with a different row, there are no dependencies. However, numerous tasks are created, as many as rows are in the matrix; and, these tasks are usually very small due to the low amount of non-zeros per row, thus introducing a non-negligible overhead for the runtime. In addition, the workload unbalance is inherent to this approach since the number of computations performed by each task depends on the number of non-zero elements.

```
for ( r = 0; r < nRows; r++){
    sval = 0.0;
    #pragma oss task ...
    {
        for ( c = 0; c < nCols; c++) {
            val = VAL_A[ROW_A[r]+c];
            col = COL_A[ROW_A[r]+c];
            sval += val* X[col]*ALPHA;
        }
        Y[r] = sval + Y[r] * BETA;
    }
}
```

Fig. 1. Pseudo-code and schema for one task per row approach.

3.2 Blocking

Blocking implementation consists of splitting the matrix into smaller blocks and creating one task per block. With this strategy we ensure the reuse of the same entries of the array y within the task, thus improving data locality. Nevertheless, blocking the matrix requires a preprocessing in order to create the blocks in CSR format, which may add an overhead to the total run time. Moreover, all the blocks that comprise the same rows in the matrix update the same positions of the array y, turning into data dependencies. An additional question to take into account with this approach is the changes required in the code in order to apply blocking, since restructuring the matrix and dealing with the new data dependencies make the programming difficult. Moreover, the block size to be used when blocking the matrix needs to be calculated in advance, requiring a previous analysis to determine it.

This approach is based on the code developed in [28], where an improved version of the conjugate gradient method is presented.

3.3 Taskloop

Keeping the use of coarser tasks, we propose the use of *taskloop*. In this case, each task will perform the matrix-vector multiplication on a fixed number of rows. The *taskloop* construct is used to distribute the rows in different tasks and the clause *grainsize* is used to determine the number of rows processed by each task. The main advantage of this approach is its simplicity, although the *grainsize* needs to be determined to maximize the use of the cores. However, it is important to note that the number of non-zeros may be highly unbalanced depending on the matrix. In our case, the *grainsize* is set in order to create one chunk per core, thus it is calculated as *#rows/#cores*. In this way, we ensure that all cores are used and the overhead due to tasks creation is minimum. Thus, it can be used as a baseline.

```
#pragma oss taskloop
            grainsize (nRows / #cores)
for ( r = 0; r < nRows; r++){
    sval - 0.0;
    for ( c = 0; c < nCols; c++) {
        val = VAL_A[ROW_A[r]+c];
        col = COL_A[ROW_A[r]+c];
        sval += val* X[col]*ALPHA;
    }
    Y[r] = sval + Y[r] * BETA;
}
```

Fig. 2. Pseudo-code and schema for *taskloop* approach.

3.4 Grouping

Finally, aiming to keep using coarse tasks but trying to adapt to the different amount of non-zero elements per row, we propose to apply the *grouping* approach of Valero-Lara et al. [16,22]. In this case, we create groups of rows according to a limit (given by the architecture, e.g. L1 size, L2 size, ...) and each group is processed by a different task. The main drawback of this approach is that it requires extra calculations in order to create the groups and this makes the code less readable. Also, using this approach one core is busy computing the next group and creating tasks.

4   Performance Analysis

In this section, we present performance results for all the presented approaches in order to show the benefits/drawbacks of each one.

We have used a set of 12 characteristic matrices obtained from the SuiteSparse Matrix Collection [7] (formerly the University of Florida Sparse Matrix Collection)[2].

Although we analyze all the matrices of our test set, we pay particular attention at the *in-2004* matrix as the main test case, due to its characteristics. The *in-2004* matrix is a non-symmetric square matrix with 1,382,908 rows and 16,917,053 non-zero elements. Additionally, as reported in Table 1, it has rows with no elements (minimum 0) and other rows with quite a few elements (maximum 7753). These features made us consider this matrix as an "extreme" test case in which sparsity in unevenly present.

A graphical representation of the in-2004 example matrix is shown in the last column of Table 1.

Performance Results

We have run our tests on Marenostrum 4 and Dibona clusters; we have used a single node of Marenostrum 4 Supercomputer, featuring two sockets Intel Xeon Platinum 8160 CPU with 24 cores each at 2.10 GHz for a total of 48 cores per node. Regarding memory hierarchy, each core has 32 KB L1 and 1 MB L2 caches, and 33 MB L3 cache shared among the 24 cores per socket. Regarding Dibona, each node presents two sockets ARM Thunder X2 (ARMv8 NEON) CPU with 32 cores each running at 2.0 GHz for a total of 64 cores per node. In this case, only one socket has been considered for our tests. The memory hierarchy characteristics for this platform are 32 KB of L1 cache, 256 KB L2 cache, and 32 MB L3 cache.

All tests are compiled with mcxx 2.3.0 (with GCC 6.4.0 or Intel icc 17.0.4 if available) and OmpSs-2 2018.06 (nanos6 2.4); for those tests that use MKL functions, MKL 2017.4 is used. Each test is run 20 times given the short time required for the computation on SpMV; from this measurements, the first repetition is discarded and only used as a warm-up phase. The reported values are calculated as the median of the remaining 19 repetitions, which measure exclusively the computation of the SpMV, leaving outside the initialization of the operands. Moreover, in each repetition cache memory is flashed to avoid data reuse between consecutive tests. In order to palliate possible NUMA effects on the overall execution time, affinity is set via *taskset* and $numactl - -interleave = all$ is used to spread across the sockets.

Figure 3-Left graphically illustrates execution time for single-threaded MKL (*mkl_dcsrmv*), and the multi-threaded one (*mkl_sparse_d_mv*) as reference. The

---

[2] Input matrices from the UFMC are: cant, conf5_4-8x8-05, consph, cop20k_A, eu-2005, Ga41As41H72, in-2004, mac_econ_fwd500, mpi1, pdb1HYS, Si41Ge41H72, webbase1-M.

single-threaded MKL routine implements SpMV as described in Eq. 1 on a sparse matrix stored in CSR format, however, the multi-threaded MKL routine performs the same operation in parallel, but it requires the use of specific MKL structures to deal with the CSR matrix. Note that the order of the matrices in the x differs from 1, showing decreasing performance to ease the reading of the plots.

Table 1. Set of matrices used in SpMV tests. Information provided for each matrix: matrix ID, name in the SuiteSparse Matrix Collection, domain, number of rows (and columns), number of non-zero elements, maximum non-zeros per row, minimum non-zeros per row, average non-zeros per row, image of the matrix.

ID	Name	Domain	#rows	NNZ	Max.	Min.	Avg.	Matrix
m1	cant	FEM Cantilever	62,451	2,034,917	40	1	32	
m2	conf5_4-8x8-05	Quantum chromodynamics	49,152	1,916,928	39	39	39	
m3	consph	FEM concentric spheres	83,334	3,046,907	66	1	36	
m4	cop20k_A	Accelerator cavity design	121,192	1,362,087	24	0	11	
m5	eu-2005	Small web crawl of .eu domain	862,664	19,235,140	6,985	0	22	
m6	Ga41As41H72	Real-space pseudo potential method	268,296	9,378,286	472	1	34	
m7	**in-2004**	Small web crawl of .in domain	1,382,908	16,917,053	7,753	0	12	
m8	mac_econ_fwd500	Macroeconomic model	206,500	1,273,389	44	1	6	
m9	mip1	Optimiation problem	66,463	5,209,641	713	1	78	
m10	pdb1HYS	Protein data bank 1HYS	36,417	2,190,591	184	1	60	
m11	Si41Ge41H72	Real-space pseudo potential method	185,639	7,598,452	531	1	40	
m12	webbase1-M	Web connectivity matrix	1,000,005	3,105,536	4,700	1	3	

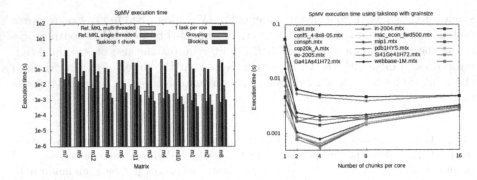

Fig. 3. Execution time for SpMV with different approaches on Intel Xeon: *one-task-per-row*, *grouping*, *blocking* and *taskloop* (Left). Execution time for 1, 2, 4, 8, and 16 chunks per core (Right).

Performance results show that the reference single-threaded MKL routine and the *one-task-per-row* approach, provide longer execution times.

For the *one-task-per-row* approach, this behavior was already predicted when presenting this strategy since many tasks are created (as many as rows) and its granularity is too fine, introducing a relevant overhead.

According to these results the best options to parallelize SpMV are *grouping*, *multi-threaded MKL*, *blocking* and *taskloop* strategies. *Grouping* (with a limit equal to 25% of L2 cache, being this the best limit tested) provides the worst performance among these three options. *MKL multi-threaded* presents a behavior similar to *Grouping*, although it performs better for very unbalanced matrices (m4, m5, m7, and m12), being slower than *taskloop* on all the tested matrices.

Blocking seems the best option in terms of execution time in some of the cases. However, execution time is considerably high for those matrices that have a highly unbalanced number of non-zeros per row (m4, m5, m7, and m12) and, more important, the preprocessing time needed to block the input matrix as CSR subblocks makes it unfeasible since this preprocessing requires an execution time between 2 and 3 orders of magnitude greater than the SpMV execution time. Finally, *taskloop* provides good results in all cases and, besides, eases the parallelization of SpMV thanks to its simplicity, facilitating the maintainability of the code.

In the light of the presented performance results, we consider the *taskloop* approach the most suitable one in order to parallelize SpMV. This selection is based on several reasons such as i) the fact that it is the easiest approach since it only requires using the *taskloop* construct, ii) it is also easily optimizable because, although it requires a previous analysis, testing different grain sizes on the platform is enough to attain a reasonable behavior, iii) it follows the OpenMP standard, so portability is ensured even if OmpSs is not available on other platforms.

Figure 4 (first) contains the trace of the execution of SpMV (using *in-2004* as an input) based on the taskloop strategy when a grainsize of $\#rows/\#cores$

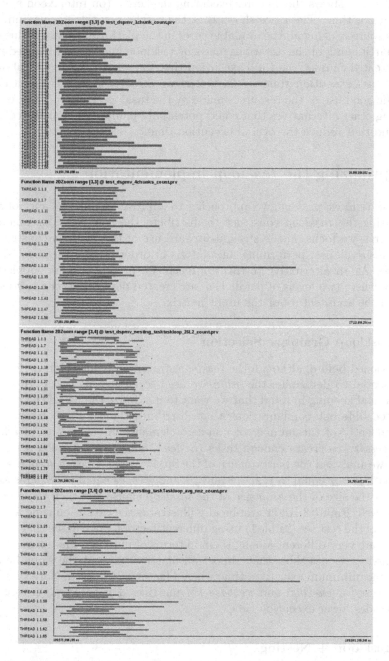

Fig. 4. Traces for SpMV when applying *taskloop* with 1 (first) and 4 chunks (second) per core, *taskloop* + *nesting* with *th = 25% L2* (third) and *th = avg nnz* per chunk (fourth) optimizations to taskloop approach.

is used. Axis y shows the 48 cores executing the kernel (on Intel Xeon platform) and axis x is time. The trace shows that the taskloop construct maximizes the use of resources, using all the available cores in the platform. However, due to the static partitioning of the iterations made by taskloop and the unbalanced nature of the created chunks, the total execution time for a few tasks is well above the average task execution time ($\sim 24,000\,\mu s$ vs. $8,000\,\mu s$). In this scenario, and given the good use of the resources made by the taskloop construct, we consider exploring other alternatives that could potentially palliate the imbalance among tasks and thus reduce the overall execution time.

5   Optimizing the *taskloop* implementation

In this section, we present two approaches to improve the load balance of SpMV when using the *taskloop* construct to distribute the computations among the cores. First, we focus on the straight-forward use of the *taskloop* construct and the *grainsize* clause, performing an analysis in order to find the most suitable *grainsize*. As an alternative to this approach, we present a more sophisticated strategy where two levels of parallelism are created depending on a few features either of the architecture or the input matrix.

5.1   Taskloop Grainsize Selection

As mentioned before, although the *taskloop* strategy provides high performance, it is essential to determine the *grainsize* used to create the tasks. To find this number, and keeping in mind that we want to maximize the use of the resources, we tested different configurations that distribute the number of rows evenly (independently of the number of non-zero elements in each row). In addition, it is necessary to create enough tasks to "feed" all the available cores, for this reason, we analyzed the performance of the SpMV when creating $\#cores * factor$ tasks, with *factor* equal to 1, 2, 4, 8 and 16, and $\#cores$ equal to 48. This formula computes the size of the *grainsize* of the *taskloop* clause and then the number of tasks as well. Figure 3-Right graphically illustrates the execution time for all the matrices of the test set (Table 1) using different factors. We can see that, even the matrices are very different among them in terms of number of non-zero elements and sparsity, results show that almost all matrices present the same behavior, finding the minimum execution time when a factor of 4 is used. Note that this is not the case for *eu-2005* and *webbase-1M* matrices. For these matrices a factor of 8 provides lower execution times.

5.2   Taskloop + Nesting

Finally, we present *taskloop + nesting* as an alternative to create tasks with a more regular number of non-zero elements, thus trying to mimic the behavior of *grouping* but reducing the overhead introduced by the thread in charge of creating the groups.

In this scenario, first we need to replace the *taskloop* construct used to create the chunks by a *task* construct. This change allows us to know the first and last row that is processed in a specific chunk and, consequently, the number of non-zeros of the chunk can easily be calculated. Despite this change, we set the number of rows to be processed by a task to *#rows/#cores*, which mimics the behavior of setting the *grainsize* clause for the first level *taskloop* to the same number. Then, a second level of parallelism is created in order to balance the workload among the created tasks when necessary. The idea is subdividing those tasks created at the first level that have a huge number of non-zeros into smaller tasks that can be balanced better. To this end, every time a task is created at the first level we check if the number of non-zeros of the chunk being processed is greater than a threshold *th*. This idea is presented in Fig. 5.

```
nChunks = get_num_chunks(nRows);
for ( nc = 0; nc < nChunks; nc++){
  #pragma oss task
  {
     nnzT = number_of_non_zeros_in_chunk(nc);
     init_row = get_init_row(nc);
     end_row = get_end_row(nc);
     #pragma oss taskloop
                num_tasks(nnzT/th)
                if (nnzT > th)
     for(r = init_row; r < end_row; r++){
            sval = 0.0;
            for ( c = 0; c < nCols; c++){
                val = VAL_A[ROW_A[r]+c];
                col = COL_A[ROW_A[r]+c];
                sval += val * X[col] * ALPHA;
            }
            Y[r] = sval + Y[r] * BETA;
     }
  }
}// End of pragma
}
```

Fig. 5. Pseudo-code and schema for *taskloop + nesting* approach.

To set the threshold value we have followed two different strategies, one focused on the architecture features and one that takes into account the sparsity of the matrix. In the first case, we set the threshold to a specific value that depends on the L2 cache size, more specifically, we perform the tests setting the threshold to 25% and 50% of L2 capacity. For the second case, we calculate the average number of non-zeros per chunk, this is the total amount of non-zero elements in the matrix divided by the number of cores of the platform. In both cases, if the number of non-zero elements of the chunk is greater than the threshold *th*, the task is split in as many tasks as necessary, each of them in charge of *th* elements.

To make a deeper analysis, Fig. 4 shows the traces for the following strategies on *in-2004* matrix: *taskloop* with 4 chunks per core, *taskloop + nesting* with *th*=25% of L2 cache, and *taskloop + nesting* with *th*=average of nnz per chunk. Axis *y* shows the 48 cores running SpMV kernel on Intel Xeon platform, while axis x shows the execution time. All traces are in the same scale; this is, the total time represented by axis x is the same in all cases.

After the analysis of the traces for *in-2004* matrix, we can state that applying nesting may be beneficial in order to compact the trace by splitting the most time consuming tasks in smaller ones. In this specific case, the approach focused on architecture features, setting the threshold to 25% of L2 cache, allows to compact the trace by creating smaller tasks, which are scheduled in a more balanced way and, consequently, help to reduce the overall execution time. However, setting the threshold to the average number of non-zeros per row, generates similar imbalance to that seen in *taskloop*.

We extend the analysis to all the matrices of the test set (see Fig. 6). We use the performance of the *taskloop one chunk per core* approach as a reference. For well structured matrices, where the number of non-zero elements per row remains almost constant, the *taskloop 4 chunks per core* approach is able to achieve good performance; almost negligible overhead is introduced and workload is well distributed thanks to the nature of the matrices (m1, m2, and m3). However, for very unbalanced matrices (m5, m7, m9, and m12), using *taskloop + nesting* based on L2 capacity is able to outperform the previous approach, achieving about 60% faster executions with respect to the reference parallel implementation. Regarding the *taskloop + nesting* approach based on the average number of non-zeros per chunk, we see that performance is similar to that attained in the other nested approaches except for a few matrices (m6, m9, m11), where the execution time is considerably increased. Figure 6 also includes the percentage of improvement for *taskloop 4 chunks per core* and *taskloop + nesting* based on L2 capacity (higher is better) with respect to the parallel reference code. Results show that the gains when cache capacity is taken into account are relevant especially for very unbalanced matrices; however, for balanced matrices the *taskloop 4 chunks per core* approach provides better results.

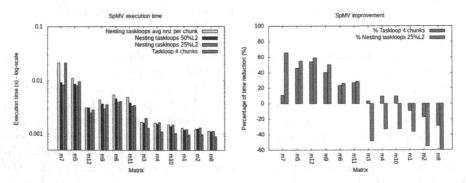

Fig. 6. Execution time (left) and percentage gain (right) for SpMV when applying optimizations to *taskloop* on Intel Xeon platform.

When comparing these results with those obtained for ThunderX2 (Fig. 7), we observe a similar behavior. The only exceptions are m6, m9 and m11 matrices. For those matrices, slightly higher performance is attained with taskloop with 4 chunks when Intel Xeon is used.

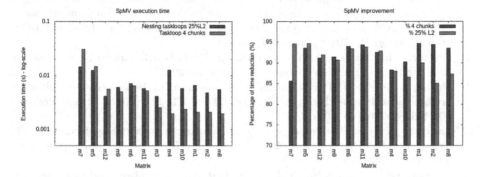

Fig. 7. Execution time (left) and percentage gain (right) for SpMV when applying optimizations to *taskloop* on ThunderX2 platform.

6 Conclusions and Future Work

Performance results show that making a static and homogeneous partition of the rows by using *taskloop* is able to achieve a good result on well-balanced sparse matrices. However, on other matrices where we find an important unbalanced sparsity, the use of *taskloop* + *nesting* presents a much better behavior, achieving an important time reduction in some cases. Both approaches are faster than the multi-threaded MKL counterpart.

In this scenario, we plan as future work to combine both strategies via the *final* clause in other to choose the most appropriate one, depending on the input matrix with the aim of attaining higher performance in each case.

References

1. cuSparse. https://docs.nvidia.com/pdf/CUSPARSE_Library.pdf
2. OmpSs-2. https://pm.bsc.es/ftp/ompss-2/doc/spec/OmpSs-2-Specification.pdf
3. Alnæs, M.S., et al.: The FEniCS project version 1.5. Archive of Numerical Software **3**(100) (2015). https://doi.org/10.11588/ans.2015.100.20553
4. Amestoy, P.R., Duff, I.S., L'excellent, J.Y.: Multifrontal parallel distributed symmetric and unsymmetric solvers. Comput. Methods Appl. Mechanics Eng. **184**(2–4), 501–520 (2000)
5. Anzt, H., Sawyer, W., Tomov, S., Luszczek, P., Yamazaki, I., Dongarra, J.: Optimizing Krylov subspace solvers on graphics processing units. In: Fourth International Workshop on Accelerators and Hybrid Exascale Systems (AsHES), IPDPS 2014. IEEE, IEEE, Phoenix, AZ, May 2014 (2014)

6. Balay, S., et al.: PETSc Web page (2018). http://www.mcs.anl.gov/petsc
7. Davis, T.A., Hu, Y.: The university of florida sparse matrix collection. ACM Trans. Math. Softw. **38**(1), 1:1–1:25, December 2011. https://doi.org/10.1145/2049662. 2049663, http://doi.acm.org/10.1145/2049662.2049663
8. Dongarra, J.J., Hammarling, S., Higham, N.J., Relton, S.D., Valero-Lara, P., Zounon, M.: The design and performance of batched BLAS on modern high-performance computing systems. In: International Conference on Computational Science, ICCS 2017, 12–14 June 2017, Zurich, Switzerland. pp. 495–504 (2017). https://doi.org/10.1016/j.procs.2017.05.138
9. Dongarra, J.J., Heroux, M.A., Luszczek, P.: HPCG Benchmark : a New Metric for Ranking High Performance Computing Systems (2015)
10. Duran, A., et al.: OMPSS: a proposal for programming heterogeneous multi-core architectures. Parallel Processing Letters **21**(2), 173–193 (2011). https://doi.org/ 10.1142/S0129626411000151
11. Langr, D., Tvrdík, P.: Evaluation criteria for sparse matrix storage formats. IEEE Trans. Parallel Distrib. Syst. **27**(2), 428–440 (2016). https://doi.org/10.1109/ TPDS.2015.2401575
12. Li, X.S.: An overview of SuperLU: algorithms, implementation, and user interface. ACM Trans. Math. Software **31**(3), 302–325 (2005)
13. Llort, G., Servat, H., Gonzalez, J., Giménez, J., Labarta, J.: On the usefulness of object tracking techniques in performance analysis. In: International Conference for High Performance Computing, Networking, Storage and Analysis, SC 2013, Denver, CO, USA - November 17–21, 2013, pp. 29:1–29:11 (2013)
14. Ohshima, S., Katagiri, T., Matsumoto, M.: Performance Optimization of SpMV Using CRS Format by Considering OpenMP Scheduling on CPUs and MIC. In: Proceedings of the 2014 IEEE 8th International Symposium on Embedded Multi-core/Manycore SoCs. pp. 253–260. MCSOC 2014, IEEE Computer Society, Washington, DC, USA (2014). https://doi.org/10.1109/MCSoC.2014.43, http://dx.doi. org/10.1109/MCSoC.2014.43
15. Ortega, G., Vázquez, F., García, I., Garzón, E.M.: FastSpMM: an efficient library for sparse matrix matrix product on GPUs. Comput. J. **57**(7), 968–979 (2014). http://dx.doi.org/10.1093/comjnl/bxt038
16. Valero-Lara, P., et al.: Variable batched DGEMM. In: 2018 26th Euromicro International Conference on Parallel, Distributed and Network-based Processing (PDP), pp. 363–367, March 2018. https://doi.org/10.1109/PDP2018.2018.00065
17. Valero-Lara, P., Andrade, D., Sirvent, R., Labarta, J., Fraguela, B.B., Doallo, R.: A fast solver for large tridiagonal systems on multi-core processors (Lass Library). IEEE Access **7**, 23365–23378 (2019). https://doi.org/10.1109/ACCESS. 2019.2900122
18. Valero-Lara, P., Catalán, S., Martorell, X., Labarta, J.: BLAS-3 optimized by OmpSs regions (LASs Library). In: 27th Euromicro International Conference on Parallel, Distributed and Network-Based Processing, PDP 2019, Pavia, Italy, February 13–15, 2019. pp. 25–32 (2019). https://doi.org/10.1109/EMPDP.2019. 8671545
19. Valero-Lara, P., Catalán, S., Martorell, X., Usui, T., Labarta, J.: sLASs: a fully automatic auto-tuned linear algebra library based on OpenMP extensions implemented in OmpSs (LASs Library). J. Parallel Distrib. Comput. **138**, 153–171 (2020). https://doi.org/10.1016/j.jpdc.2019.12.002
20. Valero-Lara, P., Martínez-Pérez, I., Peña, A.J., Martorell, X., Sirvent, R., Labarta, J.: cuHinesBatch: solving multiple hines systems on GPUs human brain project[*].

In: International Conference on Computational Science, ICCS 2017, 12–14 June 2017, Zurich, Switzerland, pp. 566–575 (2017). https://doi.org/10.1016/j.procs. 2017.05.145

21. Valero-Lara, P., Martínez-Pérez, I., Sirvent, R., Martorell, X., Peña, A.J.: cuThomasBatch and cuThomasVBatch, CUDA routines to compute batch of tridiagonal systems on NVIDIA GPUs. Concurrency and Computation: Practice and Experience **30**(24) (2018). https://doi.org/10.1002/cpe.4909

22. Valero-Lara, P., Sirvent, R., Peña, A.J., Martorell, X., Labarta, J.: MPI+OpenMP tasking scalability for the simulation of the human brain: human brain project. In: Proceedings of the 25th European MPI Users' Group Meeting. pp. 5:1–5:8. EuroMPI 2018, ACM, New York, NY, USA (2018). https://doi.org/10.1145/ 3236367.3236373, http://doi.acm.org/10.1145/3236367.3236373

23. Valero-Lara, P., Sirvent, R., Peña, A.J., Labarta, J.: MPI+OpenMP tasking scalability for multi-morphology simulations of the human brain. Parallel Comput. **84**, 50–61 (2019). https://doi.org/10.1016/j.parco.2019.03.006

24. Valero-Lara, P., Sirvent, R., Peña, A.J., Martorell, X., Labarta, J.: MPI+OpenMP tasking scalability for the simulation of the human brain: human brain project. In: Proceedings of the 25th European MPI Users' Group Meeting, Barcelona, Spain, September 23–26, 2018. pp. 5:1–5:8 (2018). https://doi.org/10.1145/3236367. 3236373

25. Valero-Lara, P., et al.: Simulating the behavior of the human brain on GPUs. Oil Gas Sci. Technol. - Rev. IFP Energies nouvelles **73**, 63 (2018). https://doi.org/10. 2516/ogst/2018061

26. Ye, F., Calvin, C., Petiton, S.G.: A Study of SpMV Implementation Using MPI and OpenMP on Intel Many-Core Architecture. In: VECPAR (2014)

27. Zhang, Y., Li, S., Yan, S., Zhou, H.: A cross-platform SpMV framework on manycore architectures. ACM Trans. Archit. Code Optim. **13**(4), 33:1–33:25, October 2016. https://doi.org/10.1145/2994148

28. Zhuang, S., Casas, M.: Iteration-fusing conjugate gradient. In: Proceedings of the International Conference on Supercomputing, pp. 21:1–21:10. ICS 2017, ACM, New York, NY, USA (2017). https://doi.org/10.1145/3079079.3079091

A Case Study on Addressing Complex Load Imbalance in OpenMP

Fabian Orland$^{(\boxtimes)}$ (iD) and Christian Terboven (iD)

Chair for Computer Science 12 - High-Performance Computing,
RWTH Aachen University, Aachen, Germany
{orland,terboven}@itc.rwth-aachen.de

Abstract. Load balance is an important factor that fundamentally impacts the scalability of any parallel application. In this paper we present a case study to address a complex load imbalance related to the convergence behavior of the parallel SPMD implementation of a GMRES solver used in a real world application in the field of computational fluid dynamics. In order to tackle this load imbalance in OpenMP we illustrate different approaches involving the use of nested tasks as well as nested parallel regions. Furthermore, we evaluate these approaches on a small kernel program extracted from the original application code and show how the load balance is affected by each of these approaches.

Keywords: OpenMP · Load balance · Dynamic load balancing · Tasking · Nested parallelism · GMRES · Convergence · SPMD

1 Introduction

Currently the largest HPC systems listed in the top500 list [3] offer hundreds of thousands or even millions of cores. In order to scale any scientific application code to such large scales the application has to efficiently utilize every available hardware resource. When doing strong scaling measurements of an application the fundamental assumption is that the code can be perfectly parallelized which in reality is not always the case [5].

For shared-memory systems the OpenMP [10,14] programming interface offers a range of concepts for load balancing such as different loop schedules or the task construct. A `static` loop schedule divides the loop iterations in chunks of equal size and assigns these chunks to threads in a round-robin fashion. Using `dynamic` schedules each thread requests a chunk of iterations and upon completion requests another chunk until all loop iteration have been carried out. With a `guided` schedule the size of these chunks varies. First some large chunks are created and then for further chunks the size is decreased steadily. The OpenMP task construct allows user-defined chunks of work to be completed asynchronously which can already lead to a good load balance.

© The Author(s) 2020
K. Milfeld et al. (Eds.): IWOMP 2020, LNCS 12295, pp. 130–145, 2020.
https://doi.org/10.1007/978-3-030-58144-2_9

In this paper we want to raise attention to a special kind of load imbalance that can occur in the SPMD implementation of iterative solvers and is complex to tackle. We discovered a scenario in which loop scheduling cannot be applied and splitting the original problem into smaller subproblems executed as tasks increases the amount of computation to be performed instead of reducing it.

2   Related Work

In order to quantify load imbalances different metrics have been established. The POP project [2], an EU Centre of Excellence in HPC, defines the load balance efficiency as the ratio between the average computation time across all execution units and the maximum computation time across these. For example, a load balance efficiency of 75% indicates that 25% of the available hardware resources are not properly utilized.

Unfortunately, this metric does not give any insight into the actual load distribution. Different distributions can have the same load balance efficiency but need to be tackled in different ways in order to improve the load balance. For example, it might make a difference if there are many slightly overloaded execution units or only a few but therefor heavily overloaded. Hence, Pearce et al. [15] propose to also take statistical moments like standard deviation, skewness and kurtosis into account. We use these metrics to quantify our load balance problem in this paper.

The OpenMP load balancing constructs have already been studied in the past. Durand et al. proposed an **adaptive** schedule which dynamically determines the chunk size depending on the utilization of the machine resources and also takes NUMA affinity information into account [13]. Recently, Ciorba et al. [8] investigated the state-of-the-art loop scheduling techniques. However, in our work dynamic loop scheduling cannot be applied because the application statically creates a single work load for each thread. We show that splitting these work loads into multiple smaller units, which could then be scheduled dynamically, will actually increase the overall runtime.

In the field of social and networking analysis Adcock et. al. used tasks to split up the computation of the δ-hyperbolicity into multiple levels of small chunks which yielded good load balancing at a scale of 1000 threads [4]. Recently, tasks have been used successfully to balance the work in a Density Matrix Renormalization Group algorithm [9]. Identifying different kinds of tasks as well as assigning higher priorities to large tasks compared to small tasks lead to a more balanced execution. Based on the idea of using nested parallelism as discussed by Royuela et al. [16] we show how the load balance can be improved by implementing nested tasks as well as nested parallel regions into the code.

3   Complex Load Imbalance

During our studies on the CalculiX [1,12] application code we discovered an interesting and complex kind of load imbalance. Further investigation revealed that the issue is related to the GMRES solver [17]. Here the GMRES implementation provided by the SLATEC project is used [7,18]. Hence, in this section we will first give a brief summary of the parallel GMRES implementation first and then present the structural pattern that we found in the code leading to a load imbalance.

3.1   Generalized Minimal Residual Method

The generalized minimal residual method (GMRES) originally developed by Yousef Saad and Martin H. Schultz in 1986 [17] is a widely used iterative method to solve linear systems of the form $Ax = b$, where A is a nonsymmetric matrix. The main idea is to create a Krylov subspace $\mathcal{K}(v_1) = span\{v_1, Av_1, \ldots, A^m v_1\}$ using Arnoldi's method [6] and approximate the exact solution of the linear system by a vector in that subspace which minimizes the residual norm. This process is repeated until the solution convergences up to a certain tolerance.

3.2   Parallel GMRES

In the CalculiX code the governing equations of the Computational Fluid Dynamics problem are discretized using the finite volume method [11]. The simulation is discretized in time by individual timesteps called increments. To obtain a steady state solution for the primary variables, such as velocity, temperature and pressure, several inner iterations are performed in which the physical conservation laws are solved in their transient form until they converge to a steady solution [12]. In each of these inner iterations multiple nonsymmetric linear equation systems have to be solved. The size of these systems is determined by the number of elements the mesh is composed of. Typically, millions of elements are used to discretize a given geometry. In order to solve these large systems the GMRES method is applied in parallel as follows:

Consider a single of these systems at an inner iteration k given by

$$A[u^{k-1}]u^k = b[u^{k-1}], \tag{1}$$

where $u^k \in \mathbb{R}^n$ is the velocity field at the end of the inner iteration k. Both the left hand side matrix $A \in \mathbb{R}^{n \times n}$ and the right hand side vector $b \in \mathbb{R}^n$ depend on the solution of the previous inner iteration u^{k-1}. Let T be the number of threads used for the parallelization. The matrix A gets subdivided into a $T \times T$ grid of submatrices $A_{i,j} \in \mathbb{R}^{nblk \times nblk}$ with $i, j \in \{1, 2, ..., T\}$ and the vectors u and b are split correspondingly into

$$A = \begin{pmatrix} A_{1,1} & \cdots & A_{1,T} \\ \vdots & \ddots & \vdots \\ A_{T,1} & \cdots & A_{T,T} \end{pmatrix}, \quad u = \begin{pmatrix} u_1 \\ \vdots \\ u_T \end{pmatrix}, \quad b = \begin{pmatrix} b_1 \\ \vdots \\ b_T \end{pmatrix}, \tag{2}$$

where the size of each submatrix $A_{i,j}$ is determined as $nblk = \lceil \frac{n}{T} \rceil$. Splitting the system in this fashion leads to T smaller subsystems

$$A_{1,1}[u^{k-1}] \cdot u_1^k + A_{1,2}[u^{k-1}] \cdot u_2^k + \ldots + A_{1,T}[u^{k-1}] \cdot u_T^k = b_1$$
$$\vdots$$
$$A_{T,1}[u^{k-1}] \cdot u_1^k + A_{T,2}[u^{k-1}] \cdot u_2^k + \ldots + A_{T,T}[u^{k-1}] \cdot u_T^k = b_T.$$

However, these systems are not independent as they are still connected by the various u_i^k for $i \in \{1, 2, \ldots, T\}$. Thus, by assuming that the solution u^k only changes slightly between each iteration one can approximate $u^k \approx u^{k-1}$ and reorder the system to yield

$$A_{1,1}[u^{k-1}] \cdot u_1^k = b_1 - \sum_{\substack{i=1 \\ i \neq 1}}^{T} A_{1,i}[u^{k-1}] \cdot u_i^{k-1}$$

$$\vdots$$

$$A_{T,T}[u^{k-1}] \cdot u_T^k = b_T - \sum_{\substack{i=1 \\ i \neq T}}^{T} A_{T,i}[u^{k-1}] \cdot u_i^{k-1}$$

As a result there are now T independent, smaller subsystems of the form

$$\tilde{A}_t \tilde{u}_t = \tilde{b}_t, \tag{3}$$

where we have $\tilde{A}_t = A_{t,t}[u^{k-1}] \cdot u_t^k$, $\tilde{u}_t = u_t^k$ and $\tilde{b} = b_t - \sum_{\substack{i=1 \\ i \neq t}}^{T} A_{t,i}[u^{k-1}] \cdot u_i^{k-1}$. So in order to solve the whole system in parallel each of these smaller subsystems is solved by a single thread using a serial GMRES implementation.

3.3   Convergence Dependent Load Imbalance

When we studied the CalculiX application we noticed a pattern occurring over the course of the whole simulation, in which one thread takes significantly longer to finish its GMRES computation than the other threads. In order to analyse this issue in more detail we isolated the solution of one of these systems and extracted a small kernel program by saving input and output data like matrices and vectors to file. In the original CalculiX code worker threads are forked and joined using the pthread API. We translated this equally into using an OpenMP parallel region so that we can use OpenMP constructs like tasks to implement solutions tackling the load imbalance later on.

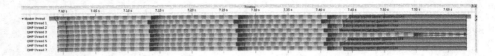

Fig. 1. Trace visualization of our GMRES kernel program using 8 OpenMP threads. Different colors correspond to different operations performed by the GMRES solver (Color figure online).

Figure 1 shows a trace of our kernel program executed with 8 OpenMP threads. We will refer to the master thread as thread 0 to match the numbering of threads in the trace correctly. On first sight the load imbalance becomes directly apparent because thread 4 takes significantly longer to finish compared to the others. We color coded different important subroutines of the GMRES implementation in the trace to highlight the iterative structure of this solver. One iteration consists mostly of applying a preconditioner in `msolve` (yellow) followed by a matrix vector product `matvec` (orange) and the orthogonalization `dorth` (pink) of the resulting vector. After 10 of such sequences the residual is calculated in `drlcal` (green) and the method is restarted in case the residual is not low enough. Based on this information we can count the number of GMRES iterations that each thread performs in the trace. While most of the threads obtain a converged solution after 31 or 32 iterations thread 4 requires 46 iterations. In order to quantify the load imbalance in our kernel program we measured load balance efficiency, standard deviation, skewness and kurtosis. All of these metrics are computed based on the runtime of the threads as well as on the number of GMRES iterations they perform. The results are shown in Table 1. First of all, we can verify that the kernel indeed has a significant load imbalance. The load balance efficiency based on runtimes ranges from 60% with 48 threads to 73% with 8 threads. Comparing these values to the load balance efficiency obtained based on GMRES iterations reveals a correlation between

Table 1. Load balance metrics obtained with our reference kernel using 8 to 48 OpenMP threads. We measured POP load balance efficiency, standard deviation, skewness and kurtosis based on runtime and GMRES iterations.

	threads	POP eff	std. dev	skewness	kurtosis
runtime	8	73%	0.065	2.192	2.959
	16	71%	0.024	3.555	10.790
	32	67%	0.012	3.531	14.152
	48	60%	0.013	4.144	17.011
iterations	8	72%	4.841	2.227	3.039
	16	69%	3.849	3.493	10.492
	32	67%	3.211	3.803	14.647
	48	68%	3.041	4.010	15.803

them. In most cases the values are nearly the same, except for the execution with 48 threads. Here we now have two slow threads while for the other executions we only have one. Furthermore, in both slow threads we find a single call to the subroutine `dorth` which suddenly takes much longer to complete compared to all other calls to this routine in the whole execution. This leads to lower efficiency value based on runtime than on GMRES iterations.

The standard deviation is not really comparable because runtime and iterations are measured in different units and have different magnitudes. However, skewness and kurtosis can be compared. We recognize that we get nearly the same results for all numbers of threads when comparing values based on runtimes and iterations. A positive skewness indicates that only a few number of threads are overloaded. The high kurtosis values indicate that variances are caused by infrequent extreme changes, i.e. by the one (or two) slow thread(s).

Even though the subsystems that each thread has to solve are of equal size in our case, the different convergence behavior leads to a load imbalance. This kind of imbalance is hard to tackle because it is difficult to predict the required number of GMRES iterations prior to the execution.

4 Load Balance Strategies

In order to improve the load balance of our parallel GMRES kernel program we implemented different ideas. The first idea uses OpenMP tasks to create multiple smaller subsystems to be solved in parallel. The second idea creates tasks conditionally only in the unbalanced phase of the execution. Lastly, the third idea is similar to the second one but instead of conditionally creating tasks it uses nested parallel regions in the unbalanced phase of the execution. In the following subsections each idea will be presented in more detail.

4.1 Tasking

In the first approach we use the OpenMP task construct. The idea is relatively simple: Instead of creating only a single subsystem to be solved by each thread we create multiple. Each subsystem is expressed as one OpenMP task. Depending on how many tasks we create a single task will shrink meaning that the subsystem to be solved will be smaller. In case a thread encounters a subsystem that converges slower than the other ones, the other threads can be kept busy by the OpenMP runtime scheduling another task from the pool of tasks to them. As a result we expect the total execution to be more balanced among the threads than with the original work distribution.

4.2 Conditional Nested Tasks

Our second approach directly tackles the unbalanced part of the execution. In our example (Fig. 1) this is the point at which all threads except thread 4 are finished with their computation. The idea is to conditionally split the remaining work in the slow thread into tasks that can be executed by the idling threads as well.

Therefore, we identified some subroutines of the GMRES solver that can be potentially parallelized. In all of these subroutines most work is done in some loops that can trivially be parallelized. We illustrate the implementation of our approach by the example of the `matvec` subroutine.

```
1  do i=1,n
2      y(i)=a(ja(i)+1)*x(ia(ja(i)+1))
3      do j=ja(i)+2,ja(i+1)
4          y(i)=y(i)+a(j)*x(ia(j))
5      enddo
6  enddo
```

Listing 1.1. Original `matvec` loop performing a sparse matrix vector product.

The original Fortran code is shown in Listing 1.1. It shows the main loop that iterates over the rows of a sparse matrix **a** stored in CSR format. For each row of **a** it computes the inner product of that row with the column vector **x** and stores the result in the corresponding location in the result vector **y**. The computation for each row is completely independent from the other rows so we can easily parallelize the outer **do** loop.

```
1      nThreads = OMP_GET_NUM_THREADS()
2  !$OMP ATOMIC READ
3      addThreads = freeThreads
4      if (addThreads .GT. 0.75 * nThreads) then
5          gs = int((n-1) / (addThreads+1)) + 1
6          do k=1,n,gs
7  !$OMP TASK SHARED(x,y,n,nelt,ia,ja,a,isym) IF(gs.ne.n)
8              do i=k,min(k+gs-1,n)
9                  y(i)=a(ja(i)+1)*x(ia(ja(i)+1))
10                 do j=ja(i)+2,ja(i+1)
11                     y(i)=y(i)+a(j)*x(ia(j))
12                 enddo
13             enddo
14 !$OMP END TASK
15         enddo
16 !$OMP TASKWAIT
17     else
18 ! serial matvec
19     endif
```

Listing 1.2. Our modified `matvec` loop performing a sparse matrix vector product with conditionally spawning nested tasks.

Our modifications to the code to implement our load balancing strategy are shown in Listing 1.2. We keep track of the number of threads that already finished their GMRES computation by atomically increasing a global variable `freeThreads`. Before we start computing the matrix vector product we atomically read this variable and save it in the variable `addThreads` (line 3).

If more than 75% of all threads are already finished with their own GMRES computation we consider to be in the unbalanced phase of the execution (line 4). In our example with 8 threads this corresponds to at least 7 threads that are already finished. Based on the number of `freeThreads` we determine the grainsize (gs) (line 5) in order to split the outer do loop into as many OpenMP tasks as there are freeThreads, including the slow running thread of course (lines 6–15). So each task corresponds to a number of rows the matrix vector product is performed on.

If less than 75% of all threads have finished their own computation we consider to still be in the balanced phase. In this case we default to the original serial matvec implementation (line 18). This should avoid any overhead the task creation may introduce when we know that only one task would be created anyways.

4.3   Conditional Nested Parallel Region

Our third and last approach is very similar to our second approach. It also conditionally splits the remaining work of the slow thread in the unbalanced phase between the other threads. However, as there is a certain overhead of creating nested tasks we use nested parallel regions as an alternative in this approach. Again we present the implementation of our approach by the example of the matvec subroutine. For the original Fortran code we refer to Listing 1.1.

```
1    nThreads = OMP_GET_NUM_THREADS()
2    addThreads = 0
3  !$OMP ATOMIC CAPTURE
4    addThreads = freeThreads
5    freeThreads = 0
6  !$OMP END ATOMIC
7    if (addThreads .LE. 0.75 * nThreads) then
8  !$OMP ATOMIC
9      freeThreads = freeThreads + addThreads
10 !$OMP END ATOMIC
11     addThreads = 0
12   endif
13
14 !$OMP PARALLEL DO PRIVATE(i,j) NUM_THREADS(1+addThreads)
15   do i=1,n
16     y(i)=a(ja(i)+1)*x(ia(ja(i)+1))
17     do j=ja(i)+2,ja(i+1)
18       y(i)=y(i)+a(j)*x(ia(j))
19     enddo
20   enddo
21 !$OMP END PARALLEL DO
22
23   if (addThreads .GT. 0) then
24 !$OMP ATOMIC
25     freeThreads = freeThreads + addThreads
26 !$OMP END ATOMIC
27   endif
```

Listing 1.3. Our modified matvec loop performing a sparse matrix vector product with conditionally creating a nested parallel region.

Our modifications in order to implement this third approach are shown in Listing 1.3. Again we track the number of threads that already completed their own GMRES computation in a global variable freeThreads. Before performing the matrix vector product loop we atomically read the value of freeThreads and save it in another variable addThreads indicating how many additional threads we can use for the following computation (line 4). In this approach we have to make sure that we also set `freeThreads` to zero to make sure no other slow thread sees the `freeThreads` and would create additional nested threads as well (line 5). Then again we evaluate our condition to determine if we are already in the unbalanced phase or not (line 7).

If we are in the balanced phase then we logically release all additional threads that we would have used to speed up computation on the current thread by performing an atomic update on `freeThreads` (line 9) and setting `addThreads` to zero. Conversely, if we are in the unbalanced phase `addThreads` holds the value of other idling threads at this point in the computation (line 13).

It follows the main `do` loop that performs the matrix vector product. This time we embedded it into a nested parallel region (lines 14–21). Depending on the evaluation of our condition to distinguish between the balanced and unbalanced phase this region will be executed with a different number of threads (line 14). If we are in the balanced phase `addThreads` $= 0$ and the parallel region will only be executed by the current thread. However, if we are in the unbalanced phase `addThreads` > 0 and the parallel region will be executed by the current thread together with some additional threads depending on how many are currently idling. In our example with 8 threads this will be all the other 7 threads.

After the parallel region has been executed we need to make sure to logically release the additional threads again by performing an atomic update on `freeThreads` (line 25). Of course this only needs to be done if we have really used them so only if `addThreads` > 0 (line 23). Otherwise we can save the atomic update operation.

5   Results

In this section we will present some performance results obtained with our kernel program. For each of our three implemented approaches we will show how it affects the load balance of our kernel.

All measurements were done on one node of the CLAIX-2018 cluster system of RWTH Aachen University. Such a node is a two-socket system equipped with two Intel Xeon Platinum 8160 processors. Each processor provides 24 cores running with a clock frequency of 2.1 GHz and 192 GB of memory. In order to fully exploit the memory bandwidth of this NUMA architecture threads are placed onto cores according to the policy of `KMP_AFFINITY=scatter`. To compile the programs we used the Intel Fortran compiler version 19.0.1.144 2018 which also provides an OpenMP runtime. For performance analysis we used Score-P 6.0, Cube 4.5 (release preview) and Vampir 9.8.0.

5.1   Tasking

Performance results obtained with the version of our kernel program that implements tasking as described in Sect. 4.1 are shown in Table 2. The kernel was executed with 8 OpenMP threads. We created a different number of tasks per thread and measured the load balance, the number of instructions executed as well as the time spent inside the GMRES kernel accumulated over all threads. First of all we recognize that the more tasks we create the closer the load balance approaches 100%. So in terms of load balancing this approach is nearly optimal. However, this approach also comes with a huge drawback. Already if we create 5 tasks per thread the accumulated time spent inside the kernel over all threads increases by 62%. Though with 10 tasks per thread this runtime only increases by 51%. In the extreme case of creating 150 tasks per thread the time spent in the kernel is 87% higher than in the reference case of using just 1 task per thread. In all cases where the runtime increases there are also more instructions executed than in the reference case. This clearly indicates that the convergence of the GMRES method plays an important role. The systems to be solved are much smaller than in the reference case. For example, when creating 150 tasks per thread an individual system is only of size 1280×1280 compared to 192000×192000 in the reference case. Unfortunately, overall more work has to be done to obtain the same solution. So this approach does not improve the load balance in a sensible way.

Table 2. Performance results of our tasking approach with 8 OpenMP threads.

Tasks per thread	Load balance	instructions	time (accumulated)
1	74%	3.83×10^{10}	3.73 s
5	89%	5.63×10^{10}	6.05 s
10	96%	5.71×10^{10}	5.63 s
50	99%	6.61×10^{10}	6.59 s
100	99%	6.41×10^{10}	6.76 s
150	99%	6.25×10^{10}	6.98 s

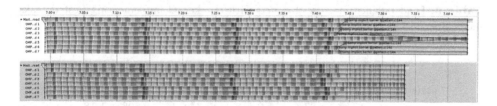

Fig. 2. Trace comparison of our reference GMRES kernel (top) and the conditional nested tasks version (bottom) both using 8 OpenMP threads.

5.2   Conditional Nested Tasks

In order to evaluate our second approach to tackle the load imbalance in our kernel we obtained a trace of the execution. A comparison between the original kernel and the one implementing conditional nested tasks is shown in Fig. 2. The balanced phase of the execution is almost identical in both traces. However, the unbalanced phase is significantly shorter using nested tasks compared to the reference. While thread 4 originally finished after roughly 630 ms it is now already finished after roughly 540 ms. This is a speedup of 1.16 compared to the reference. Moreover, the load balance has improved to 89%(+16%). The standard deviation in the runtimes is almost halved. This indicates that indeed the runtime on the slow thread got shorter while the runtimes on the other threads get longer because they now additionally spend time with computations inside the nested tasks. So overall the runtimes are now closer together than before. The skewness and kurtosis are also slightly lower than in the reference execution. This means the characteristics of the runtime distribution among the threads are still the same. We still have only one slow thread. However, this thread is now faster.

We obtained similar results for executions with a higher number of threads. Table 3 shows load balance metrics obtained for thread numbers ranging from 8 to 48. By comparing these results with the reference results shown in Table 1 we can see that the load balance efficiency is improved in all cases. While for 8 and 16 threads we yield an improvement of 16% we only get 11% with 32 threads and 4% with 48 threads. The same trend can be observed for the speedup factors. With 8 and 16 threads we yield a speedup of 1.16 and 1.18 respectively. However, with 32 threads only a speedup of 1.09 is obtained. Even worse when running with 48 threads the runtime is still the same as in the reference execution. This might be an impact of the overhead when frequently spawning nested tasks because each individual task is quite small and only operates on vectors with roughly 667 elements. The statistical moments are all slightly lower compared to the reference. Again this means that in all cases the runtime characteristics of the load imbalance stay the same. But the individual runtimes of each thread are now closer to the average.

Table 3. Load balance metrics obtained with our kernel implementing nested tasks using 8 to 48 OpenMP threads. We measured POP load balance efficiency, standard deviation, skewness, kurtosis and the speedup compared to the reference kernel.

	threads	POP eff	std. dev	skewness	kurtosis	speedup
nested tasks	8	89%	0.035	2.029	2.557	1.16
	16	87%	0.012	3.349	9.808	1.18
	32	78%	0.009	3.033	11.691	1.09
	48	64%	0.013	4.119	16.670	1.00

Finally, we also verified our results. In all cases the converged solution is equal to the original solution in the reference case with respect to machine precision (16 digits). The number of GMRES iterations that each thread performs have also not changed.

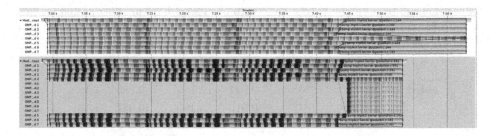

Fig. 3. Trace comparison of our reference GMRES kernel (top) and the conditional nested parallel regions version (bottom) both using 8 OpenMP threads.

5.3 Conditional Nested Parallel Region

A comparison between the original kernel and the one implementing conditional nested parallel regions is shown in Fig. 3. In the balanced phase we do not recognize any differences between the reference execution and the execution with nested parallel regions, except that these regions are visible in the trace even when they are executed by just one thread. However, in the unbalanced phase the runtime of the kernel is significantly shorter. Thread 4 obtains the converged solution after roughly 540 ms. This is a speedup of roughly 1.16 compared to the reference execution. The load balance is also significantly improved and is now at 88% (+15%). Furthermore, the statistical moments are also improved. The standard deviation almost got halved. This means that the variance in the individual runtimes of the threads are now smaller. The skewness is still positive and only slightly lower than before which shows that there is still only one overloaded thread. The kurtosis is also only slightly lower indicating that there are still infrequent large variances in the runtimes caused by the one slow thread.

Similar results are obtained with higher numbers of threads, ranging from 8 to 48, as shown in Table 4. In all cases the load balance efficiency is improved. Using 8 and 16 threads we yield an improvement of 15% and 16% respectively. However, with 32 threads we only yield a plus of 8%, which is also 3% less than with nested tasks. Using 48 threads we only get 3% improvement. The speedup values show a similar behavior. With 8 threads we get a speedup of roughly 1.16 which is identical to the nested task approach. But with 16 or more threads the nested parallel regions approach becomes a little bit slower than nested tasks. Using 16 threads we yield a speedup of 1.13 which is 5% slower than nested tasks. With 32 threads the speedup is only 1.02 and 7% slower than nested tasks. This becomes worse when using 48 threads. Here we yield a speedup of 0.95 which is a 5% slowdown compared to the reference execution. The statistical moments are all slightly lower compared to the reference case. However, they have still the same order of magnitude and are all positive. The similar skewness and kurtosis imply that still the load imbalance is caused by one overloaded thread.

Moreover, the kernel still computes the correct solution. The converged solution is identical with the original one up to machine precision (16 digits). The number of GMRES iterations performed by each thread also remains the same.

Table 4. Load balance metrics obtained with our kernel implementing nested regions using 8 to 48 OpenMP threads. We measured POP load balance efficiency, standard deviation, skewness, kurtosis and the speedup compared to the reference kernel.

	threads	POP eff	std. dev	skewness	kurtosis	speedup
nested regions	8	88%	0.034	2.165	2.883	1.16
	16	87%	0.015	3.461	10.087	1.13
	32	75%	0.011	3.218	11.350	1.02
	48	63%	0.015	3.734	13.424	0.95

In order to execute the kernel with nested parallel regions correctly the environment needs to be configured in a special way. First of all, we set OMP_NESTED = 1 to enable nested parallelism. Furthermore, we set KMP_HOT_TEAMS_MODE = 1 which will keep the nested threads in the team for faster reuse as multiple nested regions are quickly executed one after another. Related to this we also set KMP_BLOCKTIME = 0 which causes threads to instantly go to sleep state instead of waiting the default 200 ms after completing the execution of a parallel region. On the one hand this makes sure that outer level threads do not spend cpu time with idling. On the other hand this global environment variable also affects the nested threads, so that they will also instantly go to sleep state after executing a nested parallel region. Since we are rapidly executing lots of nested regions it would be much better if the blocktime could be set for each nesting level separately. Unfortunately, this is not possible with the current Intel OpenMP runtime.

Lastly, we pinned the kernel to a set of physical cores corresponding to the KMP_AFFINITY=scatter setting using taskset. The number of cores is equal to the number of outer level threads the kernel is executed with. Otherwise the nested threads could be scheduled on one of the remaining free physical cores of our system if there are some, for example when running with only 8 threads. However, the intent of our implementation is to mimic a similar behavior as with nested tasks. So by restricting the execution to as many physical cores as there are threads initially, we make sure that nested threads can only be scheduled to the same set of physical cores as the outer level threads.

6   Future Work

Our current approach using nested parallelism has some drawbacks. Currently, the condition when to trigger the nested parallelism is hard-coded into the subroutines of the GMRES solver. Nested tasks or threads are spawned as soon as more than 75% are idling. For the presented load imbalance, where mostly only a single thread is heavily overloaded, this condition works quite well. However, for other cases with multiple slow threads it might not be suitable. Hence, we would like to also investigate arbitrary thresholds to trigger nested parallelism.

Moreover, the results presented in this paper focus only on the execution of a small kernel program extracted from the CalculiX application. Our results on the kernel look promising to also speedup the whole CalculiX application as the presented load imbalance pattern can be found over the course of the whole simulation. Hence, we want to verify the applicability of our approach using the whole CalculiX application in the future.

After that it might be interesting to identify similar load imbalances in implementations of iterative methods other than GMRES. If the load imbalance is similar to the pattern presented in this paper we expect our approach to be applicable as well.

Finally, our approach tackles the load imbalance when it already occurred. Thus, we are also interested in investigating the root cause of this imbalance. If we know what the imbalance is caused by we could tackle it directly and avoid the need to spawn nested tasks or nested regions at all.

7 Conclusions

In this work we presented a very special kind of load imbalance that can occur in the parallel implementation of iterative methods used to solve systems of linear equations in an SPMD fashion. If each thread solves an independent subsystem different convergence behavior of these systems may induce a load imbalance between the threads.

We identified such a pattern in the CalculiX code in which one thread consistently has to perform more solver iterations than all the other threads thus reducing the load balance to 73% and implemented three different approaches to tackle the load imbalance: Splitting the problem into more even smaller subproblems leads to a perfectly balanced workload but also to a higher computational complexity and thus a longer runtime. Conditionally spawning nested tasks or nested parallel regions in the unbalanced phase of the execution both yield comparable results when running with 8 or 16 threads. Here we got a speedups between 1.13 and 1.18. But when running with 32 or 48 threads the kernel does not scale as well anymore so that in the worst case our approach slightly slowed the kernel down. Moreover, we investigated different statistical moments which indicate that the characteristics of the load imbalance are the same for all number of threads. In all cases we mostly have a single overloaded thread. Since the nested regions approach requires a special environment configuration, interferes with the thread scheduling of the OpenMP runtime and yielded a small application slowdown, we recommend to prefer nested tasks whenever possible.

Finally, our approach is directly implemented into the GMRES solver. It is independent from the CalculiX application code and can in general be used by other applications, that use the GMRES method in a similar way, as well.

Acknowledgements. Part of this work was performed under the POP2 project and has received funding from the European Union's Horizon 2020 research and innovation programme under grant agreement 824080.

References

1. CALCULIX A Free Software Three-Dimensional Structural Finite Element Program. http://www.calculix.de/. Accessed 22 May 2020
2. Performance Optimisation and Productivity (POP) - A Centre of Excellence in HPC. https://pop-coe.eu. Accessed 22 May 2020
3. Top500 list - november 2019. https://www.top500.org/list/2019/11/?page=1. Accessed 22 May 2020
4. Adcock, A.B., Sullivan, B.D., Hernandez, O.R., Mahoney, M.W.: Evaluating OpenMP tasking at scale for the computation of graph hyperbolicity. In: Rendell, A.P., Chapman, B.M., Müller, M.S. (eds.) IWOMP 2013. LNCS, vol. 8122, pp. 71–83. Springer, Heidelberg (2013). https://doi.org/10.1007/978-3-642-40698-0_6
5. Amdahl, G.M.: Validity of the single processor approach to achieving large scale computing capabilities. In: Proceedings of the April 18–20, 1967, Spring Joint Computer Conference, pp. 483–485. AFIPS 1967 (Spring), Association for Computing Machinery, New York, NY, USA (1967). https://doi.org/10.1145/1465482.1465560
6. Arnoldi, W.E.: The principle of minimized iterations in the solution of the matrix eigenvalue problem. Q. Appl. Math. **9**(1), 17–29 (1951). https://doi.org/10.1090/qam/42792
7. Brown, P.N., Hindmarsh, A.C.: Reduced storage matrix methods in stiff ODE systems. Appl. Math. Comput. **31**, 40–91 (1989). https://doi.org/10.1016/0096-3003(89)90110-0
8. Ciorba, F.M., Iwainsky, C., Buder, P.: Openmp loop scheduling revisited: making a case for more schedules. In: de Supinski, B.R., Valero-Lara, P., Martorell, X., Mateo Bellido, S., Labarta, J. (eds.) Evolving OpenMP for Evolving Architectures, pp. 21–36. Springer, Cham (2018)
9. Criado, J., et al.: Optimization of condensed matter physics application with OpenMP tasking model. In: Fan, X., de Supinski, B.R., Sinnen, O., Giacaman, N. (eds.) IWOMP 2019. LNCS, vol. 11718, pp. 291–305. Springer, Cham (2019). https://doi.org/10.1007/978-3-030-28596-8_20
10. Dagum, L., Menon, R.: OpenMP: an industry-standard API for shared-memory programming. IEEE Comput. Sci. Eng. **5**(1), 46–55 (1998). https://doi.org/10.1109/99.660313
11. Dhondt, G.: The Finite Element Method for Three-dimensional Thermomechanical Applications. Wiley, Chichester (2004)
12. Dhondt, G.: CalculiX CrunchiX USER'S MANUAL version 2.16, November 2019
13. Durand, M., Broquedis, F., Gautier, T., Raffin, B.: An efficient OpenMP loop scheduler for irregular applications on large-scale NUMA machines. In: Rendell, A.P., Chapman, B.M., Müller, M.S. (eds.) IWOMP 2013. LNCS, vol. 8122, pp. 141–155. Springer, Heidelberg (2013). https://doi.org/10.1007/978-3-642-40698-0_11
14. OpenMP Architecture Review Board: OpenMP Application Program Interface Version 5.0. https://www.openmp.org/wp-content/uploads/OpenMP-API-Specification-5.0.pdf (2018)
15. Pearce, O., Gamblin, T., de Supinski, B.R., Schulz, M., Amato, N.M.: Quantifying the effectiveness of load balance algorithms. In: Proceedings of the 26th ACM International Conference on Supercomputing, pp. 185–194. ICS 2012, Association for Computing Machinery, New York, NY, USA (2012). https://doi.org/10.1145/2304576.2304601

16. Royuela, S., Serrano, M.A., Garcia-Gasulla, M., Mateo Bellido, S., Labarta, J., Quiñones, E.: The Cooperative Parallel: A Discussion About Run-Time Schedulers for Nested Parallelism. In: Fan, X., de Supinski, B.R., Sinnen, O., Giacaman, N. (eds.) IWOMP 2019. LNCS, vol. 11718, pp. 171–185. Springer, Cham (2019). https://doi.org/10.1007/978-3-030-28596-8_12
17. Saad, Y., Schultz, M.H.: GMRES: a generalized minimal residual algorithm for solving nonsymmetric linear systems. SIAM J. Sci. Stat. Comput. **7**(3), 856–869 (1986)
18. Seager, M.: A SLAP for the masses. Technical report, Lawrence Livermore National Laboratory (1988)

Tools

On-the-fly Data Race Detection with the Enhanced OpenMP Series-Parallel Graph

Nader Boushehrinejadmoradi[✉], Adarsh Yoga, and Santosh Nagarakatte

Rutgers University, New Brunswick, NJ 08901, USA
{naderb,adarsh.yoga,santosh.nagarakatte}@cs.rutgers.edu

Abstract. This paper proposes OMP-RACER, a dynamic apparent data race detector for OpenMP programs. Apparent data races are those races that manifest in a program considering the logical series-parallel relations of the execution. By identifying apparent races, OMP-RACER can detect races that occur not only in the observed schedule but also in other schedules for a given input. Our key contribution is a data structure to capture series-parallel relations between various fragments of an OpenMP program with both structured and unstructured parallelism directives, which we call the Enhanced OpenMP Series-Parallel Graph (EOSPG). OMP-RACER maintains information about previous accesses with each memory access and uses the EOSPG to check if they can logically execute in parallel. OMP-RACER detects more races with similar overheads when compared to existing state-of-the-art race detectors for OpenMP programs.

Keywords: OpenMP · Data races · Series-parallel relations · EOSPG.

1 Introduction

Data races are common in OpenMP programs as with any multithreaded program. Data races can cause non-determinism, make the execution dependent on the memory model, and cause debugging issues. Two accesses are said to constitute a data race if they access the same memory location, one of them is a write, and they can execute in parallel. Data races can be classified into apparent races and feasible races [17]. Data races that manifest when we consider the computation, synchronization, and parallel constructs are termed feasible races. Although there is a large body of work on detecting feasible races [10,20,24], they detect races in a given schedule (*i.e.*, interleaving). Detecting feasible races also requires interleaving exploration either systematically or through prioritization [6,16]. In contrast, data races that occur in an execution of a program primarily considering the parallel constructs, but without taking the actual computation into account, are termed apparent races. An apparent race may not be a feasible race in scenarios where the computation itself may change when the parallel threads are scheduled in a different order. Every apparent race is also a feasible race for Abelian programs [8].

© Springer Nature Switzerland AG 2020
K. Milfeld et al. (Eds.): IWOMP 2020, LNCS 12295, pp. 149–164, 2020.
https://doi.org/10.1007/978-3-030-58144-2_10

To detect apparent races, one needs a data structure that represents the logical series-parallel relations between various fragments of the program. Further, any race detector also needs to maintain access history metadata with each memory location that records previous accesses to that location. Prior work on detecting apparent races has primarily focused on task-parallel programs [9,21,22,27,30], which have structured parallelism. This paper focuses on detecting apparent races in OpenMP programs with both work-sharing and tasking directives.

This paper proposes OMP-RACER, an on-the-fly apparent data race detector for OpenMP programs. To encode the logical series-parallel relations between various fragments of the execution in the presence of both structured and unstructured directives (e.g., taskwait and dependencies), we propose a new data structure that we call the Enhanced OpenMP Series-Parallel Graph (EOSPG). It enhances the OpenMP Series-Parallel Graph (OSPG), which we previously proposed for profiling serialization bottlenecks [4], with support for unstructured directives. Specifically, the EOSPG encodes the nesting depth of the tasks that enables it to capture the logical series-parallel relations for a larger class of OpenMP programs than prior state-of-the-art.

The EOSPG accurately encodes logical series-parallel relations between any two fragments of an OpenMP execution (where a fragment is the longest sequence of serial instructions without any OpenMP directives encountered in the dynamic execution). This logical series-parallel relation encoded by the EOSPG is a property of the program for a given input. It enables OMP-RACER to detect races not just in a given schedule but also in other schedules for a given input. It can alleviate the need for exploring schedules with race detection, which is an advance compared to per-schedule detectors based on vector clocks [10,13,24]. The EOSPG supports a large subset of directives in the OpenMP specification. It still does not support undeferred tasks and their interaction with dependency clauses, which we plan to explore in future work.

Apart from constructing the EOSPG during the execution of the program, OMP-RACER also maintains access history metadata with every memory location. On a memory access, OMP-RACER consults the per-location access history metadata and uses the EOSPG to check if the current access can logically happen in parallel using least common ancestor (LCA) queries (see Sect. 3). OMP-RACER provides two modes: a precise mode and a fast mode. In the precise mode, OMP-RACER detects data races when the program uses taskwait directives with no restrictions. The metadata per-memory location is proportional to the nesting level of tasks. In the fast mode, OMP-RACER performs a quick execution to construct the EOSPG and identifies whether the program uses taskwaits in a fully nested manner, which results in structured parallelism. Subsequently, it performs an execution to detect races by maintaining a constant amount of information per-memory location. In our experiments, the fast mode detects all data races in the DataRaceBench suite [14] without any false positives. The performance overhead of OMP-RACER in its fast mode is comparable to a single execution of Archer [2]. Further, Archer generally requires multiple executions of the same program with the same input to detect a given data race while OMP-RACER does not. OMP-RACER is open source and publicly available [5].

Contributions. This paper proposes EOSPG, a novel data structure, to encode logical series-parallel relations for an OpenMP program with both structured and unstructured directives. This paper presents mechanisms to construct and use the EOSPG to detect data races that occur not only in the observed schedule but also in other possible schedules for a given input.

2 Overview of OMP-RACER

This section provides an overview of race detection with OMP-RACER. We use the program in Fig. 1(a) that uses different OpenMP directives to compute the sum of an array in parallel to illustrate OMP-RACER. It uses worksharing (*i.e.*, `single` and `for`) and tasking directives (*i.e.*, `task`) to add parallelism to the program. This example has a data race due to insufficient synchronization between child tasks and the implicit task executing the single directive (lines 12–24 in Fig. 1(a)). The thread encountering the taskwait directive only waits for its child tasks to complete but does not wait for its descendant tasks, which results in unstructured parallelism [19]. The dynamic execution trace with the memory accesses generated when the program is executed on a machine with two threads is shown in Fig. 1(b). The two accesses involved in the data race are executed by the same thread in this schedule. However, OMP-RACER can detect this race because it uses the logical series-parallel relation.

Enhanced OpenMP Series-Parallel Graph. OMP-RACER executes on-the-fly with the program and constructs the EOSPG during program execution. EOSPG is an extension of the OSPG [4]. The EOSPG is an ordered directed acyclic graph (DAG) that captures the dynamic execution of an OpenMP program as a set of program fragments. A fragment is the longest sequence of instructions in the dynamic execution of the program between two OpenMP directives. Each fragment executes serially in a thread or a task. By design, each program fragment is a leaf node in the EOSPG. The intermediate nodes of the EOSPG encode the series-parallel relation between the leaf nodes. EOSPG captures the logical series-parallel relations between any pair of fragments in the program for a given input. Given any two fragments, we can identify if they may execute in parallel by performing a least common ancestor (LCA) query between the leaf nodes corresponding to the two fragments.

Nodes in an EOSPG. The EOSPG generated for the example program is shown in Fig. 1(c). Each W-node represents a fragment of the execution. The intermediate nodes can be one of the following types: S-node, P-node, or an ST-node (see Sect. 3). The subtree under the S-node executes in series with the siblings and their descendants to the right. Similarly, the subtree under the P-node executes in parallel with the siblings and their descendants on the right. In the EOSPG, ST-nodes captures the fact that the subtree under the ST-node has encountered a taskwait directive. As taskwait only serializes a task's immediate children, it is necessary to count the nesting depth of the tasks. Hence, each ST-node and P-node maintain a value (e.g., st_val) to account for the nesting depth. Each P-node contributes a value of 1 to the nesting depth. Each ST-node that has seen a taskwait serializes the immediate children and nullifies the contribution of one P-node under it. Hence, the value of the ST-node starts at 0, and upon encountering a taskwait, it changes to -1.

Checking if Two Accesses can Execute in Parallel. In the absence of ST-nodes and dependencies, two W-nodes, W_i and W_j, where W_i is to the left of W_j, logically execute in parallel if the left child of the least common ancestor (LCA) of W_i and W_j on the path to W_i is a P-node. In the presence of ST-nodes, the procedure is slightly more involved (see Sect. 3). When the left child of the LCA on the path to W_i is an ST-node, we compute the sum of the values related to nesting depth maintained with each ST-node and P-node from W_i to the left child of the LCA. If this sum is greater than zero, then the two nodes execute in parallel. Otherwise they execute serially.

In Fig. 1(c), W-nodes W2 and W5 logically execute in parallel because the left child of the LCA node S3 is the P-node P1. Intuitively, these are parallel chunks of a dynamic for loop. A pair of W-nodes, W8 and W10, in Fig. 1(c) execute in parallel because the left child of the LCA node (i.e., S4) is the ST-node ST1 and the sum of st_val values from W8 to ST1 is 1, indicating a logical parallel relation. In contrast, W-nodes W9 and W10 execute in series because the left child of the LCA node (i.e., S4) is the ST-node ST1. However, the sum of st_val values from W9 to ST1 is 0. Intuitively, the taskwait on line 22 serializes their execution.

Metadata for Data Race Detection. To detect races, OMP-RACER maintains access history metadata with each memory location. To store access histories, it has two modes: a fast mode and a precise mode. In the fast mode, it performs a complete execution of the program to first check if all taskwaits are fully nested (i.e., they create a taskgroup, where each parent task waits for its child tasks with a taskwait), and there are no critical sections. In such cases, it treats all ST-nodes as S-nodes and maintains two parallel reads and a write with each memory location. In precise mode, OMP-RACER maintains additional information about two reads and writes with each ST-node that is present on the path from the W-node to the root of the EOSPG. The execution has an apparent race if the current operation happens in parallel with the previous conflicting operations to the same memory location in the access history metadata associated with the root node or the access history metadata associated with each of the ST-nodes on the path from the current node to the root of the EOSPG.

Illustration of Race Detection. Figure 1(b) provides the dynamic execution trace and the updates to the access history metadata for each memory location using the precise mode for the example program in Fig. 1(a). The write operation to psum[1] at line 18 of the example program corresponds to the W-node, W8. Upon this write operation, the metadata associated with psum[1]

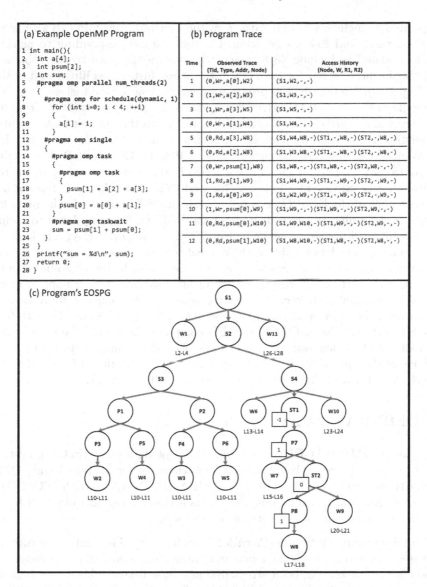

Fig. 1. (a) Example OpenMP program with a write-read apparent data race on variable psum[1] at lines 18 and 23. (b) The execution trace of the example program when executed with two threads. The first column specifies the ordering of the observed trace. The second column specifies the memory access as a 4-tuple comprised of thread id, memory access type, memory access location, and the W-node performing the access. The third column illustrates the access history maintained by OMP-RACER for the corresponding memory access as a 4-tuple with the node identifier, W-node corresponding to the latest write, and two W-nodes corresponding to two parallel read accesses (- denotes the empty set). (c) The program's EOSPG. The code fragment each W-node represents is shown below it. The square boxes next to some EOSPG nodes represent the value indicating the nesting depth in the presence of taskwaits.

is updated to include W8. The path from the root of the EOSPG to W8 has two
ST-nodes: ST1 and ST2. In addition, the metadata corresponding to psum[1]
is also updated to include W8 for each ST-node on the path to the root node,
resulting in three entries for psum[1] in the access history (as illustrated at time
7 in Fig. 1(b)). Eventually, the program execution reaches the taskwait directive
at line 22 in Fig. 1(a). OMP-RACER updates the st_val of node ST1 from 0 to
-1 to record the presence of a taskwait. Later, when the implicit task executing
the single directive performs a read operation on psum[1] at line 23 in Fig. 1(a),
the W-node representing the current read is W10. OMP-RACER retrieves the
metadata for psum[1], which includes access histories corresponding to the root
node of the EOSPG and ST-nodes ST1 and ST2. Since the path from W10 to
the root node of the EOSPG does not contain any ST-nodes, only the metadata
entry corresponding to the root node of the EOSPG, S1, is updated to include
the current read access (time 12 in Fig. 1(b)). Next, OMP-RACER looks for
possible data races by checking if the current read operation happens in parallel
with any previous write accesses recorded in the access history metadata. In our
example, OMP-RACER checks if the current read access may happen in parallel with the previously recorded write operation corresponding to W-node W8.
In this case, the LCA of W8 and W10 is S4. The left child of S4 on the path to W8
is an ST-node ST1. Next, OMP-RACER computes the sum of the st_val values
from W8 to ST1, which evaluates to 1. Thus, W8 and W10 may execute in parallel,
and one of the operations is a write operation, which results in OMP-RACER
reporting an apparent race on the memory access to psum[1].

3   OMP-RACER Approach

The goal of OMP-RACER is to detect apparent data races that manifest not
just in a given schedule but also in other schedules for a given input. OMP-
RACER constructs the Enhanced OpenMP Series-Parallel Graph (EOSPG) to
represent series-parallel relations, maintains access history metadata with each
memory location, and checks them to catch races.

Enhanced OpenMP Series-Parallel Graph. EOSPG is a data structure that
captures series-parallel relations between various fragments of an OpenMP execution in the presence of both structured and unstructured directives. It builds
on our prior work, the OpenMP Series-Parallel Graph (OSPG) [4]. Specifically,
the OSPG assumed that taskwaits are fully nested. According to the OpenMP
specification [19], the taskwait directives need not be fully nested. EOSPG is
an enhancement of OSPG to handle directives that can result in unstructured
parallelism such as taskwaits and other features such as dependencies.

Definition. EOSPG is a directed acyclic graph (DAG), $G = (V, E)$, where the
set V consists of four types of nodes, W-nodes, S-nodes, P-nodes, and ST-nodes.
Thus, $V = V_w \cup V_p \cup V_s \cup V_{st}$. The set of edges, $E = E_{pc} \cup E_{dep}$, where E_{pc} denotes
the parent-child edges between nodes and E_{dep} denotes the dependency edges.
The EOSPG has a root S-node which has a unique directed path consisting

of only E_{pc} edges to all other nodes. A node's depth is defined as the number of edges on the path consisting of E_{pc} edges from the root node to it. Nodes with the same parent are referred to as sibling nodes. E_{dep} edges are between two sibling nodes. Thus an E_{pc} edge between a pair nodes, (v_1, v_2), establishes a parent-child relation between the two nodes, where v_1 is the parent node of v_2. Moreover, sibling nodes in an EOSPG are ordered from left to right, which corresponds to the logical ordering of operations in the program.

In contrast to the OSPG, the EOSPG has a new type of node (ST-nodes). Further, each P-node and ST-node maintains additional information to encode the nesting depth that is required to correctly identify series-parallel relations in the presence of the taskwait directive. The state is maintained with each node is called st_val, which is an integer in $\{-1, 0, 1\}$.

W-node. Similar to the OSPG, a W-node represents a serial fragment of dynamic execution in the program. By construction, a W-node is always a leaf node in the EOSPG. A fragment either starts from the beginning of the program or when the execution encounters an OpenMP directive. The fragment continues until the program ends, or it reaches another OpenMP directive. In the absence of any OpenMP directives in the program's execution, the entire program is serially executed. Hence, the EOSPG of a sequential program consists of a single W-node that is a direct child of the root S-node. A W-node has an st_val of zero.

S-node and P-node. These nodes encode the logical series-parallel relations between W-nodes. An S-node establishes a serial relation (whereas a P-node establishes a parallel relation) between all its descendant W-nodes and all right siblings and their descendant W-nodes. A P-node and an S-node have an st_val of one and zero, respectively. The st_val of a P-node is one because a P-node creates a parallel strand of execution and contributes a level to nested parallelism.

ST-node. This node also encodes the logical series-parallel relations between W-nodes. Unlike S-nodes or P-nodes, the logical series-parallel relation between W-nodes in the subtree under an ST-node and its right siblings and their descendants depends on whether there has been a taskwait and the nesting depth of the node. Effectively, for an ST-node, its descendant W-nodes are partitioned into two subsets. First, W-nodes that execute serially with all right siblings and the descendants of the ST-node. Second, W-nodes that run in parallel relative to the right siblings and their descendants of the ST-node. The OSPG did not have any ST-nodes [4]. We added this node to the OSPG to enable capturing the logical series-parallel relations in the presence of OpenMP directives that do not fall under structured parallelism. ST-nodes are used whenever creating a P-node or an S-node is not sufficient to capture the logical series-parallel relations between program fragments.

Construction of the EOSPG. A program's EOSPG is constructed incrementally and in parallel during program execution. Each executing thread adds nodes to a subtree of the EOSPG. Different threads will operate on different subtrees of the EOSPG and updates can be done with limited use of synchronization.

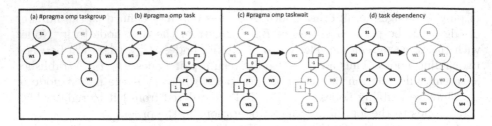

Fig. 2. EOSPG construction for different OpenMP directives. The nodes before encountering a directive are greyed out after the EOSPG is updated.

Except for the handling of the ST-nodes, the construction of the EOSPG is similar to the construction of the OSPG [4]. Here, we highlight the changes to the construction algorithm to capture the logical series-parallel relation that were not supported in the original OSPG design. Figure 1(c) illustrates the EOSPG for the program in Fig. 1(a) after the program completes execution.

Handling Task Synchronization Directives in the EOSPG. OpenMP supports task-based parallelism using the task directive. During program execution, when the currently running task, whether implicit or explicit, encounters a task directive, the current task creates a new child task, becoming its parent task. The child task may execute in parallel with the continuation of the parent task. Moreover, OpenMP provides several options to synchronize task execution. These options include the taskgroup directive, the taskwait directive, and task dependencies.

Taskgroup Directive. A taskgroup directive enforces a serial ordering between the structured block associated with the taskgroup and the code fragments that execute after the taskgroup. Namely, the code following the taskgroup waits for the completion of all created tasks and their descendants within the taskgroup's structured block. As illustrated in Fig. 2(a), the EOSPG captures this serial relation by adding an S-node, S2, when the program trace encounters the beginning of a taskgroup. All the fragments in the taskgroup are contained in the subtree rooted at node S2. Moreover, the fragment executing after the taskgroup will be the right siblings of newly created S-node, depicted as W-node W3 in Fig. 2(a). Therefore, creating the S-node S2 captures the serial relation between all fragments executing within the taskgroup and all the fragments executing after it.

Taskwait Directive. A taskwait directive specifies a serial ordering between the task encountering the directive and its children. However, unlike the taskgroup directive, a taskwait does not enforce a serial ordering with the parent task and its grandchildren and descendant tasks. While fully nested taskwaits produce a behavior similar to that of a taskgroup, it becomes more challenging to correctly capture series-parallel relations when taskwaits are not fully nested.

To capture the series-parallel relations induced by the taskwait directive correctly, we also need to take the nesting level into account. Further, during the dynamic execution, we do not know whether the execution will see a taskwait directive in the future. Hence, whenever a parent task encounters a task directive and creates its first child task in the program or spawns a new task after a taskwait, we add an ST-node, followed by a P-node to the program's EOSPG as illustrated in Fig. 2(b). We create an ST-node at this point in the execution because we do not know a priori the nesting level of the newly created child task and whether at each nesting level, including the current one, the execution will encounter a taskwait directive. The subsequent P-node captures the parallel relation between the newly created child task and its sibling tasks, if any.

An ST-node partitions the W-nodes under its subtree into two subsets because a taskwait does not serialize all the W-nodes in the subtree. (1) W-nodes that execute serially with all right siblings of the ST-node and their descendants. (2) W-nodes that run in parallel relative to the right siblings of the ST-node and their descendants. To determine if a W-node is a member of the first or the second subset, we use the nodes' st_val values on the path to the ST-node. Intuitively, st_val values on the path to the ST-node, capture the nesting level and the number of encountered taskwaits. Whenever an ST-node is created, its st_val is initially set to zero (Fig. 2(b)). If later during the execution, the task that created the ST-node encounters a taskwait, we capture this information by setting the st_val of the corresponding ST-node to -1 (Fig. 2(c)). To capture the nesting level under an ST-node's subtree, the newly created P-node, which is the immediate child of the ST-node, will have an st_val of one.

Key Invariant in the Presence of ST-nodes. For a pair of W-nodes, (W_i, W_j), where W_i is under the subtree of ST-node ST_k and W_j is either a right sibling or a descendant of a right sibling of ST_k, the pair of W-nodes execute in parallel if the sum of the st_val values of the EOSPG nodes on the path from ST_k to W_i is a positive integer. Otherwise, the two W-nodes execute in series.

Task Dependencies. In OpenMP, sibling tasks logically execute in parallel. However, with task dependencies, OpenMP supports user-defined ordering between sibling tasks. We capture the serial ordering produced by task dependencies in the EOSPG by adding E_{dp} edges between P-nodes that correspond to dependent tasks. For example, consider two sibling tasks $t1$ and $t2$ where $t2$ is dependent on $t1$. The EOSPG captures this task dependency as follows. By construction, each task has a corresponding P-node in the EOSPG, labeled as P1 and P2 in Fig. 2(d). The E_{dp} edge, $(p1, p2)$, captures the underlying task dependency. The dependency of two sibling tasks can be checked by looking for a path comprised of E_{dp} edges between the corresponding P-nodes.

To check if a pair of W-nodes, (W2, W4) in Fig. 2(d), execute in series due to a task dependency, we first check if they are sibling tasks. This is accomplished by computing the LCA. If the LCA node is not an ST-node, then they are not sibling tasks, and the dependency edges are ignored. A task dependency only serializes the sibling tasks, which does not imply the serialization of its nested descendants. If the LCA is a ST-node, then we identify the corresponding P-nodes to check the if pair of W-nodes are at the same nesting level; we use the sum of the st_val values of EOSPG nodes on the path from W2 to the LCA.

The pair of W-nodes execute in series if this sum equals to 1, and there exists a directed path comprised of E_{dp} edges between the two sibling P-nodes.

Checking Series-Parallel Relations. Using the EOSPG, we can check if two W-nodes logically execute in parallel. Given a pair of W-nodes, W_l and W_r where W_l is to the left of W_r, this procedure is as follows. (1) Compute the least common ancestor (LCA) of the two nodes W_l and W_r. (2) Identify the left child of the LCA on the path to W_l. If this left child is a S-node or a W-node, then the two nodes logically execute in series. (3) If the left child of the LCA on the path to W_l is a P-node, check if the two W-nodes under consideration are serialized by dependency edges. Identify the child of the LCA on the path to W_r. If there is a directed path between these two P-nodes and are at the same nesting level, they execute in series. Otherwise, they logically execute in parallel. (4) If the left child of the LCA on the path to W_l is a ST-node, check if the two nodes are serialized by fully nested taskwaits. Determine the count of the st_val values on the path from W_l to the child of the LCA. If this count is greater than 0, then two nodes execute in parallel. Otherwise, they execute in series.

Metadata. OMP-RACER maintains access history metadata with each shared memory address. In the fast mode when the taskwait directives are properly nested and the program does not use locks, then OMP-RACER maintains three W-nodes corresponding to the previous write and two previous reads (R_1 and R_2) per-memory location similar to prior work [22,30]. The invariant maintained by OMP-RACER is that if any future memory access is involved in a data race with prior n reads to the same memory location $R_{1..n}$, then it will also have a data race with R_1 or R_2. This invariant is maintained by choosing (R_1, R_2) such that, $L = LCA(R_1, R_2)$, is closer to the root node than $L' = LCA(R_1, R_K)$ or $L'' = LCA(R_2, R_K)$ for any $R_K \in R_{1..n}$.

In the precise mode, OMP-RACER stores a number of W-nodes per shared memory location that increases proportionally to the size of the lockset and the number of active ST-nodes in the program. When the EOSPG has ST-nodes, maintaining only two read accesses for the entire program to detect the first data race is no longer sufficient. Consider two parallel reads, (R_1, R_2) that occur in tasks that are at an outer nesting level of the program and a parallel read that occurs in a task at an inner nesting level, R_3. Maintaining the earlier invariant results in keeping (R_1, R_2) in the access history. Leading to potentially missing data races that involve R_3. For example, this could happen if the outer nesting level is synchronized with a taskwait that does not synchronize the inner nesting level, as depicted in Fig. 1(a) (lines 14–23). Hence, OMP-RACER maintains two additional reads and one write for each active ST-node in the program. To detect data races in the presence of locks, OMP-RACER tracks the set of locks held before an access (*i.e.*, lockset [8]) and maintains up to two W-nodes for prior parallel reads (R_1, R_2) and up to two W-nodes for prior parallel writes (W_1, W_2) for each lockset per memory location [22,30].

Metadata Updates and Checks on Each Access. On every memory access, the metadata for that memory location is retrieved, checked for races, and is updated. In the precise mode, the metadata is a list of access history entries. Each entry is uniquely identified by the lockset and a node of the EOSPG (*i.e.*, either root node or a ST-node). Each entry consists of a lockset, a node of the OSPG (*i.e.*, a root or an ST-node), two reads, and two write operations. On a memory access with a lockset (l_c) in a W-node W_c, the metadata is checked as follows. OMP-RACER iterates over the list of access histories to retrieve a 6-tuple (lockset, node, R_1, R_2, W_1, W_2). For every entry, if the intersection of the lockset of the access history and l_c is non-empty, OMP-RACER checks if the current node W_c and previous reads/writes in the access history are conflicting and can logically execute in parallel. If so, it reports an apparent race. Subsequently, the metadata is updated as follows. Starting from W_c, traverse the EOSPG to the root node and identify all ST-nodes on the path to the root node. For every ST-node encountered and the root node, OMP-RACER creates or retrieves a new entry from the list of access history entries that corresponds to the current lockset. This entry contains four W-nodes. If the LCA of W_c and one of the existing nodes is closer to the root than the existing LCA of the nodes, then W_c is added to the access history. Otherwise, information about W_c is already subsumed by the existing information in the access history.

In the fast mode, OMP-RACER runs the program once to construct the EOSPG and to identify whether the program uses locks and uses taskwaits in a properly nested manner. During the construction of the EOSPG, when an ST-node completes execution, if the *st_val* of the all ST-nodes is -1, then the program contains properly nested taskwait directives. In the subsequent race detection execution, the access history per-memory location contains two reads and a write operation. A current access is an apparent data race if it is conflicting with the prior access in the access history and can happen in parallel.

Scaling to Long Running Applications. Our approach can scale to long running applications because it is not necessary to maintain the entire EOSPG in memory. The EOSPG and the access history metadata can be cleared at the end of the parallel directive. Further, any EOSPG node can be deallocated even before the end of the parallel directive when it does not have any reference in the access history metadata space.

4   Experimental Evaluation

Prototype. OMP-RACER prototype supports C/C++ OpenMP programs. It uses LLVM-10's OpenMP runtime and the OMPT interface to construct the EOSPG. It also includes an LLVM pass to instrument memory accesses. OMP-RACER constructs a program's EOSPG and performs data race detection on-the-fly during execution. OMP-RACER has two modes: a precise and a fast mode. The precise mode detects data races even when the program uses locks and imposes no restriction on how taskwaits are used in the program, which can have significant overheads. In the fast mode, OMP-RACER first checks if the program has fully nested taskwaits. If so, it uses a constant amount of metadata per memory location in the subsequent execution for race detection.

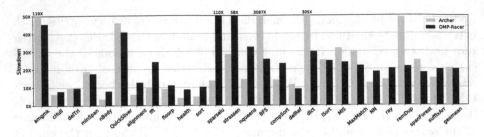

Fig. 3. small Performance slowdown of OMP-RACER and Archer with various PBBS, BOTS, and Coral application suites.

It is significantly faster. We report all evaluation results with the fast mode. OMP-RACER prototype is publicly available [5].

Benchmarks. We evaluate the detection abilities of OMP-RACER with DataRaceBench1.2.0 [14]. OMP-RACER does not support the target directive and SIMD parallelization, yet. Out of 116 programs, 106 do not contain these directives. To measure performance overheads, we use a suite of 26 OpenMP applications from Coral, BOTS, and PBBS benchmarks suites. We performed all experiments on a Ubuntu 16.04 machine with a 16-core Xeon 6130 processor running at 2.1 GHz and with 32 GB of memory. We use the latest version of Archer [2] with LLVM-10, which is the state-of-the-art for OpenMP programs, to compare the detection abilities and overheads with OMP-RACER.

Detection Ability. We compare OMP-RACER and Archer's effectiveness in detecting races using DataRaceBench. OMP-RACER detects data races in all the 106 programs from a single execution and does not produce any false positives (*i.e.*, 100% detection rate). As we detect apparent races, OMP-RACER detects races that do not manifest in a particular schedule. Archer did not detect many of the races in a single execution. When we ran Archer with multiple threads and multiple times, it detected 95% of the races. We observed that Archer misses races in some programs (*e.g.*, DRB013) when executed with a low number of threads. Archer does not precisely capture the semantics of task synchronization and task dependency, which results in false negatives. In summary, OMP-RACER is more effective in detecting races compared to Archer.

Performance Overheads. Figure 3 reports the performance overhead of OMP-RACER and Archer with our performance applications. The runtime overhead of OMP-RACER in its fast mode, on average, is 20×. The overhead of Archer is 21×. When the program performs significant recursive decomposition (*e.g.*, with Strassen and SparseLU), OMP-RACER has higher runtime overhead compared to Archer. The height of the EOSPG is proportional to the nesting level of the program. An increase in height can increase the cost of performing LCA queries, which results in higher overheads.

We also measured the impact of increasing the number of threads and the costs of EOSPG creation. The overhead of OMP-RACER decreases with the increase in the number of threads with scalable applications as the instrumentation code is executed in parallel. The average cost of constructing the EOSPG is 1.12× on average compared to the baseline program without any instrumentation. Hence, performing an initial execution to check if the taskwaits are properly nested in the fast mode is inexpensive compared to the cost of overall race detection.

5   Related Work

Race detection has been widely studied for parallel programs. These include both approaches that rely on static analysis [3,7,26] and dynamic analysis [9–12,15,18,21–25,30]. Static analysis tools can detect races for all inputs. However, they report false positives due to conservative analyses. Among dynamic analysis tools, Eraser [23] uses locksets to identify data races. Subsequent approaches have used happens-before relation with vector clocks [13] to detect races [10,24]. ThreadSanitizer [24] makes numerous trade-offs to scale vector-clocks to large applications.

Our work is inspired by prior approaches that use logical series-parallel relations for fork-join programs, which include labeling [11,15,18] and construction of series-parallel graphs [1,9,21,22,25,28–30]. OMP-RACER proposes a novel series-parallel graph (*i.e.*, EOSPG) to accurately capture series-parallel relations induced by the directives according to the OpenMP specification.

Among OpenMP tools for dynamic race detection, ROMP [11] and Archer [2] are closely related. ROMP [11] expands upon offset-span labeling to support OpenMP directives, including tasking and task synchronization. Asymptotically, the operations in the EOSPG are comparable to ROMP's offset-span labeling since the length of labels and the depth of the EOSPG grow proportional to the nesting level of the program. However, the public prototype of ROMP is not mature to run with large applications. Archer [2] builds upon ThreadSanitizer by extending it to support OpenMP semantics. As Archer is a per-schedule detector, it is necessary to run an application with Archer multiple times and with multiple thread counts to detect races. Compared to Archer, OMP-RACER is able to detect more races that not only occur in the observed schedule but also in other possible schedules for a given input from a single execution.

6   Conclusion

This paper makes a case for detecting apparent races in OpenMP programs using logical series-parallel relations. The Enhanced OpenMP Series-Parallel Graph precisely models logical series-parallel relations for a significant portion of the OpenMP specification, which makes it useful for building numerous performance analysis and debugging tools. It supports both work-sharing and tasking directives. The ability to detect races not only in the observed schedule but also in other possible schedules for a given input with OMP-RACER can alleviate the need for repeated executions and interleaving exploration. Our preliminary results with OMP-RACER are promising and we plan to support more features from the OpenMP specification in the future.

Acknowledgments. We thank the reviewers for their feedback. This paper is based on work supported in part by NSF CAREER Award CCF–1453086, NSF Award CCF-1908798, and NSF Award CCF-1917897.

References

1. Agrawal, K., Devietti, J., Fineman, J.T., Lee, I.T.A., Utterback, R., Xu, C.: Race detection and reachability in nearly series-parallel dags. In: Proceedings of the Twenty-Ninth Annual ACM-SIAM Symposium on Discrete Algorithms, p. 156–171. SODA 2018 (2018)
2. Atzeni, S., et al.: Archer: effectively spotting data races in large OpenMP applications. In: 2016 IEEE International Parallel and Distributed Processing Symposium (IPDPS), pp. 53–62. IPDPS 2016 (2016)
3. Basupalli, V., et al.: ompVerify: polyhedral analysis for the OpenMP programmer. In: Chapman, B.M., Gropp, W.D., Kumaran, K., Müller, M.S. (eds.) IWOMP 2011. LNCS, vol. 6665, pp. 37–53. Springer, Heidelberg (2011). https://doi.org/10.1007/978-3-642-21487-5_4
4. Boushehrinejadmoradi, N., Yoga, A., Nagarakatte, S.: A parallelism profiler with what-if analyses for OpenMP programs. In: Proceedings of the International Conference for High Performance Computing, Networking, Storage, and Analysis, pp. 16:1–16:14. SC 2018 (2018)
5. Boushehrinejadmoradi, N., Yoga, A., Nagarakatte, S.: Omp-racer data race detector (2020). https://github.com/rutgers-apl/omprace
6. Burckhardt, S., Kothari, P., Musuvathi, M., Nagarakatte, S.: A randomized scheduler with probabilistic guarantees of finding bugs. In: Proceedings of the 15th International Conference on Architectural Support for Programming Languages and Operating Systems, pp. 167–178. ASPLOS (2010)
7. Chatarasi, P., Shirako, J., Kong, M., Sarkar, V.: An extended polyhedral model for SPMD programs and its use in static data race detection. In: Ding, C., Criswell, J., Wu, P. (eds.) LCPC 2016. LNCS, vol. 10136, pp. 106–120. Springer, Cham (2017). https://doi.org/10.1007/978-3-319-52709-3_10
8. Cheng, G.I., Feng, M., Leiserson, C.E., Randall, K.H., Stark, A.F.: Detecting data races in cilk programs that use locks. In: Proceedings of the 10th ACM Symposium on Parallel Algorithms and Architectures, pp. 298–309. SPAA (1998)
9. Feng, M., Leiserson, C.E.: Efficient detection of determinacy races in cilk programs. In: Proceedings of the 9th ACM Symposium on Parallel Algorithms and Architectures, pp. 1–11. SPAA (1997)
10. Flanagan, C., Freund, S.N.: Fasttrack: efficient and precise dynamic race detection. In: Proceedings of the 30th ACM SIGPLAN Conference on Programming Language Design and Implementation, pp. 121–133 (2009)
11. Gu, Y., Mellor-Crummey, J.: Dynamic data race detection for OpenMP programs. In: Proceedings of the International Conference for High Performance Computing, Networking, Storage, and Analysis, pp. 61:1–61:12. SC 2018 (2018)
12. Jannesari, A., Bao, K., Pankratius, V., Tichy, W.: Helgrind+: an efficient dynamic race detector. In: 2009 IEEE International Symposium on Parallel Distributed Processing, pp. 1–13 (2009)

13. Lamport, L.: Time, clocks, and the ordering of events in a distributed system. Commun. ACM, pp. 558–565 (1978)
14. Liao, C., Lin, P.H., Asplund, J., Schordan, M., Karlin, I.: Dataracebench: a benchmark suite for systematic evaluation of data race detection tools. In: Proceedings of the International Conference for High Performance Computing, Networking, Storage and Analysis, pp. 11:1–11:14. SC 2017 (2017)
15. Mellor-Crummey, J.: On-the-fly detection of data races for programs with nested fork-join parallelism. In: Proceedings of the 1991 ACM/IEEE Conference on Supercomputing, pp. 24–33. Supercomputing (1991)
16. Nagarakatte, S., Burckhardt, S., Martin, M.M., Musuvathi, M.: Multicore acceleration of priority-based schedulers for concurrency bug detection. In: Proceedings of the 33rd ACM SIGPLAN Conference on Programming Language Design and Implementation, pp. 543–554. PLDI (2012)
17. Netzer, R.H.B., Miller, B.P.: What are race conditions?: Some issues and formalizations. ACM Lett. Program. Lang. Syst. pp. 74–88 (1992)
18. Nudler, I., Rudolph, L.: Tools for the efficient development of efficient parallel programs. In: Proceedings of the 1st Israeli conference on computer system engineering (1988)
19. OpenMP Architecture Review Board: Openmp 5.0 complete specification, November 2017. https://www.openmp.org/wp-content/uploads/OpenMP-API-Specification-5.0.pdf
20. Pozniansky, E., Schuster, A.: Efficient on-the-fly data race detection in multithreaded c++ programs. In: Proceedings of the Ninth ACM SIGPLAN Symposium on Principles and Practice of Parallel Programming, pp. 179–190. PPoPP (2003)
21. Raman, R., Zhao, J., Sarkar, V., Vechev, M., Yahav, E.: Efficient data race detection for Async-finish parallelism. In: Proceedings of the 1st International Conference on Runtime Verification, pp. 368–383. RV (2010)
22. Raman, R., Zhao, J., Sarkar, V., Vechev, M., Yahav, E.: Scalable and precise dynamic datarace detection for structured parallelism. In: Proceedings of the 33rd ACM SIGPLAN Conference on Programming Language Design and Implementation, pp. 531–542. PLDI (2012)
23. Savage, S., Burrows, M., Nelson, G., Sobalvarro, P., Anderson, T.: Eraser: a dynamic data race detector for multi-threaded programs. In: Proceedings of the 16th ACM Symposium on Operating Systems Principles, pp. 27–37. SOSP (1997)
24. Serebryany, K., Iskhodzhanov, T.: Threadsanitizer: Data race detection in practice. In: Proceedings of the Workshop on Binary Instrumentation and Applications, pp. 62–71. WBIA (2009)
25. Utterback, R., Agrawal, K., Fineman, J.T., Lee, I.T.A.: Provably good and practically efficient parallel race detection for fork-join programs. In: Proceedings of the 28th ACM Symposium on Parallelism in Algorithms and Architectures. SPAA 2016 (2016)
26. Ye, F., Schordan, M., Liao, C., Lin, P.H., Karlin, I., Sarkar, V.: Using polyhedral analysis to verify OpenMP applications are data race free. In: 2018 IEEE/ACM 2nd International Workshop on Software Correctness for HPC Applications (Correctness), pp. 42–50 (2018)
27. Yoga, A., Nagarakatte, S.: Atomicity violation checker for task parallel programs. In: Proceedings of the 2016 International Symposium on Code Generation and Optimization, pp. 239–249. CGO (2016)
28. Yoga, A., Nagarakatte, S.: A fast causal profiler for task parallel programs. In: Proceedings of the 2017 11th Joint Meeting on Foundations of Software Engineering, pp. 15–26. ESEC/FSE 2017 (2017)

29. Yoga, A., Nagarakatte, S.: Parallelism-centric what-if and differential analyses. In: Proceedings of the 40th ACM SIGPLAN Conference on Programming Language Design and Implementation, p. 485–501. PLDI 2019 (2019)
30. Yoga, A., Nagarakatte, S., Gupta, A.: Parallel data race detection for task parallel programs with locks. In: Proceedings of the 2016 24th ACM SIGSOFT International Symposium on Foundations of Software Engineering, pp. 833–845. FSE (2016)

AfterOMPT: An OMPT-Based Tool for Fine-Grained Tracing of Tasks and Loops

Igor Wodiany[1]([⊠]), Andi Drebes[2], Richard Neill[1], and Antoniu Pop[1]

[1] Department of Computer Science, The University of Manchester, Manchester, UK
{igor.wodiany,richard.neill,antoniu.pop}@manchester.ac.uk
[2] Inria and École Normale Supérieure, Paris, France
andi.drebes@inria.fr

Abstract. We present AfterOMPT, a new trace-based tool for analyzing the execution of OpenMP applications using the OMPT interface to capture accurate information on loop partitioning, distribution of iteration spaces across workers, task scheduling, and synchronization events. In contrast to previous works that rely on specific, instrumented runtime libraries, our tool is able to collect information from any runtime implementing the OMPT interface. In order to visualize the information from the collected traces, we have extended the Aftermath performance analysis tool with appropriate renderers for OMPT events. We also propose an extension of the OMPT interface for the collection of more detailed information on scheduled OpenMP loops. Experimental results show a tracing overhead of under 5% for the majority of studied benchmarks, increasing more significantly for those with highly fine-grained workloads.

Keywords: OpenMP · OMPT · Performance analysis · Tracing

1 Introduction

There are many factors that impact the performance of OpenMP [15] programs which may result in an inefficient utilization of the executing system, such as a limited amount of parallelism exposed by the application itself, interactions with the runtime system, locality of memory accesses, and sub-optimal use of explicit parallel constructs. Such performance bottlenecks are difficult or even impossible to detect using static analysis and thus require tracing of dynamic events and post-mortem analysis. In order to precisely identify the source of performance issues, it is further necessary to be able to attribute such events to specific instances of parallel constructs and to the OpenMP workers.

This work was supported by the grant EuroEXA H2020-754337. Antoniu Pop is funded by the RAEng University Research Fellowship. Igor Wodiany is supported by the Department of Computer Science Kilburn Scholarship and the University of Manchester Presidents Award.

© Springer Nature Switzerland AG 2020
K. Milfeld et al. (Eds.): IWOMP 2020, LNCS 12295, pp. 165–180, 2020.
https://doi.org/10.1007/978-3-030-58144-2_11

Aftermath [5] is a trace-based tool for performance analysis of parallel programs and has been extended for OpenMP programs in prior work [4]. The tool provides developers with accurate traces for loop and task execution and is able to capture synchronization events. Its ability to trace and visualize the distribution of loop iteration spaces across workers allows programmers to track the origin of work imbalance caused by inappropriate chunk sizes, unsuited loop scheduling strategies or a mismatch between data placement and work distribution on machines with non-uniform memory access. However, Aftermath relies on an instrumented version of the OpenMP runtime to generate traces. This comes with a cost for setting up the execution environment and bears the risk of an outdated runtime library, as the instrumentation likely requires updating with every new version of the runtime.

With the inclusion of the OpenMP Tools (OMPT) interface [7] in the OpenMP standard, it became possible to develop portable profiling tools that can be attached to any compatible runtime. The OMPT interface defines a set of callbacks that are invoked by the runtime for specific events throughout the execution. Tools can use this interface to capture information associated to these events and to write this information to a trace file. In order to eliminate the need for a specific, instrumented runtime for Aftermath tracing and thus provide a portable tool for OpenMP performance analysis, we have developed *AfterOMPT*, a library that implements the OMPT callbacks to collect dynamic events and write them to a trace file using the Aftermath tracing API. We have further extended Aftermath with OMPT-specific rendering functions that enables the visualization of such traces.

While the set of callback functions specified by the OMPT interface covers a basic set of OpenMP events, it is unsuited to capture dynamic information about the distribution of loop iteration spaces across workers: the OMPT work callback (`ompt_callback_work`) can only capture an aggregated execution of all iterations assigned to a specific worker, without any loop-specific details. The more recent dispatch callback (`ompt_callback_dispatch`) is an attempt to mitigate this issue, but potentially incurs a high overhead as is called at the beginning of each loop iteration.

Langdal et al. [10] identified similar issues with OMPT in the context of Grain Graphs, a chronogram-based tool for visualizing OpenMP applications in the form of hierarchical graphs. Although their work provides specific implementation details and detailed overhead analysis, it lacks concrete examples on how information obtained from those callbacks can be used to optimize the performance of applications.

In this work, we provide concrete case studies to make a case for extending the tracing interface. Specifically, this paper makes the following contributions:

- We present *AfterOMPT*, a new Aftermath-based tool implementing the OMPT interface for portable and detailed performance analysis.
- We present two case studies to support an extension of the tracing interface with loop-related OMPT callbacks.

– We provide experimental results showing that the instrumentation overhead is below 5% for the majority of our studied benchmarks.

The rest of the paper is organized as follows. Section 2 introduces Aftermath and sets the terminology that AfterOMPT borrows from Aftermath. In Sect. 3, we discuss the implementation of our profiling tool and use of existing and proposed OMPT callbacks. We then present two case studies in Sect. 4 illustrating how AfterOMPT can be used to collect and inspect OpenMP traces. Tracing overhead is analyzed in Sect. 5. Related work, concluding remarks and directions for future work are presented in Sect. 6 and Sect. 7.

```
for(int k = 0; k < 2; k++) {
  #pragma omp parallel
  {
    #pragma omp for schedule(static, 2) // First loop
    for(int i = 0; i < 32; i++) { foo(); }
    foo();
    #pragma omp for schedule(dynamic, 2) // Second loop
    for(int i = 0; i < 32; i++) { foo(); }
    foo();
  }
}
```

Listing 1.1. Example with two loop constructs

2   Aftermath

Aftermath[1] is a free and open source tracing and visualization tool for performance analysis. The project has transitioned from a tool supporting a specific set of parallel frameworks [4,5] to a framework-independent toolbox for building specialized tools for performance analysis. Multiple models can co-exist at the same time and are supported by an extensible, template-based type system for the definition of the trace format, trace processing and the in-memory data model. The four main components of the tool are:

– A *type system*, offering a declarative description of on-disk and in-memory tracing data structures and their relationships, from which functions for creation, management, storage and processing of trace data are generated.
– A *tracing library* that defines set of functions to create, write and read Aftermath trace files used for the instrumentation of runtimes and for building data capturing tools.
– A *rendering library* providing a set of functions to visualize trace data in graphical user interfaces or tools for bulk rendering.
– A *configurable graphical user interface (GUI)*, used for trace inspection and performance analysis by the end user. The GUI is defined by a customizable interface file that assembles different graphical widgets and a data-flow graph for trace processing, both of which can be modified on-the-fly during execution. Multiple GUI definitions and data-flow graphs can co-exist, providing specialized tools for specific frameworks or specific types of analyses.

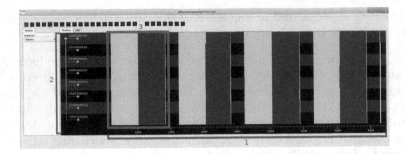

Fig. 1. Visualization of iteration periods from Listing 1.1 in the Aftermath GUI: (1) Timeline; (2) Worker Threads/Cores; (3) Execution of a single loop instance (Color figure online)

It is worth noting that the timeline in the Aftermath GUI is hierarchical and nodes (e.g., worker threads, cores) can be collapsed, so that statistics shown on a lane are the accumulated values. As an example, consider three CPUs, with the first one spending 40% of the time in function f, the second one spending 30% of the time also in f, and the third one spending 60% of the time in function g for the same time interval associated to a pixel. The non-collapsed view would show three lanes: two with the pixel in the colour associated to f and another one with the pixel in the colour associated to g. When collapsed, the dominant function becomes f and the pixel would be rendered with the colour of f. Using this approach a large number of cores can be divided into smaller groups and the user can expand/collapse nodes to adjust granularity of the displayed data.

Previous support for OpenMP in Aftermath relied on a specific, instrumented OpenMP runtime to generate the trace files. In this paper, we present an OMPT-based tool that can be used to trace any runtime supporting OMPT. To this end, we extended the Aftermath type system to represent OMPT events and implemented callbacks with calls to Aftermath's tracing library. Since our OMPT-based tool is intended to entirely replace the legacy OpenMP support in Aftermath based on the instrumented runtime library, we refer to both our tool and Aftermath simply as Aftermath for the remainder of the paper.

Throughout the paper, we use the terms *loop instance, iteration set, iteration period, task instance* and *task period* introduced in [4] and defined as follows. We say that a parallel loop is *instantiated* when control flow reaches the instructions associated with a static definition of a parallel loop in the source code and its iteration space is distributed across workers according to its scheduling strategy. Each such encounter is defined as a *loop instance*. Similarly, we speak of a *task instance* when referring to the dynamic instructions executed by a task statically defined in the source code. The iteration space of a loop instance is split into *iteration sets*, each of which is assigned to exactly one worker. The iteration set corresponds directly to the loop chunk. The execution of an iteration set consists

---

[1] https://www.aftermath-tracing.com/.

of one or more *iteration periods*, defined as contiguous intervals of execution of dynamic instructions of the loop associated to the loop instance. For flat loops each *iteration set* consists of exactly one *iteration period*, that corresponds to the execution of a specific loop chunk. For loops containing loops' nests the *iteration set* is split between multiple *iteration periods*, representing execution on the given nest level. Similarly, execution of a *task instance* is split into one or more *task periods*.

To illustrate these concepts, consider the Listing 1.1 where two loops are each executed twice. This results in four *loop instances* in total—two for the first loop and two for the second loop. Each instance is split into 16 distinct *iteration sets* with each set containing two iterations invoking the function foo(). Since the loop body does not contain nested parallel regions and does not spawn tasks, each *iteration set* will be associated with one continuous *iteration period*.

A visualization of the execution is given in Fig. 1. The four distinct loop instances are presented as beige and green regions executing on a total of 8 worker threads, each identified by their thread ID on the left side of the figure. Those coloured regions represent alternating *iteration periods*, in this case corresponding directly to loop chunks (*iteration sets*). The thin yellow line after each loop instance represents the loop's implicit barrier, while the rightmost yellow line represents the barrier at the end of the parallel section.

3   Tracing Using OMPT Callbacks

In this section, we present the implementation of AfterOMPT based on the OMPT interface. We discuss which OMPT callbacks are used and what information is captured through the interface. We also present workarounds for cases in which additional information is required, but is not provided by OMPT.

3.1   Labeling Instances

The ability to associate dynamic events with specific instances of OpenMP constructs and to combine the data captured from multiple callbacks requires a mechanism to reliably identify particular instances. AfterOMPT implements a labeling mechanism for this, associating each instance of a supported OpenMP construct with a unique label that identifies it. Each label is composed of two components: the thread ID of the worker instantiating the construct and the value of the worker's monotonically increasing sequence counter. Since the thread ID and the counter value are unique and private to a worker, workers can generate labels independently and concurrently without any need for synchronization. Once an instance has been created, its label is stored within an associated task data structure. Any related event that is captured through an OMPT callback function afterwards has access to the task's data and can thus store the serialized event data along with a reference to the instance in the trace file.

3.2   Tracing Loops

The current OMPT interface provides very limited information on loops via the
ompt_callback_work callback function. Neither the loop bounds nor the partitioning of the iteration space into chunks are exposed, which prevents tracing
the distribution of the iteration space using OMPT alone. While this issue was
identified in [10], and we base our work on that proposal, we propose further
changes to the callback signatures necessary to generate more complete traces.

```
typedef void (*ompt_callback_loop_begin_t) (
    ompt_data_t* parallel_data , ompt_data_t* task_data ,
    int flags ,
    int64_t lower_bound , int64_t upper_bound ,
    int64_t increment ,
    int num_workers ,
    void* codeptr_ra );

typedef void (*ompt_callback_loop_end_t) (
    ompt_data_t* parallel_data , ompt_data_t* task_data );
```

Listing 1.2. Callback signatures for loop tracing

For loop tracing, AfterOMPT uses two callbacks with signatures as defined
in Listing 1.2, one invoked at the beginning of the loop and one invoked at the
end of the loop. In line with the work of Langdal et al. those callbacks replace the
current work callback whenever a loop is executed. However, rather than using
the endpoint argument as the authors proposed, we use two distinct callbacks
with names ending with *_begin and *_end. This simplifies the implementation
by reducing the data required to be traced at the end of the loop, as work-sharing
information is instead provided implicitly through the bounds, the increment, the
number of workers and the flags indicating the schedule. This defines a compact
representation from which the distribution across workers can be recovered by
the callback function, compared to an explicit set of chunks and distribution.

The codeptr_ra argument refers to an address of an instruction of the loop
body and can be used as a unique identifier for the source code location of the
instantiated loop construct.

In order to trace loop chunks, we propose an additional callback function
with the signature shown on Listing 1.3. In contrast to the signature proposed by
Langdal et al., we do not include a parameter marking the final chunk, since this
chunk is always followed by the loop end event and can thus be recovered post-
mortem. We also omit the loop chunk creation time parameter, as we currently
do not use it, however we aim to investigate potential use cases in the future.

Using this information, iteration sets can be recovered by mapping each
occurrence of the loop chunk event into the new iteration set. To recover iteration periods we consider four cases: (1) The new period starts when the chunk
gets dispatched and finishes when the next chunk gets dispatched; (2) The new
period starts when the chunk gets dispatched and finishes when the loop ends;
(3) The new period starts when the loop at the nest level n ends and finishes
when the loop at the nest level $n-1$ ends; (4) The new period spans the execution time between the end of one loop and the start of the another loop at the
same nest level, e.g., for{ for{} /* Period (4) */ for{} }.

```
typedef void (*ompt_callback_loop_chunk_t) (
  ompt_data_t* parallel_data, ompt_data_t* task_data, int64_t
  lower_bound, int64_t upper_bound);
```

Listing 1.3. Callback signature for the tracing of loop chunks

3.3 Tracing Tasks

While the detailed tracing of loops requires an extension of the OMPT interface, tasks can be traced using the existing callbacks `ompt_callback_task_create` and `ompt_callback_task_schedule`. These events are captured as discrete events in the trace, with the task instance beginning and end events associated post-mortem, to reduce the run-time overhead. All instances of a given task construct can also be retrieved post-mortem by iterating over all task-creation events for the task's address, as provided by the `codeptr_ra` parameter within the task creation callback function. Tasks periods can be easily determined from scheduling points captured through the task schedule callback.

3.4 Tracing Synchronization Events and Regions

Barriers, taskwait states, critical sections, master, single and parallel regions can be accurately traced by recording the information provided by the associated OMPT callbacks and by matching the invocations of the callbacks indicating the beginning of an event with the invocation of the callback indicating its end.

4 Case Studies

We now present two case studies using the tracing interface and show that AfterOMPT provides performance insights which are unavailable to developers without the proposed extensions of the OMPT interface for loop-related callbacks. In the first study, we show how an uneven distribution of work across the iteration space of a parallel loop can be inspected with our tool. The second study shows how AfterOMPT can be used to assess the effect of pipeline parallelism on the performance of an application.

4.1 Experimental Setup

We implemented new callbacks for dynamic loops and loop chunks, and static loops in the LLVM 9.0 OpenMP runtime[2]. This work is based on the implementation of the Aftermath instrumented OpenMP runtime [4].

For static loops, each worker can determine its part of the iteration space independently from the others, solely based on its thread ID, the chunk size, the loop bounds and the loop increment. Since this does not require invocation of

---

[2] Artifacts and sources available at: https://github.com/IgWod/ompt-loops-tracing.

the OpenMP runtime, static loops cannot be traced from within the runtime and require static instrumentation by the compiler. We have therefore used the modified version of Clang proposed in [10], where the compiler inserts the required callback directly into static loops within the application.

An alternative approach, not used in this paper, that does not require the modified compiler involves setting the compile-time schedule to *runtime* (with `schedule(runtime)`) and then runtime schedule to *static* with a specific chunk size. This forces the application to distribute the work using the runtime functions—the same ones that are used by the dynamic scheduling.

For trace recording, processing and visualization, we have extended the latest branch of Aftermath with new types representing OMPT events. To leverage the existing OpenMP support in Aftermath and to avoid code duplication with our new OMPT-based implementation, we have also added an extra processing step in the Aftermath GUI that converts OMPT events into native Aftermath OpenMP types. Finally, AfterOMPT comes as a standalone library that implements required callbacks with Aftermath tracing API to capture required data.

All experiments have been carried out on a platform with two Intel Xeon Silver 4116 processors, each of which has 12 cores (24 threads) running at 2.10 GHz. The 112 GiB memory is split across 2 NUMA nodes. The system was running Ubuntu 18.04.4 LTS with kernel version 4.15 and Hyper-Threading enabled.

For the case studies, we have limited the execution to 12 threads (6 physical cores) on a single socket in order to improve readability of the visualized traces and to exclude any NUMA-specific effects. The subsequent overhead analysis has been carried out using all 48 threads (24 physical cores).

4.2   Identifying Slow Iterations in Unbalanced Loops

The first case study demonstrates how AfterOMPT's loop tracing capabilities can be used to inspect a non-uniform distribution of work across the iteration space of a parallel loop. We illustrate this on the integer bucket sort (*IS*) from the NAS Parallel Benchmark suite [3], version 3.4 with a custom data set.

The bucket sort algorithm sorts a sequence of N integer values by distributing these values into K buckets, sorting each bucket individually and concatenating the sorted buckets into a final, sorted sequence. The distribution into the buckets is based on the maximum value $V_{\max}$ of the input sequence: a value v is put into the bucket with the index $\left\lfloor (K-1) \cdot \frac{v}{V_{\max}} \right\rfloor$. The amount of work required to sort a bucket depends on the number of values in the bucket, which in turn depends on the distribution of values of the input sequence.

The *IS* benchmark consists of three parallel loops in the main processing function. Two loops distribute keys into buckets and one loop sorts one bucket per iteration. In the following analysis, we show how AfterOMPT can be used to determine an uneven data distribution in the *IS* benchmark and to determine for which iterations the amount of work differs substantially.

To this end, we have first changed the range of generated integer values to $(1048576, 1064960)^3$. Since this range does not start at zero and does not end at the hard-coded V_{max} of the implementation, the buckets for low and high values remain empty, while the buckets for "medium" values each receive a significant part of the keys.

With the default parameters, the execution takes 2.58 s for the input class C and the input range adjusted to the interval above. A visualization of the loop iteration intervals from the execution trace is given in Fig. 2a. We have outlined

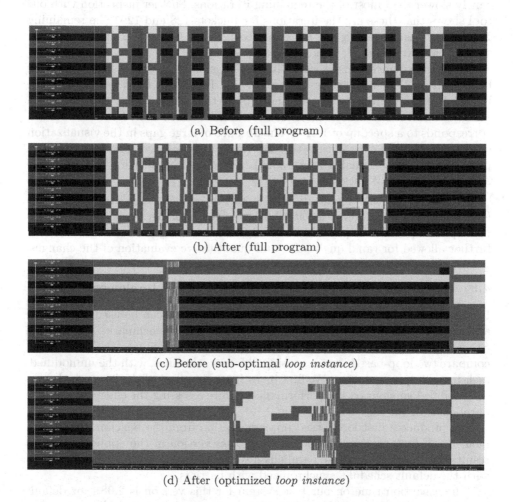

(a) Before (full program)

(b) After (full program)

(c) Before (sub-optimal *loop instance*)

(d) After (optimized *loop instance*)

Fig. 2. *Iteration periods* before and after changing the number of buckets in *IS* with bucket sorting loop instances marked in red (Color figure online)

---

[3] Partial verification of this changed dataset fails as it relies on pre-defined ranks for keys at specific locations, but full verification passes, so that we can assume that the algorithm executes correctly.

in red the first three loop instances which are sorting the buckets. For each such instance, only two workers have significant iteration periods, indicated by the green and beige intervals within the red rectangles. For the remaining workers the visualization shows the alternating black and gray of the background, which means that these workers are mostly idle. Outside of the red rectangles, the loops process keys with a constant amount of work per iteration.

The zoomed visualization on the first imbalanced loop instance given in Fig. 2c confirms the imbalance and clearly shows that two iterations are significantly slower than most of the remaining iterations. Further inspection with our tool shows that these are the iterations for buckets 128 and 129. The remaining 1022 iterations processing the buckets 0 to 127 and 130 to 1023 are very short, since these sort empty, or almost empty buckets.

The performance can be easily improved, simply by increasing number of buckets from 1024 to 4096 as this effectively distributes the work for a single bucket from the initial settings to more buckets and thus more workers. With a higher number of buckets, the execution time can be reduced to 2.11 s, which corresponds to a speedup of 1.22×. The absence of large gaps in the visualization of the trace in Fig. 2b confirms the improved work balance. The long iteration periods from the original settings could be reduced by a factor of 3 with the increased number of buckets.

In conclusion, the visualization of *iteration periods* helped identifying the loop imbalance and allowed for attribution of the intervals to specific iterations of a specific parallel loop in the code. Repeated tracing with changed settings further allowed for rapid qualitative and quantitative evaluation of the changes.

4.3   Comparison of Loop-Based and Task-Based Implementations

In the second case study, we illustrate how AfterOMPT can be used to evaluate and compare different implementations of the same benchmark. We use the *SparseLU* benchmark of the Barcelona OpenMP Task Suite (BOTS) [6] and compare two loop-based versions, using different schedules, with the unmodified, task-based implementation. We first investigate the effect of the loop schedule in our modified versions on the performance, before assessing the effects of pipeline parallelism of the task-based version.

We produce a first loop-based implementation from the benchmark by commenting all task pragmas in the *for-omp-tasks* version of the application. This results in a benchmark whose parallelism is exposed solely through parallel loops with the default schedule, synchronized with barriers.

The execution time on our test system for this version is 2.08 s for default input size ($S1 = 50 \times 50$, $S2 = 100 \times 100$). The visualization of the execution trace provided in Fig. 3a reveals significant work imbalance. Inspection of the iteration periods shows that the bulk of the execution time is spent in the code region executing the bmod function.

To mitigate the work imbalance, we have changed the default static schedule (no schedule specified) to a dynamic schedule with a chunk size of a single

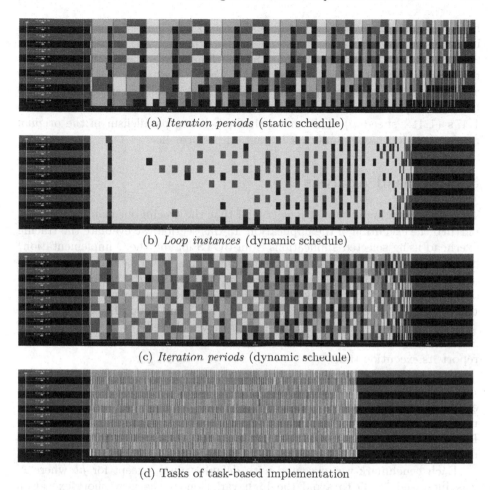

(a) *Iteration periods* (static schedule)

(b) *Loop instances* (dynamic schedule)

(c) *Iteration periods* (dynamic schedule)

(d) Tasks of task-based implementation

Fig. 3. Traces for loop-based and task-based implementations of *SparseLU* (Color figure online)

iteration (`schedule(dynamic, 1)`). This decreases the execution time to 1.81 s, corresponding to a speedup of 1.15×. Although this represents a significant improvement, the gaps in the visualization of the execution trace after modification shown in Fig. 3b indicate that there is still potential for improvement. To identify the cause of the remaining imbalance, we investigate the *iteration periods* shown in Fig. 3c. The duration of the periods is relatively uniform, indicating that the distribution of work is even across iterations. However, the barriers between loop instances have a significant impact as they cause a significant fraction of the workers to idle if the number of available iterations is not a multiple of the number of workers. Furthermore, the available parallelism decreases over time, leaving more and more workers idle towards the end of the execution. Since the number of iterations is data-dependent, any statically configured chunk size or loop schedule will lead to imbalance for certain problem instances.

The original, unmodified version the benchmark uses the parallel loops only to spawn parallel tasks. The barrier only synchronizes task creation, but not completion, thus exposing pipeline parallelism which allows all the workers to be kept busy for most of the time (Fig. 3d) and reduces the execution time to 1.47 s (1.41× speedup). This shows that pipelining parallelism in the original implementation has a significant impact on performance.

5   Overhead Analysis

To obtain meaningful traces, it is crucial that the tracing mechanism does not perturb the execution of the application. In this section, we evaluate the tracing overhead using selected applications from BOTS [6] and the C implementation[4] of the NPB 2.3 [3] benchmarks. In our experiments, we trace threads, task creation, task execution, the beginning and end of loops, and the beginning and end of the execution of loop chunks via the callback functions thread_{begin,end}, task_create, task_schedule, loop_{begin,end} and loop_chunk.

To stress the tracing mechanism for loops, we selected *CG*, *EP*, *LU*, *MG* and *SP*, excluding *BT* and *FT* as they failed to build[5], as well as *IS* as it does not report its execution time.

For task-based benchmarks, we selected *alignment*, *fft*, *fib*, *floorplan*, *health*, *nqueens*, *sort*, *sparselu* and *strassen* from BOTS. The *uts* benchmark was excluded as we encountered frequent application segmentation faults when running it on the experimental machine. We used the *omp-tasks-tied* version for the BOTS benchmarks, except *alignment* and *sparselu* for which this version was unavailable, and the *for-omp-tasks-tied* version was used instead.

Each benchmark was executed with default values, except for *fib* where N was increased to 35 to avoid the high variation of the very short execution for the default value. The largest available input files were used for the BOTS benchmarks that require input files, except for *uts*, where *small.input* was used. The NPB benchmarks operated on the C input class, with the exception of *SP* which was given the A input class in order to avoid excessive experiment duration. Each benchmark was executed 50 times, where for the same reason *SP* was instead executed 20 times.

Figure 4 shows the relative mean increase of the execution time when tracing is enabled, compared to the execution without tracing. The reported values were obtained by dividing the execution time of each run of the benchmark with the tool attached, by the mean execution time of 50 runs of the baseline (no tool attached). The value above each bar indicates the mean relative change and error bars indicate the standard deviation.

---

[4] https://github.com/benchmark-subsetting/NPB3.0-omp-C.
[5] The compilation error is caused by the potential bug in the unofficial C port of the benchmarks and does not appear in the official Fortran implementation.

The relative overhead for three of the loop-based NPB benchmarks, *CG*, *EP* and *MG*, was very low, with all three recording an increased execution time of under 3%. A higher relative overhead was recorded for the remaining two NPB benchmarks *LU* and *SP*: averaging 6.0% ± 4.0% for *LU*, and 35.2% ± 5.7% for *SP*. The increased relative overhead for these benchmarks is due to their large number of very fine-grained loop-chunks (especially for *SP*), resulting in a large number of invoked callbacks relative to the overall work done.

The overhead results varied across the task-based BOTS benchmarks, with values under 3% for *alignment*, *fft*, *sort*, *sparselu* and *strassen*, and values up to 24% for the remaining benchmarks. As with the NPB results, the more significant relative overheads resulting for these benchmarks is due to their large number of short-lived task instances, thereby invoking significantly more tracing-callbacks relative to their workload. Analysis of the *floorplan* benchmark shows that the average duration of an AfterOMPT tracing-callback was around 200 cycles, compared to the average total duration of a task instance (including the tracing overhead) of around 2400 cycles. All of these measures include the overhead of the OMPT interface itself. For more details, including cases with empty callbacks and OMPT disabled, we refer to [10].

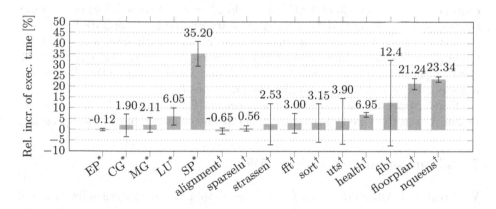

Fig. 4. Profiling overhead for the selected benchmarks from NPB 2.3 and BOTS (*loop-based, †task-based)

In conclusion, the average overhead of AfterOMPT was found to be under 5% for the majority of the benchmarks (9 out of 15), increasing to under 7% for two further benchmarks, and greater than 10% for only four of the most fine-grained benchmarks. As the AfterOMPT tracing infrastructure incurs an overhead of only around 200 cycles per callback invocation, its generally low impact on the overall program execution time—while dependent on the workload granularity—means that it is highly suitable for tracing and analysing many target OpenMP applications. Moreover the overhead does not depend on number of threads, as synchronization within the tool is kept to minimum—one critical section per thread initialization —meaning each thread is traced independently.

6   Related Work

Langdal et al. [10] were first to investigate extending the OMPT interface with loop related callbacks. While they discuss implementation details and overhead analysis for the potential new loop callbacks, they do not provide detailed use cases to support proposed changes. We complement their work by presenting detailed scenarios, showing how information associated with those callbacks are useful in practice.

Their work was done in the context of Grain Graphs [12]. Compared to Aftermath, Grain Graphs is a chronogram-based application that represents OpenMP programs in a hierarchical graph form. It allows detection of limited parallelism, load imbalance and synchronization issues, however the visual representation does not attribute profiled constructs to specific cores. Aftermath presents traces on per worker timelines allowing to detect additional anomalies, such as problems related to NUMA.

Score-P [8,11] is a profiling and event tracing infrastructure for HPC applications. It allows tracing of OpenMP applications with either by POMP2 [9] instrumentation using source-to-source compiler or with OMPT interface. It generates traces in the formats (OTF2 or CUBE4) compatible with several analysis tools such as Vampir [13] or TAU [13] toolkit. However Score-P does not support tracing of loops using OMPT with granularity offered by AfterOMPT.

Extrae [1], a tool for capturing execution trace with interfaces for MPI, OpenMP, pthreads, OmpSS and CUDA. Captured data can be later viewed with Paraver [16] visualization tool. Although data collection using OMPT interface is supported, it has the same limitations as Score-P.

Finally Intel VTune [2] does not support OMPT and uses VTune instrumentation API in the OpenMP runtime in addition to the sampling based profiling.

7   Conclusion and Future Work

We presented AfterOMPT, an OMPT-based tool for tracing, visualization and performance analysis of OpenMP applications that is portable across OpenMP runtimes. We motivated an extension of the OMPT interface that allows for fine-grained analysis of parallel loops. We showed that our tool allows for a detailed analysis of both loop-based and task-based applications. With a tracing overhead as little as 200 cycles per OMPT callback function, the resulting increase in the execution time is less than 5% for many benchmarks and only leads to a significant increase for very fine-grained work sharing. In the future we plan to extend our tool further with the visualization of tasks trees and also integrate OpenMP hardware event profiling proposed before in [14].

References

1. Extrae. https://tools.bsc.es/extrae. Accessed 25 May 2020
2. Intel VTune Profiler. https://software.intel.com/content/www/us/en/develop/tools/vtune-profiler.html. Accessed 25 May 2020
3. Bailey, D.H.: The NAS parallel benchmarks. Int. J. Supercomput. Appl. **5**(3), 63–73 (1991)
4. Drebes, A., Bréjon, J.-B., Pop, A., Heydemann, K., Cohen, A.: Language-centric performance analysis of OpenMP programs with aftermath. In: Maruyama, N., de Supinski, B.R., Wahib, M. (eds.) IWOMP 2016. LNCS, vol. 9903, pp. 237–250. Springer, Cham (2016). https://doi.org/10.1007/978-3-319-45550-1_17
5. Drebes, A., Pop, A., Heydemann, K., Cohen, A.: Interactive visualization of cross-layer performance anomalies in dynamic task-parallel applications and systems. In: 2016 IEEE International Symposium on Performance Analysis of Systems and Software (ISPASS), pp. 274–283. IEEE (2016)
6. Duran, A., Teruel, X., Ferrer, R., Martorell, X., Ayguade, E.: Barcelona OpenMP tasks suite: a set of benchmarks targeting the exploitation of task parallelism in OpenMP. In: 2009 International Conference on Parallel Processing, pp. 124–131. IEEE (2009)
7. Eichenberger, A.E., et al.: OMPT: an OpenMP tools application programming interface for performance analysis. In: Rendell, A.P., Chapman, B.M., Müller, M.S. (eds.) IWOMP 2013. LNCS, vol. 8122, pp. 171–185. Springer, Heidelberg (2013). https://doi.org/10.1007/978-3-642-40698-0_13
8. Feld, C., Convent, S., Hermanns, M.-A., Protze, J., Geimer, M., Mohr, B.: Score-P and OMPT: navigating the perils of callback-driven parallel runtime introspection. In: Fan, X., de Supinski, B.R., Sinnen, O., Giacaman, N. (eds.) IWOMP 2019. LNCS, vol. 11718, pp. 21–35. Springer, Cham (2019). https://doi.org/10.1007/978-3-030-28596-8_2
9. Itzkowitz, M., Mazurov, O., Copty, N., Lin, Y., Lin, Y.: An OpenMP runtime API for profiling. OpenMP ARB White Paper (2007). http://www.compunity.org/futures/omp-api.html
10. Langdal, P.V., Jahre, M., Muddukrishna, A.: Extending OMPT to support grain graphs. In: de Supinski, B.R., Olivier, S.L., Terboven, C., Chapman, B.M., Müller, M.S. (eds.) IWOMP 2017. LNCS, vol. 10468, pp. 141–155. Springer, Cham (2017). https://doi.org/10.1007/978-3-319-65578-9_10
11. Lorenz, D., Dietrich, R., Tschüter, R., Wolf, F.: A comparison between OPARI2 and the OpenMP tools interface in the context of Score-P. In: DeRose, L., de Supinski, B.R., Olivier, S.L., Chapman, B.M., Müller, M.S. (eds.) IWOMP 2014. LNCS, vol. 8766, pp. 161–172. Springer, Cham (2014). https://doi.org/10.1007/978-3-319-11454-5_12
12. Muddukrishna, A., Jonsson, P.A., Podobas, A., Brorsson, M.: Grain graphs: OpenMP performance analysis made easy. In: Proceedings of the 21st ACM SIGPLAN Symposium on Principles and Practice of Parallel Programming, pp. 1–13. ACM (2016)
13. Müller, M.S., et al.: Developing scalable applications with Vampir. VampirServer and VampirTrace. In: PARCO, vol. 15, pp. 637–644 (2007)
14. Neill, R., Drebes, A., Pop, A.: Accurate and complete hardware profiling for OpenMP. In: de Supinski, B.R., Olivier, S.L., Terboven, C., Chapman, B.M., Müller, M.S. (eds.) IWOMP 2017. LNCS, vol. 10468, pp. 266–280. Springer, Cham (2017). https://doi.org/10.1007/978-3-319-65578-9_18

15. OpenMP Architecture Review Board: OpenMP Application Programming Interface (Version 5.0) (2018)
16. Pillet, V., Labarta, J., Cortes, T., Girona, S.: Paraver: a tool to visualize and analyze parallel code. In: Proceedings of WoTUG-18: Transputer and OCCAM Developments, vol. 44, pp. 17–31 (1995)

Co-designing OpenMP Features Using OMPT and Simulation Tools

Matthew Baker[1](✉), Oscar Hernandez[1], and Jeffrey Young[2]

[1] Oak Ridge National Laboratory, Oak Ridge, TN, USA
{bakermb,oscar}@ornl.gov
[2] Georgia Institute of Technology, Atlanta, Georgia
jyoung9@gatech.edu

Abstract. The design of future HPC systems is trending towards more heterogeneity with different types of accelerators, special purpose instructions sets, system-on-chip designs, complex memory hierarchies, and multiple memory coherence domains. This complexity exacerbates the design challenges and testing of programming models which aim to provide a high-level interface while also producing high performance programs. In this paper we describe how to use full-system architectural simulation of OpenMP applications to provide a platform for experimenting with OpenMP extensions on future architecture designs. Furthermore, we put forward the concept of integrating the OpenMP Tools API (OMPT) in conjunction with other tools (performance, emulators, etc.) to help speed up the use of architectural simulators with new OpenMP implementations. In this work, we evaluate an initial implementation of this simulation testbed design using gem5, an open source full system simulation, with the EPCC OpenMP micro-benchmarks that are instrumented with OMPT. We show that OMPT can be a powerful tool for the codesign of future systems models and programming model features.

Keywords: OpenMP · HW/SW codesign · Full system simulation · OpenMP Tools API

1 Introduction

As we design new OpenMP specifications (e.g. OpenMP 5.1, 6.0, etc), we need to evaluate how proposed OpenMP extensions will work on future systems. For example, we are seeing a trend in next-generation systems towards more diverse types of accelerators, special purpose instructions on multicores for HPC and AI, and novel memories and interconnects that may have "extreme NUMA" properties. New features of the OpenMP specification, especially those related to performance portability, need to keep up with these new system trends. For example, the new loop constructs, variants, metadirectives, and affinity and thread management need to be extended to have the ability to program devices of different types and to schedule tasks on heterogeneous devices. As these possibilities arise,

© Springer Nature Switzerland AG 2020
K. Milfeld et al. (Eds.): IWOMP 2020, LNCS 12295, pp. 181–194, 2020.
https://doi.org/10.1007/978-3-030-58144-2_12

we need to evaluate if the latest features in OpenMP 5.0 (e.g. memory management API, data affinity, etc) can manage this diverse set of architectural designs on the node efficiently.

We belive that full-system (FS) simulation (with gem5) is key to studying programming models like OpenMP and for improving the co-design process for performance and power studies on future architectures. Full-system simulation incorporates a Linux kernel and full support for code generated by OpenMP compilers and associated OpenMP runtimes. This full software stack allows programs to run on top of simulated architecture models at cycle-level detail while capturing all the dynamic behavior on the target platform. However, this process is expensive in terms of exploration time; we need to improve the simulation process by designing new techniques for speeding up these typically slow simulations. Our key contributions that differentiate our work from previous studies is a focus on using new features with the OpenMP Tools API to find regions of interest and sample these regions with detailed simulations and to demonstrate how the OpenMP tool chain can be connected to a simulation infrastructure.

Full-system simulators can help to provide a "full-stack" approach to model architectures, programming models and runtimes, and applications in a way that promotes co-design of hardware and software with the major limitation of extreme slowdowns of 10,000x or more versus native execution. Our approach is different from other existing simulators like SST which improve simulation speed by abstracting away hardware features that may impact language design (e.g., tasking for OpenMP runtimes, orchestration of multiple devices, etc.). Instead, simulators like gem5 rely on a complicated process for checkpointing *regions of interest* and then resetting simulation state with more detailed CPU models. In the context of OpenMP programs, our definition of *regions of interest* refers to parallel execution regions, typically bounded by OpenMP constructs and delineated by implicit or explicit thread synchronization points (e.g., an `omp barrier` call) to guarantee consistent state across all threads.

As a first step to addressing this slowdown, we have been investigating techniques to define small enough regions of interest and to use sampling to evaluate critical parts of these regions. The OpenMP tools API provides a runtime-based method to execute arbitrary code as "callbacks" when specific OpenMP pragmas are encountered. As an example, we have just recently used the `ompt_callback_parallel_begin_t` API call from a custom Clang/LLVM build to trigger a checkpoint for gem5 simulations whenever a parallel region, such as `#pragma omp parallel for` is encountered. This arbitrary, runtime-driven code instrumentation allows us to scope detailed simulations explicitly to relevant OpenMP pragma regions we are interested in. We are currently investigating how this technique can be used to skip the first few loop iterations of the parallel region (to allow for cache warm-ups for detailed simulations) and to sample relevant loop or thread iterations for a highly multi-threaded application. With miniapps like toypush from the XGC code, we are also looking at how to potentially use the OpenMP Tools API to sample every other iteration of a parallel region and how to switch between detailed simulations with a few threads and less-detailed simulations with many threads.

In this paper, we describe the available tools and techniques available to evaluate Arm SVE architectures with gem5 and Arm's Instruction Emulator, and we detail how OMPT can be used to speed up architectural simulators. Results show that it is possible to simulate OpenMP constructs using OMPT, and that OMPT tools can enable more efficient testing of different architectural features such as vector length. We also note how users can drive the selection of large, parallel regions of interest for simulation and emulation by annotating their OpenMP code with pragmas and running with OMPT libraries.

Figure 1 shows the general overview of how the OpenMP Tools API, Arm's Instruction Emulator (ArmIE), and simulators can be integrated to select and simulate regions of interest on simulated future architectures. In this workflow, the OMPT API is used to dynamically link with both an OpenMP executable and multiple generated tools for working with the gem5 simulator by either placing simulation checkpoints or by switching between simulation modes. It should be noted that these tool libraries can be swapped out at *runtime*, allowing for more flexible analysis of application codes. We plan to cover compiler analysis in future work, so we note here that static compiler analysis and related projects like the LLVM-based codelet extraction tool, CERE [4], can be used as an alternate means of selecting ROI.

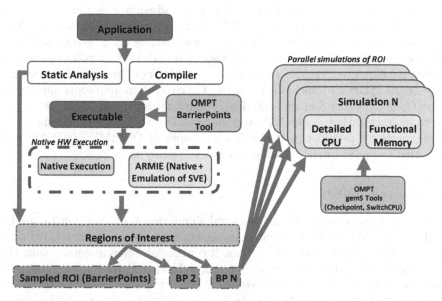

Fig. 1. Using OMPT and ArmIE to select regions of interest

2   Background and Related Work

Based on Fig. 1 we go into more detail about the OpenMP Tools, emulation, and simulation components for selecting and analyzing regions of interest with an application. In our discussion, we define **simulation** to include detailed architectural models with some sort of timing model (e.g., cycle- or event-driven) while **emulation** focuses on modeling software and kernel correctness without providing detailed timing information.

2.1   OpenMP Tools Interface

OpenMP compilers lowers directives to transform code that invokes custom runtime libraries to manage the OpenMP environment, and to create threads or initialize devices, assign work to them, and/or offload computations to devices. The lack of a defacto OpenMP runtime layer has hindered the development of third-party tools for OpenMP application development because it requires either modifying the application source code or writing binary specific instrumentation for implementations. In OpenMP 5.0 [9], the OpenMP tools interface (OMPT) [5] was adopted as an interface specification for profiling and tracing tools that support the OpenMP programming model. It is designed to permit tools to gather or query information about a program's OpenMP execution by tracking OpenMP states or triggering event callbacks. OMPT is implemented inside the OpenMP runtime library. The main advantage is that it leverages the OpenMP runtime to track OpenMP states and events. By doing so, OMPT does not require modification of the application's source code because all instrumentation is independent of the user's code. Instead, OMPT relies on callback handles implemented via the runtime. It also does not interfere with compiler analysis and optimizations while providing the context to map tools information to the OpenMP execution context. The design and implementation allows for a tool to interact with an OpenMP program via *LD_PRELOAD* or through static linking. Section 4 provides more details on the specific OpenMP 5.0/OMPT callbacks that are used in the creation of OpenMP analysis tools.

2.2   Gem5 Simulator

Gem5 [1] is a cycle-accurate architectural simulation tool that can be used to simulate detailed models of system components like caches, memory, GPU accelerators, networks and processor designs. It consists of different components that can simulate an instruction set architecture (ISA) and its implementation in hardware, and these components can be used to run applications in a traditional Linux environment via a QEMU-like front-end. Of importance to our recent investigations for OpenMP codesign, gem5 also provides SVE models for forthcoming Arm SVE hardware [8,11] and accelerator support via a ROCm GCN 3 Advanced Processing Unit (APU) model [6].

For our evaluations, we are focused on using recently integrated Arm SVE support within gem5 which provides an SVE-based processor model that supports vector lengths of 128 to 2048 bits. In addition to providing detailed memory models (not evaluated in this work), gem5 also provides two types of widely used CPU models: 1) AtomicSimpleCPU provides a very simple in-order CPU model that implements atomic accesses to memory and that provides approximate time for caching of data accesses to memory. The Atomic CPU model is suitable for "fast-forward" execution and providing cache warm-up capabilities for more detailed simulation models. 2) O3CPU implements a detailed out-of-order CPU that is very similar to today's 64-bit processors with five pipeline stages and accurate timing via the execution of simulated instructions in the execution phase of the pipeline. The O3CPU model can be used to execute SVE 64-bit instructions based on the AArch64 instruction set with fine-grained detail at the cost of long simulation times.

2.3   Arm Instruction Emulator

ArmIE is an emulator tool that is built around the DynamoRio [2] dynamic binary instrumentation tool, and it supports multiple clients for memory tracing, instruction tracing and counting, and basic block and code introspection. Since ArmIE does not provide a detailed timing model, it cannot be used to provide a detailed performance vision of codes. However, it can be used to count and investigate the SVE instructions that would be executed on SVE-enabled hardware and can be used as an extra validation platform for comparing against SVE statistics and instruction counts from gem5. Specifically, ArmIE can be used for the following tasks: 1) predicting cache performance with SVE code 2) vector utilization for SVE/non-SVE code, and 3) analyzing SVE gather/scatter versus contiguous accesses. We use ArmIE in the experimental evaluation to help validate statistics (specifically the number of SVE instructions and total instructions) from our gem5 results, and we note some incongruities between the two tools. Section 2.3 shows the execution of one of the EPCC kernels, SIMDBench, with ArmIE emulating a 1024-bit wide SVE hardware support.

```
#Run ArmIE with vector width of 1024 bits and count normal and SVE instructions
$ armie -msve-vector-bits=1024 -i libinscount_emulated.so -- simdbench
Client inscount is running

#SVE instructions are reported and counted
SVE: 0x00000000004017c4 0x04a0e3e9
...
#Application executes to completion
...


SIMD time     = 435.020924 microseconds +/- 9.786090
SIMD overhead = 435.020924 microseconds +/- 9.786090
#ArmIE reports the total number of instructions and SVE instructions
18577013 instructions executed of which 48719 were emulated instructions
```

Listing 1: ArmIE Execution for SIMDBench

2.4 Future Work - Measuring ROI in OpenMP Applications with BarrierPoint

A BarrierPoint [3] (BP) is a sampled region of interest that is typically delineated by a synchronization point in a multi-threaded program. Based on SimPoints sampling and clustering techniques developed to speed up architectural simulation by finding and simulating regions of interest [7,10], the BarrierPoint technique extends this capability by creating candidate ROI based on parallel regions within OpenMP programs that have similar runtime characteristics. More recent work by Arm Research [12] extended this functionality to also support constructs with explicit synchronization of threads such as #pragma omp barrier and implicit synchronization such as at the end of a *parallel for* region or after #pragma omp single. These added capabilities led to a further 4.3x speedup in simulation times when compared to the initial BarrierPoint technique.

```
#pragma omp parallel private(j)  ──▶   Implicit Task
{                                       Creation Point
    for (j = 0; j < innerreps; j++) {
    #pragma omp for simd simdlen(8)
    for (i = 0; i < itersperthr * nthreads; i++)
    {
        C[i] = A[i]*B[i];
    }
    }                    ──▶   Implicit Synchronization (IS)
}
```

Fig. 2. Mapping BarrierPoints to OMPT callbacks

Importantly, BarrierPoint can be used with OpenMP semantics and barriers to specify ROI and to help guide user-driven codesign and architectural exploration. Figure 2 shows an example of how BarrierPoints can be used to delineate ROI and speed up analysis. The parallel region creates an implicit task for the parallel region body where all the threads will execute, and the threads all synchronize again at the end of this region. This is the outer BarrierPoint. In between, assuming no variable dependencies, each thread can execute the outer loop redundantly in parallel. We use the combined directive #pragma omp for simd to define an inner BarrierPoint because #pragma omp simd (without a for) does not imply any synchronization and does not have OMPT callback handles for measuring the inner loop as a region of interest. #pragma omp barrier (not shown in Fig. 2) also can be used to create an explicit synchronization point for a BarrierPoint. More recent work by Arm Research has shown that independent loop iterations may also be sampled (i.e., simulate every N iterations) and then used to reconstruct representative behavior for the entire parallel loop region.

3 Sample OMP Tools for Codesign

Here we briefly discuss some of the types of OpenMP tools we envision for codesign and demonstrate how one or two of them can be used for emulation and simulation studies. Specifically, we envision 3 different types of tools and demonstrate the usage of one of them, the gem5 tool, to show how it can be used to improve the usage of architectural simulation. We specifically envision that OMPT can be used for triggering added events and monitoring in several ways: 1) Simulation with gem5 can be improved by using OMPT to create checkpoints for simulation of smaller regions of interest and for switching CPU models at runtime. 2) For emulation with ArmIE, OMPT can be used to scope tracing and analysis to a specific region using ArmIE's ROI functionality and the insertion of START and STOP tracing macros at the beginning and end of OpenMP regions. Listing 2 shows an example of how OMPT can be used to trigger region-of-interest tracing with ArmIE. 3) While it is not detailed here, we have also tested using OMPT callbacks with native execution for either starting or stopping PAPI counter-based profiling.

```
//Use a global flag to specify when a region starts or stops
int roiEnabled = 0;
//Define tracing assembly instructions
#define __START_TRACE() { asm volatile (".inst 0x2520e020"); }
#define __STOP_TRACE() { asm volatile (".inst 0x2520e040"); }

static void
on_ompt_callback_parallel_begin(
 ompt_data_t *parallel_data,
 ompt_data_t *encountering_task_data,
 int flags,
 const void *codeptr_ra) {

    if(roiEnabled == 0) {
        __START_TRACE();
        roiEnabled = 1;
    }
    else { // end the ROI
        __STOP_TRACE();
        roiEnabled = 0;
    }
}
```

Listing 2: OMPT ArmIE Example

Since detailed O3 gem5 simulations are too slow to run an entire benchmark, a benchmark is normally run using a sampling technique like SimPoint or BarrierPoint. Alternatively, a benchmark can be run in a low-detail mode, such as "SimpleAtomic" mode, checkpointed near the region of interest, and then restarted in a higher fidelity mode. Integrating this technique with OMPT requires that a benchmark be run twice - once in a low detail mode to identify all regions of interest and generate checkpoints using our custom OMPT gem5 tool and once to simulate from the generated checkpoints. After these checkpoints are made, they can be filtered to remove checkpoints that include initialization and cleanup, rather than compute kernels which are of actual interest. Listing 3 shows how we use OMPT to drop checkpoints and switch CPU models for OpenMP-based ROI, specifically for `#pragma omp parallel for` regions.

```
static void
on_ompt_callback_parallel_begin(
  ompt_data_t *parallel_data,
  ompt_data_t *encountering_task_data,
  int flags,
  const void *codeptr_ra)
{
  //Create a gem5 checkpoint to allow for stopping and
  //restarting the simulation
  m5_checkpoint(0,0);

  //This callback could also be used in a separate tool to switch
  //from a less detailed to a more detailed model.
  //switch_cpu
}
```

Listing 3: OMPT gem5 Example

4   Experimental Setup

We focus our experiments on variants of the EPCC benchmark to detail the overheads for running OpenMP code with gem5 and also to demonstrate using OpenMP Tools API to generate checkpoints and run detailed simulations in parallel.

Specifically we run the following benchmarks: 1) Syncbench with the OMP PARALLEL FOR and BARRIER sub-tests. 2) A new variant of Syncbench called "Overhead" that runs each of these two sub-tests without any loop computation - this test just measures the amount of time to run OpenMP parallel regions. 3) SIMDbench - a simplistic OMP PARALLEL FOR implementation that does matrix multiplication on two 16K input matrices. This test was designed as a simple example that can be vectorized using a SIMD OpenMP pragma implemented by the Arm compiler and that can be executed with ArmIE and gem5 using SVE instructions. Listing 4 shows the code for this test. SIMD-Bench is run with 20 outer reptitions and 1024 repetitions, since it can be vectorized using SVE instructions. Overhead and Syncbench are each run with 1 outer and inner repetition to allow for simulation with gem5.

```
//This function is run outerreps number of times
void testsimd() {
    int i, j;
    #pragma omp parallel private(j)
    {
        for (j = 0; j < innerreps; j++) {
        //Vectorize the inner loop explictly with simdlen
        #pragma omp for simd simdlen(8)
        for (i = 0; i < itersperthr * nthreads; i++) {
            C[i] = A[i]*B[i];
        }
        }
    }
}
```

Listing 4: SIMDbench Code Description

All code is compiled with the Arm 20.0 HPC compiler and the -mcpu = generic -march = armv8-a+sve flags to produce SVE-based code for execution with gem5 and ArmIE. ArmIE 20.0 is used for all emulation tests, and gem5's gem5-20 release branch is used for all gem5 testing. Each of the benchmarks is run with 1,2,4, and 8 OpenMP threads and the wall-clock time is measured as well as statistics provided by ArmIE like instruction counts, SVE instruction counts, and opcode (histogram of types of instructions) counts. An Arm TX2 machine is used for native and ArmIE experiments, and the gem5 tests are run in parallel on an x86 cluster at ORNL.

4.1 ArmIE Emulator Setup

ArmIE 20.0 is used to generate timings for basic emulated analysis with two tools: 1) *inscount_emulated* is used to execute SVE instructions and to measure the total time taken for execution and the total number of instructions executed and SVE instructions executed. 2) *opcodes_emulated* is used to generate the number of opcodes generated as well as the total number of SVE opcodes and instructions that are generated as a percentage of the overall instructions. Each of these tools takes in a vector length as demonstrated in Sect. 2.3.

4.2   Simulator Setup

The gem5 simulator itself consists of a C++ code that handles the main execution of the simulator. To configure the simulated machine a python script is used. This script will set up the specific hardware configuration of a simulated machine such as the number of CPUs, what size and kind of caches are utilized, and how the cores and caches are connected and how these connect to memory.

For these experiments a simulated Arm machine is created with 8 cores, SVE registers 512 bits wide, and 4GB of DDR memory. A virtual disk image provided by Arm with gem5, which is loaded with Linaro Linux, is added to this machine and edited to add the EPCC benchmarks.

As mentioned in Sect. 3, two separate OMPT tools are used to drop checkpoints and to switch to more detailed CPU models (Atomic to O3) for simulation of regions of interest with gem5. Multiple gem5 simulation runs can be started simultaneously to do a detailed simulation of each of the benchmarks and specific configurations (i.e., different tests or runs with different vector lengths or numbers of OpenMP threads) and OMPT is used at the end of the region of interest to dump statistics files that can then be collated and parsed.

The gem5 stats.txt file provides in-depth and detailed statistics of hardware behavior in the region of interest. The statistics used in this paper focus on host_seconds or wall clock time, but we also measure statistics like sim_seconds and an aggregation of vec_insts across all cores in the simulator. These statistics can be used to calculate how efficiently codes operate with Arm SVE and what kind of overheads exist when running OpenMP pragma regions in simulation.

5   Results

Figures 3, 4, and 5 all show the normalized simulation/emulation time for the three EPCC benchmarks, Overhead, Syncbench, and SIMDBench. For each of these, the wall-clock time is normalized to the native execution of the benchmark on the ThunderX2 (TX2) platform. For example, Syncbench's Parallel For test with 2 OpenMP threads runs in 29 ms on the native TX2 machine, 764 ms with ArmIE's instruction count emulation tool, and 1210 ms with a detailed O3 simulation model on gem5. We show this normalization to demonstrate the slowdown from emulation and simulation with different test parameters.

Figure 3 and Fig. 4 have similar slowdowns for both the Parallel For and Barrier tests, but we can identify several interesting trends. As the number of threads is increased, the overhead of the gem5 simulations dramatically increases due to the serial nature of multi-threaded CPU simulation within gem5. Interestingly, with 1 OpenMP thread gem5 is quite fast, beating out the ArmIE emulation tool while also providing more detailed statistics.

These plots also demonstrate that the overhead for ArmIE is relatively consistent as the number of threads is increased to 8 threads, with a slowdown of around 31–35 for ArmIE, as compared to the slowdown of 2267x to 3459x with gem5's O3 model.

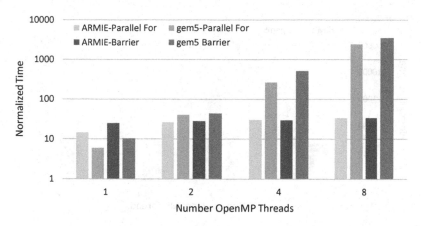

Fig. 3. Normalized simulation time - overhead benchmark

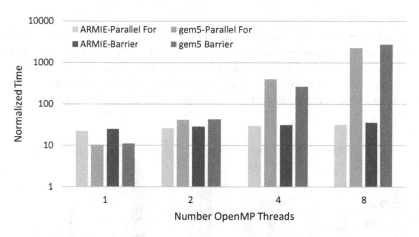

Fig. 4. Normalized simulation time - syncbench benchmark

SIMDBench includes much more computation and less synchronization and idle delay time than either of the other benchmarks, so simulation time also suffers more drastically as thread count increases. Slowdowns vary from 22.96x to 67.29x for ArmIE's instruction count tool while gem5 takes anywhere from 816.94x longer to ˜193,000x longer to run SIMDBench with 1024 inner iterations and 20 outer iterations. In practical terms, an 8 thread gem5 simulation takes 893.49 ms of measured wallclock time while ArmIE takes 0.31 ms and native execution takes 4.64 ns.

We also use ArmIE's opcode tool to evaluate how the percentage of instruction opcodes varies with vector length and number of OpenMP threads, shown in Fig. 6. Since we compiled SIMDBench with an explicit `#pragma omp for simd simdlen(8)` pragma, we would expect that 8 quadwords or 512 bits would be the best-performing vector length for a target architecture executing this code.

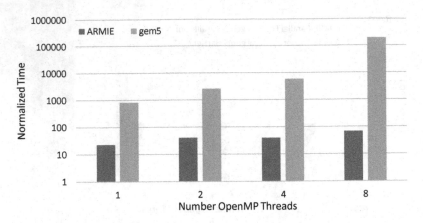

Fig. 5. Normalized simulation time - SIMDBench benchmark

This figure does indeed show that as vector length increases to 512 bits, the percentage of SVE instructions increases to a maximum of 46% with 1024 bit vector lanes and 1 OpenMP thread. The vector length does not strictly correlate with improved performance. However, having a higher percentage of vector instructions likely leads to better performance on SVE-enabled architectures.

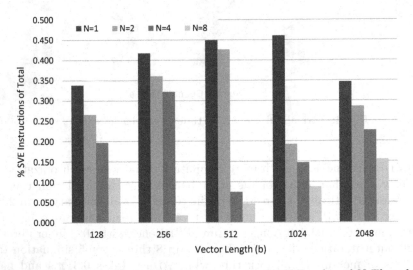

Fig. 6. SVE opcode % of total instructions with SIMDBench and N Threads

6   Conclusion

In this paper we have demonstrated that it is possible to use the OpenMP tools API to control the execution of the EPCC benchmarks with an instruction emulator and architectural simulator. This was done in an automated fashion that did not require the rebuilding of binaries in a way that would prevent the application from running on hardware that supports an ArmV8+SVE instruction set. Evaluations of simple microbenchmarks show that gem5 simulation overheads increase dramatically due to the serial nature of the simulation engine, with overheads of up to 193,000x versus a native, non-SVE benchmark execution. For this reason, we need to further improve techniques like those proposed in this work for using both emulation and simulation in a productive manner to limit simulation and analysis time with increasingly complicated architectural models.

Using tools like gem5, OMPT, and in the future, BarrierPoint-based tools, we plan to build better methodologies for extracting regions of interest from OpenMP codes and for simulating them in a detailed and accurate fashion with architectural simulators.

Acknowledgments. This research was funded by the Laboratory Directed Research and Development (LDRD) Program of the Oak Ridge National Laboratory managed by UT-Battelle, LLC, for the U.S. Department of Energy under Contract DE-AC05-00OR22725. This research also used resources of the Oak Ridge Leadership Computing Facility at the Oak Ridge National Laboratory, which is supported by the Office of Science of the U.S. Department of Energy under Contract No. DE-AC05-00OR22725.

References

1. Binkert, N., et al.: The gem5 simulator. SIGARCH Comput. Archit. News **39**(2), 1–7 (2011). https://doi.org/10.1145/2024716.2024718
2. Bruening, D., Garnett, T., Amarasinghe, S.: An infrastructure for adaptive dynamic optimization. In: International Symposium on Code Generation and Optimization, CGO 2003, pp. 265–275, March 2003. https://doi.org/10.1109/CGO.2003.1191551
3. Carlson, T.E., Heirman, W., Van Craeynest, K., Eeckhout, L.: Barrierpoint: Sampled simulation of multi-threaded applications. In: 2014 IEEE International Symposium on Performance Analysis of Systems and Software (ISPASS). pp. 2–12 (2014)
4. Castro, P.D.O., Akel, C., Petit, E., Popov, M., Jalby, W.: Cere: LLVM-based codelet extractor and replayer for piecewise benchmarking and optimization. ACM Trans. Archit. Code Optim. **12**(1) (2015). https://doi.org/10.1145/2724717
5. Eichenberger, A.E., Mellor-Crummey, J., Schulz, M., Wong, M., Copty, N., Dietrich, R., Liu, X., Loh, E., Lorenz, D.: OMPT: an OpenMP tools application programming interface for performance analysis. In: Rendell, A.P., Chapman, B.M., Müller, M.S. (eds.) IWOMP 2013. LNCS, vol. 8122, pp. 171–185. Springer, Heidelberg (2013). https://doi.org/10.1007/978-3-642-40698-0_13
6. Gutierrez, A., et al.: Lost in abstraction: pitfalls of analyzing GPUs at the intermediate language level. In: 2018 IEEE International Symposium on High Performance Computer Architecture (HPCA), pp. 608–619, February 2018. https://doi.org/10.1109/HPCA.2018.00058

7. Hamerly, G., Perelman, E., Calder, B.: Comparing multinomial and k-means clustering for SimPoint. In: 2006 IEEE International Symposium on Performance Analysis of Systems and Software, pp. 131–142 (2006)
8. Kodama, Y., Odajima, T., Matsuda, M., Tsuji, M., Lee, J., Sato, M.: Preliminary performance evaluation of application kernels using arm SVE with multiple vector lengths. In: 2017 IEEE International Conference on Cluster Computing (CLUSTER), pp. 677–684, September 2017. https://doi.org/10.1109/CLUSTER.2017.93
9. Pennycook, S.J., Sewall, J.D., Hammond, J.R.: Evaluating the impact of proposed OpenMP 5.0 features on performance, portability and productivity. In: 2018 IEEE/ACM International Workshop on Performance, Portability and Productivity in HPC (P3HPC), pp. 37–46, November 2018. https://doi.org/10.1109/P3HPC.2018.00007
10. Perelman, E., Hamerly, G., Van Biesbrouck, M., Sherwood, T., Calder, B.: Using SimPoint for accurate and efficient simulation. ACM SIGMETRICS Perform. Eval. Rev. **31**(1), 318–319 (2003)
11. Rico, A., Joao, J.A., Adeniyi-Jones, C., Van Hensbergen, E.: Arm HPC ecosystem and the reemergence of vectors: Invited paper. In: Proceedings of the Computing Frontiers Conference, CF 2017, pp. 329–334. ACM, New York (2017). https://doi.org/10.1145/3075564.3095086
12. Tairum Cruz, M., Bischoff, S., Rusitoru, R.: Shifting the barrier: extending the boundaries of the barrierpoint methodology. In: 2018 IEEE International Symposium on Performance Analysis of Systems and Software (ISPASS), pp. 120–122 (2018)

NUMA

sOMP: Simulating OpenMP Task-Based Applications with NUMA Effects

Idriss Daoudi[1,2]([✉]) [iD], Philippe Virouleau[1,2], Thierry Gautier[2],
Samuel Thibault[1], and Olivier Aumage[1]

[1] INRIA, LaBRI, Université de Bordeaux, IPB, CNRS, Bordeaux, France
idriss.daoudi@inria.fr
[2] LIP, ENS-Lyon, UCBL-Lyon 1, Inria, Lyon, France

Abstract. Anticipating the behavior of applications, studying, and designing algorithms are some of the most important purposes for the performance and correction studies about simulations and applications relating to intensive computing. Often studies that evaluate performance on a single-node of a simulation don't consider Non-Uniform Memory Access (NUMA) as having a critical effect. This work focuses on accurately predicting the performance of task-based OpenMP applications from traces collected through the OMPT interface. We first introduce TiKKi, a tool that records a rich high-level representation of the execution trace of a real OpenMP application. With this trace, an accurate prediction of the execution time is modeled from the architecture of the machine and sOMP, a SimGrid-based simulator for task-based applications with data dependencies. These predictions are improved when the model takes into account memory transfers. We show that good precision (10% relative error on average) can be obtained for various grains and on different numbers of cores inside different shared-memory architectures.

Keywords: OpenMP tasks · NUMA architecture · Performance modeling · Simulation

1 Introduction

Simulation tools are of significant interest in the field of application development. They allow, among other things, to understand whether an application has been designed efficiently, and to test limits and sensitivity of hardware characteristics for components such as CPUs and memory buses. They can be an important predictive tool for evaluating existing and non-existing systems in procurements.

OpenMP is probably the most commonly used programming language for shared-memory paradigms in HPC applications. On these architectures, the increasing number of cores leads to the need for a complex memory hierarchy, which implies Non-Uniform Memory Access (NUMA) timings from each core to each memory location. To benefit the most from such a platform, it is thus not enough that several blocks of operations are made to execute in parallel on

© Springer Nature Switzerland AG 2020
K. Milfeld et al. (Eds.): IWOMP 2020, LNCS 12295, pp. 197–211, 2020.
https://doi.org/10.1007/978-3-030-58144-2_13

different cores. It is also essential that these blocks of operations are executed on CPU cores close to the memory node in which the data they access is located. The placement of data, therefore, has a primary effect on the performance of the application. This makes simulating task-based applications on shared memory architectures a challenging endeavor, since these different NUMA-related effects must be captured accurately to perform a reliable simulation.

This work targets OpenMP applications composed of tasks with data dependencies, such as dense linear algebra routines (Cholesky, QR...). Task-based applications are indeed increasingly common, but overheads in runtime systems implementations may limit the applicability of the task model [12]. It is fundamentally important to be able to exhibit the precise performance of an OpenMP task-based application without artifacts from the runtime implementation: in addition to performance profiling [7,11], simulation is a way to achieve this goal. In previous works [24,25], we explored the simulation of task-based scheduling on heterogeneous architectures, which is now used as a reliable tool for scheduling experiments [1]. This work differs in that it targets the complications of task-based OpenMP programs that use architectures with large core counts.

To retrieve the information necessary to replay and predict an application's performance, we developed a tool called TiKKi[1] on top of the OMPT API, that records all profiling events required to construct a task graph. We then created a simulator named sOMP[2], using the SimGrid framework, to address the problem of predicting the performance of a task-based parallel application on shared memory architectures. sOMP finely models the platform to simulate data transfer contentions accurately, and takes data locality into account to predict the execution time from various scenarios of data placements. Although SimGrid is designed to simulate distributed memory architectures, we adapted the possibilities offered by this tool to execute tasks on simulated shared-memory NUMA platforms. To summarize, this paper presents the following contributions:

1. We introduce TiKKi an OMPT-based tracing tool to extract the high-level information necessary for the simulation;
2. We introduce a modeling of a NUMA machine using the SimGrid framework;
3. We develop sOMP, an implementation of the simulator that leverages the S4U API tool from SimGrid;
4. We propose a model to refine the simulations that uses the link parameters of the simulated platform to model the effects of contention and data access;
5. We show a small relative error of the simulation for various architectures (Intel and AMD) while taking into account the locality effects of the data. The simulation itself is found to be much faster than real executions.

2   Related Work

Many simulators have been designed for predicting performance in a variety of contexts, in order to analyze application behavior. Several simulators have been

---

[1] https://gitlab.inria.fr/openmp/tikki/-/wikis/home.
[2] https://gitlab.inria.fr/idaoudi/omps/-/wikis/home.

developed to study the performance of MPI applications on simulated platforms, such as BigSim [29], xSim [10], the trace-driven Dimemas tool [13], or MERP-SYS [6] for performance and energy consumption simulations. Some others are oriented towards cloud simulation like CloudSim [4] or GreenCloud [18].

Other studies are oriented towards the simulation on specific architectures, such as the work by Aversa and al. [2] for hybrid MPI/OpenMP applications on SMP, and task-based applications simulations on multicore processors [15,22, 24,26]. All these studies present approaches with reliable precision, but, as with Simany [16], no particular memory model is implemented.

Many efforts have been made to study the performance of task-based appli-cations, whether with modeling NUMA accesses on large compute nodes [8,14], or with accelerators [25]. Some studies have a similar approach to our work, whether in the technical sense, like using SimGrid's components for the simula-tion of parallel loops with various dynamic loop scheduling techniques [20], or in the modeling sense, such as simNUMA [19] on multicore machines (achieving around 30% precision error on LU algorithm) or HLSMN [23] (without consid-ering task dependencies). But to our knowledge, no currently available simula-tor allows the prediction of task-based OpenMP applications performances on NUMA architectures, while taking into account data locality effects. To build our simulator, it was necessary to develop new tools and models that employ an extraction process of OMPT traces, but also manage task dependencies, data locality, and memory access effects.

3   sOMP: Simulating Task-Based OpenMP Applications

Since our goal is to build a simulator for existing OpenMP task-based applica-tions on multicore NUMA architectures, we will use two tools. First, the TiKKi tool leverages the OMPT API [9] to record events of a running OpenMP appli-cation. Secondly, the generated traces are then processed by the sOMP tool to perform an offline simulation on top of the SimGrid [5] generic engine. For this work, sOMP extends SimGrid with the modeling of NUMA architectures.

To perform the simulations, tasks and their dependencies are re-computed by collecting information contained in the post mortem execution trace generated by TiKKi. We then introduce a communications-based model to take into account NUMA effects, to produce improved simulations.

3.1   TiKKi: Tracing with OMPT

OMPT [9] is the OpenMP API for performance tools integrated in OpenMP since its revision 5.0 [3]. OMPT allows developers to instrument tools with trace-based methodologies.

The libKOMP [28] OpenMP runtime has an embedded trace and monitor-ing tool, based on the work of de Kergommeaux et al. [17]. The tool, called TiKKi, was developed using the initial OMPT API [9] available in an older ver-sion of the LLVM OpenMP runtime with extensions. We have updated it to match the OMPT specification of the current standard [3]. TiKKi captures all events required to construct the program's task graph, and records them to a file. It also enriches the recording with performance information. For instance, task attributes may contain locality information [28], and hardware performance counters may be registered, in addition to time, within specific events (task creation, task termination...). Hence, TiKKi can generate several output forms of execution traces: task graph as a .dot file, Gantt chart as an R script, or a specific file format for the simulations performed by sOMP. In the current OpenMP standard, it is impossible to recover the information about data size: we are doing this explicitly for the moment, but the standard could be improved to expose this information, the implementation is usually easy.

The structure of the execution trace is a sequence of parallel regions, where the events of each task are recorded. When TiKKi processes the trace, it generates a sequence of sOMP input files, one per parallel region. Each of these can then be simulated as a separate task graph.

3.2 Modeling of NUMA Architectures with SimGrid

SimGrid. [5]. The specific objective of SimGrid is to facilitate research in the field of programming and running parallel applications on distributed computing platforms, from a simple network running in a workstation to the computing grids. It provides the basic functionalities for the simulation of heterogeneous distributed applications in distributed environments.

The operating principle is as follows: an *actor*, *i.e.* an independent stream of execution in a distributed application, can perform several *activities*, such as computations or communications, on a *host*, representing some physical resource with computing and networking capabilities. Several *actors* can communicate, and all classical synchronization mechanisms such as barriers, semaphores, mutexes, and conditional variables are provided.

From a platform description point of view, SimGrid provides the building blocks for a detailed description of each element of a distributed system, such as the computing *hosts* mentioned above, *routers*, *links*..., but also the routing on the platform, *i.e.* which path is taken by communications between two hosts. These elements have arguments that allow configuration and tuning of the platform in order to simulate different scenarios.

NUMA Architecture Modeling. While SimGrid is initially designed for simulating applications running on distributed architectures, we divert its use to simulate NUMA platforms.

The approach to model these architectures is as follows. The CPU cores are considered to be computing units interconnected by a network of links. Cores are thus grouped into NUMA nodes and sockets according to the actual architecture topology and these groups are interconnected with links to ensure access to the memory.

The model we consider in this work does not take into account the memory topology exhaustively. The addition of even more architectural components would result in better precision, but also contribute to increasing the complexity of the problem and the simulation time. We had to make a compromise between accuracy and cost of the simulation: we could simulate more architectural elements, and that would be precise and expensive, or simulate very few elements which would be inexpensive but imprecise.

Notably, we do not model the L1/L2 cache, because all data sizes considered in this work exceed L1/L2 cache sizes, and their behavior will thus be caught already well enough when measuring task execution time without contention. Therefore, we model a NUMA architecture using elements sketched in Fig. 1a, and we employ the concepts defined by SimGrid to model these components.

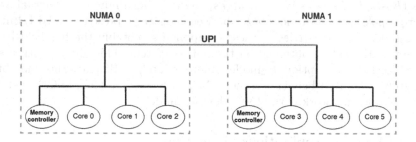

Fig. 1. NUMA machine modeling

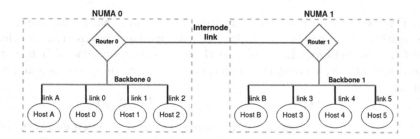

Fig. 2. Model using SimGrid components

Modeling with SimGrid. SimGrid offers the possibility of describing a platform with the XML format. Any platform must contain basic essential elements such as *hosts*, *links*, *routers*, etc. SimGrid requires the explicit declaration of the routes and links between these components in order to simulate communications between *hosts*.

We map the cores of a processor with SimGrid *hosts*. These represent a computing resource on which *actors* can run. From there, as depicted in Fig. 2, we can model a NUMA node by a group of *hosts*, each having a *link* to a *backbone*-type link. The latter makes it possible to model the intra-node contention and connect the group of *hosts* to a *router*, which allows communications with other NUMA nodes. Regarding the memory controller, we chose to model it with a "fake" *host* (memory controller host) that does not perform any computation: this component only receives communications which simulate accesses to the machine's memory. Every *link* and *route* is referenced by an ID and can be tuned with parameters such as latency and bandwidth, allowing them to match the real machine's characteristics. We will discuss the tuning of those parameters in Sect. 5.3.

In the end, sOMP provides SimGrid with an assembly of simulated components (*hosts, links, backbones, routers, routes*) which mimics the actual architecture topology: for instance *routes* between *routers* represent real UPI/Infinity Fabric links. The properties of these components (notably the bandwidth) are then set to the values obtained on the native system. This allows, with a simple architecture description, to model different Intel/AMD platforms and obtain accurately simulated behavior as described in Sect. 5.3. The SimGrid network model used in this work is the LV08 default model.

3.3   Task-Based Applications Simulation

Here we use two components to model a task-based application: first, only the task computational time is modeled, then the memory access costs are taken into account.

Task Execution Simulation. At runtime, we assume that a task mainly executes arithmetic instructions interleaved with memory instructions (typically load/store instructions). Let's assume that the execution time of a task t_i is decomposed into (ie, we neglect interactions between memory accesses and computations):

$$Time(t_i) = T_{Computations}(t_i) + T_{Memory}(t_i) \qquad (1)$$

where $T_{Computations}(t_i)$ represents the time spent in the sequential execution of the task t_i with data local to the core executing the task. The term $T_{Memory}(t_i)$ represents the penalty due to a remote memory access on a NUMA architecture, which depends on the data location on the machine as well as the core that initiates the access. We consider that $T_{Computations}(t_i)$ is the execution time that we collect from a sequential execution, which thus does not suffer from NUMA effects. This time can also be collected from regression-based models [24].

As a first step, the sOMP model considers that $T_{Memory}(t_i) = 0$. Hence, we only simulate tasks computation time without any consideration for memory access and data locality. Such a model is well adapted for computation-bound applications.

Communications-Based Model. When the application is more memory-bound and is executed on NUMA architectures, the time to perform memory accesses should be taken into account. Our model considers the set of memory accesses made by a task, groups them by task operands (e.g. matrix tiles), and takes into account the machine topology and the capacity of links between components.

The grouping allows matching with SimGrid's programming model which is oriented towards distributed memory platforms: we model the task memory accesses with data transfers for the task operands, i.e., as SimGrid *communications*. Since application tasks usually access to the content of all operands in an interleaved pattern, we make these communications concurrent and let SimGrid account for contention on the simulated links.

$T_{Memory}(t_i)$, the communications time of the task operands, which allows to improve the simulation accuracy, can then be written as:

$$T_{Memory}(t_i) = \max_{j=0}^{n-1} T_{Comm}(a_{i,j}) \tag{2}$$

where n is the number of memory accesses, $a_{i,j}$ is the j-th operand of task t_i and $T_{Comm}(a_{i,j})$ the time to transfer $a_{i,j}$ depending on its location and the core performing task t_i.

Moreover, the memory access modes (read, write, or read-write) allows us to take into account the cost of each communication differently: for read-write type operations, we double the communication time since these are composed of two distinguished transfers of the same tile.

To summarize, we express memory accesses to task operands as sets of concurrent SimGrid communications. SimGrid can then take into account the concurrency between the various communications of all tasks executing at the same time on the platform, with respect to the network characteristics, as depicted in Fig. 2. This allows us to model the actual concurrency observed in real platforms [21]. SimGrid can thus determine for each communication how its duration $T_{Comm}(a_{i,j})$ gets affected by contention. These are then gathered by Eq. (2) into $T_{Memory}(t_i)$ which influences the simulated execution time according to Eq. (1). All of this is driven by the machine model and the defined latency and bandwidth values of the intra and inter-node links (obtaining those values will be discussed in Sect. 5.2).

4   Implementation

To simulate the execution of task-based applications on the architecture model presented in Sect. 3.2, we need to develop a scheduling algorithm to manage task dispatching, execution, and dependencies on SimGrid *hosts*, with support of memory accesses for the communications-based model.

4.1   sOMP Architecture

Since we exploit a trace file from a sequential execution of the application, we first need a parser to extract all the useful pieces of information contained in the generated file with the TiKKi tool in .rec format (from GNU Recutils). This file gives details on the executed tasks and provides their name, submission order, dependencies, logical CPU number and memory node on which the task was executed, submission/start/end time, the nature of memory transfers performed by the task, the data on which these operations happened, and their size.

After parsing the trace file, we proceed with inserting tasks in a submission queue (FIFO) that the sOMP scheduler handles. The scheduler submits the tasks for execution by the simulated cores (hosts). The scheduler's task submission works according to two constraints: tasks must be ready, i.e., all their dependencies have been satisfied, and *hosts* workers must be idle, i.e., they are not currently executing another task. We use a centralized task queue for now which is similar to the one performed by a typical OpenMP runtime. Other scheduling policies can be tested in the future to try to improve the application performances relating to that field. We do not use the SimDAG (deprecated) and disk support of Simgrid since they do not allow us to finely control data transfers and interactions on the memory bus.

On each simulated core, a SimGrid actor (called *worker*) picks tasks one by one for simulation. The worker first simulates the memory accesses of the task: for every operand access, it triggers a message with the corresponding size (in bytes). The worker then waits for the completion of the transfer of all messages, which will increase SimGrid's internal clock, taking into account the latency and bandwidth of the traversed links and the contention induced on those links by concurrent accesses. The worker then simulates the task's execution by advancing the internal clock of SimGrid by a time equal to the task's real execution time, obtained from the TiKKi trace. Once the execution of a task is completed, the worker is responsible for activating the submission of the successors of the finished task to the scheduler, if all their dependencies have been satisfied.

4.2   Managing Data Locality

In the communications-based model, we store the NUMA node number on which each data allocation and initialization task was executed, and thus the NUMA node on which the data was effectively allocated. Since the other (computation) tasks will need to access those pieces of data, their NUMA locations are crucial to properly model the accesses.

When modeling the access to an operand with a communication, we not only define a payload size corresponding to the size of the operand, but also specify the source and recipient of the communication. This corresponds to modeling data accesses according to their location: the communication is performed between the memory controller *host* of the NUMA node where the operand was effectively allocated, and the core *host* that executes the task. Notably, if the core is in the NUMA node where storage is assigned, the communication will take place only on the local backbone, thus modeling the reduced contention.

5 Evaluation

The KASTORS [27] benchmark suite has been designed to evaluate the implementation of the OpenMP dependent task paradigm, introduced as part of the OpenMP 4.0 specifications. It includes several benchmarks. The experiments presented here are based on the PLASMA subset of the KASTORS benchmark suite, which provides three matrix factorization algorithms (Cholesky, LU, QR) extracted from the PLASMA library [27]. Experiments with the KASTORS benchmarks were performed on two machines:

- dual-socket **Intel Xeon Gold 6240**, 24.75MB L3 cache, 36 cores, **Cascade-Lake** microarchitecture with 1 NUMA node per socket, and 18 cores per NUMA node;
- dual-socket **AMD EPYC 7452**, 128MB L3 cache, 64 cores, **AMD Infinity** architecture with 4 NUMA nodes per socket, and 8 cores per NUMA node.

5.1 Methodology

In order to evaluate our simulator performance, we carry out various tests with the KASTORS benchmarks on the machines presented above. We choose different matrix sizes and different tile sizes in order to observe the accuracy of our simulator when confronted with a variety of scenarios.

To measure the reliability of the simulations by comparing simulation time (T_{sim}) with real execution time (T_{native}), we do not consider the absolute values of the metric, but set a metric that defines the precision error of sOMP compared to native executions: $PrecisionError = (T_{native} - T_{sim})/T_{native}$. Therefore, when the precision error is positive, it means that we "under-simulate" the actual execution time, in other terms our prediction is optimistic. A negative precision error means that we "over-simulate", hence a pessimistic prediction.

5.2 Latency and Bandwidth Measurements

To model a NUMA machine, providing the link's latency and bandwidth corresponding to the real values in the architecture is essential. As stated before, we consider that all of our memory transfers only involve the L3 cache and the DRAM, since all the representative tile sizes exceed the conventional sizes of the L1 and L2 caches (respectively around 64 Kb and 256 Kb). Therefore, we have set data sizes at least equal to the size of L2 cache in our experiments. To carry out our measurements, we used two benchmarks: BenchIT combined with x86membench and Intel Memory Latency Checker v3.8 to confirm the results.

The latency and bandwidth measurements inside a NUMA node for a data size just beyond the size of the L2 cache are attributed to the intra-node links, while measurements with data sizes just beyond the size of the L3 cache are attributed to the backbone. For inter-node links, we performed tests to measure values corresponding to the UPI/Infinity Fabric links latencies/bandwidths for Intel/AMD simulations: 147 ns/221 ns, and 45 GBps/70 GBps.

5.3 Results

In order to evaluate the simulator, we carry out tests on dense linear algebra applications in different data size scenarios and check the sOMP precision error, both in the case with only task execution modeling, and with the addition of the communications-based model

Our first tests aim to verify the reliability of the simulator for several tile sizes. We compare a real execution time to the simulated time for a matrix with a size of 16384 × 16384 and different tile sizes (512 × 512, 768 × 768, and 1024 × 1024) on the machines presented in Sect. 5.2. We perform tests using a single core up to using all cores on a node. As presented in Fig. 3(left), on the

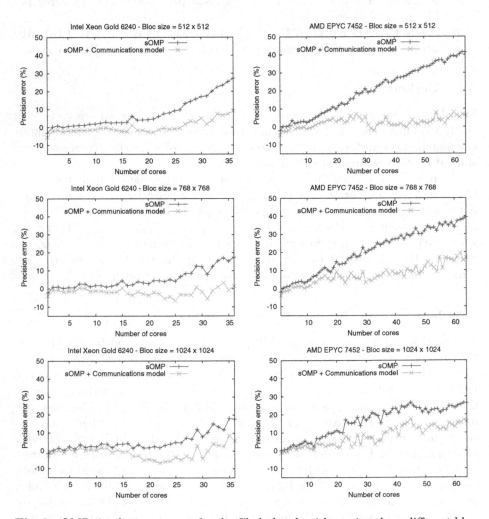

Fig. 3. sOMP simulator accuracy for the Cholesky algorithm using three different bloc sizes on the two architectures, for the same matrix size 16384 × 16384.

Intel architecture the variation in the number of cores influences the accuracy of the simulator regardless of tile size.

On the Intel architecture, we achieve ±5% error of precision on the Cholesky algorithm when running on a single socket (up to 18 cores) and using the task execution model only. Additionally using the second socket contributes to an increase in precision error, especially when approaching full machine usage.

However, we observe that the communications model introduced compensates for the loss of precision, notably when the majority of the cores of the two sockets are used. This is highlighted in tests with AMD architecture (Fig. 3(right)), where the communication model provides excellent precision compared to task execution alone, especially for fine-grain simulations —under 10% error up to 32 cores and less than 20% at full node in all configurations—. The difference in precision between the two machines is due to the nature of each architecture: Intel with a single NUMA domain per socket generates less memory effects than the four NUMA domains socket AMD.

The simulator's behavior, when coupled with the communications model, allows us to confirm the reliability of the developed NUMA modeling, and also, observe the impact of memory-related effects on the execution of the application when disabling communications. In algorithms where tasks are handling fewer data, sOMP default model allows us to obtain better accuracy, as depicted in Fig. 4 for the LU algorithm. The tile size is fixed (768 × 768) and two matrices of 8192 and 16384 are simulated. For the task execution model the error of precision remains lower than 15 model based on communications, it is possible to efficiently improve the simulations even for a large number of cores with an error contained in the interval [−5%, 5%] regardless of the problem size. Therefore, we can achieve better overall precision on the LU algorithm compared to other simulators such as simNUMA (30% average error).

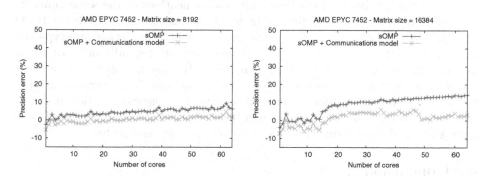

Fig. 4. sOMP simulator accuracy for the LU algorithm using two different matrix sizes and a tile size of 768 × 768 on AMD EPYC 7452

For the QR algorithm, the precision is influenced widely by the size of the problem: in Fig. 5, we fix the tile size (768 × 768) and vary the size of the matrix. In the first case (matrix size of 8192 × 8192 and a tile size of 768 × 768), the error remains below 10% on average. However, for the matrix size 16384×16384 (four times bigger) the precision error grows linearly from -5% to about 37%, with an average of 21%. We also observe that the communications model contributes less to improving accuracy compared with tests for the Cholesky algorithm. This is related to the nature of the task graph of the QR algorithm, which is slightly different: first, the arithmetic intensity of the kernels is more significant, so data accesses have less impact on the execution time. Next, QR kernels handle more data per task, some of which are temporary, generating significant cache-related effects that are not supported by the current version of the simulator and will be addressed in further work.

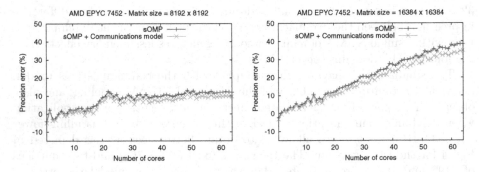

Fig. 5. sOMP simulator accuracy for the QR algorithm using two different matrix sizes and a tile size of 768×768 on AMD EPYC 7452

Finally, simulation with sOMP provides considerable time savings compared to actual execution. The simulation time is primarily linked to the number of tasks and the number of cores that emit communications at the same time. At the full scale (all cores) and fine grain blocking (matrix size of 16384×16384 and tile size of 512×512) and with the default model, simulations are typically $30\times$ faster. With the communications model, they are typically only $5\times$ faster on the Intel system and $2.5\times$ faster on the AMD system which has twice as many cores emitting communications at the same time. The overhead created by the communications-based model highlights the concerns mentioned earlier in adding too many architectural elements. Furthermore, SimGrid uses only one core, so several simulations can be run simultaneously on a multicore laptop.

6   Conclusion

This work focuses on simulating OpenMP task-based applications on shared memory architectures. On such structures, taking memory effects into account is crucial to obtain accurate simulations of linear algebra applications. Modeling the execution time of the tasks only is not sufficient.

We introduced a model to simulate the effects of memory accesses by leveraging the communications features offered by the SimGrid framework. Although

SimGrid is oriented towards simulations of distributed architectures, we showed that we could divert its use to model a shared-memory machine, and to build a simulator for linear algebra applications based on parallel tasks with data dependencies, offering a good trade-off between the cost and the accuracy of the simulations.

We showed that the communications model consistently reduces the precision error, regardless of the number of cores or the architectures. Within a processor, the simulator initially obtains an average relative error of around 15%; the communications model lowers this to less than 5% for the LU algorithm. Therefore, we have shown that it is necessary to consider memory access metrics in the architecture model to reduce precision errors.

Moreover, we observed that variations in the number of cores and granularity deeply impact simulation accuracy within a socket. Two effects are involved: concurrent memory access contention, and data movements between caches. Even if our machine model does not capture the detailed connectivity between the cores, we were able to simulate the contention delays accurately. However, we do not yet model data movements between caches, as depicted in results with the QR algorithm. Capturing this second effect is the subject of on-going work. We can also take into account more architecture components and simulate other applications such as SpMVM, BiCGStab... In the longer run, it will be useful to combine this work with simulations of MPI and GPUs to achieve the simulation of hybrid MPI/OpenMP applications on heterogeneous architectures.

Acknowledgments. This work is partially supported by the Hac Specis INRIA Project Lab. Experiments presented in this paper were carried out using the PlaFRIM experimental testbed, supported by Inria, CNRS (LABRI and IMB), Université de Bordeaux, Bordeaux INP and Conseil Régional d'Aquitaine (see https://www.plafrim.fr/).

References

1. Agullo, E., Beaumont, O., Eyraud-Dubois, L., Kumar, S.: Are static schedules so bad? A case study on cholesky factorization. In: IPDPS 2016. Proceedings of the 30th IEEE International Parallel & Distributed Processing Symposium, IPDPS 2016, Chicago, IL, United States. IEEE (May 2016)
2. Aversa, R., Di Martino, B., Rak, M., Venticinque, S., Villano, U.: Performance prediction through simulation of a hybrid MPI/OPENMP application. Parallel Comput. **31**(10), 1013–1033 (2005). openMP
3. Board, O.A.R.: Openmp application programming interface - version 5.0. https://www.openmp.org (2018)
4. Calheiros, R.N., Ranjan, R., Beloglazov, A., De Rose, C.A.F., Buyya, R.: CloudSim: a toolkit for modeling and simulation of cloud computing environments and evaluation of resource provisioning algorithms. Software: Pract. Exp. **41**(1), 23–50 (2011)
5. Casanova, H.: Simgrid: a toolkit for the simulation of application scheduling. In: Proceedings First IEEE/ACM International Symposium on Cluster Computing and the Grid, pp. 430–437 (2001)

6. Czarnul, P., et al.: MERPSYS: an environment for simulation of parallel application execution on large scale HPC systems. Simul. Model. Pract. Theory **77**, 124–140 (2017)
7. Daumen, A., Carribault, P., Trahay, F., Thomas, G.: SCALOMP: analyzing the scalability of OpenMP applications. In: Fan, X., de Supinski, B.R., Sinnen, O., Giacaman, N. (eds.) IWOMP 2019. LNCS, vol. 11718, pp. 36–49. Springer, Cham (2019). https://doi.org/10.1007/978-3-030-28596-8_3
8. Denoyelle, N., Goglin, B., Ilic, A., Jeannot, E., Sousa, L.: Modeling non-uniform memory access on large compute nodes with the cache-aware roofline model. IEEE Trans. Parallel Distrib. Syst. **30**(6), 1374–1389 (2019)
9. Eichenberger, A.E., et al.: OMPT: An OpenMP tools application programming interface for performance analysis. In: Rendell, A.P., Chapman, B.M., Müller, M.S. (eds.) IWOMP 2013. LNCS, vol. 8122, pp. 171–185. Springer, Heidelberg (2013). https://doi.org/10.1007/978-3-642-40698-0_13
10. Engelmann, C.: Scaling to a million cores and beyond: using light-weight simulation to understand the challenges ahead on the road to exascale. Fut. Gener. Comput. Syst. **30**, 59–65 (2014)., special Issue on Extreme Scale Parallel Architectures and Systems, Cryptography in Cloud Computing and Recent Advances in Parallel and Distributed Systems, ICPADS 2012 Selected Papers
11. Feld, C., Convent, S., Hermanns, M.-A., Protze, J., Geimer, M., Mohr, B.: Score-P and OMPT: navigating the perils of callback-driven parallel runtime introspection. In: Fan, X., de Supinski, B.R., Sinnen, O., Giacaman, N. (eds.) IWOMP 2019. LNCS, vol. 11718, pp. 21–35. Springer, Cham (2019). https://doi.org/10.1007/978-3-030-28596-8_2
12. Gautier, T., Perez, C., Richard, J.: On the impact of OpenMP task granularity. In: de Supinski, B.R., Valero-Lara, P., Martorell, X., Mateo Bellido, S., Labarta, J. (eds.) IWOMP 2018. LNCS, vol. 11128, pp. 205–221. Springer, Cham (2018). https://doi.org/10.1007/978-3-319-98521-3_14
13. Girona, S., Labarta, J.: Sensitivity of performance prediction of message passing programs. J. Supercomput. **17**, 291–298 (2000). https://doi.org/10.1023/A:1026567408307
14. Haugen, B.: Performance analysis and modeling of task-based runtimes. Ph.D. thesis (2016)
15. Haugen, B., Kurzak, J., YarKhan, A., Luszczek, P., Dongarra, J.: Parallel simulation of superscalar scheduling. In: 2014 43rd International Conference on Parallel Processing, pp. 121–130 (2014)
16. Heinrich, F.: Modeling, Prediction and Optimization of Energy Consumption of MPI Applications using SimGrid. Theses, Université Grenoble Alpes, May 2019
17. de Kergommeaux, J.C., Guilloud, C., de Oliveira Stein, B.: Flexible performance debugging of parallel and distributed applications. In: Kosch, H., Böszörményi, L., Hellwagner, H. (eds.) Euro-Par 2003. LNCS, vol. 2790, pp. 38–46. Springer, Heidelberg (2003). https://doi.org/10.1007/978-3-540-45209-6_9
18. Dzmitry, K., Pascal, B., Samee, K.U.: GreenCloud: a packet-level simulator of energy-aware cloud computing data centers. J. Supercomput. **62**, 1263–1283 (2012)
19. Liu, Y., Zhu, Y., Li, X., Ni, Z., Liu, T., Chen, Y., Wu, J.: SimNUMA: simulating NUMA-architecture multiprocessor systems efficiently. In: 2013 International Conference on Parallel and Distributed Systems, pp. 341–348, December 2013
20. Mohammed, A., Eleliemy, A., Ciorba, F.M., Kasielke, F., Banicescu, I.: Experimental verification and analysis of dynamic loop scheduling in scientific applications. In: 2018 17th International Symposium on Parallel and Distributed Computing (ISPDC), pp. 141–148. IEEE (2018)

21. Porterfield, A., Fowler, R., Mandal, A., Lim, M.Y.: Empirical evaluation of multi-core memory concurrency (2009)
22. Rico, A., Duran, A., Cabarcas, F., Etsion, Y., Ramirez, A., Valero, M.: Trace-driven simulation of multithreaded applications. In: IEEE International Symposium on Performance Analysis of Systems and Software (IEEE ISPASS), pp. 87–96 (2011)
23. Slimane, M., Sekhri, L.: HLSMN: high level multicore NUMA simulator. Elec-trotehnica Electronica, Automatica **65**(3), 170–175 (2017)
24. Stanisic, L., et al.: Fast and accurate simulation of multithreaded sparse linear algebra solvers. In: The 21st IEEE International Conference on Parallel and Dis-tributed Systems. Melbourne, Australia, December 2015
25. Stanisic, L., Thibault, S., Legrand, A., Videau, B., Méhaut, J.F.: Faithful per-formance prediction of a dynamic task-based runtime system for heterogeneous multi-core architectures. Concur. Comput. Pract. Exper. **27**(16), 4075–4090 (2015)
26. Tao, J., Schulz, M., Karl, W.: Simulation as a tool for optimizing memory accesses on NUMA machines. Perform. Eval. **60**(1–4), 31–50 (2005)
27. Virouleau, P., et al.: Evaluation of OpenMP dependent tasks with the KASTORS benchmark suite. In: DeRose, L., de Supinski, B.R., Olivier, S.L., Chapman, B.M., Müller, M.S. (eds.) IWOMP 2014. LNCS, vol. 8766, pp. 16–29. Springer, Cham (2014). https://doi.org/10.1007/978-3-319-11454-5_2
28. Virouleau, P., Roussel, A., Broquedis, F., Gautier, T., Rastello, F., Gratien, J.-M.: Description, implementation and evaluation of an affinity clause for task directives. In: Maruyama, N., de Supinski, B.R., Wahib, M. (eds.) IWOMP 2016. LNCS, vol. 9903, pp. 61–73. Springer, Cham (2016). https://doi.org/10.1007/978-3-319 45550-1_5
29. Zheng, G., Kakulapati, G., Kalé, L.V.: BigSim: a parallel simulator for performance prediction of extremely large parallel machines. In: 18th International Parallel and Distributed Processing Symposium 2004. Proceedings, p. 78. IEEE (2004)

Virtflex: Automatic Adaptation to NUMA Topology Change for OpenMP Applications

Runhua Zhang$^{(\boxtimes)}$, Alan L. Cox, and Scott Rixner

Rice University, Houston, TX 77005, USA
{rz18,alc,rixner}@rice.edu

Abstract. Advances in PCI-Express and optical interconnects are making "rack-scale computers" possible, but these computers will undoubtedly exhibit Non-Uniform Memory Access (NUMA) latencies. Ideally, a hypervisor for rack-scale computers should be able to dynamically reconfigure a virtual machine's processing and memory resources, *i.e.*, its NUMA topology, to satisfy each application's evolving demands. Unfortunately, current hypervisors lack support for such dynamic reconfiguration. To that end, this paper introduces Virtflex, a multilayered system for enabling unmodified OpenMP applications to adapt automatically to NUMA topology changes. Virtflex provides a novel NUMA page placement reset mechanism within the guest OS and a novel NUMA-aware superpage ballooning mechanism that spans the guest OS-hypervisor boundary. The evaluation shows that Virtflex enables applications to adapt efficiently to NUMA topology changes. For example, adding resources incurs an average runtime overhead of only 7.27%.

Keywords: Virtualization · NUMA · OpenMP

1 Introduction

Advances in PCI-Express and optical interconnect technologies are making it possible to consider the construction of "rack-scale computers", where the whole rack can be considered a single computer [13]. When communication latency is low enough (and bandwidth is high enough), it becomes practical to build disaggregated servers in which there are pools of processors, memory, and I/O devices within the rack that can be carved up as necessary to suit the demands of each application. Nonetheless, such rack-scale computers will undoubtedly exhibit Non-Uniform Memory Access (NUMA) latencies [3].

In principle, a machine virtualization system, like Xen or VMware ESXi should be ideal for flexibly allocating a rack's resources among its users' applications, while providing stronger isolation than container-based systems, like Docker. In particular, a hypervisor for rack-scale computers should make it possible to dynamically construct or *reconfigure* high-performance virtual machines

© Springer Nature Switzerland AG 2020
K. Milfeld et al. (Eds.): IWOMP 2020, LNCS 12295, pp. 212–227, 2020.
https://doi.org/10.1007/978-3-030-58144-2_14

that provide each application with the appropriate processing, memory, and I/O resources as the application's requirements evolve over time. Unfortunately, current hypervisors provide inadequate support for NUMA architectures. In particular, they do not adequately support the dynamic reconfiguration of a virtual machine's NUMA topology, *i.e.*, its processing and memory resources [1, 2, 7].

This paper introduces Virtflex, a multilayered system for enabling *unmodified* OpenMP applications to adapt automatically to NUMA topology changes. Specifically, Virtflex provides synergistic enhancements to the GNU OpenMP runtime, the Linux guest operating system (OS), and the Xen hypervisor that enable the OpenMP runtime to recognize the addition or removal of processing and memory resources from the underlying virtual machine (VM) and adapt thread and memory page placement to these changes. These enhancements include a novel NUMA page placement reset mechanism within the guest OS and a novel NUMA-aware superpage ballooning mechanism that spans the guest OS-hypervisor boundary.

To evaluate the efficacy and overhead of Virtflex, this paper presents an analysis of its impact on the execution of a variety of well-known, unmodified OpenMP applications from the HPC Challenge and NPB 3.3.1 benchmark suites. While these applications do not have changing resource requirements over the course of their execution, they enable a clear evaluation of the impact of topology change on performance. The innovations of Virtflex are effective on both traditional NUMA architectures and rack-scale computers, so the applications are evaluated on a traditional NUMA architecture. This makes it easier to understand the performance characteristics of the overall system by using familiar hardware.

The rest of this paper is organized as follows. Section 2 provides background. Section 3 describes the design and implementation of Virtflex. Section 4 evaluates the efficacy and overhead of Virtflex. Section 5 discusses related work, and Sect. 6 concludes the paper.

2   Background

2.1   Virtualization

Virtualization is the technique that allows multiple tenants to use one physical machine for resource consolidation. In hypervisor-based virtualization, the privileged hypervisor controls access to the physical hardware resources and manages the virtual machines. Virtual machines run with full-blown operating systems and share the hardware resources of the physical machine.

A virtual CPU (vCPU) represents a period of time a virtual machine can run on a physical CPU core. The hypervisor schedules vCPUs to time-share physical cores just like processes are scheduled on CPUs in operating systems. vCPU can also be scheduled to different CPU cores if necessary. Xen and Linux allow hot-add or hot-remove vCPUs of a virtual machine, which increases the flexibility of vCPU furthermore.

Memory virtualization is accomplished by adding a layer of address translation. Guests cannot access machine physical addresses directly for isolation and security reasons. Instead, virtual addresses in the guests are translated into guest physical addresses first, then another page table (the nested page table in AMD processors or the extended page table in Intel processors) is used to translate the guest physical address into machine physical addresses. The hypervisor has complete control of the nested/extended page table. When a page fault occurs in the guest, the hardware page table walker performs a 2-dimensional page walk, walking two page tables at once. And the guest virtual address to machine physical address translation is cached in the TLB.

2.2   Linux NUMA Support Limitations

Linux exposes NUMA policies to user applications through libnuma. For example, applications can choose to use a "first-touch" policy, where memory is allocated on the NUMA node in which the first accessing thread runs, or "interleaved", where memory is allocated across all NUMA nodes in a round-robin fashion. Selecting the appropriate allocation policy can boost the performance of memory-intensive applications by up to 50%.

Unfortunately, the libnuma interface assumes a static NUMA topology. It provides functions for placing memory and threads on specific nodes. When the topology can change, this interface is not only ineffective, but can be incorrect, as the nodes that memory and threads are placed on can disappear.

Linux also provides autoNUMA, which will automatically migrate pages across NUMA nodes in an attempt to achieve better performance. AutoNUMA periodically unmaps pages in an application's address space and uses the ensuing soft page faults to collect statistics about local and remote accesses. When remote accesses happen twice in a row to a page, autoNUMA will migrate that page to the node that made the remote accesses. AutoNUMA is turned on by default in Linux.

While autoNUMA does not necessarily assume a static NUMA topology, it is designed for the case where most of the memory pages are already in the right place. When the topology changes, autoNUMA can take a long time to adapt. First, it takes time for autoNUMA to scan the entire address space of an application (tens of minutes for an application with a large working set). Second, the statistics collected by autoNUMA will need to be invalidated upon a change in topology, forcing it to restart its accounting mechanisms, further delaying reconfiguration upon a topology change.

Currently, virtualization systems, including Xen, Linux KVM, and ESXi, all handle NUMA architectures in one of two ways. In one approach, the hypervisor simply hides the underlying NUMA topology from the guests and provides the guests with the illusion of *uniform memory access* (UMA) latency. Any resource exchange (processors and memory) between the hypervisor and the guests is oblivious to the NUMA topology. Moreover, this approach prevents applications from doing any NUMA-related optimization. In the other approach, Xen's vNUMA, the hypervisor places a guest within a static partition of the NUMA topology, and exposes this subset of the NUMA topology to the guest as a virtual NUMA topology. On the upside, applications and the guest OS are able to perform NUMA optimizations. However, the downside is that guests are locked within this subset of the NUMA topology. Moreover, any resource exchange between a guest and the hypervisor will potentially make the static vNUMA topology inaccurate, invalidating NUMA-related optimizations by applications or the OS.

In virtualized systems, memory ballooning is a mechanism that enables memory exchange between the hypervisor and the guest. It requires the balloon driver running in the guest OS to cooperate with the hypervisor. To reclaim memory from the guest, the hypervisor instructs the guest's balloon driver to "inflate" the balloon by allocating memory from the guest operating system. The balloon driver then transfers this memory to the hypervisor and the hypervisor unmaps it from the guest. To restore memory to the guest, the hypervisor instructs the guest's balloon driver to "deflate" the balloon by freeing memory that the hypervisor first transfers back to the balloon driver (and maps to the guest). Note that the memory that the hypervisor gives back to the balloon driver is unlikely to be the same physical memory that it originally took.

Ballooning is a simple, yet effective, mechanism often used in the context of memory overcommitment. However, there are some challenges when using ballooning in NUMA systems, especially when the NUMA topology can change. First, the current implementation of Linux's balloon driver for Xen is not NUMA aware; it treats all memory as one uniform pool. Ballooning is known to often disturb a guest's NUMA topology [9], so it is therefore recommended to turn off ballooning when vNUMA is used. Second, ballooning is slow, exchanging memory at around 1 GB/s. Finally, ballooning splits nested page table entries. On creating a guest, Xen tries to use 1 GB and 2 MB page mappings in the nested page table instead of 4 KB mappings to reduce the cost of guest physical to machine physical address translation [6]. But ballooning will split the large pages into 4 KB pages.

3   Virtflex Design and Implementation

Virtflex operates at three levels: the hypervisor, the guest OS, and the application's runtime library.

3.1   Hypervisor-Guest OS Boundary

In Virtflex, when the hypervisor decides to change the topology of a guest, the hypervisor communicates this information to the guest through Xenstore. The hypervisor changes the available guest memory on each node of a guest and sets a topology change indicator in Xenstore. vCPUs are hot-added to/removed from the guest accordingly. If this is a node de-population, the balloon driver in the guest OS inflates the balloon on nodes that are being de-populated and issues a *new* memory migration hypercall to migrate the non-reclaimable memory of that node to a remaining node. Note that non-reclaimable memory is memory that the balloon driver cannot allocate on the node, since it is in use by the kernel. If this is a node population, the balloon driver in the guest first uses the hypercall to migrate non-reclaimable memory back to the correct physical location, then deflates the balloon, making the rest of the memory available to the guest.

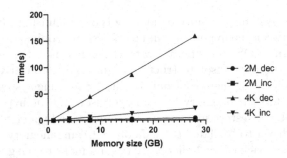

Fig. 1. Ballooning performance 4 K/2 M

NUMA-awareness is vital for ballooning to be used to change the guest's NUMA topology. NUMA-aware ballooning requires the hypervisor to have control over the available memory with per-node granularity instead of per-VM granularity. Virtflex's balloon driver separates the management of each NUMA node by having one balloon for each NUMA node, which allows Virtflex to guarantee that pages exchanged by the guest and hypervisor are from the same node. This prevents the balloon driver from disrupting the guest's NUMA topology.

To use ballooning to achieve rapid topology change, it must be possible to quickly exchange memory. Virtflex modifies the Xen balloon driver to operate on 2 MB regions instead of individual 4KB pages to improve ballooning performance. There have been previous attempts to implement superpage ballooning in KVM and ESXi to improve performance. Hu [12] proposed a hugepage ballooning mechanism in KVM, changing the ballooning granularity from 4 KB to 2 MB. VMware similarly has attempted to change the ballooning granularity [4]. However, neither of these are NUMA-aware.

The main bottleneck of ballooning in Xen is the hypervisor's updates to 4 KB granularity nested page table entries. Virtflex modifies the nested page table management in Xen to operate on larger pages. This reduces the number of nested page table entries Xen has to work on by a factor of 512. Using larger pages also reduces memory allocation/deallocation overheads, the number of guest machine frame numbers that need to be exchanged between the guest OS and hypervisor, and the number of hypercalls guests have to make. Together, these large page ballooning optimizations yield more than a ten-fold improvement in ballooning performance in Xen.

Figure 1 shows the performance comparison between Virtflex's superpage ballooning and regular 4 KB ballooning. In our experiments, Virtflex's superpage ballooning outperforms regular 4 KB ballooning by 33.4x to 39.1x for decrease reservation and 13.4x to 22.3x for increase reservation. Our ballooning mechanism does support 1 GB ballooning granularity in the hypervisor. However, due to restrictions on large memory allocations in Linux, Virtflex's balloon driver in Linux can only use 2 MB superpages for ballooning.

When the NUMA topology changes, entire NUMA nodes are added or removed. Memory ballooning can never entirely remove a complete NUMA node. Linux stores unreclaimable memory in every node. Experiments reveal that Linux stores around 100 MB of such unreclaimable memory: around 64 MB is used for storing the node's `struct page`'s, around 15 MB is used for the slab allocator, and there is a small amount of free memory that is unreclaimable because of fragmentation.

Rather than making intrusive modifications to the Linux kernel, Virtflex migrates this unreclaimable guest kernel memory to alternate nodes. The memory is migrated via the nested page table. Once the balloon driver balloons the target node down to the point where only unreclaimable memory remains, the guest passes the guest's physical memory range of this node to the hypervisor through a hypercall. After that, the hypervisor scans the corresponding range in the nested page table in two passes.

In the first pass, the hypervisor write-protects any valid leaf entries in that range. The hypervisor also encodes a special migration type for those entries. Write-protection makes any page fault from the guest on this range trap in the hypervisor. The hypervisor's page fault handler recognizes such faults and waits for the migration to complete before resuming. In the second pass, the hypervisor allocates pages from the destination node, copies the content from the old pages to the new pages and updates the nested page table to reflect the change. After the update to the page table entry, the hypervisor signals the migration's completion to any page fault handler that is waiting. Finally, Xen frees the old pages.

After the kernel memory migration, guests are left with a minimal node that has all of its CPUs disabled by the hypervisor and a small amount of unreclaimable memory. This allows Linux to continue to operate unmodified. When the hypervisor wants to re-populate such a node, it does so in the reverse order. The hypervisor first moves the remaining memory of that node back to the right place. Then ballooning populates the remaining memory of the node. Finally, all the CPUs from the node are enabled again by the hypervisor.

One issue with this strategy is dealing with pages that are shared between the hypervisor and the guest. In particular, there are two shared pages per vCPU that are used to deliver interrupts. After those pages are allocated at boot time, the guest's physical frame numbers are passed to the hypervisor. The references to these pages, and other shared pages are potentially scattered throughout the hypervisor. Virtflex simply skips all shared pages for correctness. A better solution would be to restructure the Xen hypervisor to centrally manage all shared pages so that access to them can easily be restricted during migration.

3.2 Guest OS-Application Boundary

After the hypervisor changes the topology of a guest, applications running in that guest have to adapt to the new topology to take advantage of the added resources or minimize the impact of the lost resources. Specifically, applications have to redistribute their threads and memory accordingly. Virtflex introduces a page placement reset system call that simplifies applications' memory adaptation.

To adapt to the topology change, applications have to know when a topology change occurs. Virtflex provides a simple Linux proc file system interface that is used to notify applications of NUMA topology changes. With this mechanism, it is up to applications to decide when to adapt.

Virtflex modifies the OpenMP library to watch for topology changes and reconfigure applications, as necessary. OpenMP applications often have parallel sections interleaved with serial sections. Before launching a team of threads for each parallel section, the runtime checks for topology change. If the topology has changed, the OpenMP runtime recalculates the number of threads to be launched and reassigns thread affinity from the OMP_PLACES list accordingly if necessary. After the new team of threads is ready, OpenMP issues the memory reset system call before launching those threads. Around 200 lines of code in total are modified for the GCC 7.3.0 implementation of OpenMP to work with Virtflex. And we expect the same amount of work for integrating Virtflex to other OpenMP implementations like LLVM. With these changes, any application written in OpenMP can adapt to topology change automatically.

Thread adaptation for OpenMP applications is achieved by using the OMP_DYNAMIC directive in the GNU OpenMP implementation. OMP_DYNAMIC allows the OpenMP runtime to adjust the number of OpenMP threads to the number of available cores on the fly. As for memory layout adaptation, Virtflex introduces a page placement reset system call that enables applications to adapt their memory layout to a new topology. Depending on the original policy of a memory region, Virtflex takes two possible actions, next-touch and re-interleave, to redistribute memory. For memory regions that use the default first-touch policy, next-touch is used; while for memory regions that use the interleave policy, re-interleave is used.

There are three possible ways to set NUMA placement traits for an OpenMP application, the first way is to use Linux's default first-touch policy; the second way is via administrator tools like numactl; the third way will be introduced by OpenMP 5.0, using custom allocators. Custom allocators can define the "partition" trait for the placement of allocated memory. Specifically, users can specify "nearest" to place memory in the nearest storage location (or NUMA node) to the thread that requested the allocation; "blocked" partitions memory into same size parts with one part on each of the NUMA nodes; "interleaved" interleaves memory to NUMA nodes; "environment" defers the placement decision to be made during execution.

Regardless of how NUMA placement is set in the user-space, these traits are/will be reflected by setting NUMA policies of memory regions in the kernel space. Since Virtflex's memory reset operates at the kernel level, Virtflex is/will be able to recognize those NUMA placement traits and take next-touch or re-interleave actions accordingly.

Similar to Linux's first-touch policy, next-touch uses thread accesses to determine on which node a memory page is placed. It protects all of the page table entries within the application's address space. When a page fault occurs, the handler determines whether the access is remote or local by comparing the current thread's node with the node where the page resides. For a local access, the page fault handler simply removes the protection and resumes the access. For a remote access, the page fault handler migrates the page to the node where the access came from. This works for any memory regions that are accessed by a single thread, including thread local storage.

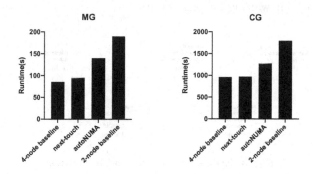

Fig. 2. Next-touch vs. baseline runtimes

Figure 2 shows the comparison between next-touch and autoNUMA in terms of the speed of topology change adaptation. For autoNUMA and next-touch results, the CPUs on nodes 2 and 3 are enabled after applications initialize their memory on nodes 0 and 1. This creates a fictitious node-expansion topology change. The OpenMP runtime adjusts the number of threads to all logical cores available (56 threads in this case), and applications use autoNUMA or next-touch (MG and CG are first-touch applications and re-interleave is not included in this experiment.) to adapt their memory layouts. The adaptation overhead for next-touch is 10.74% and 0.97% for the NPB MG.D and CG.D applications, respectively. While for autoNUMA this adaptation overhead is 63.68% and 32.18%, respectively.

AutoNUMA adapts to topology changes much slower because autoNUMA is designed for the case where most of the memory pages are in the correct place. For the default setting, autoNUMA only scans 256 MB of application memory every scan period (each scan period ranges from 1 s to 60 s). That means for MG.D (the total amount of memory touched during execution is around 26.5 GB), it takes at least 106 s to scan the whole address space. And since autoNUMA requires two remote accesses in a row to migrate a page, the actual adaptation time doubles the scanning time. Tuning the scanning rate to be more aggressive may shorten the adaptation time but with the cost of larger overhead for handling page faults between topology changes.

In contrast, instead of scanning an application's address space gradually, next-touch unmaps the entire address space at once and does not require repeated accesses to trigger migration. Thus, pages can be migrated as soon as the first remote access occurs after a topology change.

Some memory regions that are accessed by multiple threads need to be interleaved to avoid a bandwidth bottleneck. For these memory regions, instead of using the fault-driven next-touch, Virtflex uses re-interleave, which redistributes the memory pages across the nodes in the new topology. While next-touch needs to temporarily protect the page table entries to guide where pages should be migrated to, re-interleave can place pages immediately in the correct nodes deterministically without waiting for page faults.

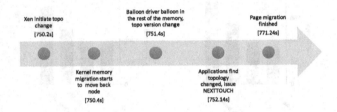

Fig. 3. Events timeline for end-to-end test

Virtflex provides two versions of the re-interleave policy: a serialized version that uses the thread that makes the re-interleave syscall to re-interleave pages, and a parallel version that uses multiple kernel threads on different NUMA nodes to achieve faster re-interleaving. Virtflex also uses some heuristics to reduce interconnect traffic in the parallel version. In particular, it avoids assigning remote nodes to migrate local pages. While the parallel version re-interleaves memory faster, it will slow down other applications running in the guest because of its CPU and memory bandwidth consumption.

Virtflex provides applications with a simple topology change notification interface and a page placement reset system call to reallocate memory across the new topology. The page placement reset system call takes different actions, namely, next-touch or re-interleave, according to the memory regions' original placement policies. However, for OpenMP applications, the application does not need to be aware of any of this, as it is completely handled by the OpenMP runtime library.

3.3   End-to-End Operation

Figure 3 shows the series of events that takes place in Virtflex for node population. First, Xen initiates a topology change by writing new node targets in Xenstore and setting the topology change indicator. Note that this topology change would be triggered by control software running in Domain 0 of Xen. The control software could choose to initiate a topology change based upon information about the system—including, but not limited to, node utilization, new guests starting, or existing guests stopping—and resource policies—including, but not limited to, information about guest priorities and desired resources.

Once the control software initiates a topology change, the balloon driver in the guest is woken up. The balloon driver first kicks off the guest kernel memory migration, migrating the unreclaimable memory of an unpopulated node to its correct physical location. Afterward, the balloon driver reacquires the remaining memory from the hypervisor. It updates the topology version once ballooning and kernel memory migration have finished. After applications realize the topology has changed, the OpenMP runtime redistributes the threads and initiates the page placement reset. Pages are migrated to the correct place during the execution of the next parallel section. Note that the OpenMP runtime system only checks for topology changes during serial sections. To give a quantitative sense of the timing of these events, the events in Fig. 3 are annotated with timestamps (system uptime, shown in brackets) from an execution of CG.D.

4   Evaluation

This section shows the end-to-end effects of combining the hypervisor, guest OS, and runtime adaptation mechanisms when a NUMA topology change occurs. The results show that Virtflex is able to adapt to topology changes rapidly, close to the ideal case.

Experiments were conducted on an AMD EPYC 7551P-based machine running Xen 4.11 and Linux 4.18. Internally, this chip is organized as 4 NUMA nodes with 8 processor cores (16 threads) each. Each node has 2 2666 MHz DDR4 channels with 16 GB of memory; each memory channel has a max bandwidth of 21.325 GB/s. The four NUMA nodes are fully connected by AMD's Infinity Fabric, which has a bidirectional bandwidth of 42.6 GB/s over each link. Remote accesses take about 1.6 times longer than local accesses.

One hardware thread on each NUMA node was reserved for Xen's Dom0. All of the 4-node VMs had 56 vCPUs and the 2-node VMs had 28 vCPUs. For the bare-metal experiments, all 64 hardware threads on the machine were used. In all cases, the number of threads for the application was set to the number of vCPUs.

The following OpenMP applications were evaluated: NPB 3.3.1 class C and D benchmarks with runtimes greater than 10 s and memory usage less than our machine's total physical memory size, and HPC Challenge's RandomAccess ("GUPS"). While most NPB benchmarks perform well with first-touch placement, GUPS performs best with interleaved placement. To demonstrate the generality of Virtflex's mechanisms, two non-OpenMP applications were modified and evaluated, fluidanimate and streamcluster, from Parsec 3.0. These two applications performed best with interleaved placement.

For the expansion of the guest's NUMA topology, VMs were created with 4 NUMA nodes, 2 of the nodes are populated while the other two are unpopulated (the majority of the memory is ballooned out and vCPUs are hot-removed). Applications start running within 2 nodes and later Xen populates the other 2 nodes while the application is running. For the reduction of the guest's topology, applications start running in a fully populated 4 node VM, later two of the nodes are de-populated.

The result of the topology expansion case is shown in Fig. 4. The x-axis shows during which iteration the topology change occurs and the y-axis shows the runtime of the application. Note that the x-axis is showing the time at which the application recognizes the topology change, which is after the hypervisor initiates the change. The two horizontal lines show the performance with fixed 2-node and 4-node topologies. The ideal case is one in which an application is able to adapt to a topology change instantaneously with no overhead. If the topology change occurred at the start of the benchmark, in the ideal case, the runtime would be the same as the fixed 4-node topology runtime. Similarly, if the topology change occurs at the end of execution, the runtime would be equal to the fixed 2-node topology runtime. If the topology changes in the middle of the run, in the ideal case, the performance should vary linearly between the two fixed cases. The gap between Virtflex's performance in the figure and this ideal case reflects Virtflex's end-to-end topology change adaptation overhead.

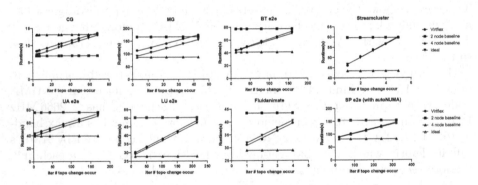

Fig. 4. End-to-end topology change (add nodes) adaptation

Topology change adaptation overhead is on average 7.27%. However, this percentage heavily depends on the total runtime of the application. The absolute slowdown is primarily a function of the memory usage of the application, because for most applications page migration accounts for the majority of the overhead. Table 1 lists the total amount of memory touched during the execution of tested applications. Applications whose pages are migrated mainly by re-interleave suffer less overhead than applications that mainly use next-touch. This is because next-touch uses a fault-driven approach: pages are migrated upon a subsequent page fault. In contrast, re-interleave directly migrates pages to their destination nodes when the page placement reset system call is performed, so there is no added page fault overhead.

Table 1. Total amount of memory touched of tested applications

Application	CG.C	BT.C	SP.C	Fluidanimate
Memory touched (MB)	892.03	701.63	177.74	894.4
Application	MG.D	UA.C	LU.C	Streamcluster
Memory touched (MB)	27098.01	484	602.72	107.73

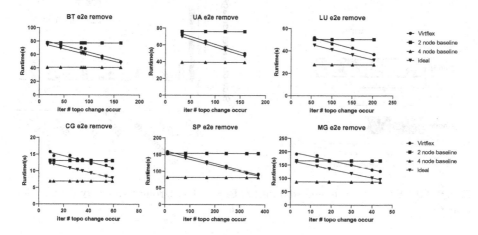

Fig. 5. End-to-end topology change (remove nodes) adaptation

Figure 5 shows the results for the reverse process, taking away nodes while applications are running. Arguably, taking away nodes while applications are running is less likely to happen than adding nodes. For example, it can occur in cases where VMs are not cooperating with the hypervisor.

In this set of experiments, applications are started in a 4-node VM, but the VM is reduced to 2 nodes while applications are running. In such cases, the order of events in the topology change timeline (Fig. 3) is reversed. For the ideal situation, if a topology change occurs at time 0, the application's runtime should be equal to the 2-node baseline. If the topology change occurs at the end, the application's runtime should be equal to the 4-node baseline.

Figure 5 shows that Virtflex's adaptation line is close to the ideal adaptation line. The average overhead for the remove case is 19.39%. However, compared to the node population case, the gaps between the ideal line and Virtflex are slightly larger. There are two reasons for this. First, removing nodes generally takes more time than adding nodes. Xen's balloon driver zeroes pages before giving them to hypervisor to prevent information leakage. Second, since next-touch uses a fault-driven approach to migrate pages, the migration time depends on how many cores are faulting on pages. In the node removal case, instead of using vCPUs from 4 nodes, migration can only use vCPU from 2 nodes to perform next-touch (Fig. 6).

As for the overhead on applications that are not subject to topology changes, as shown in Fig. 7, the performance impact is minimal. In this experiment, applications are pinned to nodes 0 and 1 while the guest topology changes from 2 nodes to 4 nodes or from 4 nodes to 2 nodes.

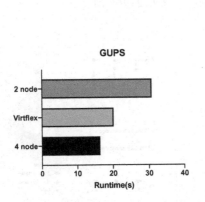

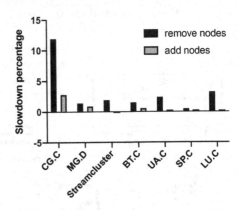

Fig. 6. GUPS topology change adaptation time

Fig. 7. Background topology change slowdown

Adding nodes causes little to no slowdown for most applications, while the slowdown from removing nodes is more visible. (In the streamcluster case, the average adding nodes runtime is slightly less than the native 2 node run, but not statistically significant.) Besides the fact that the expanding node time is around 1/3 to 1/4 of the removing node case, when adding nodes, the scheduler is likely to schedule the balloon driver on node 2 or 3 to reduce the CPU competition with applications. In the removing case, since the balloon driver first removes the vCPUs then does the ballooning, the balloon driver is competing with applications for the vCPUs of nodes 0 and 1. The absolute slowdowns for removing nodes on all applications are around 1–2 s, comparable to the standalone superpage ballooning time.

5   Related Work

Researchers have developed NUMA-aware schedulers for OpenMP, including a multi-level task scheduler [15] and a dynamic loop scheduler [10]. Broquedis, *et al.* further developed interfaces to maintain thread-memory affinity for OpenMP applications on NUMA machines [8]. Their system uses next-touch to migrate memory to the correct NUMA node, but it requires guidance from the programmer. Overall, these works are complimentary to Virtflex, as they deal with OpenMP memory and thread placement on static NUMA topologies and do not react to topology changes.

Hyper-V, KVM, and Xen do not support dynamic changes to the guest's NUMA topology [1,2,7]. Similarly, VMware is only able to change the guest's NUMA topology when the virtual machine is power cycled [5].

Apart from various performance analyses on virtualized NUMA systems (Han [11] and Song [18]), most research that focuses on optimization for virtualized NUMA systems takes one of the following two approaches: (1) hiding the NUMA topology from the guests and handling all optimizations in the hypervisor [14,16,17,19,20] or (2) exposing the topology to the guest and letting the guest OS and applications do all NUMA optimization [1].

The closest research to Virtflex is XPV [9]. XPV is an interface that exposes the NUMA topology to guests and is able to track topology changes. They abandoned the ACPI table that vNUMA uses to express NUMA topology, which only allows setting NUMA topology at boot time. This work mainly focuses on three situations that invalidate the guest NUMA topology: ballooning, vCPU scheduling, and memory flipping. Every time the guest NUMA topology changes, the guest OS will get notified through their interface. However, changing the ACPI table to this new interface in the guest requires invasive kernel modifications. As a result, the bootstrap, page allocator and scheduler code have to be changed for the guest OS to work with the new interface. In contrast, Virtflex takes a different approach in which the hypervisor presents empty nodes to the guests. This eliminates the need for invasive kernel modifications in order to adapt to topology changes. Furthermore, in XPV, the application itself must respond to topology changes, placing the burden of dealing with toplogy changes on the programmer. In contrast, Virtflex provides toplogy-free interfaces like next-touch and re-interleave that can easily be encapsulated within the OpenMP runtime to adapt to topology changes.

6   Conclusions

This paper has presented Virtflex, a NUMA virtualization solution that allows unmodified OpenMP applications to adapt automatically to NUMA topology changes. Virtflex provides a novel NUMA page placement reset mechanism within the guest OS and a novel NUMA-aware superpage ballooning mechanism that spans the guest OS-hypervisor boundary. Virtflex enables applications to adapt to added resources with an average runtime overhead of only 7.27%. Furthermore, Virtflex's innovations are valuable in a variety of contexts, both in virtualized and non-virtualized systems. The NUMA-aware balloon driver is arguably the way ballooning should be done on all NUMA machines, and superpage ballooning should be used over traditional 4 KB granularity ballooning in any situation. The memory-reset system call enables applications to change their memory placement at runtime.

References

1. Hyper-V NUMA support. https://www.silviodibenedetto.com/hyper-v-series-configure-numa/. Accessed 9 Jan 2020
2. KVM NUMA support. https://access.redhat.com/documentation/en-us/red_hat_enterprise_linux/7/html/virtualization_tuning_and_optimization_guide/sect-virtualization_tuning_optimization_guide-numa-numa_and_libvirt. Accessed 9 Jan 2020
3. The Gen-Z Consortium. https://genzconsortium.org/. Accessed 24 May 2020
4. VMware hugepage ballooning. https://www.spinics.net/lists/kernel/msg1968363.html. Accessed 2 Jan 2020
5. VMware NUMA topology. https://www.vmware.com/content/dam/digitalmarketing/vmware/en/pdf/techpaper/vmware-vsphere-cpu-sched-performance-white-paper.pdf. Accessed 2 Jan 2020
6. Xen Hugepage Support. https://wiki.xenproject.org/wiki/Huge_Page_Support. Accessed 31 Dec 2019
7. Xen NUMA support. https://wiki.xen.org/wiki/Xen_NUMA_Roadmap. Accessed 9 Jan 2020
8. Broquedis, F., Furmento, N., Goglin, B., Wacrenier, P.-A., Namyst, R.: Forest-GOMP: an efficient OpenMP environment for NUMA architectures. Int. J. Parallel Prog. **38**(5–6), 418–439 (2010)
9. Bui, B., et al.: When extended para - virtualization (XPV) meets NUMA. In: Proceedings of the Fourteenth EuroSys Conference 2019, EuroSys 2019, New York, NY, USA, 2019, pp. 7:1–7:15. ACM (2019)
10. Eichenberger, A.E., et al.: OMPT: an OpenMP tools application programming interface for performance analysis. In: Rendell, A.P., Chapman, B.M., Müller, M.S. (eds.) IWOMP 2013. LNCS, vol. 8122, pp. 171–185. Springer, Heidelberg (2013). https://doi.org/10.1007/978-3-642-40698-0_13
11. Han, J., Ahn, J., Kim, C., Kwon, Y., Choi, Y., Huh, J.: The effect of multi-core on HPC applications in virtualized systems. In: Guarracino, M.R., et al. (eds.) Euro-Par 2010. LNCS, vol. 6586, pp. 615–623. Springer, Heidelberg (2011). https://doi.org/10.1007/978-3-642-21878-1_76
12. Hu, J., Bai, X., Sha, S., Luo, Y., Wang, X., Wang, Z.: Hub: hugepage ballooning in kernel-based virtual machines. In: Proceedings of the International Symposium on Memory Systems, pp. 31–37. ACM (2018)
13. Intel. Rack Scale Design. https://www.intel.com/content/www/us/en/architecture-and-technology/rack-scale-design-overview.html. Accessed 24 May 2020
14. Liu, M., Li, T.: Optimizing virtual machine consolidation performance on NUMA server architecture for cloud workloads. In: 2014 ACM/IEEE 41st International Symposium on Computer Architecture (ISCA), pp. 325–336. IEEE (2014)
15. Olivier, S.L., Porterfield, A.K., Wheeler, K.B., Spiegel, M., Prins, J.F.: OpenMP task scheduling strategies for multicore NUMA systems. Int. J. High Perform. Comput. Appl. **26**(2), 110–124 (2012)
16. Rao, D.S., Schwan, K.: VNUMA-MGR: managing VM memory on NUMA platforms. In: 2010 International Conference on High Performance Computing, pp. 1–10. IEEE (2010)
17. Rao, J., Wang, K., Zhou, X., Xu, C.-Z.: Optimizing virtual machine scheduling in NUMA multicore systems. In: 2013 IEEE 19th International Symposium on High Performance Computer Architecture (HPCA), pp. 306–317. IEEE (2013)
18. Song, W., Jung, H.-J., Ahn, J.H., Lee, J.W., Kim, J.: Evaluation of performance unfairness in NUMA system architecture. IEEE Comput. Archit. Lett. **16**(1), 26–29 (2016)

19. Voron, G., Thomas, G., Quéma, V., Sens, P.: An interface to implement NUMA policies in the xen hypervisor. In: Proceedings of the Twelfth European Conference on Computer Systems, EuroSys 20177, New York, NY, USA, 2017, pp. 453–46. ACM (2017)
20. Wu, S., Sun, H., Zhou, L., Gan, Q., Jin, H.: VPROBE: scheduling virtual machines on NUMA systems. In: 2016 IEEE International Conference on Cluster Computing (CLUSTER), pp. 70–79. IEEE (2016)

Compilation Techniques

Using OpenMP to Detect and Speculate Dynamic DOALL Loops

Bruno Chinelato Honorio$^{(\boxtimes)}$ (ID), João P. L. de Carvalho (ID), Munir Skaf (ID),
and Guido Araujo (ID)

IC and IQ – UNICAMP, Campinas, Brazil
{bruno.honorio,joao.carvalho,guido}@ic.unicamp.br, skaf@unicamp.br

Abstract. Production compilers such as GCC, Clang, IBM XL and the Intel C Compiler employ multiple loop parallelization techniques that help in the task of parallel programming. Although very effective, these techniques are only applicable to loops that the compiler can statically determine to have no loop-carried dependences (DOALL). Because of this restriction, a plethora of Dynamic DOALL (D-DOALL) loops are outright ignored, leaving the parallelism potential of many computationally intensive applications unexplored. This paper proposes a new analysis tool based on OpenMP clauses that allow the programmer to generate detailed profiling of any given loop by identifying its loop-carried dependences and producing carefully selected execution time metrics. The paper also proposes a set of heuristics to be used in conjunction with the analysis tool metrics to properly select loops which could be parallelized through speculative execution, even in the presence of loop-carried dependences. A thorough analysis of 180 loops from 45 benchmarks of three different suites (cBench, Parboil, and Rodinia) was realized using the Intel C Compiler and the proposed approach. Experimental results using static analysis from the Intel C Compiler showed that only 7.8% of the loops are DOALL. The proposed analysis tool exposed 39.5% May DOALL (M-DOALL) loops which could be eventually parallelized using speculative execution, as exemplified by loops from the Parboil sad program which produced a speedup of 1.92x.

Keywords: Compilers · Loop-carried dependences · Debugging · Profiling

1 Introduction

For decades, multicore and manycore parallel architectures have been successfully employed to deliver performance to data-parallel applications [28]. This success is mainly due to substantial work on compiler-based techniques that identify and exploit parallelism opportunities in applications' code [42]. State-of-the-art compiler-based techniques can statically prove that many loops are

Supported by CCES (Center for Computing in Engineering and Sciences) and FAPESP (São Paulo Research Foundation). Grant Numbers: 2013/08293-7, 2019/04536-9, 2016/15337-9 and 2019/01110-0.

free of loop-carried dependences[1] (DOALL) by analyzing their control and data dependences [5,20,31,37]. Most production-ready compilers such as the GNU Compiler Collection (GCC) [14], the C language family front-end (Clang) for LLVM [30], the IBM XL Compiler [25] and Intel's C Compiler (ICC) [26] already implement such parallelization techniques. Besides, application programming interfaces (APIs) such as OpenMP [36] simplify this task by giving programmers control over *which* and *how* loops are parallelized without requiring them to *write* parallel code.

Most production compilers provide loop parallelization methods that are very effective in exploiting DOALL loops, making the ability to detect such loops a central technique in the effective usage of the parallelism available in today's machines. To achieve that, compilers rely on alias analysis which determines if two memory references access the same address and thus are dependent [10]. As a consequence, the quality of the dependence analysis is based on the quality of the alias analysis. Despite the many years of active research [10–12,16,17,19,40], alias analysis remains difficult to verify [38] and requires trade-offs in time/memory *vs.* precision to be implemented in practice [9,21,45]. Static alias analysis for both flow-sensitive and insensitive cases was proven to be NP-Hard [22,29].

Although compilers have been successful in parallelizing DOALL loops, they are oblivious to loops that *do* have loop-carried dependences (DOACROSS), potentially leaving a significant amount of parallelism unexplored [8]. Instead of only relying on information available at compile-time, an alternative to static alias analysis is to leverage dynamic information that can be collected at runtime [4,35]. Previous work focused on dynamic memory disambiguation techniques that couples trace scheduling with compile-time inserted assertions [35]. Other works proposed actual runtime checks that direct control-flow to aggressively parallelize versions of code when dynamic disambiguation determines that two memory references are not aliased [4]. Subsequent works exploited out-of-order execution features, such as speculative execution of branch dependent code, to improve parallelism and efficiency of runtime dependence checks [2,23,33,39].

As Wu et al. show in [43], dynamic memory disambiguation indeed improves program coverage and is more effective than static alias analysis. Nevertheless, such improvements come at the cost of more pressure to processors' micro-architectural structures (e.g. caches). More specifically, program size increases due to code duplication[2] from runtime checks [2,4,23,33,39] and compensation code from traces [35]. This extra code adds needless pressure to a processor micro-architecture even when memory ambiguity is rare or nonexistent [4,35]. This paper leverages dynamic memory disambiguation to precisely find runtime dependences. It aims at detecting two potential classes of parallelizable loops: (a) Dynamic DOALL loops (D-DOALL), which are loops that a compiler failed to statically prove, but may have no loop-carried dependences at runtime; and (b) Dynamic DOACROSS loops (D-DOAX) that have dynamic loop-carried dependences at runtime. In such cases, because of the dynamic nature of these

---

[1] Dependences that arise across different loop iterations.
[2] Code duplication can be avoided in some cases, but not always [13].

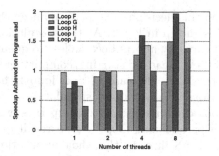

Fig. 1. Speedup achieved by Parboil sad program when different loops are speculated.

dependences, privatization and speculative execution via hardware transactional memory (HTM) [18] can be used to parallelize such loops. HTM is widely available on modern commodity processors from Intel [27], IBM [24], and most recently on ARM processors [3]. Alongside a memory disambiguation analysis, this paper proposes a set of metrics governed by a group of heuristics that allows users to properly choose D-DOAX loops with speed-up potential. This paper makes the following contributions:

- An OpenMP based tool, LoopAnalyzer, integrated into LLVM compiler framework [30], that automatically instruments loops with calls to a custom runtime (see Sect. 3). The runtime collects a set of metrics (see Sect. 3.1) that couples dynamic dependence information with source code location for precise application profiling reports (see Sect. 3.3);
- A set of heuristics that, guided by LoopAnalyzer's profiling reports, allows programmers to properly select loops for parallel speculative execution or privatization (see Sect. 4).
- A thorough dependence analysis and discussion of loops from 45 applications of three well-known benchmarks: cBench [15], Parboil [41], and Rodinia [7]. The evaluation in Sect. 4.2 covered up to 180 loops that are responsible for, at least, 10% of CPU time.
- An artifact [1], which will be open-sourced at publication time.

1.1 Motivating Example

Program sad is among the benchmarks that LoopAnalyzer detected to have loops with potential for D-DOALL parallelism. From all the loops in sad, loop F has shown to be a good candidate for parallelization through speculative execution using hardware transactions (see Sect. 4.2). However loop F exhibit early cache evictions (see Sect. 3.1), which prevents it from taking advantage of HTM (see Sect. 2). Fortunately, F has several nested loops within it (G, H, I, J) and the programmer can determine which nesting level could benefit the most from speculative execution. As described in Sect. 3.1, this paper proposes several metrics to help the programmer in this decision. The performance achieved by speculating each nested loop in F is shown in Fig. 1. As the speculation is moved to deeper loop nest levels, HTM capacity aborts become less frequent as transaction sizes decrease. However, the overhead of starting/committing transaction becomes more noticeable. Therefore, in the case of sad, loop H has the best trade-off in terms of reducing capacity aborts and speculation overhead (see Sect. 4.2). According to the proposed heuristics, nested loop H is exactly the loop chosen to be speculated when parallelizing loop F. As a result, when loop H is speculated and parallelized with 8 threads, the whole application achieves a speedup of 1.92x. This shows how effective HTM-enabled speculation of D-DOALL loops can be when LoopAnalyzer's criteria are met.

The remainder of the paper is organized as follows. Section 2 briefly discusses the fundamental ideas on data-dependence and hardware transactional memory support. Section 3 presents LoopAnalyzer, explains its components, and shows how they are integrated into a new OpenMP clause. Section 4 makes an in-depth discussion of the results obtained with LoopAnalyzer on finding parallelization opportunities. Final and concluding remarks are presented in Sect. 5.

2   Background

Data dependences arise when different statements, or different instances of a statement in the case of loops, access the same memory address and one of the accesses is a write operation [31, 32]. Let S_1 and S_2 be two memory statements accessing the same memory address such that S_1 performs a memory read and S_2 be a memory write. If S_1 executes after S_2, in program order, then a True dependence[3] exists between statements S_1 and S_2. Alternatively, if S_1 executes before S_2 in the program order then the dependence between S_1 and S_2 is said to be an Anti-dependence[4]. Now assuming that both S_1 and S_2 write to the same memory address, then an Output dependence[5] exists. Loop-carried dependences (LCDs) are a special case of those data dependence types that arise between statement instances from different loop iterations [32]. LCDs constrain the order in which loop iterations are allowed to execute in parallel without violating program order semantics [35].

Hardware support for speculative execution in the flavor of transactional memory (HTM) is available on commodity processors for a couple of years already [24, 27, 34, 44]. Most recently, ARM announced the introduction of HTM support to their processors [3]. Hardware transactions are exposed to programmers as new instructions from ISA (*Instruction-Set Architecture*) extensions. HTM instructions are used to explicitly *start*, *commit*, or *abort* transactions. A hardware transaction only commits if throughout its execution no data conflicts happen. Aborts might happen not only due to data conflicts but also

---

[3] a.k.a. Flow or Read-After-Write (RAW) dependence.
[4] a.k.a. Write-After-Read (WAR) dependence.
[5] a.k.a. Write-After-Write (WAW) dependence.

Table 1. The proposed metrics of `LoopAnalyzer`.

Metric	Description
Number of visits	The number of times a loop was visited and fully executed
Total number of iterations	Average number of iterations a single loop visit has
Innermost loop indicator	Indicates if a loop is the innermost in a loop nest
First Eviction Iteration (FEI)	Indicates in which iteration of a loop the first cache line eviction happens
Total number Of Loop-Carried Dependences (LCD)	The sum of unique loop-carried dependences (LCD) of a loop
Total Loop-Carried Probability (LCP)	The accumulated loop-carried probability (LCP) of all unique LCDs of a loop

because hardware transactions can exhaust the hardware's speculative capacity [34]. Existing HTM-ready processors store speculative state on their cache hierarchy, usually on first or second-level caches [34]. Due to capacity constraints and restrictions on the instructions that are allowed to execute inside transactions, there are no guarantees that a transaction will eventually commit. Thus, HTM runtimes are best-effort implementations, and programmers need to provide a fallback code path to handle aborted transactions. The most common (but not the most effective) fallback mechanism is to acquire a global lock to serialize transactions that persistently fail [6].

3   Extending OpenMP to Enable Loop Profiling

The main goal of `LoopAnalyzer` is to discover loops that can be parallelized but static analysis in mainstream compilers considered non-profitable to do so because of may-dependences. Thusly, at runtime, `LoopAnalyzer` can determine if a loop is D-DOALL or D-DOAX for a given set of program inputs. Moreover, `LoopAnalyzer` also measures each loop's CPU time and how much, percentage-wise, it contributes to the overall execution time of an application. However, this information alone is not enough to determine if a loop is a good candidate for parallelization (see Sect. 4.2). For example, in the case the loop is detected to be D-DOALL, the programmer cannot assure it is a DOALL loop, as a dependence might arise if a different input is used. Therefore, a group of metrics was chosen to help users of `LoopAnalyzer` to quickly determine if a loop is a good candidate for parallelization.

3.1   Metrics

Table 1 shows the proposed metrics. A high number of visits implies high overhead for parallel runtime libraries, possibly causing a slowdown if a loop is parallelized. The total number of iterations is a desirable metric because it relates to how much work is available to be divided between worker threads. The size of innermost loops constrains how effective hardware transactions will be when executing iterations speculatively. Hardware-based transactions have capacity limitations in most commercially available HTM implementations [44]. FEI is computed via a custom software simulation of the cache level associated with the speculative state of hardware transactions [34]. Cache evictions cause hardware transactions to abort in all commercially available HTM implementations [34]. Capacity aborts increase the overhead and affect the overall performance of applications. If a loop has FEI of one, then every transaction will abort and roll-back for retry. Due to the best-effort nature of HTMs, this will force every transaction to be serialized. FEI is a simple way to estimate the number of iterations a transaction can execute without suffering compulsory aborts. LCD is used because since the analysis is dynamic, different dependences can manifest in each loop iteration due to conditional branches within a loop's body. Low LCP means that dependences happen rarely, meaning that it is possible to execute a loop speculatively in parallel for the majority of its iterations.

3.2   General Overview of the Profiling Tool

LoopAnalyzer is comprised of three components: DOVEC, DOPROF, and DOCHECK. DOVEC uses the Intel C Compiler (ICC) with the vectorization report flags[6] on to collect whether a loop was vectorized. If the loop was vectorized it is categorized as a DOALL loop, otherwise is said to be a may-DOALL loop (M-DOALL). The ICC report feature is the only functionality not provided by LoopAnalyzer. Although ICC offers a better vectorization report, dependence analyzers from other compilers could also be adapted to LoopAnalyzer.

DOPROF performs profiling of loops and collects the following loop information: CPU time, the total number of visits, average execution time of each visit, and the average number of iterations. Loops that contribute to less than 10% of total CPU time are discarded because the goal was to capture loops with the best possible payback.

DOCHECK leverages on the proposed OpenMP clause check to look for loop-carried dependences at runtime (see Sect. 3.3). Adding check to a loop will instrument it with calls to a custom runtime library (see Sect. 3.4) that collects dependence information of each visit to the loop. The output of DOCHECK is the group of metrics discussed in Sect. 3.1 that summarizes the speculative potential of each loop. DOCHECK reports if a loop has loop-carried dependences and categorizes the loop as either dynamic DOALL (D-DOALL) or dynamic DOACROSS (D-DOAX), for the given set of program input data (see Subsect. 4.1). If the loop is D-DOALL, it means it did not present any data dependence during the whole execution in all of its visits. For D-DOAX loops, DOCHECK also shows its LCD, LCP, and FEI. It also shows innermost loop information for both loop types. DOCHECK takes as input the output from both DOVEC and DOPROF and automatically annotates loops with the check clause. The output of DOCHECK is then fed to a table generator that presents the loops sorted in the following order: CPU Time, LCD, LCP, and FEI.

---

[6] -q-opt-report5 and -qopt-report-phase=vec.

3.3   The Check Clause

As Table 2 shows, check has four attributes: dependence, first, verbose and time. dependence classifies the loop as D-DOALL or D-DOAX and collects the number of LCDs, LCP, FEI and indicates if a loop is an innermost loop in a loop nest. With dependence every loop visit is instrumented to collect the total number of unique LCDs and LCPs. It is the optimal choice for analyzing a significant amount of loops in a neatly summarized way. The dependence attribute can be used in any type of loop (for, while or do-while loops), and is capable of instrumenting canonical as well as non-canonical loops[7]. Due to the high memory overhead of memory disambiguation analysis, it is recommended to annotate with dependence just one loop at a time.

Table 2. The different attributes of the check clause.

Attribute	Operation
Time	Reports file name, line number, CPU time, iterations and visits
Dependence	Reports LCD, LCP, FEI, INNER for all loop visits
First	Reports if the loop has at least one LCD or not
Verbose	Reports the location of the loop dependence

Listing 1.1. Using verbose on a loop.

```
1  #pragma omp parallel \
2    check(verbose)
3  for(i=0; i < N; ++i){
4    const int value = img[
       i];
5    if(histo[value] <
       UINT8_MAX)
6    {
7      ++histo[value];
8    }
9  }
```

Listing 1.2. verbose report.

```
1
2  for(i=0; i < N; ++i){
3    .
4    .
5  +--> if (histo[value]...
6  |  .
7  |  .
8  +<-- >--< ++histo[value];
9    .
```

The first attribute aims at checking if a loop has *any* loop-carried dependence. With first the dependence analysis of subsequent memory access is skipped once the first loop-carried dependence is detected. After the first LCD is detected the loop continues to run without any instrumentation. The information gathered with first is the same as with dependence, but only up to the first LCD found. This allows for much faster execution and shorter analysis time.

The verbose attribute shows the exact source code location of loop-carried dependences, thus allowing programmers to identify the precise code region that

---

[7] A loop is canonical if and only if it has a single induction variable, a simple test expression, and its induction variable is never modified in the loop body.

should be executed speculatively. As an example, consider the loop in Listing 1.1, extracted from the `histo` benchmark in the Parboil suite. Listing 1.2 shows the report generated when loop in Listing 1.1 is annotated with `verbose`. The `>--<` arrows represent loop-carried dependences within the same program line while `+-->/+<--` arrows show the dependence relation across different lines. `verbose` is recommended for loops that have a small number of LCDs, as loops with high LCD counts are associated with hard to parallelize loops and will generate long reports.

The `time` attribute has considerably lower runtime overhead compared to other `check` attributes such as `verbose` and `dependence`, thus it can be used to instrument many, or even all loops in an application. Depending on the input size of the data and loop nesting level, the runtime overhead will increase proportionally to the trip-count.

All loops can be instrumented without any source-code changes by specifying the `-fdoprof` flag to `LoopAnalyzer`.

Listing 1.3. For-loop after a `check` source-to-source transformation.

```
1  { //START OF PROFILING
2    unsigned long __indvar = 0;
3    __enterLoopRegion();
4    for(...){
5      __start_iter_prof(__indvar++);
6
7      //Loop body
8
9      __stop_iter_prof();
10   }
11   __exitLoopRegion(INNER,SUMMARY);
12 } //END OF PROFILING
```

3.4   Implementation of the Check Clause

We extended the OpenMP language support in Clang to add the `check` clause and its attributes. Source-to-source transformation passes add calls to a custom runtime (`check-rt`) which are later used in an LLVM IR pass (`OMPCheckPass`) to instrument load/store instructions within loops. Moreover, any functions that are called within annotated loops also need to be instrumented.

Listing 1.3 shows how a for-loop looks like after `check`'s source-to-source transformations. `__enterLoopRegion` is an initializer function that passes to `check-rt` the stack pointer and program counter (PC) at the start of the loop. `start_iter_prof` passes the current iteration of the loop. Loop iteration information is key to enable the collection of metrics such as FEI and to identify the LCDs themselves, as discussed shortly.

start_iter_prof and stop_iter_prof mark the boundaries of a loop's body. Only variables declared within the loop body are not instrumented. All exit points of a function are annotated with a call to function_exit. All metrics are summarized when __exitLoopRegion is called at the end of each loop visit. The first argument indicates if the loop is the innermost (INNER) or not (OUTER). The second argument is a LoopAnalyzer's dependence report mode: summarized (SUMMARY) or verbose (VERBOSE).

The check_dependence function in check-rt implements the memory disambiguation analysis to identify loop-carried dependences. Moreover, it also implements the logic to simulate the cache organization to compute FEI. This runtime function takes two arguments: (1) the program counter (PC) of the instruction accessing memory and (2) the type of memory access (read/write). Memory access information is stored in a two-level map data-structure, one map for reads, and another for writes. The first level maps memory addresses to another map that associates the PC of the access with the last iteration that accessed the same address. Dependences are stored in a separate map that associates the PC of memory accessing instruction with a list of dependence records. A dependence record keeps the pair of PCs of each dependent instruction along with the dependence type and probability (LCP).

4   Experimental Results

This section shows how LoopAnalyzer is used to uncover parallelism opportunities that are not discovered by typical compile-time static analysis. We also discuss a set of heuristics that allows users to identify parallelizable loops guided by the metrics extracted with LoopAnalyzer.

4.1   Methodology

The experimental results aim to show the latent parallelism that a state of the art compiler misses due to the conservative nature of its static analysis. In order to assess LoopAnalyzer capabilities, three benchmark suites widely studied in the literature are used, namely cBench [15], Parboil [41], and Rodinia [7]. cBench is a collection of open-source sequential programs, while Parboil and Rodinia are sets of computing applications with multiple implementations for different parallel models, such as CUDA, OpenMP and OpenCL. The unoptimized sequential versions of Parboil's applications were used. Rodinia does not provide a sequential version of its applications, thus the OpenMP parallelized code without the pragmas was used. In total, 180 loops from 45 benchmarks were analyzed by our LoopAnalyzer tool. These loops do not cover all loops existing in each application. Only loops that account for at least 10% of total CPU time are discussed.

The results reported in this section represent the mean of 10 executions[8] of the DOPROF step of LoopAnalyzer, since DOCHECK's reports are the same for the

---

[8] Average variance across measurements was lower than 0.5% of the mean.

specific input of parameters used. All applications were compiled with Clang 4.0 and Intel C Compiler (ICC) 19.1 with the highest optimization level (-O3) enabled. All applications were compiled from the same source code in both compilers. cBench applications were executed with the default input size and repeat loop iterations set to 1, because rerunning the application would not reveal different loop-carried dependences. For Parboil, sad used large, bfs used 1M, mri-q, histo and spmv used large, cutcp and tpacf used small. The default input was used in Rodinia. The experiments discussed next were conducted on a machine powered by a Intel® Xeon™ E5-2620 2.1 GHz processor and 64 GB of RAM.

4.2   Identifying Parallelization Opportunities via LoopAnalyzer

Figure 2(a) shows the breakdown of loops classified either as DOALL or M-DOALL by ICC's static analysis. Only 7.2% of the loops analyzed were categorized as DOALL (3 from cBench, 3 from Parboil, and 7 from Rodinia). The results with our LoopAnalyzer tool runtime analysis reveal that there is a significant amount of potential parallel loops that are not uncovered by ICC's static analysis, as Fig. 2(b) shows. Out of the 167 M-DOALL loops (92.2%), 44 loops (26.4%) were categorized as D-DOALL[9] and 123 (73.6%) as D-DOAX[10] for the input data of the corresponding benchmarks. Although a significant percentage of loops (26.4%) revealed to be D-DOALL, this does not automatically imply that performance gains via speculation of these loops are possible. Similarly, being classified as D-DOAX does not mean that a loop cannot be parallelized. The metrics proposed in this paper were designed to allow a finer-grained analysis of these loops. Besides, a set of heuristics is proposed to guide the decision of which loops should be considered for parallelization. These heuristics were designed based on

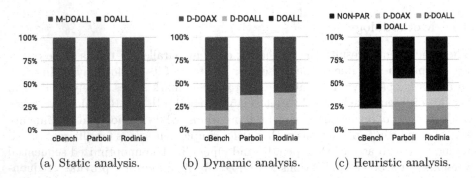

(a) Static analysis.   (b) Dynamic analysis.   (c) Heuristic analysis.

Fig. 2. Breakdown of loops according to (a) static (DOALL and M-DOALL loops), (b) dynamic analysis, and with LoopAnalyzer's classification for each benchmark suite. In (b) M-DOALL loops are further divided into D-DOALL and D-DOAX without any parallelization concern. In (c) the heuristic analysis divides loops into non-parallelizable (NON-PAR) and parallelizable (D-DOALL, D-DOAX, and DOALL).

---

[9] 12 from cBench, 12 from Parboil and 20 from Rodinia.
[10] 57 from cBench, 25 from Parboil and 41 from Rodinia.

Table 3. Detailed loop information extracted with `LoopAnalyzer` from loops in cBench (`cB`), Parboil (`Par`), and Rodinia (`Rod`) benchmark applications. Potentially parallelizable loops have IDs in bold.

	LOOPS			CPU TIME				METRICS					
ID	BENCHMARK	FILENAME	LINE	%	TOTAL(s)	MEAN(s)	TYPE	VISITS	INNER	ITER	FEI	LCP	LCD
A	(cB) consumer_jpeg_c	jcapimin.c	155	80.17	0.015589	8.66e-04	D-DOALL	18	YES	13.0	-	-	-
B	(cB) security_blowfish_e	bf.c	111	20.66	0.000107	1.08e-06	D-DOALL	99	YES	39.0	-	-	-
C	(cB) automotive_susan_c	susan.c	1458	71.49	0.012366	2.81e-05	D-DOAX	440	YES	590.0	356	21.43	10003
D	(cB) telecom_adpcm_c	adpcm.c	101	77.53	0.001421	1.82e-05	D-DOAX	78	YES	989.0	-	58.91	181
E	(cB) consumer_jpeg_d	djpeg.c	570	55.72	0.001972	1.97e-03	D-DOAX	1	YES	208.0	-	99.52	1
F	(Par) sad	sad_cpu.c	39	96.88	52.29	7.80e-01	D-DOALL	67	YES	120.0	1	-	-
G	(Par) sad	sad_cpu.c	69	96.88	52.29	6.50e-03	D-DOAX	8040	NO	33.0	20	96.97	13
H	(Par) sad	sad_cpu.c	70	96.86	52.28	1.97e-04	D-DOALL	265320	NO	33.0	-	-	-
I	(Par) sad	sad_cpu.c	74	96.29	51.96	5.93e-06	D-DOAX	8755560	NO	4.0	-	75.0	10
J	(Par) sad	sad_cpu.c	75	93.40	50.41	1.44e-06	D-DOALL	35022240	NO	4.0	-	-	-
K	(Par) tpacf	model_compute_cpu.c	32	98.78	3.24	3.31e-05	D-DOAX	97786	NO	364.0	-	38.81	5
L	(Rod) heartwall	main.c	549	99.89	69.462486	3.47e+00	D-DOALL	20	YES	51.0	-	-	-
M	(Rod) pathfinder	pathfinder.cpp	42	22.33	0.319378	3.19e-01	D-DOALL	1	NO	100.0	-	-	-
N	(Rod) backprop	backprop.c	316	11.50	0.010901	6.41e-04	D-DOAX	17	YES	61682.0	99	100.00	2
O	(Rod) hotspot3D	3D.c	161	19.74	1.005184	1.26e-03	D-DOALL	800	NO	512.0	2	-	-

observations we made during the experiments over the benchmark suites. We are working towards making them generic for most programs. The loops at Table 3 are used to guide readers in understanding the insights that lead to the choice of the proposed heuristics. Only loops that satisfy all the conditions below are considered viable candidates for parallelization:

- VISITS: The number of visits should be below 1000, due to the high overhead of OpenMP runtime calls as wells as transaction invocations.
- ITER: The number of iterations has to be at least two to mitigate threading overhead.
- LCP and LCD: If LCP is higher than 30%, then the LCD threshold is at most 15. Otherwise, the LCD threshold is at most 30.
- FEI: `D-DOALL` or `D-DOAX` loops that satisfy the above metrics and do not have FEI = 1 are immediately considered parallelizable. If FEI = 1, a search over perfectly nested loops (if they exist) is done to find a loop that satisfies the following conditions:
  - Inner Loops with Visits Below 1 Million
  - Inner Loops that have FEI higher than 1.

A high LCP means that dependences are frequent and thus some iterations inevitably need to be executed sequentially, thus reducing potential performance gains. Frequent dependences would also cause frequent transaction aborts that introduce overhead. A high LCP but a low LCD count indicates that these dependences could be removed via privatization. Low LCP and high LCD do not necessarily imply that a loop can be safely speculated as, even with a low LCP, most iterations might have at least one loop-carried dependence. For example, if a loop has 4 dependences on a loop with 100 iterations and each dependence only appears in separated chunks of 25 iterations, the accumulated LCP will only be 25%, but all iterations will have a dependence. So the higher the number of LCDs, the higher the chance of dependences appearing in all iterations.

Loops with FEI > 1 can have individual iterations speculated when the outermost loop is divided between worker threads, as long it satisfies all metrics other than FEI. Alternatively, such loops can also be strip-mined, mitigating possible loop-carried dependences by assigning dependent iterations to the same thread.

Table 3 presents only 15 out of 180 loops analyzed due to space constraints[11]. Each loop is labeled from A to R for easier referencing as Table 3 shows. As D-DOALL loops do not have dependences, denoted by "-" in their respective LCP and LCD columns in Table 3. Similarly, "-" in the FEI column is used to denote when no cache evictions happen throughout a loop's execution. Loops in Table 3 were selected because they are representative of different metrics' values that show how the heuristics work. According to the heuristics presented above, the following loops are parallelizable: A, B, E, F, L, M, N, O. The other loops are considered nonparallelizable.

Loops A, B, L, M, and O are all D-DOALL loops and they satisfy all metrics. Loops E and N are D-DOAX loops that have an LCP of 99.52% and 100% but with only 1 and 2 LCDs, respectively. However, as both have low LCD they are also good candidates for parallelization. Loop C meets all criteria except that it exceeds the LCD threshold (30) for low LCP (<30%) loops with a total of 10003 loop-carried dependences. A high LCD count does not make Loop C a good candidate for speculation because, even with a low LCP (20%), most iterations have at least one loop-carried dependence. When Loop C was executed speculatively via HTM an abort rate near 100% is observed. Loop D does not meet both LCD and LCP requirements. Loop K exceeds the VISITS threshold (1000), which could cause a significant overhead due to thread dispatching, as each thread could be (re)dispatched 97786 times.

Loops F, H, I, and J show how effective the heuristics are to identify loops with potential parallelism. Loop F is a D-DOALL loop with FEI = 1 which prevents it from being directly speculated. Therefore, speculation needs to happen in a fine-grained manner. Although LoopAnalyzer shows that this loop is an innermost loop, a quick inspection of the application code revealed that F's body consists of a single function call. The function called within F's body contains loops G, H, I, and J nested in this order. Because these loops are perfectly nested, speculation can happen at any nesting level. Speculating loop F shows no performance gains due to FEI being 1, meaning that almost every transaction aborts, serializing the loop. Loop G, has a higher FEI (20), however, capacity aborts were still frequent, explaining the modest performance gains achieved by speculating its body. Loops I and J have visits higher than 1 million and bodies consisting of a dozen of instructions, imposing a high speculation overhead due to transaction management. Loop H has the best trade-off in terms of transaction size and speculation overhead. Application (sad), when loop H is speculated and parallelized with 8 threads achieved a whole application speedup of 1.92x.

---

[11] These loops were chosen because they are representative of the values of the presented metrics.

Figure 2(c) shows that a detailed analysis using `LoopAnalyzer` combined with the proposed set of heuristics reveals that 53 (out of 167) `M-DOALL` loops are parallelizable. Combining the above-mentioned approach to the `DOALL` loops that the compile-time static analysis encountered, the cBench benchmark presented a total of 13% of potentially parallelizable loops, Parboil showed 55% of the loops having the potential to be parallelized, Rodinia showed that 40.2% of its loops have potential to be parallelized. A stark contrast when compared to the initial static analysis, which only showed as high as 10% parallelizable loops for the Rodinia benchmark.

5 Conclusion

This paper presented `LoopAnalyzer`, a loop profiling tool designed to identify loops that can be parallelized through speculative execution. A new OpenMP clause is proposed to enable `LoopAnalyzer` and simplify the task of finding loop candidates. Loops annotated with the proposed clause are automatically instrumented with calls to a custom runtime memory disambiguation and loop analysis library (`check-rt`). Experimental results show that `LoopAnalyzer` revealed that up to 53 (out of 167) `M-DOALL` loops would benefit from parallel speculative execution. Moreover, by using `LoopAnalyzer` guided by the proposed heuristics, a thorough loop dependence analysis and discussion of 45 applications showed that over 36% of loops across all applications from well-known benchmarks (cBench, Parboil, and Rodinia) have parallelism opportunities not explored by existing production-ready compilers. Exploiting these opportunities is a future goal of this work.

References

1. LoopAnalyzer Tool Repository: Available at publication time. https://github.com/BrunoChonorio/LoopAnalyzer
2. Alli, S., Bailey, C.: Compiler-directed dynamic memory disambiguation for loop structures. In: Euromicro Symposium on Digital System Design, 2004, DSD 2004, pp. 130–134 (2004). https://doi.org/10.1109/DSD.2004.1333268
3. ARM C Language Extensions Documentation, ARM Limited: Transactional Memory Extension (TME) intrinsics (2019). https://developer.arm.com/docs/101028/0009/transactional-memory-extension-tme-intrinsics. Release ACLE Q3 2019. Document Number 101028
4. Bernstein, D., Cohen, D., Maydan, D.E.: Dynamic memory disambiguation for array references. In: Proceedings of the 27th Annual International Symposium on Microarchitecture, MICRO 27, pp. 105–111. Association for Computing Machinery, New York (1994). https://doi.org/10.1145/192724.192737
5. Burke, M., Cytron, R.: Interprocedural dependence analysis and parallelization. SIGPLAN Not. **21**(7), 162–175 (1986). https://doi.org/10.1145/13310.13328
6. de Carvalho, J.P., Araujo, G., Baldassin, A.: The case for phase-based transactional memory. IEEE Trans. Parallel Distrib. Syst. **30**(2), 459–472 (2018)

7. Che, S., et al.: Rodinia: a benchmark suite for heterogeneous computing. In: 2009 IEEE International Symposium on Workload Characterization (IISWC), pp. 44–54. IEEE (2009)

8. Chen, D.K., Yew, P.C.: An empirical study on DOACROSS loops. In: Proceedings of Supercomputing 1991, pp. 620–632. IEEE (1991)

9. Chowdhury, Rezaul A., Djeu, Peter., Cahoon, Brendon., Burrill, James H., McKinley, Kathryn S.: The limits of alias analysis for scalar optimizations. In: Duesterwald, Evelyn (ed.) CC 2004. LNCS, vol. 2985, pp. 24–38. Springer, Heidelberg (2004). https://doi.org/10.1007/978-3-540-24723-4_3

10. Cooper, K.D., Kennedy, K.: Fast interprocedual alias analysis. In: Proceedings of the 16th ACM SIGPLAN-SIGACT Symposium on Principles of Programming Languages, POPL 1989, pp. 49–59. Association for Computing Machinery, New York (1989). https://doi.org/10.1145/75277.75282

11. Deutsch, A.: Interprocedural may-alias analysis for pointers: beyond k-limiting. SIGPLAN Not. 29(6), 230–241 (1994). https://doi.org/10.1145/773473.178263

12. Diwan, A., McKinley, K.S., Moss, J.E.B.: Type-based alias analysis. SIGPLAN Not. 33(5), 106–117 (1998). https://doi.org/10.1145/277652.277670

13. Doerfert, J., Grosser, T., Hack, S.: Optimistic loop optimization. In: Proceedings of the 2017 International Symposium on Code Generation and Optimization, CGO 2017, pp. 292–304. IEEE Press (2017)

14. Free Software Foundation Inc.: Using the GNU Compiler Collection (2019). https://gcc.gnu.org/onlinedocs/

15. Fursin, G., Lokhmotov, A., Plowman, E.: Collective knowledge: towards R&D sustainability. In: Proceedings of the Conference on Design, Automation and Test in Europe (DATE 2016) (March 2016)

16. Gupta, S.K., Sharma, N.: Alias analysis for intermediate code. In: GCC Developers Summit, p. 71. Citeseer (2003)

17. Hall, Mary W., Murphy, Brian R., Amarasinghe, Saman P., Liao, Shih -Wei, Lam, Monica S.: Interprocedural analysis for parallelization. In: Huang, Chua-Huang, Sadayappan, Ponnuswamy, Banerjee, Utpal, Gelernter, David, Nicolau, Alex, Padua, David (eds.) LCPC 1995. LNCS, vol. 1033, pp. 61–80. Springer, Heidelberg (1996). https://doi.org/10.1007/BFb0014192

18. Herlihy, M., Moss, J.E.B.: Transactional memory: architectural support for lock-free data structures. In: Proceedings of the 20th Annual International Symposium on Computer Architecture, pp. 289–300 (1993)

19. Hind, M., Burke, M., Carini, P., Choi, J.D.: Interprocedural pointer alias analysis. ACM Trans. Program. Lang. Syst. 21(4), 848–894 (1999). https://doi.org/10.1145/325478.325519

20. Hind, M., Burke, M., Carini, P., Midkiff, S.: An empirical study of precise interprocedural array analysis. Sci. Program. 3, 255–271 (1994)

21. Hind, M., Pioli, A.: Evaluating the effectiveness of pointer alias analyses. Sci. Comput. Program. 39(1), 31–55 (2001). https://doi.org/10.1016/S0167-6423(00)00014-9. http://www.sciencedirect.com/science/article/pii/S0167642300000149. Static Program Analysis (SAS 1998)

22. Horwitz, S.: Precise flow-insensitive may-alias analysis is NP-hard. ACM Trans. Program. Lang. Syst. 19(1), 1–6 (1997). https://doi.org/10.1145/239912.239913

23. Huang, A.S., Slavenburg, G., Shen, J.P.: Speculative disambiguation: a compilation technique for dynamic memory disambiguation. In: Proceedings of the 21st Annual International Symposium on Computer Architecture, ISCA 1994, pp. 200–210. IEEE Computer Society Press, Washington, DC (1994). https://doi.org/10.1145/191995.192012

24. IBM Corporation: IBM Power ISA, Version 3.0 B (2017)
25. IBM Corporation: IBM XL C/C++ for Linux: Compiler Reference, Version 16.11 (SC27-8047-01) (2018)
26. Intel Corporation: Intel® C++ Compiler Developer Guide and Reference (Version 19.1) (2019)
27. Intel Corporation: Intel® Architecture Instruction Set Extensions Programming Reference (2020). Reference Number 319433–038
28. Kirk, D.B., Wen-Mei, W.H.: Programming Massively Parallel Processors: A Hands-on Approach. Morgan Kaufmann, Burlington (2016)
29. Landi, W., Ryder, B.G.: Pointer-induced aliasing: a problem classification. In: Proceedings of the 18th ACM SIGPLAN-SIGACT Symposium on Principles of Programming Languages, pp. 93–103 (1991)
30. Lattner, C., Adve, V.: LLVM: a compilation framework for lifelong program analysis & transformation. In: Proceedings of the International Symposium on Code Generation and Optimization: Feedback-Directed and Runtime Optimization, CGO 2004, pp. 75–86. IEEE Computer Society, Washington, DC (2004). http://dl.acm.org/citation.cfm?id=977395.977673
31. Maydan, D.E., Hennessy, J.L., Lam, M.S.: Efficient and exact data dependence analysis. SIGPLAN Not. **26**(6), 1–14 (1991). https://doi.org/10.1145/113446.113447
32. Maydan, D.E., Hennessy, J.L., Lam, M.S.: Effectiveness of data dependence analysis. Int. J. Parallel Program. **23**(1), 63–81 (1995)
33. Moshovos, A., Breach, S.E., Vijaykumar, T.N., Sohi, G.S.: Dynamic speculation and synchronization of data dependences. SIGARCH Comput. Archit. News **25**(2), 181–193 (1997). https://doi.org/10.1145/384286.264189
34. Nakaike, T., Odaira, R., Gaudet, M., Michael, M.M., Tomari, H.: Quantitative comparison of hardware transactional memory for Blue Gene/Q, zEnterprise EC12, Intel Core, and POWER8. SIGARCH Comput. Archit. News **43**(3S), 144–157 (2015). https://doi.org/10.1145/2872887.2750403
35. Nicolau, A.: Run-time disambiguation: coping with statically unpredictable dependencies. IEEE Trans. Comput. **38**(5), 663–678 (1989). https://doi.org/10.1109/12.24269
36. OpenMP Architecture Review Board: OpenMP application program interface version 5.0 (November 2018). http://www.openmp.org
37. Padua, D.A., Wolfe, M.J.: Advanced compiler optimizations for supercomputers. Commun. ACM **29**(12), 1184–1201 (1986). https://doi.org/10.1145/7902.7904
38. Robert, Valentin, Leroy, Xavier: A formally-verified alias analysis. In: Hawblitzel, Chris, Miller, Dale (eds.) CPP 2012. LNCS, vol. 7679, pp. 11–26. Springer, Heidelberg (2012). https://doi.org/10.1007/978-3-642-35308-6_5
39. Sato, T.: Speculative resolution of ambiguous memory aliasing. In: Proceedings Innovative Architecture for Future Generation High-Performance Processors and Systems, pp. 17–26 (1997)
40. Steensgaard, B.: Points-to analysis in almost linear time. In: Proceedings of the 23rd ACM SIGPLAN-SIGACT Symposium on Principles of Programming Languages, POPL 1996, pp. 32–41. Association for Computing Machinery, New York (1996). https://doi.org/10.1145/237721.237727
41. Stratton, J.A., et al.: Parboil: a revised benchmark suite for scientific and commercial throughput computing. Cent. Reliab. High-Perform. Comput. **127** (2012)
42. Wolfe, M.J.: High Performance Compilers for Parallel Computing. Addison-Wesley Longman Publishing Co., Inc., Boston (1995)

43. Wu, Y., Chen, L.L., Ju, R., Fang, J.: Performance potentials of compiler-directed data speculation. In: Proceedings of the 2003 IEEE International Symposium on Performance Analysis of Systems and Software, ISPASS 2003, pp. 22–31. IEEE Computer Society, USA (2003)
44. Yoo, R.M., Hughes, C.J., Lai, K., Rajwar, R.: Performance evaluation of intel® transactional synchronization extensions for high-performance computing. In: Proceedings of the International Conference on High Performance Computing, Networking, Storage and Analysis, SC 2013. Association for Computing Machinery, New York (2013). https://doi.org/10.1145/2503210.2503232
45. Zheng, X., Rugina, R.: Demand-driven alias analysis for C. In: Proceedings of the 35th Annual ACM SIGPLAN-SIGACT Symposium on Principles of Programming Languages, POPL 2008, pp. 197–208. Association for Computing Machinery, New York (2008). https://doi.org/10.1145/1328438.1328464

ComPar: Optimized Multi-compiler for Automatic OpenMP S2S Parallelization

Idan Mosseri[1,2], Lee-Or Alon[1,3], Re'Em Harel[3,4], and Gal Oren[1,2(✉)]

[1] Department of Computer Science, Ben-Gurion University of the Negev,
P.O.B. 653, Be'er Sheva, Israel
{idanmos,alonlee,orenw}@post.bgu.ac.il
[2] Department of Physics, Nuclear Research Center-Negev,
P.O.B. 9001, Be'er-Sheva, Israel
[3] Israel Atomic Energy Commission, P.O.B. 7061, 61070 Tel Aviv, Israel
reemharel22@gmail.com
[4] Department of Physics, Bar-Ilan University, IL52900 Ramat-Gan, Israel

Abstract. Parallelization schemes are essential in order to exploit the full benefits of multi-core architectures, which have become widespread in recent years. In shared-memory architectures, the most comprehensive parallelization API is OpenMP. However, the introduction of correct and optimal OpenMP parallelization to applications is not always a simple task, due to common parallel shared-memory management pitfalls, architecture heterogeneity and the current necessity for human expertise in order to comprehend many fine details and abstract correlations. To ease this process, many automatic parallelization compilers were created over the last decade. [2] tested several source-to-source compilers and concluded that each has its advantages and disadvantages and no compiler is superior to all other compilers in all tests. This indicates that a fusion of the compilers' best outputs under the best hyper-parameters for the current hardware setups can yield greater speedups. To create such a fusion, one should execute a computationally intensive hyper-parameter sweep, in which the performance of each option is estimated and the best option is chosen. We created a novel parallelization source-to-source multi-compiler named *ComPar*, which uses code segmentation-and-fusion with hyper-parameters tuning to achieve the best parallel code possible without any human intervention while maintaining the program's validity. In this paper we present *ComPar* and analyze its results on NAS and PolyBench benchmarks. We conclude that although the resources *ComPar* requires to produce parallel code are greater than other source-to-source parallelization compilers – as it depends on the number of parameters the user wishes to consider, and their combinations – *ComPar* achieves the best performance overall compared to the serial code version and other tested parallelization compilers. *ComPar* is publicly available at: https://github.com/Scientific-Computing-Lab-NRCN/compar.

K. Milfeld et al. (Eds.): IWOMP 2020, LNCS 12295, pp. 247–262, 2020.
https://doi.org/10.1007/978-3-030-58144-2_16

1   Introduction

Since the end of Dennard scaling [3] in 2005, there is a growing usage in multi-core architectures. These architectures can be found in a wide range of computers from wearable devices through smartphones and personal computers to high-performance computers [4]. Although these architectures can yield excellent performance in theory, in practice one should adjust his programming methods to work in parallel [5], i.e. to be executed by several processing units simultaneously. Furthermore, to fully exploit these architectures, one has to consider balancing the workload of the program between the processing units. Unfortunately, transforming a program from a sequential into a parallel one may be a very complicated and pricey task, especially when dealing with legacy codes [6]. This is due to the fact that in order to evolve a program to work in a parallel fashion, one must have a deep understanding of the code behavior and be very cautious not to change the inner logic of the program while attempting to utilize the benefits of the system. In a shared-memory setting, this is usually done via compiler optimizations and parallelization API such as OpenMP.

OpenMP [7] is a pragma (compiler directive) oriented library for shared memory parallelization. The programmer can mark structured code-block by wrapping them with directives that instruct the compiler how to perform the parallelization. At run-time, each structured code-block is divided and executed concurrently on several threads. Note that the compiler might ignore the suggested directives. In this case, the structured block that was wrapped by the ignored directive will not be executed in parallel. In addition to the directives, OpenMP offers a wide variety of run-time sub-routines and environment variables that can control the run-time specification and the fashion of the parallel execution. All of the above have an impact on the final performance of the parallel execution. To ease the burden of introducing such directives, several source-to-source (S2S) parallelization compilers that allow users to automatically parallelize their code [8] – prior to the machine-code compilation – were invented.

The automatic S2S parallelization compilers insert parallelization instructions in different fashions while preserving both the program's correctness and data coherence implied by its data dependencies. These compilers work as follows: The compilers parse the code into an Abstract Syntax Tree (AST) [9]; then, they find data dependencies by analyzing the generated tree; and afterward, they add parallel directives to certain structured code-blocks in an attempt to optimize the performance of the code. This process is done several times until convergence. At the end of the process, the tree is converted back to code in the original programming language. The following note should be highlighted in this context: Currently, no existing automatic parallelization compiler can fully replace the programmer's insight, as programmers are still able to push the performance of the parallelization further than automatic compilers. This is since some information is usually hard to automatically extract from the AST alone, and is crucial for full exploitation of the parallel performance of the code. For example, function side effects; pointer aliasing; valuable information that may be based on computational load; optimal scheduling; chunk size and the number of threads. In this work, we introduce *ComPar*: a unified multi-compiler that sweeps over different flags, OpenMP clauses and runtime library routines for each structured code-block that is suitable for parallelization using different automatic S2S parallelization compilers and fuses the best results, in terms of performance, together into one optimal code.

The rest of the paper is organized as follows: In Sect. 2 we present the related work done in regards to automatic parallelization compilers and the foundations of *ComPar*. In Sect. 3 we briefly discuss the relevant compilers for *ComPar* purposes. In Sect. 4 we present *ComPar*, and examine its performance in Sect. 5. Finally, we conclude this work and discuss future work in Sect. 6.

2 Related Work

S2S Automatic Parallelization Compilers: S. Prema et al. [10] compared several automatic parallelization compilers (not necessarily S2S) including Cetus [11], Par4All [12], Pluto [13], Parallware [14,15], AutoPar [16], and ICC [17]. They discussed the different aspects of the compilers' work fashions and showed their speedups and points of failure on ten NAS Parallel Benchmarks [18] using the Gprof performance analysis tool [19]. While Parallware and Pluto failed to parallelize the benchmarks, the authors suggested a way to overcome these points of failure with manual intervention. They observed that Par4All requires no manual intervention, while Cetus and AutoPar require minimal manual intervention, thus allowing us to consider them for this work. Harel et al. [2] focused on Cetus, Par4All, and AutoPar [16] while eliminating the need for the rest of the S2S automatic parallelization compilers. [2] briefly discussed these compilers (regarding both history and work fashion) and presented each compiler's strengths and weaknesses. Moreover, [2] tested the performance of these compilers in the Matrix Multiplication kernel and the NAS benchmark [18]. In addition, [2] pointed out the pitfalls of the selected compilers and proposed changes to their code-base, in an attempt to aid these compilers to insert more OpenMP directives. [2] also compared the compilers' performance on two different suitable hardware architectures – multi-core (Non-Uniform Memory Access) and many-core (XeonPhi, GPGPU). [2] concluded that currently there is no best S2S automatic parallelization compiler. However, there is a preferable compiler for each specific case, as the compilers behave differently either inherently (e.g. different AST analysis and precautions) or extrinsically (e.g. compilation flags of the parallelizer itself), thus finding the preferable one might be a tedious and costly task.

Hyper-parameters Tuning: The concept of auto-tuning OpenMP code is well-established [20–23], and as one can assume, the choice of each environment variable can greatly affect the performance of the code [24]. Consider for example the *dynamic* scheduling option: If the chosen *chunk_size* is too small, the resulting numerous work segments cause high overhead. Contrary, too large *chunk_size* may result in some threads that will not be assigned with any work, hence harming the parallelization performance. Therefore, these variables should be carefully tuned. One way to do this is by testing and empirically selecting the optimal ones. Sreenivasan et al. [25] proposed an auto-tuning tool for OpenMP directives. The suggested framework currently supports only changing the number of threads used for parallel regions (the more the merrier does not necessarily apply here), the *chunk_size*, and the scheduler type (*static/dynamic*). However, in addition to these control variables, recent advancements in OpenMP provides many additional variables that control the run-time environment of the program, which may increase the performance of the program when defined correctly [26]. For example, even in the context of the already used variables, [25] disregarded newer types of scheduling such as *guided*, *auto*, and *runtime*.

Code Segmentation-and-Fusion: As OpenMP directives target each optional parallel section separately (in contrast, for example, to MPI [27]), and as each one of them might have a completely different work fashion and balance, no unified compilation of an entire program using a single S2S compiler can assure the best possible performance. Thus, code segmentation into possibly parallel sections, followed by a varied S2S compilation sweep for best match in terms of performance is needed. Although not S2S, this idea was previously suggested by Shivam et al. in MCompiler [28], which divides the code into segments, chooses the best machine-code compiler for each segment, and composes the compiled segments back together. MCompiler uses the following compilers: Intel's C compiler [17], PGI's C compiler [29], GNU GCC [30], LLVM Clang [31], Polly [32], and Pluto [13]. MCompiler's code segmentation is based on identifying loops in the code. While compiling a loop nest, MCompiler attempts to optimize it using different compiler flags. Machine learning is optionally used in order to match each loop nest to the proper compiler before running the job in practice. However, the reliance of MCompiler on machine-code compilation to gain higher performance and not on S2S with an OpenMP parallelization, prevents users from retrieving the enhanced code for further development, as well as tweaking run-time variables such as the number of threads used by the computation or other parallelization-related ones. Yet, MCompiler may be used as the machine-code compiler for resulting S2S automatic parallelized code, thus achieving better performance both in terms of machine compilation as well as parallelization.

Unified Multi-compiler Approach: Concluding, [2] suggested an automatic compiler that will take the current automatic parallelization performances to the next level: Dividing the code into suitable-for-parallelization segments, choosing the best parallelization compiler for each segment while tuning the hyperparameters (both OpenMP's and the compiler's) and fusing the outperforming segments back together to a unified code. The suggested compiler is based on the assumption that there is no best compiler for an *entire* program, yet there is one for a suitable-for-parallelization individual *segment*, as each compiler is preferable for a different task under different hyper-parameters. As High-Performance Computing (HPC) resources skyrocket over the last decade, such a compute-intensive task of hyper-parameters sweep and the execution of many computations to achieve the best performing code is no longer impossible in terms of computing power and might be worthwhile and cost-effective for long-living and legacy codes. Moreover, as those codes use HPC resources constantly and on a massive scale, even modest optimizations to the codes' performances – in terms of parallelization efficiency – can dramatically reduce future unnecessary stacked costs. Ergo, in this paper, we implemented and extended the suggested compiler, named *ComPar*.

3   *ComPar*'s S2S Automatic Parallelization Compilers

As [2] concluded, AutoPar, Par4All, and Cetus are the most suitable compilers for S2S automatic parallelization (although other S2S compilers can be easily added to *ComPar* by implementing an appropriate interface). Therefore, we decided to incorporate them into *ComPar*. In the following section a brief summary of each chosen compiler is provided.

Cetus: Cetus [33] is an open-source S2S automatic parallelization compiler for C programs, which was developed by the ParaMount research group at Purdue University. Cetus compiler can verify existing OpenMP directives in a given code and perform data-dependent analysis, pointer alias analysis, and array privatization and reduction recognition. Moreover, Cetus uses a special flag to guarantee that parallelization is done only for loops above 10,000 iterations, in an attempt to prevent parallelization overhead. In cases of nested loops, the number of iterations of each loop segment will also include the number of iterations of its inner loops. However, standard compilers may not recognize Cetus' clauses. One main disadvantage of Cetus is that it does not insert OpenMP directives to loops that contain function calls.

AutoPar: AutoPar [16] is an open-source S2S automatic parallelization compiler for C and C++ programs and is developed by Lawrence Livermore National Laboratory (LLNL). Besides AutoPar's ability to automatically insert OpenMP directives to a given code, it can also ensure the correctness of the directives in a given parallel code. As was mentioned above, some additional manual information is required from the user in order to maximize the parallelization performance. Users can provide to AutoPar an annotation file describing the features of the code.

Par4All: Par4All [34] is an open-source S2S automatic parallelization compiler for C and Fortran programs, which was developed by SILKAN, MINES ParisTech, and Institute Télécom as a merge of some open-source development projects. This compiler is suitable for a broad range of hardware architectures [12], and in particular it can be used to migrate programs to multi-core processors and GPGPUs using CUDA paradigms. Furthermore, it can optimize code execution on multi-core and many-core architectures. Par4All can perform data dependencies analysis and can validate the correctness of code manipulations. Note that Par4All may change the structure of the code.

4 *ComPar*: From Theory to Practice

As was discussed in [2], each tested compiler has its advantages and disadvantages and no compiler is superior to the other compilers in all tested benchmarks. Hence, using only one compiler at a time is not enough in order to reach optimal performance. This might suggest that one should carefully fuse the abilities of all compilers in order to fully exploit the given hardware capabilities to the limit. In this paper, we suggest *ComPar* - a novel parallelization S2S compiler that follows this vision. Due to the fact that ComPar uses outputs of different S2S compilers, ComPar support is limited to these compilers. For example, since AutoPar supports parallelization over accelerators, ComPar has the ability to do the same.

4.1 Characteristics, Architecture and Workflow

ComPar is a S2S compiler that optimizes the parallelization of the code in terms of running-time that can be achieved from S2S automatic parallelization compilers without any human intervention. This is done by fusing several outputs of said compilers while selecting the best from each based on varied empirical tests. *ComPar* only requires the user to specify the desired hyper-parameters to be considered (i.e. the parameters defined by OpenMP and the different compilers) in a JSON format (an example of such file can be found in [35]). Note that although, theoretically, *ComPar* considers all available compilers' flags as well as OpenMP *parallel for* directive clauses and OpenMP run-time library routines (RTLs), some of them might affect the correctness of the program. The correctness of the generated code is based on the assumption that it is the responsibility of the user to provide reasonable *guiding* parameters, as the user is familiar with the logic of the source code, its dependencies, and the hardware at hand. For example, in cases of a source code containing pointer aliasing, the user must not provide the *no-pointer-aliasing* flag as a parameter in the JSON file. We suggest two methods to overcome this problem: (1) *ComPar*'s black-box testing functionality, which examines the functionality of an application before and after the parallelization without peering into its internal structures or workings, and (2) AutoPar's ability to ensure the correctness of OpenMP directives in a given parallel code.

The workflow of *ComPar* is as follows (summarized in the diagram in Fig. 1): First, the *Fragmentor* enumerates and annotates all loops in the given source code by their parenthesis. Next, the *Timer* adds a piece of code around each enumerated loop which will later be used to measure its execution time. Meanwhile, the *Combinator* parses three JSON files specifying which S2S compilers should be used; which compilation flags should be considered for each compiler; which OpenMP directives should *ComPar* consider adding to each parallel loop (i.e. *schedule(kind[, chunk_size])*); and which OpenMP RTL functions should *ComPar* consider adding before each loop. The *Combinator* registers a combination in the *DB* for each possible permutation of the above parameters. Consequently, for every such combination, the *Parallelizer* parallelizes the code with the compiler and flags specified by the combination, and then adds the specified directive

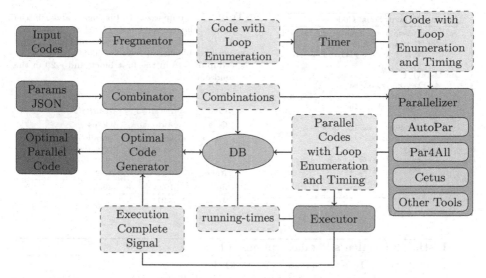

Fig. 1. Architecture and workflow of *ComPar*. Green: inputs, blue: modules, grey: transferred data type, yellow: compilers, teal: DB, red: output. (Color figure online)

clauses and RTL functions to the loops that the compiler parallelized. Each parallel code is then executed by the *Executor*, which logs its total running-time and the running-times of all of its loops in the *DB*. Finally, after all combinations are executed, the *Optimal Code Generator* chooses the parallelization scheme that produced the shortest running-time across all combinations for every individual loop and creates a parallel code version in which each loop is parallelized using its empiric optimal parallelization scheme.

Consider, for example, the following program presented in Listing 1. This source code is a tri-nested loop that multiplies elements in array x by constant α and stores the result in array y. First, *ComPar* annotates and times the loops in the given code (lines 2 and 5, for instance, in Listing 2). Then, it creates all possible combinations of the given hyper-parameters and names them. Afterward, *ComPar* generates the output source codes for each structured block as was produced by the S2S compilers with all these combinations. Next, *ComPar* chooses the combination that produced the best run-time in practice for each structured block. As one can see, *ComPar*'s output (Listing 2) is composed of both AutoPar output and Cetus output (Line 3 was generated by AutoPar, whereas lines 14–17 and 19–22 were generated by Cetus). That is, *ComPar* found that the best parallelized code that could be generated under these S2S parallelization compilers would be the fusion of both AutoPar and Cetus. Thus, *ComPar* allows the user to enjoy the advantages of these compilers, while avoiding, when possible, from their disadvantages. Table 1 summarizes the differences between each loop segment as a comparison between the two listings.

Listing 1 Daxpy Serial Code

```
1   void init(double *x, double *y, int N){
2       for (int i=0; i<N; ++i) {
3           x[i] = i*0.3; y[i] = i*0.2;}
4   }
5   int main() {
6       double *x, *y, alpha = 3.0;
7       int N =  1024*1024*256, R = 64, k,i,g;
8       x = (double *) malloc (N *
        ↪ sizeof(double));
9       y = (double *) malloc (N *
        ↪ sizeof(double));
10      init(x,y,N);
11      for(k=0; k<R; k++)
12          for (i=0; i<N; i++)
13              y[i] = alpha * x[i];}
```

Table 1. Comparison of Listings 1 and 2 in the context of the marked loops. *ComPar* chose comb' *HASH#1* and *HASH#2* for the first and second structured block respectively. This choice led to speedup of ~16 in the first block and ~29 in the second one.

File	daxpy.c	
Comb'	*HASH#1*	*HASH#2*
Comp'	Autopar	Cetus
Comp' flags	keep_going no_aliasing	parallelizeloops = 2 privatize = 2 alias = 3
Runtime	0.11	1.99
Speedup	16.62	26.96
Total (sec)	2.21	

Listing 2 ComPar's Parallel Optimized Daxpy

```
1   void init(double *x, double *y, int N) {
2       // START_LOOP_MARKER1 | COMB_ID: HASH#1 | COMPILER_NAME: autopar
3       #pragma omp parallel for firstprivate(N)
4       for (int i = 0; i <= N - 1; i += 1) {
5           x[i] = i * 0.3; y[i] = i * 0.2;} // END_LOOP_MARKER1
6   }
7   int main() {
8       double *x, *y, alpha = 3.0;
9       int N = 1024 * 1024 * 256, R = 64, k, i, g;
10      x = (double *)malloc(N * sizeof(double));
11      y = (double *)malloc(N * sizeof(double));
12      init(x, y, N);
13      // START_LOOP_MARKER2 | COMB_ID: HASH#2 | COMPILER_NAME: cetus
14      #pragma cetus firstprivate(y) private(i, k) lastprivate(y)
15      #pragma loop name main #0
16      #pragma cetus parallel
17      #pragma omp parallel for if ((10000 < ((1L + (3L * R)) + ((3L * N) *
        ↪ R)))) private(i, k) firstprivate(y) lastprivate(y)
18      for (k = 0; k < R; k++) {
19          #pragma cetus private(i)
20          #pragma loop name main #0 #0
21          #pragma cetus parallel
22          #pragma omp parallel for if ((10000 < (1L + (3L * N))))
            ↪ private(i)
23          for (i = 0; i < N; i++) {
24              y[i] = (alpha * x[i]);}} // END_LOOP_MARKER2
25  }
```

Additionally, as previously noted, the user may provide *ComPar* with a testing script that verifies the correctness of each execution according to its output (i.e *stdout* or output file). Using this script, *ComPar* rejects any combination that did not pass the tests, thus providing correctness criteria that might help with pointing out invalid hyper-parameters. The user can also use *AutoPar*'s abilities in this regard.

Assuming the correctness of the input, and the complete preservation of the entire AST under each S2S compiler, the theoretical proof of *ComPar* optimization is straight-forward. The algorithm chooses the best directive provided by the different compilers for each loop structured block. Thus, *ComPar* either improves or does not change the running-time of the parallelized algorithm that could be produced by the best compiler, i.e., in the worst case, *ComPar*'s output would be the best-parallelized code out of the codes that were generated by each of the supported compilers separately (or the serial code in case none of them succeed). We stress that a decrease, improvement or disruption of the code performance or results can be an outcome *only* of the selected parallelization paradigm per each segment, and that the code validity can be assured using *ComPar*'s black-box testing functionality and AutoPar's ability to ensure the correctness of the OpenMP directives in a given parallel code.

As was mentioned above, *ComPar* runs all possible combinations of S2S compilers and flags, thus the number of combinations is given by the number of subsets of possible flags, which is:

$$\sum_{i\in C}(2^{n_i} - 1)(2^{rtl+d} - 1)$$

where C is the group of S2S compilers, n_i is the number of flags to consider for S2S compiler i, and rtl and d are the number of run-time library routines and directives to consider adding to parallel loops, respectively.

The running-time of a single combination is the running-time of the corresponding parallel version of the input code (since the rest of the workflow's running-time is negligible compared to the Executor's running-time). Thus, the total time until *ComPar* produces its output is the sum over all the running-times of all combinations. Since *ComPar*'s running-time depends on the running-time of the given source code, if one wishes to parallelize code s, it is strongly recommended to choose a sufficiently suitable input x' for s, preferably a 'sweet-spot' in which the input is not too small to cause the parallel code to overwhelmingly suffer from parallelization overhead and not too big to cause the code to suffer from excessive running-times. Then it is recommended to run the realistic input x using the parallel code generated.

4.2   Interface

ComPar offers both command-line and GUI interfaces with a variety of options such as compilation options, i.e. whether to use a Makefile or what machine-code compiler (e.g. GCC, ICC, etc.) to use, together with the corresponding compilation flags; SLURM parameters (*ComPar* executes its jobs using the SLURM resource manager [36]); whether or not to save all the created combinations' files; where to store *ComPar*'s output; what is the name of the project and what operational mode to use, etc. *ComPar*'s GUI is divided to three modes, where each mode has its own features. For further information, please see [37].

5   Experiments and Discussion

In order to evaluate the contributions of this paper, we examined the parallelization output on different kernels of both the NAS [18] and PolyBench 4.2.1 beta [38] Parallel benchmarks. *ComPar* was compared against the different parallelization compilers and to serial executions. All of our benchmarks were executed using a single computation node with a total of 32 cores (AMD Opteron Processor 6376 [39]). Note that the number of threads utilized by the benchmark (correlates to the number of cores used) depends on each and every specification of combination. Table 2 presents the flags of the S2S compilers; the OpenMP *parallel for* directive clauses; and OpenMP run-time library routines that we tested in our experiments. Moreover, we present the resulted speedups as well as the running-times in order to ratify the truthfulness of our results (by showing that they consumed a reasonable amount of computation time in regard to the given input and hardware settings). Note that the presented running-times and speedups are the best each S2S compiler achieved using the different flag combinations and are not a result of a "vanilla" execution (i.e. without any flags).

5.1   NAS Parallel Benchmarks

The Numerical Aerodynamics Simulations (NAS) Parallel Benchmarks [18] are a group of applications, developed by NASA, to evaluate the performance of

Table 2. Parallelization compilers' flags, OpenMP *parallel for* directive clauses and OpenMP run-time library routines we tested in our experiments.

Compilers' flags	
Compiler	*Flag*
Cetus	parallelize-loops, reduction, privatize, alias
AutoPar	keep_going, enable_modeling, no_aliasing, unique_indirect_index
Par4All	O, fine-grain, com-optimization, no-pointer-aliasing
OMP *parallel for* Directive Clauses	
Clause	*Kind*
schedule	static [2, 4, 8, 16, 32], dynamic
Runtime Library Routines	
RTL Routine	*Argument*
omp_set_num_threads	2, 4, 8, 16, 32

high-performance computers. NAS Parallel Benchmarks include ten different
benchmarks [40]. In order to be consistent with [2], we tested the performance
of the compilers over the following benchmarks: Block Tri-diagonal solver (BT),
Conjugate Gradient (CG), Embarrassingly Parallel (EP), Lower-Upper Gauss-
Seidel solver (LU), Multi-Grid (MG) and Scalar Penta-diagonal solver (SP).
Similarly to [2], we did not use Fourier Transform (FT), Integer Sort (IS) and
Unstructured Adaptive mesh (UA) benchmarks, as some compilers failed to
process them. As can be observed from Figs. 2 and 3, *ComPar* always achieved
the best speedups and running-times respectively, or at least the same ones as
the best S2S compiler (which is different for each benchmark).

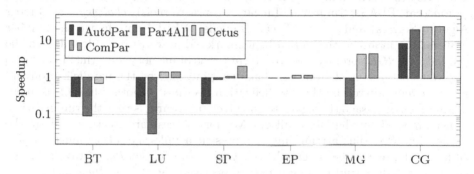

Fig. 2. NAS benchmark speedups (compared to a serial execution) achieved by the
different compilers in logarithmic scale.

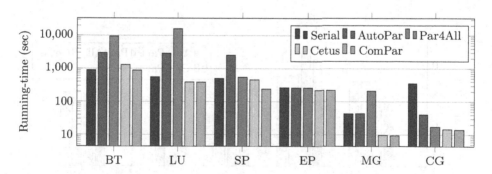

Fig. 3. NAS benchmark running-times achieved by the different compilers in logarithmic scale.

5.2 PolyBench Benchmarks

PolyBench [38, 41, 42] is a collection of 30 representative potentially compute-intensive benchmarks. It attempts to make the kernels' execution as uniform and consistent as possible. PolyBench contains a single file, tunable at compile-time, which is used for the kernel instrumentation. This file performs extra operations such as cache flushing before the kernels' execution, and can set real-time scheduling to prevent operating-system interference.

Most of the benchmarks in the same category are computationally comparable (e.g 2 mm versus 3 mm). Therefore, we chose one representative benchmark in each category (except for *Medley* which we considered redundant in this context). We tested the performance of the compilers over *correlation* (cat. Data Mining), *gemm* (cat. BLAS), 2 mm (cat. Linear Algebra Kernels), *cholesky* (cat. Linear Algebra Solvers) and *jacobi-2d* (cat. Stencils). We did not change the number of iterations in any of the chosen benchmarks. However, we evenly enlarged the (already *LARGE*) problem size by x8 (in terms of memory footprint) in order to ensure that the benefit from load-balancing imposed by the parallelization will not be overshadowed by the parallelization overhead. Another benefit of maximizing memory usage (in regard to the given hardware) is that the running-time is less affected by the Non-Uniform Memory Access architecture and by the cache hierarchy, thus attempting to represent a full-scale job as much as possible. Again, as can be observed from Figs. 4 and 5, *ComPar* always achieved the best speedups and running-times respectively, or at least the same ones as the best S2S compiler (which is different for each benchmark). As one can see, even though jacobi-2d has a single kernel loop nest, i.e. should only have a single segment, *ComPar* outperform all of the individual compilers. This is a direct result of the parameter autotuning of *ComPar*.

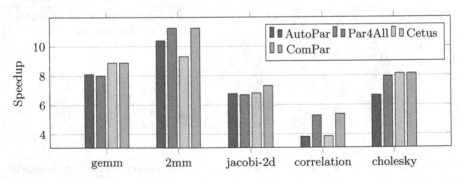

Fig. 4. Polybench benchmark speedups (compared to a serial execution) achieved by the different compilers.

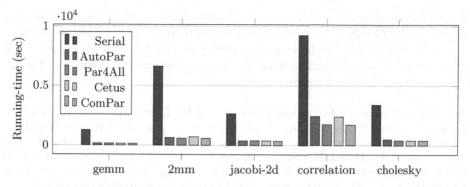

Fig. 5. Polybench benchmark running-times achieved by the different compilers.

6   Conclusions and Future Work

In this paper, we address the pitfalls of S2S automatic parallelization and how some crucial aspects of them could be resolved using *ComPar*. We briefly discussed Cetus, AutoPar and Par4All, which we found most suitable for this task. We then presented *ComPar* and analyzed its results over both the NAS and the PolyBench benchmarks. We conclude that although the resources *ComPar* consumes in order to produce efficient parallel code are greater than the resources other parallelization compilers demand – as it depends on the number of parameters the user wishes *ComPar* to consider – *ComPar* achieves the best overall performance compared to the tested parallelization compilers and the serial code version. We presented the reasons for which this usage might be worthwhile and even cost-effective.

Much work is left for the future: Adding support for Fortran programming language is one of our next goals, as *ComPar* is primarily targeting legacy large-scale serial scientific codes. One may also try to better learn the code dependencies and refine the semantically correct parallelization parameters accordingly. Additionally, since *ComPar* runtime strongly depends on the problem's size, one might develop a model that suggests users the most suitable size. Moreover, a comprehensive understanding of the hardware specs, let alone actively learning which hyper-parameters best suite each hardware using machine learning paradigms, may further enhance our speedups and shorten *ComPar*'s execution time [43]. In addition, the chosen S2S compilers are currently limited to OpenMP v2.5, hence the generated code can not utilize most of the advantages of directives from later OpenMP versions. Adding more automatic parallelization compilers might be also beneficial. Furthermore, adding more machine-code compilers might improve the current results and support additional input source codes. Currently, *ComPar* can choose the most suited compiler for different hardware architectures only under certain circumstances (see Sect. 4), while in the future we wish to explore this improvement opportunity under other circumstances. As was discussed in [28], it may be advantageous to use VTune [44] in *ComPar* in order to find the most suited automatic parallelization compiler for each code segment and the best machine-code compilers for each output file generated by *ComPar* and each hardware architecture. Nevertheless, we emphasize that *ComPar* is the first open-sourced platform for such optimizations of S2S automatic parallelization compilers, and as such could benefit from further unexplored avenues and future research.

Acknowledgments. This work was supported by the Lynn and William Frankel Center for Computer Science. Computational support was provided by the NegevHPC project [1]. The authors would like to thank Reuven Regev Farag, Gilad Guralnik, Yoni Cohen, May Hagbi, Shlomi Tofahi, and Yoel Vaizman from the Department of Software Engineering - SCE for their part in the development of *ComPar*, and to Matan Rusanovsky[1,2] for his fruitful comments and extensive evaluation of this work.

References

1. NegevHPC Project. https://www.negevhpc.com
2. Harel, R., Mosseri, I., Levin, H., Alon, L., Rusanovsky, M., Oren, G.: Source-to-source parallelization compilers for scientific shared-memory multi-core and accelerated multiprocessing: analysis, pitfalls, enhancement and potential. Int. J. Parallel Program. **48**(1), 1–31 (2020)
3. Dennard, R.H., Gaensslen, F.H., Rideout, V.L., Bassous, E., LeBlanc, A.R.: Design of ion-implanted MOSFET's with very small physical dimensions. IEEE J. Solid-State Circ. **9**(5), 256–268 (1974)
4. Blake, G., Dreslinski, R.G., Mudge, T.: A survey of multicore processors. IEEE Signal Process. Mag. **26**(6), 26–37 (2009)
5. Pacheco, P.: An Introduction to Parallel Programming. Elsevier, Amsterdam (2011)
6. Feathers, M.: Working Effectively with Legacy Code. Prentice Hall, Upper Saddle River (2004)
7. Dagum, L., Menon, R.: Openmp: an industry standard API for shared-memory programming. IEEE Comput. Sci. Eng. **5**(1), 46–55 (1998)
8. Prema, S., Nasre, R., Jehadeesan, R., Panigrahi, B.K.: A study on popular auto-parallelization frameworks. Concurr. Comput.: Pract. Exp. **31**(17), e5168 (2019)
9. Neamtiu, I., Foster, J.S., Hicks, M.: Understanding source code evolution using abstract syntax tree matching. ACM SIGSOFT Softw. Eng. Notes **30**(4), 1–5 (2005)
10. Prema, S., Jehadeesan, R., Panigrahi, B.K.: Identifying pitfalls in automatic parallelization of NAS parallel benchmarks. In: 2017 National Conference on Parallel Computing Technologies (PARCOMPTECH), pp. 1–6. IEEE (2017)
11. Dave, C., Bae, H., Min, S.-J., Lee, S., Eigenmann, R., Midkiff, S.: Cetus: a source-to-source compiler infrastructure for multicores. Computer **42**(12), 36–42 (2009)
12. Amini, M., et al.: Par4all: from convex array regions to heterogeneous computing. In: IMPACT 2012: Second International Workshop on Polyhedral Compilation Techniques, HiPEAC 2012 (2012)
13. Bondhugula, U., Ramanujam, J.: Pluto: a practical and fully automatic polyhedral parallelizer and locality optimizer (2007)
14. Parallware: The OpenMP-enabling Source-to-Source Compiler. http://www.appentra.com/products/parallware

15. Gómez-Sousa, H., Arenaz, M., Rubiños-López, Ó., Martínez-Lorenzo, J.Á.: Novel source-to-source compiler approach for the automatic parallelization of codes based on the method of moments. In: 2015 9th European Conference on Antennas and Propagation (EuCAP), pp. 1–6. IEEE (2015)
16. Liao, C., Quinlan, D.J., Willcock, J.J., Panas, T.: Semantic-aware automatic parallelization of modern applications using high-level abstractions. Int. J. Parallel Programm. **38**(56), 361–378 (2010)
17. Intel C++ Compiler for Linux Systems User's Guide. https://software.intel.com/en-us/cpp-compiler-developer-guide-and-reference
18. Bailey, D.H., et al.: The NAS parallel benchmarks. Int. J. Supercomput. Appl. **5**(3), 63–73 (1991)
19. Graham, S.L., Kessler, P.B., Mckusick, M.K.: Gprof: a call graph execution profiler. ACM SIGPLAN Not. **39**(4), 49–57 (2004)
20. Katarzyński, J., Cytowski, M.: Towards autotuning of OpenMP applications on multicore architectures. arXiv preprint arXiv:1401.4063 (2014)
21. Liao, C., Quinlan, D.J., Vuduc, R., Panas, T.: Effective source-to-source outlining to support whole program empirical optimization. In: Gao, G.R., Pollock, L.L., Cavazos, J., Li, X. (eds.) LCPC 2009. LNCS, vol. 5898, pp. 308–322. Springer, Heidelberg (2010). https://doi.org/10.1007/978-3-642-13374-9_21
22. Mustafa, D., Eigenmann, R.: Performance analysis and tuning of automatically parallelized OpenMP applications. In: Chapman, B.M., Gropp, W.D., Kumaran, K., Müller, M.S. (eds.) OpenMP in the Petascale Era, IWOMP 2011. Lecture Notes in Computer Science, vol. 6665, pp. 151–164. Springer, Heidelberg (2011). https://doi.org/10.1007/978-3-642-21487-5_12
23. Silvano, C., et al.: Autotuning and adaptivity in energy efficient HPC systems: the ANTAREX toolbox. In: Proceedings of the 15th ACM International Conference on Computing Frontiers, pp. 270–275 (2018)
24. Balaprakash, P., et al.: Autotuning in high-performance computing applications. Proc. IEEE **106**(11), 2068–2083 (2018)
25. Sreenivasan, V., Javali, R., Hall, M., Balaprakash, P., Scogland, T.R.W., de Supinski, B.R.: A framework for enabling OpenMP autotuning. In: Fan, X., de Supinski, B.R., Sinnen, O., Giacaman, N. (eds.) IWOMP 2019. LNCS, vol. 11718, pp. 50–60. Springer, Cham (2019). https://doi.org/10.1007/978-3-030-28596-8_4
26. Van der Pas, R., Stotzer, E., Terboven, C.: Using OpenMP the Next Step: Affinity, Accelerators, Tasking, and SIMD. MIT Press, Cambridge (2017)
27. Gropp, W., Gropp, W.D., Lusk, E., Skjellum, A., Lusk, A.D.F.E.E.: Using MPI: Portable Parallel Programming with the Message-Passing Interface, vol. 1. MIT Press, Cambridge (1999)
28. Shivam, A., Nicolau, A., Veidenbaum, A.V.: Mcompiler: a synergistic compilation framework. arXiv preprint arXiv:1905.12755 (2019)
29. PGI: PGI compiler user's guide (2020)
30. GNU Project. GCC online documentation (2020). https://gcc.gnu.org/onlinedocs
31. Lattner, C.: LLVM and Clang: next generation compiler technology. In: The BSD Conference, vol. 5 (2008)
32. Grosser, T., Zheng, H., Aloor, R., Simbürger, A., Größlinger, A., Pouchet, L.-N.: Polly-polyhedral optimization in LLVM. In: Proceedings of the First International Workshop on Polyhedral Compilation Techniques (IMPACT), vol. 2011, p. 1 (2011)
33. Cetus Homepage. https://engineering.purdue.edu/Cetus/
34. Par4All Homepage. http://par4all.github.io/
35. ComPar's Assets

36. SLURM. https://slurm.schedmd.com/
37. ComPar GitHub (2020). https://github.com/Scientific-Computing-Lab-NRCN/compar/blob/master/README.md
38. PolyBench Benchmarks. https://web.cse.ohio-state.edu/~pouchet.2/software/polybench/
39. AMD Opteron(tm) Processor 6376 (2013). https://www.amd.com/en/products/cpu/6376
40. Padua, D. (ed.): NAS Parallel Benchmarks. Encyclopedia of Parallel Computing, pp. 1254–1259. Springer, Boston, MA (2011). https://doi.org/10.1007/978-0-387-09766-4
41. Pouchet, L.-N., et al.: PolyBench: the polyhedral benchmark suite (2012). http://www.cs.ucla.edu/pouchet/software/polybench
42. Yuki, T.: Understanding PolyBench/C 3.2 kernels. In: International workshop on Polyhedral Compilation Techniques (IMPACT), pp. 1–5 (2014)
43. Tournavitis, G., Wang, Z., Franke, B., O'Boyle, M.F.P.: Towards a holistic approach to auto-parallelization: integrating profile-driven parallelism detection and machine-learning based mapping. ACM Sigplan Not. 44(6), 177–187 (2009)
44. Reinders, J.: VTune Performance Analyzer Essentials. Intel Press, Santa Clara (2005)

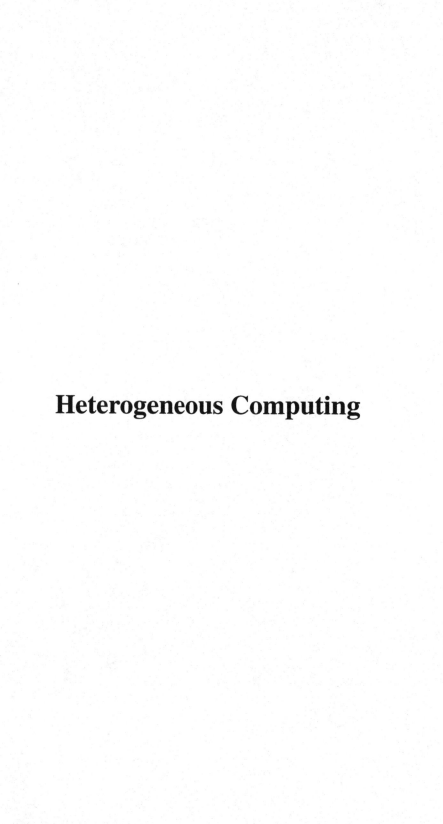

Heterogeneous Computing

OpenMP Device Offloading to FPGAs Using the Nymble Infrastructure

Jens Huthmann[1], Lukas Sommer[2([⊠])], Artur Podobas[3], Andreas Koch[2], and Kentaro Sano[1]

[1] Riken Center for Computational Science, Kobe, Japan
{jens.huthmann,kentaro.sano}@riken.jp
[2] Embedded Systems and Applications Group, TU Darmstadt, Darmstadt, Germany
{sommer,koch}@esa.tu-darmstadt.de
[3] Royal Institute of Technology, KTH, Stockholm, Sweden
artur@podobas.net

Abstract. Next to GPUs, FPGAs are an attractive target for OpenMP device offloading, as they allow to implement highly efficient, applications-specific accelerators. However, prior approaches to support OpenMP device offloading for FPGAs have been limited by the interfaces provided by the FPGA vendors' HLS tool interfaces or their integration with the OpenMP runtime, e.g., for data mapping.

This work presents an approach to OpenMP device offloading for FPGAs based on the LLVM compiler infrastructure and the Nymble HLS compiler. The automatic compilation flow uses LLVM IR for HLS-specific optimizations and transformation and for the interaction with the Nymble HLS compiler. Parallel OpenMP constructs are automatically mapped to hardware threads executing simultaneously in the generated FPGA accelerator and the accelerator is integrated into `libomptarget` to support data-mapping.

In a case study, we demonstrate the use of the compilation flow and evaluate its performance.

Keywords: FPGA · OpenMP · Device offloading · Heterogeneous · LLVM · HLS

1 Introduction

As the end of transistor scaling [30] draws near, researchers are actively pursuing and evaluating alternative emerging architectures and computing paradigms, with which they hope to continue performance scaling we have grown used to rely on. Among the more salient of these emerging architectures are reconfigurable systems, whose silicon plasticity/reconfigurability provides a partial remedy for the end of Moore's law [22] – we do not need more transistors, we just need to repurpose the existing transistor to better fit the requirements of our applications.

© Springer Nature Switzerland AG 2020
K. Milfeld et al. (Eds.): IWOMP 2020, LNCS 12295, pp. 265–279, 2020.
https://doi.org/10.1007/978-3-030-58144-2_17

Today, Field-Programmable Gate Arrays (FPGAs) are among the more popular and mature reconfigurable systems available. While early FPGAs had limited computing capabilities, and were primarily used for circuit simulation and digital signal processing, modern FPGAs – on the other hand – feature tens of TeraFLOP/s of raw single-precision performance, and are capable of rivaling both general-purpose and graphics processing units (GPUs) in power efficiency and/or raw execution performance. Furthermore, with the increased maturity of High-Level Synthesis [12] tools, using FPGAs is no longer monopolized by hardware architectures, and instead, anyone with knowledge of C/C++/Java programming can map applications onto these exciting new architectures. Today, several research groups have already mapped important High-Performance Computing (HPC) applications onto FPGAs, with benefits illustrated over existing approaches [16, 26, 33–35]. These efforts have led to several research laboratories setting up large FPGA-based testbeds to investigate the role of these reconfigurable devices in a post Exa-scale era, such as the Noctua cluster at Paderborn University or the Cygnus cluster at University of Tsukuba.

In this paper, we present the Nymble OpenMP HLS infrastructure, which is a self-contained compilation tool-kit for running (a subset of) OpenMP constructs on FPGAs, and also visualize them using the Paraver [23] visualization tool. Unlike existing OpenMP HLS approaches, which use source-to-source compilation and rely on commercial black box compilers for hardware generation, Nymble is transparent and fully transforms OpenMP code down to Register Transfer Level (RTL) Verilog code without external dependencies. This, in turn, enables users to get a better insight into what hardware is actually generated, while at the same time providing an open platform for FPGA-based OpenMP research.

Our contributions in this paper are:

- A description over the Nymble infrastructure, including details on the front-end compilation and the hardware generation & architecture, including which OpenMP constructs Nymble supports and how they are implemented,
- A use-case showing how Nymble transforms well-known OpenMP code into hardware, including empirical performance evaluation, and
- A discussion on the future of OpenMP for FPGAs, including challenges and directions.

2   Motivation

Today, FPGAs are being considered to complement (and compete with) the general-purpose processor and GPUs that currently reside in modern HPC infrastructure. Several research laboratories are already setting up large FPGA-based testbeds to investigate the role of these reconfigurable devices in a post-Exa-scale era, such as for example the Noctua cluster at Paderborn University or the Cygnus cluster at the University of Tsukuba.

Meanwhile, using these accelerators in a user-friendly way (that is, without resorting to writing RTL code), is often limited to using vendor-specific toolchains, such as for example Intel's OpenCL SDK for FPGA [8] or Xilinx SDSoC/SDAccel [32]. While these toolchains are often high-performing, they are also very tied to a specific execution model. Furthermore, adding or researching into alternative programming models using these vendor solutions (such as for example OpenMP) is challenging, because tools are closed source, and even if some aspects can be changed (such as the Board Support Package, BSP), these changes become non-trivial.

There are methods to extend functionality, such as using source-to-source methods to transcompile OpenMP [10], but these methods have no way of even remotely controlling or dictating how the underlying hardware is generated. Finally, vendor tools and road-maps are not always necessarily aligned with what we as users or researchers need, meaning that it is imperative to look at alternative approaches, in particular for guiding and doing research on OpenMP execution on future FPGAs. The Nymble OpenMP infrastructure aspires to be one such alternative for OpenMP researchers and users.

3   The Nymble OpenMP Infrastructure

The goal of this work is to develop a compilation flow that maps OpenMP target regions to FPGA-based accelerators without requiring manual intervention by the user. The compilation flow is based on the LLVM compiler infrastructure [18] and its implementation of OpenMP. In contrast to many prior approaches that use source-to-source transformations on AST-level to extract target regions for HLS (see Sect. 6 for detailed discussion), the compilation flow in this work uses LLVM IR to interact with the HLS tool. This approach facilitates code transformations that can be used to transform and optimize target regions, described in more detail in Sect. 3.1.

As the commercially available HLS-tools only provide source-level interfaces and no official interface on IR-level, the state-of-the-art academic HLS compiler *Nymble* [15] is used for the actual High-Level Synthesis of the target regions. Besides providing an IR-level interface, Nymble also supports true multi-threading in the generated accelerators [14], described in more detail in Sect. 3.2.

3.1   Compilation Flow

Figure 1 presents an overview of our compilation flow. For OpenMP device offloading, LLVM's Clang frontend uses separate compilation passes for host- and device code. For this work, the host compilation remains completely unchanged and therefore supports any host code and OpenMP host constructs that Clang supports.

The device compilation flow (shown on the right-hand side of Fig. 1) does not only support the basic `target` directive to denote target regions and the *full* range of data-mapping constructs (map-clause, `target data`-directive, array-sections, etc.), but also provides two kinds of parallelism: The `teams` or `parallel` construct can be used inside a target region to express parallelism, Sect. 3.2 explains how this parallelism is realized in hardware. Note that in our current prototype, only one of these constructs can be used at a time and nested parallelism is not supported. For the `teams` construct, the `distribute` construct is also supported to specify worksharing for a loop nest.

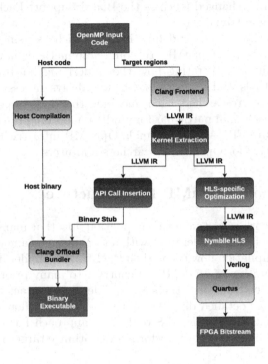

Fig. 1. Overview of the compilation flow.

Similar to many approaches investigated in the survey by Mayer et al. [21] (see Sect. 6 for detailed discussion), a binary stub for execution on the host machine is generated as one of the products of the device compilation flow. In this work, the binary stub is not only used to initiate the FPGA execution, but also to handle parallelism. Parallel constructs will spawn multiple software threads in the binary stub, these threads then interact with one hardware thread each in the FPGA-accelerator in an 1:1-relationship. This approach allows to reuse the standard mechanisms from LLVM's OpenMP runtime `libomp` to manage thread spawning and worksharing. Therefore, after generating LLVM IR in the Clang frontend, the *Kernel Extraction* splits the outlined target function into the stub to remain on the host and the actual target region kernel function for High-Level Synthesis.

The *API Call Insertion* then inserts calls to a thin wrapper library around Intel's *Open Programmable Acceleration Engine*[1] into the stub function to

---

[1] https://opae.github.io/.

transfer function arguments and initiate hardware execution. Note that, in contrast to approaches such as [17], data-management is not handled via generated API calls, but rather through a plugin for LLVM's `libomptarget`, enabling the whole range of data-mapping clauses/constructs, including array sections and uni-directional transfers (`to`/`from` clause). The stub is then compiled for the host machine (`x86-64` in our case) and included in the binary executable using the Clang Offload-Bundler [1]. At runtime, the stub is loaded by `libomptarget` and initiates the execution on the FPGA accelerator.

The extracted HLS kernel undergoes a number of transformations and optimizations before actual High-Level Synthesis (*HLS-specific Optimizations* in Fig. 1). The transformations are mainly concerned with transforming OpenMP language constructs into constructs suitable for High-Level Synthesis. Currently, the prototype supports the OpenMP API runtime functions `omp_get_thread_num`, `omp_get_num_threads`, `omp_get_team_num` and `omp_get_num_teams`, which, in addition to `teams distribute`, can be used to assign individual workloads to the different threads. Besides that, the synchronization constructs `omp critical` and `omp barrier` are also supported inside target regions and mapped to efficient implementations using hardware semaphores.

Static allocation of thread-private memory inside the target region (`alloca` in LLVM IR) is also supported by the compilation flow and HLS backend and automatically mapped to low-latency accessible local memory (SRAM) on the FPGA device. Vector datatypes are also allowed in the target regions, but arithmetic operations on vectors are realized as individual operations on each vector element, as vector operations do not provide significant benefits in FPGA hardware. Therefore, to allow for more fine-grained scheduling during HLS, we automatically partition vector-wide thread-private memories into individual local memories for each element while preserving array semantics as one of the optimization steps.

The transformed LLVM IR is then passed to the Nymble HLS backend, which performs the typical HLS steps of allocation, binding and scheduling. For this purpose, the LLVM IR is transformed into a *control dataflow graph* (CDFG) representation, as described in [15]. More details on the mapping of different constructs to hardware will be presented in the next section.

The final product of the Nymble HLS backend is an HDL (Verilog) description of the accelerator, which is passed to Intel's Quartus software for synthesis and place-and-route, eventually yielding an FPGA bitstream.

3.2   Hardware Architecture

The overall hardware architecture of the generated FPGA accelerator is depicted in Fig. 2. The *Avalon slave interface* of the compute unit (CU) that is connected to the host is used as entry point for the hardware execution. The memory mapped register file can be used to pass kernel arguments and other information (e.g., thread ID) from the software thread to the corresponding hardware thread.

For larger data, the accelerator supports two different kinds of memory:

- Small, on-chip (SRAM) local memories (*LMEM*) are directly connected to the compute unit. These memories can be used as thread-private memory.
- *External memory* (DRAM) located on the FPGA-board can be used to hold large amounts of data and also for data-exchange with the host RAM using the OpenMP data-mapping constructs via the `libomptarget`-plugin. This memory is connected to the CU via an Avalon bus, with a dedicated Avalon master port per hardware thread.

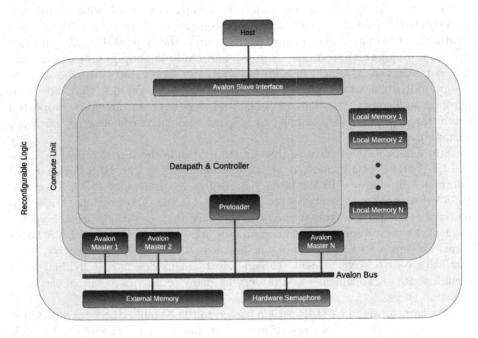

Fig. 2. Hardware architecture of the reconfigurable accelerator.

As the data-width of the external memory interface is usually higher than the size of single data-item of primitive type (e.g., `float`), vector data-types can be used in the OpenMP input code to improve the memory access efficiency. Where possible, vector-wide memory accesses are automatically mapped to Avalon burst accesses.

Another mechanism to further improve the memory access efficiency is the use of the *Preloader*. By using calls to the custom function `omp_target_preload` in the OpenMP input code to transfer data between global memory and thread-private local memory, the required data can be transferred efficiently in a single burst transfer. A more detailed discussion of the Preloader can be found in Sect. 4.1.

The Avalon bus system is also used to integrate the memory-mapped *Hardware Semaphore* that is used to realize the `omp critical` and `omp barrier` synchronization constructs.

The execution inside the *Datapath* is based on the Nymble-MT execution model presented in prior work by Huthmann et al. [14]. The unique feature of this execution model is the fact that it supports the simultaneous execution of multiple hardware threads in a *single* compute-unit, whereas most other FPGA-based approaches achieve thread-level parallelism through spatial replication of the compute-unit (e.g., [6], cf. Sect. 6 for discussion).

To allow for simultaneous execution of multiple hardware threads, the operations found in the data-flow graph of the kernel are organized into so-called *stages* according to their static HLS schedule. The different stages can operated independently by the controller, allowing multiple threads to be active in different stages simultaneously. The stage-based execution model in addition also support loop pipelining.

The threads can operate completely independently of each other in this model, also allowing threads to start and finish at different points in time. Hardware threads are launched by their software counterpart (as stated in the previous section, we use a 1:1-relationship between software- and hardware threads) through the entry point in the Avalon slave interface. Parallelism in the OpenMP execution model (threads/teams) is automatically mapped to these simultaneously operating threads by the compilation flow presented here.

A major challenge in the stage-based execution model is the integration of operations for which the latency (in clock cycles) cannot be determined statically, e.g., accesses to external memory, which we call *variable-latency operations* (VLO). These operations are scheduled assuming their minimum latency. In case a VLO exceeds the assumed latency at execution time, the execution of the encountering thread is suspended until the VLO completes. To make sure that a single thread encountering a longer-than-expected latency does not block other threads, stages containing a VLO allow for thread re-ordering, i.e., threads can overtake each other in these stages.

3.3   Performance Visualization

Just as with any other device or target platform, the optimization of application code is an important step to achieve performance on FPGAs and is often an iterative process. To assist developers in this process, the compilation flow developed in this work provides mechanisms to automatically include various performance counters directly in the generated hardware. While the full details of the hardware implementation are out of scope for this work, the performance counters were designed to be as non-invasive as possible, i.e., to not have an impact on the performance of the investigated accelerator design, e.g. by increasing the initiation interval of pipelined loops.

The performance counters allow to capture important metrics such as memory bandwidth, arithmetic operations per time-interval (e.g. GFLOPs) or hardware thread idle times and facilitate the analysis and optimization of the target regions offloaded to the FPGA. After the execution on the FPGA completes, the collected performance data is exported in the Paraver trace format for use with the popular HPC performance visualization tool Paraver [23]. The integration with a state-of-the-art HPC visualization tool makes the performance analysis of the FPGA target regions more accessible for HPC domain experts.

4 Evaluation

To demonstrate the compilation flow from OpenMP with target offloading to FPGA-based accelerators, we use a well-understood benchmark as case study. The selected application allows to test the different features of the compilation flow and architecture template by covering the supported OpenMP constructs as mentioned in the previous section, including synchronization.

For the application, a single compute unit is implemented inside the FPGA, supporting the simultaneous execution of up to four threads. The implementation of the compilation flow is based on LLVM release 9.0 and Quartus Prime version 18.1.2 is used for synthesizing the generated Verilog code to an FPGA bitstream.

The targeted FPGA is an Intel FPGA PAC D5005 card. The card is coupled via PCIe to the host processor, a quad-core Xeon Gold 5122 CPU which executes the host-portion of the applications and is also used for CPU benchmarking. Note that the performance figures always include data-transfers between host- and FPGA external memory via PCIe, initiated through `libomptarget`, i.e., the numbers reported here are end-to-end performance of the FPGA offloading.

4.1 Case Study: GEMM

As an example application, we use the general matrix multiplication (GEMM). The FPGA accelerator is compiled from a blocked version of GEMM and the different hardware threads compute distinct submatrices of the overall result matrix. Inside the computation of each thread, the computation is partially unrolled to exploit the potential of *spatial* parallelism provided by FPGAs. To reduce the number of expensive accesses to global, external memory, local memory is used to buffer inputs and intermediate results. To further improve the efficiency of memory access to the input matrices A and B, the threads preload blocks of the input matrices into the local memory using the preloader that is part of the compute unit. For users of the compilation flow, the preloading capability is available through a simple C++ template function called `omp_target_preload` (cf. Listing 1.1), which simply gets passed the relevant pointers to external and local memory and the number and type of the elements to load.

```
1  template <typename T, int ELEMENTS>
2  void omp_target_preload(size_t offset, size_t stride,
3      size_t num_transfers, void* globalSrc, void* localDst){...}
```

Listing 1.1. Definition of the `omp_target_preload`-function

The preloader will then collect the access to multiple elements in a single Avalon (burst) request, significantly improving the memory access efficiency. To further leverage the spatial parallelism, double buffering is implemented for the local memory and the preloading for the next block happens in parallel to the computation of the current block. All these optimizations have been implemented using standard OpenMP or, in case of unrolling (`pragma unroll`), compiler annotations and C++ constructs. The `omp_target_preload`-function was designed to be very generic and corresponds to a pattern often found in accelerator programming (e.g., GPU programming), the preloading of relevant input data from global memory to local memory. An usage example of the preload-function can be found in Listing 1.2.

```
1   void gemm(float* A,...){
2     [...]
3     VECTOR A_local[BUFFERING][BLOCK_SIZE];
4     omp_target_preload<float, BLOCK_SIZE>((i*DIM)+k, DIM,
          ↪ BLOCK_SIZE, (void*) A, (void*)
          ↪ &A_local[buffer%BUFFERING * BLOCK_SIZE]);
5     [...]
6   }
```

Listing 1.2. Usage example of the `omp_target_preload`-function (excerpt).

Figure 3 shows the performance of the FPGA accelerator with different numbers of hardware threads executing simultaneously in the single compute unit for matrices of dimensions 8192×8192. While the performance of the accelerator almost doubles when going from a single to two threads, the increase slows down for three and four threads, respectively. In these cases, the threads do not only compete for compute resources in the multithreaded accelerator, but also for memory bandwidth to the external memory. The comparison with the BLAS implementation from the ATLAS library [31] on the Xeon CPU shows that the accelerator with a single thread outperforms a single thread on the CPU, but is not able to keep up with an execution with four threads on the CPU, partially also due to the data-transfers between host and FPGA.

In terms of hardware resource usage, the accelerator takes up 14% of logic resources, 16% of BRAM and 18% DSPs at a frequency of 183 MHz. Despite the relative low resource usage, it does not make sense to further increase the number of threads due to the negative impact on operating frequency. Instead, the remaining resources could be utilized to duplicate the accelerator and compute on multiple compute units in parallel in future versions of the proposed architecture.

In order to validate the support for OpenMP synchronization constructs via a lock implemented in the bus-attached hardware semaphore, an alternative version of GEMM, where each thread computes parts of the result for each element of the result matrix. The computed partial result is then added to the overall result inside a `critical` region. Even though the hardware semaphore allows for efficient locking, this version of GEMM, due to the very frequent access to global memory, delivers less performance than the optimized version using local memories described above.

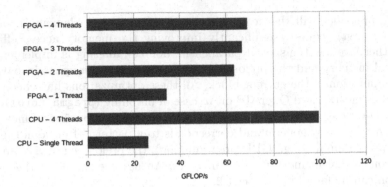

Fig. 3. Arithmetic performance of the blocked GEMM computation in GFLOP/s with different numbers of hardware threads simultaneously active in the compute unit.

5   Discussion

In this paper, we have demonstrated the Nymble infrastructure and shown that we can support a significant subset of OpenMP target offloading on FPGAs without much loss of generality, and that many of the properties (load-imbalance, scalability, etc.) materialize even in hardware. However, there are ample opportunities and future work for OpenMP on FPGAs, some of which we discuss herein.

OpenMP tasking, introduced in v3.0 (and dependent tasks in v4.0), is a construct that we would like to support in the Nymble subsystem. In theory, all necessary ingredients to support tasking is already provided by Nymble, and scheduling could be in a very software manner. However, such a solution would likely bloat the generated hardware, and a more customized approach is preferable (such as Nexus [9]), but a trade-off between consumed FPGA resources and the added performance must be performed. Alternatively, we could outsource task-management to a soft-core (e.g., a RISC-V [2]) that only orchestrates and resolves dependencies. More importantly, the FPGA allows for customizing communication between threads (and thus tasks), leading to interesting opportunities, particularly for dependent tasks.

One exciting future direction is concerning the synchronization and atomicity of operations. Today, Nymble uses a customized mutex hardware core (that is memory mapped) to support atomicity and synchronization. While this is a correct and functional way of supporting them, there are likely better ways that leverage the customization that FPGAs give us. For example, since we are working with an FPGA, we could, in theory, place the functionality of atom updates inside the external memory controller (DDR4 in our case). Similarly, rather than going through shared memory for synchronization, we could have a system-wide token bus that synchronizes all the threads (by sending and forwarding a synchronization token).

Another opportunity, unique for the FPGA, is concerning the recent memory allocations added in OpenMP. Because the memory hierarchy can be fully customized, we foresee that there are many future opportunities for tuning these for a particular performance criteria (e.g., execution time or power-consumption). For example, we could mark part of the FPGA that would be dedicated to the memory hierarchy as a partially reconfigurable region, and then *dynamically* adapt and optimize the actual hardware in real-time, such as for example changing cache sizes or replacement policies, scratchpad memories, coherency (or coherency-less) islands of memory, and so on and forth, in order to facilitate high-performance, low-latency producer/consumer patterns in (for example) the OpenMP 4.0 dependent tasks.

The representation of floating-point numbers has recently become a hot topic, with multiple authors proposing (and evaluating) new representations such as Posit [13] and Elias encoding [20]. Today, OpenMP does not contain support for setting a particular region to use a specific representation, but in the future, it might. FPGAs can execute arithmetic operations on these exciting new representations at high speed [27]. If selecting number representation will be part of future OpenMP standard, then FPGAs will be the platform that can exploit it to the fullest.

Finally, scaling OpenMP onto multiple FPGAs is an open question. On hand, we could rely on OpenMP's accelerator directives, and treat each device a discrete system with little to no access to other systems. However, on FPGAs, we can do more, and create/include special hardware to (for example) support a shared memory view across multiple FPGAs, or use tasks as containers that encapsulate produced/consumed data, that are exchanged among FPGAs.

In short, our understanding of OpenMP on FPGAs is just starting, and there are ample opportunities and future directions where this work affect OpenMP in the future.

6   Related Work

As OpenMP-based programming is very attractive for integrating FPGAs into HPC systems and toolflows, a number of previous works has presented approaches for mapping OpenMP to FPGAs. A good overview of these approaches can be found in the survey by Mayer et al. [21].

Early approaches tried to map OpenMP tasks [4,11,24,25] or worksharing constructs [6,7,19], such as `parallel for` to FPGA accelerators. As these approaches date back to the time before the OpenMP target constructs were standardized, no OpenMP constructs for specifying data mapping and device-specific execution were available for these approaches.

More recent approaches combine the OpenMP device constructs with commercially available HLS tools. Many of these works take an approach where target regions are extracted from the input program on AST-level [3,28], making OpenMP-specific optimizations before HLS difficult. The approach presented by Ceissler et al. [5] even requires the accelerator cores to be implemented in a hardware-description language and uses OpenMP only for the integration into the overall application. Only the work by Knaust et al. [17] uses IR (namely LLVM-IR) to interact with the HLS tool through an undocumented interface. However, as the data-transfers via the OpenCL API are statically generated during compile-time, their approach does not support array sections or mapping of data in only one direction (`to` or `from`), a limitation not found on our approach.

All of the tools mentioned above try to achieve a speedup over sequential execution through spatial parallelism (e.g., a dedicated accelerator core per thread) and classical HLS optimization techniques such as loop pipelining, but none of them supports actual hardware multi-threading inside the accelerator core. In contrast, in [29], OpenMP worksharing loops were mapped to multi-threaded accelerator cores. However, their threading model is much more limited than the one used in this work, as in their model, only a single thread can be active at a time and threads would only be switched when the active thread was suspended due to memory access latency.

As one of the key challenges for an effective mapping of OpenMP constructs to FPGA hardware, Mayer et al. [21] identified the code analysis and optimization across the border between compiler frontend and low-level HLS tool. With our fully integrated compilation flow from input program to Verilog, we are able to propagate information across this border and exploit knowledge of the underlying FPGA execution model for high-level, FPGA-specific transformations on IR-level in the compiler frontend.

7   Conclusion

This work presented a compilation flow for targeting FPGAs with OpenMP device offloading, in combination with a complete integration in `libomptarget` for complete data management support. The presented compile flow supports a significant subset of OpenMP for device offloading, including parallel constructs (e.g., `parallel, teams`) that are mapped to actual hardware threads executing simultaneously in the generated, multi-threaded accelerator, a unique feature of the presented approach.

By optimizing across the border between compiler front-end and the HLS-tool based on LLVM and the academic HLS-compiler Nymble, FPGA-specific optimizations were integrated in the compile flow. This insight could also be interesting for FPGA's vendor and a motivation to further open up their HLS-compiler IR interfaces for OpenMP-based compilation flows.

The case study showed that it is possible to target FPGAs from OpenMP programs, using only standard programming language constructs and annotations, without any HLS-specific extensions, and also showcased an integration of a data preloading functionality that could also be of interest on other accelerator architectures (e.g. GPUs). As described in Sect. 5, OpenMP is an interesting option for integrating FPGAs into parallel and heterogeneous applications, with a number of interesting research avenues.

References

1. Antão, S.F., et al.: Offloading support for OpenMP in Clang and LLVM. In: Third Workshop on the LLVM Compiler Infrastructure in HPC, LLVM-HPC@SC 2016, Salt Lake City, UT, USA, November 14, 2016, pp. 1–11. IEEE Computer Society (2016). https://doi.org/10.1109/LLVM-HPC.2016.006
2. Asanović, K., Patterson, D.A.: Instruction sets should be free: the case for RISC-V. Tech. rep. UCB/EECS-2014-146, EECS Department, University of California, Berkeley (2014)
3. Bosch, J., et al.: Application acceleration on FPGAs with OmpSs@FPGA. In: International Conference on Field-Programmable Technology, FPT 2018, Naha, Okinawa, Japan, December 10–14, 2018, pp. 70–77. IEEE (2018). https://doi.org/10.1109/FPT.2018.00021
4. Cabrera, D., Martorell, X., Gaydadjiev, G., Ayguadé, E., Jiménez-González, D.: OpenMP extensions for FPGA accelerators. In: Najjar, W.A., Schulte, M.J. (eds.) Proceedings of the 2009 International Conference on Embedded Computer Systems: Architectures, Modeling and Simulation (IC-SAMOS 2009), Samos, Greece, July 20–23, 2009, pp. 17–24. IEEE (2009). https://doi.org/10.1109/ICSAMOS.2009.5289237
5. Ceissler, C., Nepomuceno, R., Pereira, M.M., Araujo, G.: Automatic offloading of cluster accelerators. In: 26th IEEE Annual International Symposium on Field-Programmable Custom Computing Machines, FCCM 2018, Boulder, CO, USA, April 29–May 1, 2018, p. 224. IEEE Computer Society (2018). https://doi.org/10.1109/FCCM.2018.00058
6. Choi, J., Brown, S.D., Anderson, J.H.: From software threads to parallel hardware in high-level synthesis for FPGAs. In: 2013 International Conference on Field-Programmable Technology, FPT 2013, Kyoto, Japan, December 9–11, 2013, pp. 270–277. IEEE (2013). https://doi.org/10.1109/FPT.2013.6718365
7. Cilardo, A., Gallo, L., Mazzeo, A., Mazzocca, N.: Efficient and scalable OpenMP-based system-level design. In: Macii, E. (ed.) Design, Automation and Test in Europe, DATE 2013, Grenoble, France, March 18–22, 2013, pp. 988–991. EDA Consortium, ACM, San Jose (2013). https://doi.org/10.7873/DATE.2013.206
8. Czajkowski, T.S., et al.: From OpenCL to high-performance hardware on FPGAs. In: 22nd International Conference on Field Programmable Logic and Applications (FPL), pp. 531–534 (2012)
9. Dallou, T., Engelhardt, N., Elhossini, A., Juurlink, B.: Nexus#: a distributed hardware task manager for task-based programming models. In: 2015 IEEE International Parallel and Distributed Processing Symposium, pp. 1129–1138 (2015)
10. Filgueras, A., et al.: OmpSs@ Zynq all-programmable SoC ecosystem. In: Proceedings of the 2014 ACM/SIGDA International Symposium on Field-Programmable Gate Arrays, pp. 137–146 (2014)
11. Filgueras, A., et al.: OmpSs@ Zynq all-programmable SoC ecosystem. In: Betz, V., Constantinides, G.A. (eds.) The 2014 ACM/SIGDA International Symposium on Field-Programmable Gate Arrays, FPGA 2014, Monterey, CA, USA, February 26–8, 2014, pp. 137–146. ACM (2014). https://doi.org/10.1145/2554688.2554777
12. Gajski, D.D., Dutt, N.D., Wu, A.C., Lin, S.Y.: High-Level Synthesis: Introduction to Chip and System Design. Springer, Heidelberg (2012). https://doi.org/10.1007/978-1-4615-3636-9
13. Gustafson, J.L., Yonemoto, I.T.: Beating floating point at its own game: Posit arithmetic. Supercomput. Front. Innov. 4(2), 71–86 (2017)

14. Huthmann, J., Koch, A.: Optimized high-level synthesis of SMT multi-threaded hardware accelerators. In: 2015 International Conference on Field Programmable Technology, FPT 2015, Queenstown, New Zealand, December 7–9, 2015, pp. 176–183. IEEE (2015). https://doi.org/10.1109/FPT.2015.7393145
15. Huthmann, J., Liebig, B., Oppermann, J., Koch, A.: Hardware/software co-compilation with the Nymble system. In: 2013 8th International Workshop on Reconfigurable and Communication-Centric Systems-on-Chip (ReCoSoC), Darmstadt, Germany, July 10–12, 2013, pp. 1–8. IEEE (2013). https://doi.org/10.1109/ReCoSoC.2013.6581538
16. Huthmann, J., Shin, A., Podobas, A., Sano, K., Takizawa, H.: Scaling performance for N-Body stream computation with a ring of FPGAs. In: Proceedings of the 10th International Symposium on Highly-Efficient Accelerators and Reconfigurable Technologies, pp. 1–6 (2019)
17. Knaust, M., Mayer, F., Steinke, T.: OpenMP to FPGA offloading prototype using OpenCL SDK. In: IEEE International Parallel and Distributed Processing Symposium Workshops, IPDPSW 2019, Rio de Janeiro, Brazil, May 20–24, 2019, pp. 387–390. IEEE (2019). https://doi.org/10.1109/IPDPSW.2019.00072
18. Lattner, C., Adve, V.S.: LLVM: a compilation framework for lifelong program analysis & transformation. In: 2nd IEEE/ACM International Symposium on Code Generation and Optimization (CGO 2004), San Jose, CA, USA, March 20–24, 2004, pp. 75–88. IEEE Computer Society (2004). https://doi.org/10.1109/CGO.2004.1281665
19. Leow, Y.Y., Ng, C.Y., Wong, W.: Generating hardware from OpenMP programs. In: Constantinides, G.A., Mak, W., Sirisuk, P., Wiangtong, T. (eds.) 2006 IEEE International Conference on Field Programmable Technology, FPT 2006, Bangkok, Thailand, December 13–15, 2006, pp. 73–80. IEEE (2006). https://doi.org/10.1109/FPT.2006.270297
20. Lindstrom, P.: Universal coding of the reals using bisection. In: Proceedings of the Conference for Next Generation Arithmetic 2019, pp. 1–10 (2019)
21. Mayer, F., Knaust, M., Philippsen, M.: OpenMP on FPGAs—a survey. In: Fan, X., de Supinski, B.R., Sinnen, O., Giacaman, N. (eds.) IWOMP 2019. LNCS, vol. 11718, pp. 94–108. Springer, Cham (2019). https://doi.org/10.1007/978-3-030-28596-8_7
22. Moore, G.E.: Cramming more components onto integrated circuits. Electron. Mag. **38**(8), 114–117 (1965)
23. Pillet, V., Labarta, J., Cortes, T., Girona, S.: Paraver: a tool to visualize and analyze parallel code. In: Proceedings of WoTUG-18: Transputer and Occam Developments, pp. 17–31 (1995)
24. Podobas, A.: Accelerating parallel computations with OpenMP-driven system on-chip generation for FPGAs. In: IEEE 8th International Symposium on Embedded Multicore/Manycore SoCs, MCSoC 2014, Aizu-Wakamatsu, Japan, September 23–25, 2014, pp. 149–156. IEEE Computer Society (2014). https://doi.org/10.1109/MCSoC.2014.30
25. Podobas, A., Brorsson, M.: Empowering OpenMP with automatically generated hardware. In: Najjar, W.A., Gerstlauer, A. (eds.) International Conference on Embedded Computer Systems: Architectures, Modeling and Simulation, SAMOS 2016, Agios Konstantinos, Samos Island, Greece, July 17–21, 2016, pp. 245–252. IEEE (2016). https://doi.org/10.1109/SAMOS.2016.7818354
26. Podobas, A., Matsuoka, S.: Designing and accelerating spiking neural networks using OpenCL for FPGAs. In: 2017 International Conference on Field Programmable Technology (ICFPT), pp. 255–258 (2017)

27. Podobas, A., Matsuoka, S.: Hardware implementation of POSITs and their application in FPGAs. In: 2018 IEEE International Parallel and Distributed Processing Symposium Workshops (IPDPSW), pp. 138–145 (2018)
28. Sommer, L., Korinth, J., Koch, A.: OpenMP device offloading to FPGA accelerators. In: 28th IEEE International Conference on Application-Specific Systems, Architectures and Processors, ASAP 2017, Seattle, WA, USA, July 10–12, 2017, pp. 201–205. IEEE Computer Society (2017). https://doi.org/10.1109/ASAP.2017.7995280
29. Sommer, L., Oppermann, J., Hofmann, J., Koch, A.: Synthesis of interleaved multithreaded accelerators from OpenMP loops. In: International Conference on ReConFigurable Computing and FPGAs, ReConFig 2017, Cancun, Mexico, December 4–6, 2017, pp. 1–7. IEEE (2017). https://doi.org/10.1109/RECONFIG.2017.8279823
30. Waldrop, M.M.: The chips are down for Moore's law. Nat. News **530**(7589), 144 (2016)
31. Whaley, R.C., Petitet, A.: Minimizing development and maintenance costs in supporting persistently optimized BLAS. Softw.: Pract. Exp. **35**(2), 101–121 (2005)
32. Wirbel, L.: Xilinx SDAccel: A Unified Development Environment for Tomorrow's Data Center. The Linley Group Inc., Mountain View (2014)
33. Yang, C., et al.: Molecular dynamics range-limited force evaluation optimized for FPGAs. In: 2019 IEEE 30th International Conference on Application-Specific Systems, Architectures and Processors (ASAP), pp. 263–271 (2019)
34. Zohouri, H.R., Maruyama, N., Smith, A., Matsuda, M., Matsuoka, S.: Evaluating and optimizing OpenCL kernels for high performance computing with FPGAs. In: Proceedings of the International Conference for High Performance Computing, Networking, Storage and Analysis, SC 2016, pp. 409–420 (2016)
35. Zohouri, H.R., Podobas, A., Matsuoka, S.: High-performance high-order stencil computation on FPGAs using OpenCL. In: 2018 IEEE International Parallel and Distributed Processing Symposium Workshops (IPDPSW), pp. 123–130 (2018)

Data Transfer and Reuse Analysis Tool for GPU-Offloading Using OpenMP

Alok Mishra[1]($\boxtimes$), Abid M. Malik[2], and Barbara Chapman[1,2]

[1] Stony Brook University, Stony Brook, NY 11794, USA
{alok.mishra,barbara.chapman}@stonybrook.edu
[2] Brookhaven National Laboratory, Upton, NY 11973, USA
{amalik,bchapman}@bnl.gov

Abstract. In the high performance computing sector, researchers and application developers expend considerable effort to port their applications to GPU-based clusters in order to take advantage of the massive parallelism and energy efficiency of a GPU. Unfortunately porting or writing an application for accelerators, such as GPUs, requires extensive knowledge of the underlying architectures, the application/algorithm and the interfacing programming model, such as CUDA, HIP or OpenMP. Compared to native GPU programming models, OpenMP has a shorter learning curve, is portable and potentially also performance portable. To reduce the developer effort, OpenMP provides implicit data transfer between CPU and GPU. OpenMP users may control the duration of a data object's allocation on the GPU via the use of target data regions, but they do not need to. Unfortunately, unless data mappings are explicitly provided by the user, compilers like Clang move all data accessed by a kernel to the GPU without considering its prior availability on the device. As a result, applications may spend a significant portion of their execution time on data transfer. Yet exploiting data reuse opportunities in an application has the potential to significantly reduce the overall execution time. In this paper we present a source-to-source tool that automatically identifies data in an OpenMP program which do not need to be transferred between CPU and GPU. The tool capitalizes on any data reuse opportunities to insert the pertinent, optimized OpenMP `target data` directives. Our experimental results show considerable reduction in the overall execution time of a set of micro-benchmarks and some benchmark applications from the Rodinia benchmark suite. To the best of our knowledge, no other tool optimizes OpenMP data mappings by identifying and exploiting data reuse opportunities between kernels.

Keywords: Compiler optimization · GPU · Offloading · Compiler · HPC · OpenMP · Clang · LLVM · Data reuse · Data transfer

1 Introduction

GPUs are well known for their massively parallel architectures, as well as exceptional performance and energy efficiency for suitable codes. Supercomputing

© Springer Nature Switzerland AG 2020
K. Milfeld et al. (Eds.): IWOMP 2020, LNCS 12295, pp. 280–294, 2020.
https://doi.org/10.1007/978-3-030-58144-2_18

clusters like Summit [31] derive the lion's share of their compute power from GPUs. Each of the 4,608 nodes of Summit is configured with 2 IBM POWER9 processors and 6 NVIDIA Tesla V100 GPUs. For the last two decades, GPUs are the preferred accelerator in the high performance computing (HPC) sector, where they serve as a co-processor to accelerate general-purpose scientific and engineering application codes. Today, they expedite computational workloads in cutting-edge scientific research in diverse areas such as Physics, Bioinformatics, Chemistry, Climate Modeling, Machine Learning, and much more.

In the HPC context, GPUs are generally considered to be auxiliary processors that are attached to a CPU. A block of code which will run on the device is called a kernel[1]. Since such a kernel often contains critical computations, most application developers expend considerable time and effort to optimize it. Yet both CPU and GPU have their own separate memories, and data must be transferred between them. Orchestrating data motion between the CPU and GPU memories is of vital importance since data transfer is expensive and can often become a major bottleneck in GPU computing. Efficiently managing data transfers is moreover quite burdensome for the application developer. This is the issue we address in our work.

1.1 GPU Offloading Using OpenMP

OpenMP [9] is a directive-based application programming interface that can be used in a Fortran, C or C++ application code to create a parallel program. It is designed for portability, enjoys wide vendor support, and has a much smaller learning curve than native programming models, like CUDA [25] and HiP [3]. From version 4.0 onward, OpenMP supports accelerator devices in a host-device model, for which it offers *"target offloading"* features. The specification provides several options to allow its users to control the duration of a data object's allocation on the GPU, via the use of `target data` directives. Compared to other directive-based methods like OpenACC [32], OpenMP has a broader user community and is more widely available. Features for offloading to devices are under active improvement, as are the implementations [27] in numerous compilers, including Clang/LLVM [21], GCC [12], Intel [17], and Cray [8].

An advantage that OpenMP provides over most native GPU programming models is that it enables implicit data transfer for GPU kernels. Users can choose whether or not to handle data transfer explicitly; in the latter case, the OpenMP compiler will manage the data motion. Unfortunately, compiler support for implicit data transfer is in need of improvement.

1.2 The Problem

All compilers that we had access to and which support OpenMP GPU offloading, like Clang and GCC, handle an implicit data transfer by moving all data needed for kernel computation without considering its availability on the device.

---

[1] In this paper the term kernel is always used in reference to a GPU kernel.

Thus, all data used in the kernel are transferred both to and from the device at the start and end of the kernel's execution, respectively. In consequence, applications may spend a significant portion of their execution time on data transfer itself. Automatically determining which data does not need to be transferred to the GPU (because it is already there) or from the GPU (when it has not been changed or is no longer required) could lead to better performance by reducing the amount of data transferred and hence the overall execution time. Such an optimization could largely avoid the performance penalty currently associated with the implicit transfer approach and ultimately help increase the fraction of codes that can utilize a GPU by reducing the developer effort. Although there are tools available which perform source-to-source transformations for GPU offloading [22,28], to the best of our knowledge no such tool exists that identifies and exploits opportunities for data reuse between kernels.

1.3   Our Solution

We have developed a Clang-based tool to perform static data reuse analysis between kernels. We selected Clang because it is the front end for the LLVM framework which is now a building block of all major compiler frameworks. The target applications of this tool are those which already use OpenMP for offloading computation to GPU. This tool performs the following actions:

- It identifies all kernels in an application that uses OpenMP for GPU offloading.
- It identifies the data that needs to be transferred between the CPU and GPU for each kernel.
- It automatically recognizes data reuse opportunities between multiple kernels.
- It inserts the pertinent OpenMP target data directives into the original source code to precisely manage data transfers between the host and the device.

Currently, our tool considers traditional data management and not data management through unified memory [20,24]. Optimizing GPU data management through unified memory is planned as future work. We also currently assume that all CPU-GPU data transfers for an input application code is handled by our tool, therefore, there are no explicit data transfers.

The rest of this paper is organized as follows: Sect. 2 provides motivating examples to describe common scenarios in user code which can benefit from data reuse. Section 3 gives a detailed explanation of our strategy for automatically generating code to exploit data reuse opportunities between kernels. Section 4 describes the experimental setup for our research. Section 5 provides a detailed analysis of the results from our experiments using the tool. Section 6 looks at related work and discussion about probable usage of the tool and we conclude in Sect. 7. Future work and planned extensions are discussed in Sect. 8.

2   Motivating Examples

For this work, we analyzed the Rodinia benchmark suite [4] to find example codes where data can be reused on a GPU. The use cases are defined in Sect. 4.

To motivate the utility of our tool, we discuss here two common scenarios in a user code which can profit from data reuse:

Loops: If a kernel is called from within a loop, there is a high probability that data is reused in multiple calls to that kernel. Any data used inside these kernels are potential candidates for reuse. Our tool analyzes data in all such kernels to decide how to efficiently transfer data between the CPU and GPU. As can be seen in Code 1.1, Kernel 1 is called within a while loop and Array_A is reused by every call of the kernel. Similarly Kernel 2 is called within a for loop, and Array_B is reused in every subsequent call to the kernel.

Close Proximity: We define two kernels to be in close proximity to each other if they are both called from the same function. In such a case there is also a high possibility of data reuse between the kernels. As can be seen in Code 1.2, 3 kernels are called inside function func1, and the array Array_A is used inside all 3 kernels in different ways. All kernels called within a loop are, by default, considered to be in close proximity to their subsequent calls. Our tool has the ability to detect data reuse in two kernels if they are in close proximity.

```
while(iter < MAX_ITER) {
    // Kernel 1
    #pragma omp target teams distribute parallel for
    for(int i=0; i<N; i++)
        // Compute on Array_A;
    iter++;
}
for(iter = 0; iter < MAX_ITER; iter++) {
    // Kernel 2
    #pragma omp target teams distribute parallel for
    for(int i=0; i<N; i++)
        // Compute on Array_B;
}
```

```
void func1 (Array_A) {
    // Kernel 1
    #pragma omp target ...
        // Assigning Array_A

    // Kernel 2
    #pragma omp target ...
        // Updating Array_A

    // Kernel 3
    #pragma omp target ...
        // Using Array_A
}
```

Code 1.1. Code snippet for kernels called from inside loops

Code 1.2. Code snippet for proximity of kernels

3 Data Reuse Optimization

In this section, we outline the key steps of our approach.

3.1 Problem with OpenMP Implicit Data Transfer

When an OpenMP program begins, an implicit target data region for each device surrounds the whole program [2]. Each device has a device data environment that is defined by its implicit target data region. Any declare target directives, and directives that accept data-mapping attribute clauses, determine how an original variable in a data environment is mapped to a corresponding variable in a device data environment. If a user chooses not to map any data to the device explicitly, then the data is implicitly managed by the compiler. Compilers, such as Clang, identify all variables used in a `target` region and move any data associated with them to the device. The compilers we studied do not take into consideration whether the data is already available on the device. Once the kernel execution is over, all array data is moved back to the host, irrespective of whether or not the data was updated on the kernel or needed beyond the kernel.

3.2 Our Approach

Our tool automatically identifies the data which need to be moved between the host and the device for each OpenMP kernel, and then searches for any data reuse opportunity between these kernels. It then inserts pertinent `target data` directives, which complies with OpenMP Specification 5.0 [7], to precisely manage data transfers between CPU and GPU. The goal of our tool is to modify the original source code (C/C++) by inserting explicit data transfers between the CPU and GPU, optimized to avoid any unnecessary data motion between them. Two advantages of this approach are:

- The user can accept, modify or reject the changes introduced by our tool.
- The updated code can be compiled using any compiler with OpenMP GPU offloading support.

3.3 Implementation

We implemented our framework using Clang/LLVM version 8.0.0 [5]. During the design stage for the tool, we had to decide whether to apply our analysis and optimization in Clang or on the LLVM IR. Yet the LLVM IR is relatively low-level and generally unsuitable for any approach that involves modification to source code. Once LLVM IR has been generated and optimizations are applied to it, it would be quite difficult to pinpoint the location of the source code where we need to insert directives. Thus, we decided to apply our analysis using the Clang Abstract Syntax Tree (AST) [19].

Table 1. Nodes identified as kernels

Clang AST node	OpenMP directive
OMPTargetDirective	omp target
OMPTargetParallelDirective	omp target parallel
OMPTargetParallelForDirective	omp target parallel for
OMPTargetParallelForSimdDirective	omp target parallel for simd
OMPTargetSimdDirective	omp target simd
OMPTargetTeamsDirective	omp target teams
OMPTargetTeamsDistributeDirective	omp target teams distribute
OMPTargetTeamsDistributeParallelForDirective	omp target teams distribute parallel for
OMPTargetTeamsDistributeParallelForSimdDirective	omp target teams distribute parallel for simd
OMPTargetTeamsDistributeSimdDirective	omp target teams distribute simd

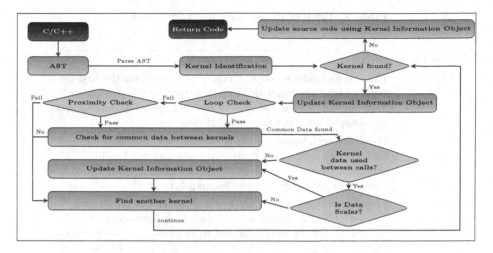

Fig. 1. Workflow for identifying data transfer opportunities and data reuse in an application using OpenMP for GPU offloading

Clang supports source to source translation, via libTooling [6], even though it is not primarily used for this purpose. In the Clang/LLVM framework [19] most of the analysis is performed on the LLVM Intermediate Representation (IR) and not on the AST. As a result, we had to re-implement some standard analyses such as live variable analysis, data flow graph and code transformation at the AST level for our tool. Consequently, we parse the AST to collect all required information related to the kernels and data variables used in them.

Figure 1 illustrates how our implementation in Clang accurately identifies data reuse opportunity between kernels. First, we parse the AST and identify the kernels in the application. To achieve this, we search for all nodes in the AST as specified in Table 1. For this, we have defined our own Kernel Information Object, which contains information about each identified kernel, e.g., a unique id assigned to the kernel, start and end location of the kernel, function from which the kernel is called, data used inside the kernel, etc. We subsequently use this class to identify variables accessed inside the kernels. The variables are classified into five groups as shown in Table 2 and stored in the Kernel Information Object, to be used during "common data" analysis and for generating the source code.

For each kernel, we implement live variable analysis using the Clang AST, focusing only on variables used inside a kernel. While traversing the AST, we store information about the source code location related to all the variables declared and accessed. Next, we check whether the kernel is called from within a loop and also check for proximity to other kernels, as defined in Sect. 2. Once kernels are identified to be in close proximity to each other, we analyze them to find common data which can be reused across multiple kernels. We use pattern matching on all variables accessed inside the sets of kernels that are in close

Table 2. Types of variables for live variable analysis.

Data types	Description
alloc	These are variables *assigned inside* the kernel for the first time. Data which falls under this category need not be transferred from the host to the device. During code generation these data are mapped with the map type "alloc"
to	These are variables *assigned before* but *accessed* inside the kernel. Data which falls under this category need to be transferred from the host to the device. During code generation these data are mapped with the map type "to"
from	These are variables that are *updated inside* the kernel and *accessed after* the kernel call. Data which falls under this category needs to be transferred from the device to the host. During code generation these data are mapped with the map type "from"
tofrom	These are variables that are *assigned before* a kernel call, *updated inside* it and *accessed after* the kernel execution is complete. Data which falls under this category need to be transferred both ways between the host and the device. During code generation these data are mapped with the map type "tofrom"
private	Finally, we have variables which are defined and used *only inside* the kernel. Data which falls under this category does not need to be transferred between the host and the device. During code generation these data are not mapped

proximity to each other, to check for potential data reuse. After identifying common data between kernels, we update the Kernel Information Object. Finally, we use the results of our analysis to update the original source code, inserting the pertinent `target data map` directives to transfer data between the host and the device explicitly.

4   Experimental Setup

To evaluate our benchmarks, we used the SeaWulf computational cluster at Stony Brook University [30]. We ran our tool on four microbenchmarks (Table 3) and six benchmark applications (Table 4) defined in the Rodinia benchmark suite [4]. We selected only those benchmarks from the Rodinia suite, which has GPU offloading support with OpenMP and more than one kernel as part of the code. We modified these benchmarks by removing all data transfer directives so that our tool could introduce new code for them automatically. For each application, we compared two versions:

- **Base Code:** – This is the basic code with implicit data transfer. It does not contain any explicit data transfers.

Table 3. Micro-benchmarks used in the experimentation.

Benchmarks	Description
Three Matrix Multiplication (3 mm)	This is the most basic implementation of multiplying three large matrices. This is a benchmark where two kernels are reusing same data. The experiment used matrices of size 5000 × 5000 each
Gauss Seidel Method (gauss)	The method for solving linear equations is an iterative method, in which the values for the given variables keep changing until a certain threshold of variance is reached. The experiment used a matrix of size $2^{13} \times 2^{13}$
Laplace Equation (laplace)	The equation in two dimensions with finite differences using jacobi iteration. The experiment used a matrix of size 2000 × 2000
Single-Precision A·X Plus Y (saxpy)	SAXPY is a function in the standard Basic Linear Algebra Subroutines (BLAS) library. In its simplest form this is a benchmark where two kernels are reusing same data. The experiment used two vectors of size 2^{27} each

Table 4. Updated benchmarks from the Rodinia benchmark suite

Application	Description
Breadth First Search (bfs) [15]	**Graph Algorithm** domain. This benchmark provides the GPU implementations of BFS algorithm which traverses all the connected components in a graph
Hotspot [16]	**Physics Simulation** domain. We re-implemented the transient differential equation solver from HotSpot using target offloading directives for GPU
k-Nearest Neighbor (knn) [11]	**Data Mining** domain. In the implementation it finds the k-nearest neighbors from an unstructured data set
LU Decomposition (lud)	**Linear Algebra** domain. This benchmark is a good example where multiple kernels care called from within a loop and some data shared by these kernels are also used on the host
Needleman Wunsch (nw) [29]	**Bioinformatics** domain. Needleman-Wunsch is a nonlinear global optimization method for DNA sequence alignments
Particle Filter (p-filter) [14]	**Medical Imaging** domain. This particular implementation is optimized for tracking cells, particularly leukocytes and myocardial cells

– **Optimized Code:** – This is the corresponding code in which our data reuse optimization has been applied to generate explicit data transfers.

We ran the two versions of a benchmark 10 times each and collected information on the amount of data transferred and the total execution time. In its current version, OpenMP in Clang uses CUDA to implement GPU offloading. Our tool is based on Clang/LLVM version 8.0, using OpenMP offloading with CUDA 10.0 in the backend. Therefore, during our experiments, we also tracked how many times the following CUDA APIs related to data transfer are invoked:

– *cuMemAlloc* - Allocates bytes of linear memory on the device and returns a pointer to the allocated memory.
– *cuMemFree* - Frees the memory space which must have been returned by a previous call to cuMemAlloc.
– *cuMemcpyHtoD* - Synchronous copies the specified amount of data from host memory to device memory.
– *cuMemcpyDtoH* - Synchronously copies the specified amount of data from device memory to host memory.

We ran these experiments on an NVIDIA Tesla V100 [26] GPU using a PCI-e connector between the CPU and GPU.

```
#pragma omp target data map(alloc:temp[0:N][0:N])
{ ←————(data reuse region starts)
#pragma omp target data map(to:A[0:N][0:N],B[0:N][0:N])
#pragma omp target teams distribute parallel for collapse(2)
    for(int i=0; i<N; i++) {
        for(int j=0; j<N; j++) {
            temp[i][j] = 0;
            for(int k=0; k<N; k++)
                temp[i][j] += A[i][k]*B[k][j];
        }
    }
#pragma omp target data map(to:C[0:N][0:N]) map(from:D[0:N][0:N])
#pragma omp target teams distribute parallel for collapse(2)
    for(int i=0; i<N; i++) {
        for(int j=0; j<N; j++) {
            D[i][j] = 0;
            for(int k=0; k<N; k++)
                D[i][j] += temp[i][k]*C[k][j];
        }
    }
} ←————(// data reuse region ends)
```

Code 1.3. Example of multiplying three matrices reusing data. Code shown in red is generated automatically by our tool.

5 Results and Analysis

Code 1.3 gives a sample output of our tool when applied to a benchmark code multiplying three matrices. Here the code marked in red is auto-generated by our tool. In this particular example, two kernels use, and reuse data from the

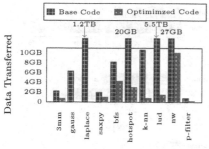

Data transfer between CPU and GPU

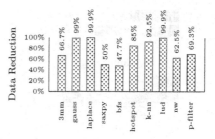

% Reduction in size of data transferred when reusing data on GPU

Fig. 2. Comparison of data transferred between CPU and GPU for different benchmarks

array *temp*. Arrays A, B and C only need to be transferred to the device. Since they are not updated on the GPU, we do not need to transfer their values back to the host. Array *temp* is needed only on the GPU, while array D needs to be returned to the host. The array *temp* is assigned on the GPU, so we do not need to transfer its data from the host to the device. We ran the base codes and optimized codes and collected the amount of data transferred between the host and device. We determined that more than 2 GB of data was transferred between the host and device in the base case.

In contrast, in our optimized code, only 763 MB of data was transferred. As can be observed in Fig. 2, there is a reduction of 66.67% in data transfer, accomplished by automatically adding three lines of OpenMP *target data* directives to manage data transfer (cf. Code 1.3). After running our tool on all the benchmark applications, we collected the amount of data transferred for the base and optimized code for each of them, and found that in all cases, less data was transferred in the optimized code than in the base code. This can clearly be observed in Fig. 2.

For Rodinia's *LU-Decomposition* benchmark, in the base case 5.5 TB (TeraByte!) of data was transferred between the host and the device, as compared to 1.5 GB in the optimized code. This is a huge reduction of 99.97%. Also, the *Laplace Equation* micro-benchmark transferred 1.2 TB of data in the base case, in comparison to only 61 MB in the optimized code (99.99% reduction). As evident from Fig. 2(b), we observed a tremendous reduction in the amount of data transferred between the host and device, with BFS being the lowest at 47.7%.

We then took a closer look at the number of times the CUDA data transfer APIs are called for each application. As shown in Fig. 3(C), *Laplace Equation* called each of the four APIs – cuMemAlloc, cuMemFree, cuMemcpyHtoD and cuMemcpyDtoH around 25000 times in its base case. Upon further analysis of the base code, we discovered that it was calling a kernel from inside a loop which iterated for 5000 times. Of the four arrays and one variable which were used inside the kernel, only the variable was used both on the host and the device. In our optimized code, the data transfer for the arrays was moved outside the

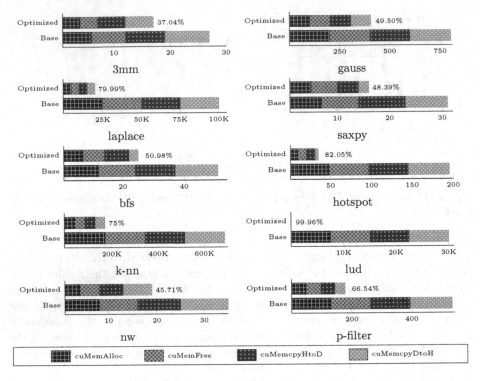

Fig. 3. Number of calls to data transfer CUDA APIs. The % at the tip of optimized code represent reduction in total number of calls when compared to base code.

loop, dramatically reducing the number of times the data was moved between the host and device. In our optimized code, each of the four concerned APIs were only called around 5000 times. To achieve this, our tool added just one *target data* directive. Figure 3 shows the reduction in the number of times the APIs are called, with a maximum of 99.96% reduction in LU-Decomposition and a minimum of 45.71% reduction in Needleman Wunsch.

We next calculated the time it took to perform the data transfer and the time taken to execute the kernel computations. The result is shown in Fig. 4. It can be seen that the kernel execution time in both base and optimized code is almost identical. This is expected, as we did not make any changes to the kernel code itself. In Figs. 4(A), 4(B), 4(E), 4(I) and 4(J), we observe that the majority of the execution time is consumed in the kernel computation rather than in data management. However, the K-Nearest Neighbor algorithm, Fig. 4(G), spends 4.382 s in cuMemAlloc, 2.958 s in cuMemFree, 0.209 s in cuMemcpyHtoD and 0.193 s in cuMemcpyDtoH, with overall 7.743 s for data management, which is almost 91x the kernel computation time of 0.085 s. After applying our optimization, data management was improved by 71% to just 2.26 s. In Fig. 4(G) we do not even see the compute bar as it is insignificant compared to the data management time.

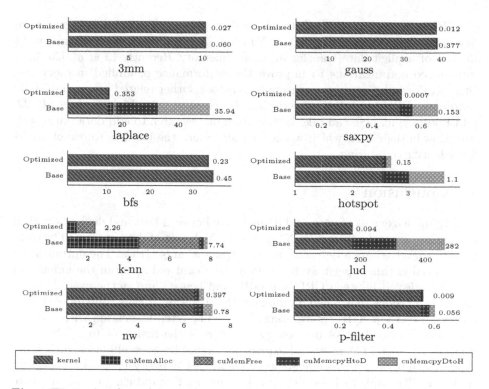

Fig. 4. Time taken (in sec) for different data management APIs and kernel computation time on V100 GPU. The numbers at the tip of each graph represent the time taken for data transfer only (in sec).

For the LU-Decomposition, Fig. 4(H), the base case requires 282.514 s for data management, which is almost 1.63x the kernel compute time of 173.441 s. But after our optimization it consumes only 94.28 ms, which is a 99.96% improvement over the base case. We also observe considerable improvement in data transfer time for Laplace (99.01%), SAXPY (99.54%), HotSpot (85.95%) and Particle Filter (83.96%).

6 Related Work

Optimizing GPU memory management where data movement must be managed explicitly has been explored in a variety of research. Jablin *et al.* [18] provide a fully automatic system for managing and optimizing CPU-GPU communication for CUDA programs. Gelado *et al.* [13] present a programming model for heterogeneous computing to simplify and optimize GPU data management. Recently Barua *et al.* [1] introduce static analysis of explicit data transfers already inserted into an OpenMP code. Current research in the field do not provide insight into utilizing data reusability on GPU for implicitly managed data between multiple kernels.

Although there are several studies on data placement in heterogeneous memory system, like Dullor *et al.* [10] or Yu *et al.* [33], unfortunately they ignore the impact of implicit data transfer in unified memory. Recently Li *et al.* [20] have introduced optimizations to improve the performance of unified memory and their work can be used in extension to our tool. Other related research on fully automatic GPU offloading of code by Mishra *et al.* [23], Mendonça *et al.* [22] and Poesia *et al.* [28], can take benefit from our research to add data reuse optimization in their tool, which would further reduce the barriers to use of GPUs for scientific computing.

7   Conclusion

Careful management of data and its mapping between host and device is critical for the use of accelerators in HPC, given the high cost of data motion. The complexities involved are a deterrent to the exploitation of GPUs. The optimization introduced in this paper may result in a significant reduction in the amount of data transferred between CPU and GPU and hence improve the overall execution time of codes that relied on implicit data transfer. It thus contributes to the ease of use of OpenMP by avoiding the penalty often associated with implicit transfers. To the best of our knowledge, this is the first tool to apply static analysis in order to identify and exploit data reuse between offload kernels in an OpenMP program. The same strategy could clearly easily be used to optimize an OpenMP compiler's handling of such transfers. By producing modified source code, as we have chosen to do, we give the user the option of accepting, improving or rejecting our generated code, and we enable them to use their compiler of choice for further building their code.

8   Future Work

The tool is under constant improvement, and a number of extensions are planned or already under way:

- We are working on exploiting unified memory for data management between the host and the device.
- We also need to further analyze data usage to determine which data can be pinned to the GPU, to reduce multiple data allocations. We are also considering how to handle data between multiple GPUs.
- Discussion is also going on for managing complex structures, sub-structures and sub-arrays and handling data between multiple GPUs as well.
- Most importantly, we are planning to improve our proximity analysis to analyze kernels beyond a single function. This could be facilitated by extending the `target data` directive of OpenMP, so that the user only prescribes the data region without the need to explicitly define the map clause. This would let the compiler automatically handle the data movement, potentially reusing data on the GPU. Any kernel called from such a data region would be considered a candidate for data reuse and be analyzed as such.

Acknowledgement. This research was supported by the Exascale Computing Project (17-SC-20-SC), a collaborative effort of the U.S. Department of Energy Office of Science and the National Nuclear Security Administration. The authors would like to thank Stony Brook Research Computing and Cyberinfrastructure, and the Institute for Advanced Computational Science at Stony Brook University for access to the SeaWulf computing system, which was made possible by a \$1.4M National Science Foundation grant (#1531492). Special thanks to our colleague Dr. Chunhua Liao from Lawrence Livermore National Laboratory for his initial feedback and helpful discussions.

References

1. Barua, P., Shirako, J., Tsang, W., Paudel, J., Chen, W., Sarkar, V.: OMPSan: static verification of OpenMP's data mapping constructs. In: Fan, X., de Supinski, B.R., Sinnen, O., Giacaman, N. (eds.) IWOMP 2019. LNCS, vol. 11718, pp. 3–18. Springer, Cham (2019). https://doi.org/10.1007/978-3-030-28596-8_1
2. Bercea, G.T., et al.: Implementing implicit OpenMP data sharing on GPUs. In: Proceedings of the Fourth Workshop on the LLVM Compiler Infrastructure in HPC, pp. 1–12 (2017)
3. C++ Heterogeneous-Compute Interface for Portability (2016). https://github.com/ROCm-Developer-Tools/HIP
4. Che, S., et al.: Rodinia: a benchmark suite for heterogeneous computing. In: 2009 IEEE International Symposium on Workload Characterization (IISWC), pp. 44–54. IEEE (2009)
5. Clang 8.0 (2019). http://releases.llvm.org/8.0.1/tools/clang/docs/index.html
6. Clang, Libtooling (2019). http://clang.llvm.org/docs/LibTooling.html
7. Consortium, O., et al.: OpenMP specification version 5.0 (2018)
8. Cray, C.: C++ reference manual, s-2179 (8.7). Cray Research (2019). https://pubs.cray.com/content/S-2179/8.7/cray-c-and-c++-reference-manual/openmp-overview
9. Dagum, L., Menon, R.: OpenMP: an industry standard API for shared-memory programming. IEEE Comput. Sci. Eng. **5**(1), 46–55 (1998)
10. Dulloor, S.R., et al.: Data tiering in heterogeneous memory systems. In: Proceedings of the Eleventh European Conference on Computer Systems, pp. 1–16 (2016)
11. Garcia, V., Debreuve, E., Barlaud, M.: Fast k nearest neighbor search using GPU. In: 2008 IEEE Computer Society Conference on Computer Vision and Pattern Recognition Workshops, pp. 1–6. IEEE (2008)
12. GCC Support for the OpenMP Language (2019). https://gcc.gnu.org/wiki/openmp
13. Gelado, I., Stone, J.E., Cabezas, J., Patel, S., Navarro, N., Hwu, W.M.W.: An asymmetric distributed shared memory model for heterogeneous parallel systems. In: Proceedings of the Fifteenth International Conference on Architectural Support for Programming Languages and Operating Systems, pp. 347–358 (2010)
14. Goodrum, M.A., Trotter, M.J., Aksel, A., Acton, S.T., Skadron, K.: Parallelization of particle filter algorithms. In: Varbanescu, A.L., Molnos, A., van Nieuwpoort, R. (eds.) ISCA 2010. LNCS, vol. 6161, pp. 139–149. Springer, Heidelberg (2011). https://doi.org/10.1007/978-3-642-24322-6_12
15. Harish, P., Narayanan, P.J.: Accelerating large graph algorithms on the GPU using CUDA. In: Aluru, S., Parashar, M., Badrinath, R., Prasanna, V.K. (eds.) HiPC 2007. LNCS, vol. 4873, pp. 197–208. Springer, Heidelberg (2007). https://doi.org/10.1007/978-3-540-77220-0_21

16. Huang, W., Ghosh, S., Velusamy, S., Sankaranarayanan, K., Skadron, K., Stan, M.R.: Hotspot: a compact thermal modeling methodology for early-stage VLSI design. IEEE Trans. Very Large Scale Integr. (VLSI) Syst. **14**(5), 501–513 (2006)
17. Intel C++ Compiler Code Samples (March 2019). https://software.intel.com/en-us/code-samples/intel-c-compiler
18. Jablin, T.B., Prabhu, P., Jablin, J.A., Johnson, N.P., Beard, S.R., August, D.I.: Automatic CPU-GPU communication management and optimization. In: Proceedings of the 32nd ACM SIGPLAN Conference on Programming Language Design and Implementation, pp. 142–151 (2011)
19. Lattner, C., Adve, V.: LLVM: a compilation framework for lifelong program analysis & transformation. In: Proceedings of the International Symposium on Code Generation and Optimization: Feedback-Directed and Runtime Optimization, p. 75. IEEE Computer Society (2004)
20. Li, L., Chapman, B.: Compiler assisted hybrid implicit and explicit GPU memory management under unified address space. In: Proceedings of the International Conference for High Performance Computing, Networking, Storage and Analysis, pp. 1–16 (2019)
21. LLVM Support for the OpenMP Language (2019). https://openmp.llvm.org
22. Mendonça, G., Guimarães, B., Alves, P., Pereira, M., Araújo, G., Pereira, F.M.Q.: DawnCC: automatic annotation for data parallelism and offloading. ACM Trans. Archit. Code Optim. (TACO) **14**(2), 13 (2017)
23. Mishra, A., Kong, M., Chapman, B.: Kernel fusion/decomposition for automatic GPU-offloading. In: Proceedings of the 2019 IEEE/ACM International Symposium on Code Generation and Optimization, pp. 283–284. IEEE Press (2019)
24. Mishra, A., Li, L., Kong, M., Finkel, H., Chapman, B.: Benchmarking and evaluating unified memory for OpenMP GPU offloading. In: Proceedings of the Fourth Workshop on the LLVM Compiler Infrastructure in HPC, pp. 1–10 (2017)
25. Nvidia, C.: Nvidia cuda c programming guide. Nvidia Corp. **120**(18), 8 (2011)
26. NVIDIA Tesla: Nvidia tesla v100 GPU architecture (2017)
27. OpenMP Compilers & Tools (April 2019). https://www.openmp.org/resources/openmp-compilers-tools
28. Poesia, G., Guimarães, B., Ferracioli, F., Pereira, F.M.Q.: Static placement of computation on heterogeneous devices. Proc. ACM Program. Lang. **1**(OOPSLA), 50 (2017)
29. Poesia, G., Guimarães, B.C.F., Ferracioli, F., Pereira, F.M.Q.: Static placement of computation on heterogeneous devices. Proc. ACM Program. Lang. **1**(OOPSLA), 50:1–50:28 (2017). Article 50
30. Seawulf, Computational Cluster at Stony Brook University (2019). https://it.stonybrook.edu/help/kb/understanding-seawulf
31. Vazhkudai, S.S., et al.: The design, deployment, and evaluation of the coral pre-exascale systems. In: SC18: International Conference for High Performance Computing, Networking, Storage and Analysis, pp. 661–672. IEEE (2018)
32. Wienke, S., Springer, P., Terboven, C., an Mey, D.: OpenACC—first experiences with real-world applications. In: Kaklamanis, C., Papatheodorou, T., Spirakis, P.G. (eds.) Euro-Par 2012. LNCS, vol. 7484, pp. 859–870. Springer, Heidelberg (2012). https://doi.org/10.1007/978-3-642-32820-6_85
33. Yu, S., Park, S., Baek, W.: Design and implementation of bandwidth-aware memory placement and migration policies for heterogeneous memory systems. In: Proceedings of the International Conference on Supercomputing, pp. 1–10 (2017)

Toward Supporting Multi-GPU Targets via Taskloop and User-Defined Schedules

Vivek Kale[1](✉), Wenbin Lu[2], Anthony Curtis[2], Abid M. Malik[1],
Barbara Chapman[1,2], and Oscar Hernandez[3]

[1] Brookhaven National Laboratory, Upton, NY 11973, USA
vkale@bnl.gov
[2] Stony Brook University, Stony Brook, NY 11794, USA
[3] Oak Ridge National Laboratory, Oak Ridge, TN 37830, USA

Abstract. Many modern supercomputers such as ORNL's Summit,
LLNL's Sierra, and LBL's upcoming Perlmutter offer or will offer multiple, e.g., 4 to 8, GPUs per node for running computational science and
engineering applications. One should expect an application to achieve
speedup using multiple GPUs on a node of a supercomputer over a single GPU of the node, in particular an application that is embarrassingly parallel and load imbalanced, such as AutoDock, QMCPACK and
DMRG++. OpenMP is a popular model used to run applications on
heterogeneous devices of a node and OpenMP 5.x provides rich features for tasking and GPU offloading. However, OpenMP doesn't provide significant support for running application code on multiple GPUs
efficiently, in particular for the aforementioned applications. We provide
different OpenMP task-to-GPU scheduling strategies that help distribute
an application's work across GPUs on a node for efficient parallel GPU
execution. Our solution involves using OpenMP's construct taskloop to
generate OpenMP tasks containing target regions for OpenMP threads,
and then having OpenMP threads assign those tasks to GPUs on a node
through a schedule specified by the application programmer. We analyze
the performance of our solution using a small benchmark code representative of the aforementioned applications. Our solution improves performance over a standard baseline assignment of tasks to GPUs by up to
57.2%. Further, based on our results, we suggest OpenMP extensions
that could help an application programmer have his or her application
run on multiple GPUs per node efficiently.

© Springer Nature Switzerland AG 2020
K. Milfeld et al. (Eds.): IWOMP 2020, LNCS 12295, pp. 295–309, 2020.
https://doi.org/10.1007/978-3-030-58144-2_19

Keywords: OpenMP · Tasks · Offload · Multi GPUs · AutoDock · Load balancing · User-defined scheduling · High-performance · Parallel

1 Introduction

Modern supercomputers for running computational science and engineering applications are often comprised of compute nodes with accelerator devices. Many of the supercomputers ranked on the latest Top500 list (http://www.top500.org) and the Green500 list (http://www.green500.org) in November 2019 are equipped with an accelerator component such as the NVIDIA GPU. A compute node in such a supercomputer often has multiple accelerators to further improve the power-to-performance ratio. For example, ORNL's supercomputer Summit has 6 NVIDIA Volta-100 GPUs per compute node [5], and LBL's Perlmutter will have nodes with 4 NVIDIA A100 GPUs and 2 AMD Milan GPUs [4]. This node architecture allows application programs to offload multiple computational kernels onto independent devices simultaneously and achieve significant performance. Supercomputers with such a node architecture are often considered as a leading candidate for running applications, in particular those applications that are embarrassingly parallel and load imbalanced, and employing Monte Carlo algorithms [3, 26].

Accelerator programming languages such as CUDA, OpenCL, OpenMP, and OpenACC are often used to offload kernels to devices [28]. OpenMP is one of the most commonly used parallel programming models for on-node programming. The current version of OpenMP, OpenMP 5.0, provides GPU offloading support [1]. However, multi-GPU OpenMP offload is limited by mapping a target region for an accelerator to a specified device number of one of multiple devices on a node explicitly when a target region is created. How can we create suitable software for applications to take advantage of multiple GPUs on a node in a generic way, without mapping to specific devices, to leverage multiple GPUs on the node and improve performance portability on systems with a different number of devices per node?

This paper explores how to program multiple GPUs within a node by looking at different task-to-GPU scheduling strategies to map computations to multiple devices. Our solution involves using OpenMP's tasking construct `taskloop` to generate OpenMP tasks containing target regions for OpenMP threads, and then having OpenMP threads assign or schedule those tasks to GPUs on a node through a schedule specified by the application programmer, or a user such as a performance engineer helping optimize an application. We analyze the performance of our solution using a small OpenMP performance benchmark code representative of the applications with Monte Carlo methods, in particular AutoDock [15] and DMRG++ [13]. Applying our solution to our benchmark, we improve performance over a standard baseline assignment of tasks to GPUs up to 57.2%. Further, based on our results, we suggest OpenMP extensions that could help application programmers have their applications use multiple GPUs per node efficiently through OpenMP. We make the following contributions in this work:

1. OpenMP task-to-GPU scheduling strategies that help distribute an application's computations across GPUs on a node, which provide significant performance benefit over basic or naive approaches of assigning computations to GPUs;
2. a framework for developing user-defined task-to-GPU scheduling strategies;
3. OpenMP extension proposals to support our approach of programming multiple accelerators within a single node through taskloop and user-defined schedules.

2   Motivation Through Use Case Applications

Distributing work and data across multiple GPUs on a node is challenging. We have discovered applications that require work decomposition, often exemplified by the computational motif, or pattern, of Monte Carlo Methods [3,26], to be straightforward to map to multiple devices get significant performance benefit from doing so. Below is a summary of applications that can benefit of a task decomposition approach to deal with load imbalances across multiple GPUs. We focus the first application due to its timeliness.

2.1   Autodock

In 2019, the emergence of a novel coronavirus (SARS-CoV-2) caused the Coronavirus Disease 2019 (COVID-19). This virus has become a major threat worldwide due to its highly contagious nature. Molecular docking is one of the important steps used in identifying candidate drugs against a virus like SARS-CoV-2.

AutoDock is a family of applications that perform this kind of docking. AutoDock 4 [15] is the sequential version that is the baseline for improvements due to parallelism. AutoDock Vina [24] achieves approximately two orders of magnitude speed-up over AutoDock 4 through threaded parallelism, while also significantly improving the accuracy of binding predictions. AutoDock 4.2 [22], or Autodock-GPU, is based on OpenCL and simulates the molecular docking process by predicting the ligand-receptor interactions. It uses a Lamarckian Genetic Algorithm (LGA) to perform docking by offloading independent LGA executions to a GPU.

During the docking of the receptor protein and the ligand molecule, Autodock-GPU searches for a pose that has a satisfyingly low energy state, which will be predicted by a scoring function. This is achieved by searching in the space of the receptor-ligand pair's conformational coordinates (position, orientation, and torsion), using LGA. The search stops automatically after either reaching a small standard deviation of the current best pose, a large number of generations, or a large number of scoring function evaluations, whichever comes first.

In Autodock-GPU, the receptors are rigid and are modeled by static grid maps. This limits the sizes of the search spaces, and makes the number of rotatable bounds in the ligand one of the most influential factors on the search difficulty. Due to the randomness of the genetic algorithm, experiments have shown that the larger search space is correlated with higher variations in the time it takes to find a good pose for a given receptor-ligand pair.

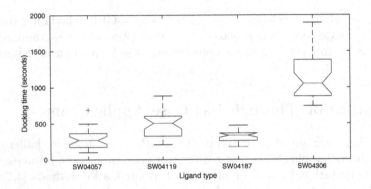

Fig. 1. Variation in docking time when running the OpenCL version of Autodock-GPU on NVIDIA Tesla V100, with local-search method ADADELTA.

We benchmarked Autodock-GPU on an NVIDIA Tesla V100 GPU, and recorded the docking times for four different ligands on the same receptor, 30 runs for each pair. In the results presented in Fig. 1, large variations are observed: the difference in run time for the same pair can vary from two times to more than four times. Similar results can be observed for ligands with fewer amounts of rotatable bounds, but with smaller variations.

Table 1. Mean, standard deviation and coefficient of variation of the docking time of the tested ligands. The result of ligand SW04057 includes several outliers that were not plotted in Fig. 1.

Ligand	Rotatable bounds	μ	σ	Coefficient of variation
SW04057	36	531.51 s	818.66 s	1.54
SW04119	22	494.38 s	185.39 s	0.37
SW04187	17	324.31 s	67.518 s	0.21
SW04306	36	1131.1 s	300.50 s	0.27

When docking is performed in a multi-GPU setup, each GPU typically processes its own set of receptor-ligand pairs independently. Although this process is embarrassingly parallel, the distribution of the docking times shown in Table 1 suggests that we should expect variations of at least 20% of the mean docking time. In the absence of a load balancing scheduler that distributes the receptor-ligand pairs dynamically, the work could become unevenly distributed and thus result in inefficient utilization of the GPUs.

2.2 DMRG++

Density Matrix Renormalization Group (DMRG++) [13] is a condensed matter physics code which is used to study superconductive properties of materials. One of the main computations of the application is a Hamiltonian matrix-vector multiplication, where the elements of the Hamiltonian matrix contain vectors of different sizes with symmetrical values to the diagonal part of the matrix that are only known at runtime. The Hamiltonian matrix-vector operation can be significantly optimized through using `taskloop` as it's a sparse matrix-vector multiplication and using OpenMP target regions to accelerate the inner matrix-vector multiplications of each of element on multiple GPUs.

2.3 Formulating Our Problem with a Representative Benchmark

We develop an OpenMP benchmark kernel code in C that represents the afore-mentioned applications' computational pattern and that identifies their perfor-mance bottlenecks[1]. Through this benchmark code, we apply the technique that we want to experiment with. The benchmark code takes as input (1) a max-imum problem dimension n of each computation and (2) the number of such computations C. The benchmark's work is to perform a set of C square rooted vector multiplications, each of which are on vectors of sizes chosen randomly from the set $\{1, 4, 9, \ldots, n * n\}$. The vector sizes are randomly generated and stored in an array of integers before the computations start. Each of these C computations resemble the multiplication of two matrices each of dimension n for protein-ligand docking pairs in Autodock. The matrix dimensions of the matrix multiplications in Autodock are of a variety of sizes and are generated at runtime.

We augment the benchmark kernel with OpenMP offload features as follows. OpenMP threads, each of which run on a core of a multi-core CPU, first ran-domly choose the vector sizes. Then, each OpenMP thread offloads its prepared work of the computations to a GPU. This offload is performed by enclosing the benchmark's computation in an OpenMP target region. Within each OpenMP task of computation, we allocate the same amount of data and the same data for running the computation on a GPU. The amount of data movement between CPU and GPU across target regions is uniform. This uniform amount of data movement is representative of the CPU-GPU data movement in the Autodock application code.

With this augmented benchmark kernel code, we make the following observa-tions. First, each vector multiplication is independent of the other, making this

---

[1] A repository for the benchmark code, which includes the strategies in this paper, is accessible at https://tinyurl.com/omp-ad-bench.

computation embarrassingly parallel. Second, the code isn't using the remaining GPUs on the node. Doing so could significantly speed up the code's execution, especially considering the baseline performance numbers shown in Sect. 2.1. Third, even if the code did use all the GPUs on the node, the code wouldn't use the GPUs efficiently due to load imbalance caused by the differently sized computations, in particular given our observations from Sect. 2.1. Given these observations, our objective is to have an application code use all computational power of the node, specifically the GPUs, all the time, given the load imbalance due to the high standard deviations of the timings across the computations. The next section covers how we try to meet the objective of using all of the GPUs all the time.

3   Using OpenMP Offload on Multiple GPUs Efficiently

The key idea of the solution is to have OpenMP threads generate work in well-defined and standard units and then have one or more OpenMP threads work together to dynamically map these units of work to GPUs. This section explains our solutions and the baseline that we compare our solution to.

A basic way to run OpenMP offload code on multiple GPUs is by pre-assigning each target region of computational work of the application to a device, i.e., GPU, ID [21]. To run a set of 100 computations of our benchmark on nodes with 6 GPUs, we can have an OpenMP thread assign the first 17 computations to GPU 0, the next 17 to GPU 1, and so on. When running T computations on a node of G GPUs, an OpenMP thread assigns the xth computation to device ID $\lceil \frac{x*G}{T} \rceil$ through adding the clause `device(x*G/T)` to the `target` construct. We call this strategy *compact*, and it is our baseline strategy.

Through a static assignment of computations to GPUs described in the previous paragraph, the benchmark code and application codes of Sect. 2.3 can have load imbalance across, and an under-utilization of, the GPUs of a node. The benchmark and application codes can utilize the GPUs more efficiently if the computations are assigned dynamically to GPUs during the application's execution [10,12,17]. To assign, or schedule, computations to GPUs dynamically, we must find a way to encapsulate the computations in standardized units of work that can be managed by the OpenMP threads to distribute to the GPUs. We use the OpenMP tasking support already available in OpenMP for this purpose.

Figure 2 illustrates the dynamic OpenMP task-to-GPU scheduling strategy, showing how OpenMP threads on a CPU manage and schedule an OpenMP task to some GPU in the set of GPUs on a node. A `taskloop` construct is applied to the loop that performs the computation in independent outer iterations, each of which contains a target region. The red trapezoids in the figure are tasks generated from the `taskloop` construct, and the grey rectangle represents the queue of `taskloop`. Each OpenMP thread on the CPU offloads a task of computation in `taskloop` to a particular GPU by dequeueing the next available GPU from a GPU queue, which is stored on the host. This GPU queue does not perform cross-GPU synchronizations, thus avoiding GPU-to-GPU communication before each execution of a task.

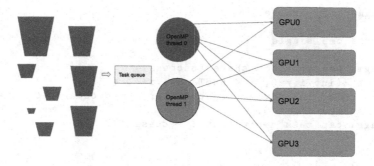

Fig. 2. Conceptual diagram of OpenMP threads scheduling tasks to GPUs.

Figure 3 shows the implementation strategy for our task-to-GPU scheduling technique. We wrap each OpenMP target region in an OpenMP task, as mentioned in the explanation of Fig. 2, and create a preceding and succeeding task for management of computational tasks for the GPU queue. These three OpenMP tasks are executed within each task in the `taskloop`. OpenMP threads of the parallel region assign the computational task of each task of the `taskloop` to GPUs through the function *gpu_scheduler_dyn()*. The function `doWork()` is the function for doing the square rooted vector multiplication computation in our benchmark.

Figure 4 shows the code change to a generic application for using the task-to-GPU dynamic scheduling strategy, which we implemented in the application code. An OpenMP thread running on the CPU invokes this function, and then waits in the `while` loop looking for an available GPU by repeatedly going through the array `occupancies` for the GPUs. Note that all the OpenMP threads are cycling through the same array `occupancies`, so atomic operations are used to avoid any data races/locks. If a GPU is busy, the thread just moves on and checks the next GPU. The thread keeps doing this until it sees the first GPU with occupancy of zero in the GPU queue. Other strategies, which may provide better load balance along with low overhead of data movement or coordination [11,14], can be defined and used by programmers or application developers alike.

4   Results

The benchmark was experimented with on SeaWulf, a cluster at Stony Brook University. We chose SeaWulf because it is representative of some of the modern supercomputers with multiple GPUs per node such as Summit, Sierra and the upcoming machine Perlmutter at NERSC, which run the applications discussed in Sect. 2. Also, the cluster was readily available for our experiments. SeaWulf has nodes with 8 NVIDIA K80 GPUs with 12 GB memory and CUDA 10.0.130 and a 28-core Intel Xeon E5-2683 v3 CPU (2 × 14-core). We use the clang/L-LVM OpenMP compiler, cloned from the GitHub master branch, commit hash

```
1  #pragma omp parallel
2  {
3  #pragma omp single
4    {
5  #pragma omp taskloop shared(success)
6      for (int i = 0; i < numTasks; i++) {
7        const int dev = gpu_scheduler_dyn(occupancies, ndevs);
8        output[i] = 0;
9  #pragma omp task depend(out : success[i])
10       {
11          success[i] = 0;
12       }
13 #pragma omp task depend(inout : success[i])
14       {
15 #pragma omp target device(dev)                                      \
16          map(to: a[0:arrSize], b[0:arrSize], c[0:arrSize])    \
17          map(tofrom: success[i:1], output[i:1], taskWork[i:1],
         occupancies[dev:1])
18          {
19             devices[dev]++;
20             if (taskWork[i] > probSize) taskWork[i] = probSize;
21             const int NN = taskWork[i];
22             output[i] = doWork(c, a, b, taskWork[i]);
23             success[i] = 1;
24          }
25       }
26 #pragma omp task depend(in : success[i])
27       {
28 #pragma omp atomic
29          occupancies[dev]--;
30       }
31    }
32  }
33 }
```

Fig. 3. Implementation for task-to-GPU scheduling.

86e3abc9. We use clang/LLVM due to its support of OpenMP features for tasking and devices. In performing our experiments, we aim to answer the question of whether sophisticated task-to-GPU scheduling on a node with multiple GPUs provides a performance benefit over the baseline approach of statically assigning tasks to GPUs.

In our experiments, we show results for four strategies of assigning OpenMP target regions to GPUs. We show the *compact* strategy which involves a straight-forward static assignment of target regions to GPUs, as discussed in Sect. 3. We show a *round-robin* task-to-GPU scheduling strategy that has OpenMP threads of the `taskloop` assigning tasks to GPUs in a round-robin fashion, with a scheduler function named `gpu_scheduler_rrb()` returning `taskID %` `ngpus`, where `taskID` is the task number taken as another input parameter

```
1 unsigned gpu_scheduler_dyn(unsigned *occupancies, int ngpus)
2 {
3   short looking = 1;
4   unsigned chosen;
5   while (looking) {
6     for (unsigned i = 0; i < ngpus; i++) {
7       unsigned occ_i;
8 #pragma omp atomic read
9       occ_i = occupancies[i];
10      if (occ_i == 0) {
11        chosen = i;
12 #pragma omp atomic
13        occupancies[chosen]++;
14        looking = 0;
15        break;
16      }
17    }
18  }
19  return chosen;
20 }
```

Fig. 4. Implementation of user-defined task-to-GPU schedule.

by the scheduler and **ngpus** is the number of GPUs on a node. Additionally, we show a *random* scheduling strategy in which an OpenMP thread assigns a task to a GPU by choosing a GPU randomly, with a scheduler function named **gpu_scheduler_ran()** returning **rand() % ngpus**. Finally, we show the *dynamic* scheduling strategy described through Fig. 4.

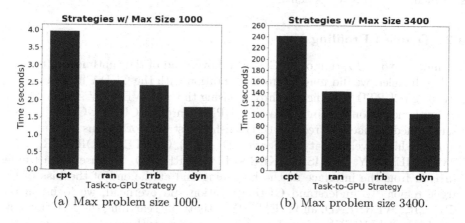

(a) Max problem size 1000.   (b) Max problem size 3400.

Fig. 5. Execution times for different task-to-GPU scheduling strategies on 8 GPUs of a node of SeaWulf.

4.1   Impact of Task-to-GPU Scheduling Strategies

We assess the impact on performance of the four different task-to-GPU assignment strategies we designed, by applying them to the benchmark code presented in Sect. 3.

Figure 5a shows results of the benchmark for 500 target regions for vector sizes from 1 to 1000^2 and run using the 8 GPUs on a SeaWulf node. We see that when we use *random*, the execution time reduces significantly from 3.96 s to 2.54 s, an improvement of 35.49%. Compared to *random*, *round robin* offers a comparable but larger improvement, 38.89% relative to compact (the baseline). When we use *dynamic*, the time decreases further, providing the best performance improvement over our baseline, 54.61%.

Figure 5b shows the results of the same square root vector addition benchmark on the same platform, this time with 500 target regions for various vectors between size 1 and 3400^2. Here, the *round-robin* strategy provides a 45.8% improvement (reducing from the baseline of 241.22 s to 130.76 s). When we use *dynamic*, the time decreases significantly, improving performance by 57.2%.

From these results, we make a few observations. First, for both problem sizes, a large amount of the performance gains come from using a task-based approach in which OpenMP threads distribute tasks across GPUs through the sophisticated task-to-GPU scheduling strategies, specifically, *random*, *round-robin* and *dynamic*. Second, *round-robin* performs slightly better than *random*, showing that a calculated and predefined strategy rather than a randomized strategy is important when using tasking, though it isn't tremendously significant. Third, *dynamic* shows a more pronounced benefit over *random* and *round-robin*, telling us that a dynamic task-to-GPU scheduling strategy, in particular one which is carefully implemented to maintain low coordination overhead, can provide a significant performance benefit.

4.2   Detailed Profiling

To understand utilization of all GPUs and overhead of the runtime and task-to-GPU scheduler, we did manual instrumentation with the CUDA Profiling Tools Interface (CUPTI), specifically through using the SOLLVE V&V suite's [2] timing implementation and interface for CUPTI. Through CUPTI, CUDA invokes user-defined callbacks to record start/finish timestamps of various events. There are many high-level activity categories: DEVICE, CONTEXT, DRIVER, RUNTIME, MEMCPY, MEMSET, KERNEL, OVERHEAD. We inserted a timing function from the interface at the beginning and at the end of the task of the target region. To understand GPU utilization and overhead, we focus on the DRIVER, OVERHEAD, and MEMCPY activity, by searching the resulting output of the SOLLVE V&V interface. We experiment with just the smaller of the two problem sizes, as for the larger of the two problem sizes, CUPTI created large amounts of overhead, making it difficult for us to understand the benefits of our approach.

Table 2 shows the timings, in nanoseconds, obtained through the CUPTI Activity API. We see that the DRIVER operations, which includes CUDA context/stream activities and synchronizations, dominate the execution time, and this is also the main source of reduction in execution time, as timings in this category are orders of magnitude larger than those in other categories. There are some variations in the MEMCPY category, which could be the result of combining GPU-to-socket locality issues and our locality-unaware schedulers. The OVERHEAD category captures the driver compiler's activity, buffer flush overhead and the instrumentation overhead. We have yet to identify the source of reductions in this category due to perturbation from the instrumentation itself. From these timings, we see that our sophisticated OpenMP task-to-GPU scheduling strategies are relevant not just from a standpoint of load balancing, but also from a standpoint of GPU resource management and reducing overhead.

Table 2. Execution activity breakdown using CUPTI (nanoseconds)

Scheduler	DRIVER	MEMCPY	OVERHEAD
Compact	23654161998	7393960	189489499
RoundRobin	16634552748	8526436	248582086
Random	17742577058	8085590	208329746
Dynamic	14229831142	6374549	171728914

5 Discussion on Results and Proposed Extensions

A key question that arises from our implementation and results is how we extend OpenMP to support of task scheduling for multi-GPUs, for ease of use by application programmers. There are different aspects to this, and we cover them in this section.

First, we need support for a single OpenMP construct to offload asynchronous target regions on multiple devices. In our implementation, we partition work across GPUs by leveraging the `taskloop` construct, associating one thread with a task of `taskloop` and then having that thread assign the task to a GPU. We used `taskloop` in our implementation for the strategy because we know through the OpenMP Community [1] that there is a potential that tasking constructs and target constructs will be unified. However, right now, a problem exists with executing each of the tasks on any of the GPUs and keeping track of the correct device contexts used by the OpenMP tasks that offload the different target regions on multiple GPUs. For example, if a CPU task is scheduled a different thread, then after a target region with a `nowait` clause is offloaded, there could be issues with the GPU contexts when running on multiple devices. We found this issue with some OpenMP implementations, where we had to comment out the `nowait` clause on the `target` construct to make our benchmark work on multiple devices. We are aware of ongoing efforts in the LLVM OpenMP community [6] to improve the support of `nowait` with tasks, in particular in the context of multiple GPUs. We expect that our results can further improve with these improvements in the OpenMP library implementation.

Second, our approach could have less overhead, and could also require less programmer effort, if OpenMP's `taskloop` construct was extended so that it could handle the scheduling of target regions to GPUs and avoid additional levels of nested tasks. In our current implementation, we have two levels of tasking. The lower level is for the target and the higher level is for coordination of the tasks of `taskloop`. We could reduce the possible overhead and reduce the programming complexity by eliminating one of these two levels. A possible extension of `taskloop` is to create a `target taskloop` construct that will automatically manage the assignment of tasks to GPUs using `grainsize` or `num_tasks` as scheduling strategies supported by OpenMP implementations and that can be specified in the construct. We may also want to extend the `taskloop` construct to support pipelines where the body of the `taskloop` can contain dependent tasks that execute on both the CPU and GPU.

Third, in this work, we showed the need for a specialized task-to-GPU scheduling strategy using atomics. Such a specialized strategy can be implemented with an OpenMP user-defined task-to-GPU schedule in a similar fashion as has been proposed in [18]. The user could define her task-to-GPU schedule in an application by implementing a function `gpu_scheduler_X()`, with a pointer to a record as a parameter to the function. The user could then specify the schedule X in a clause of `taskloop`. We note that better atomic instructions such as compare-and-swap can also help make developing such schedules easier.

Lastly, our approach can benefit from an `affinity` clause for `taskloop` which could work hand-in-hand with the proposed user-defined task-to-GPU schedules. The affinity clause would reduce data movement from CPU to GPU, and significantly improve performance when data has been mapped to a specific device. We need to assess various design issues given the application for this kind of affinity which include a study of task-to-data, task-to-device and thread-to-device affinity. For example, for Autodock, the tasks doing docking for a ligand will be assigned to the GPU on which that data already resides through the affinity clause hint, which would allow for improved locality through reuse of the data.

6   Related Work

Existing accelerator programming libraries support only a single accelerator. However, several methods deal with multiple accelerators by using the libraries together with parallel programming libraries for hosts. One example method is to spawn multiple threads using OpenMP on host, and each thread deals with one accelerator [9,16,27]. Another is to spawn multiple processes using MPI on host, with each process dealing with one accelerator [7,27].

Xu et al. [28] propose an OpenACC extension to support multiple accelerators. Although the OpenACC extension supports communication between accelerators, dividing data and tasks manually is needed. Komoda et al. [20] propose another OpenACC extension that supports dividing data and tasks into multiple accelerators. Furthermore, its compiler has a mechanism to keep data consistency on the accelerator memory automatically. However, the OpenACC extension can be used only before the loop statement. So, the OpenACC extension cannot offload data to an arbitrary device, as in our work. Scogland [25] developed directive extensions to support scheduling work on multiple GPUs and multi-cores using the a runtime called coreTStar. The extension partitions loop iterations and its data across multiple devices and CPU threads.

Matsumura et al. [8] develop an OpenACC compiler system to generate an OpenACC code for multiple accelerators from an OpenACC code for a single accelerator automatically. However, there are some limitations. For example, a loop statement that can be divided is composed only of affine access. Nakao et el. [23] develop an XcalableACC directive-based language for accelerated clusters which gives an ability to use multiple accelerators on a single node. In contrast, our work allows for sophisticated scheduling strategies that the user to define within the application code.

7 Conclusions

In this work, we presented methods to use all GPUs of a node of an HPC cluster efficiently through OpenMP, particularly for applications that are embarrassingly parallel and load imbalanced, which are characteristics of the computational pattern of Monte Carlo Methods and exemplified by the applications Autodock and DMRG++. Our solution involves encapsulating each OpenMP target region containing a computation within an OpenMP task, and then having OpenMP threads assign the OpenMP tasks to GPUs on a node through a user-level task-to-GPU schedule. Through experimenting with our approach, our results provide up to a 57.2% performance improvement. Our results suggest the usefulness of OpenMP tasking across GPUs on a node.

Our technique focuses on scheduling tasks across GPUs rather than scheduling of Thread Blocks to Stream Multiprocessors (SMs), i.e., scheduling within a GPU. An extension to our approach that combines scheduling across GPUs and scheduling within GPUs will be written for future work. We will also incorporate our techniques within relevant application codes, e.g., Autodock, DMRG++ [13, 19, 22]. We will work to propose new extensions in OpenMP, particularly implementing them in the LLVM OpenMP compiler and supporting OpenMP implementations that allow users to easily use our approach. We will look at the impact of and tune the taskloop's grain-size. Finally, we will look at using or adapting the affinity clause to easily reduce data movement overheads of our task-to-GPU scheduling strategies. The affinity clause will give a hint to the task scheduler about placing a task on the most appropriate GPU based on the GPU context.

Acknowledgements. This research was supported in part by the Exascale Computing Project (17-SC-20-SC), a collaborative effort of the U.S. Department of Energy

Office of Science and the National Nuclear Security Administration, in particular its subproject on Scaling OpenMP with LLVm for Exascale performance and portability (SOLLVE). It is also supported in part by NSF project 1409946 "Compute on Data Path". This material is based upon work supported by the U.S. Department of Energy, Office of Science, Office of Advanced Scientific Computing Research, under contract number DE-AC05-00OR22725. This research used resources of the Oak Ridge Leadership Computing Facility at the Oak Ridge National Laboratory, which is supported by the Office of Science of the U.S. Department of Energy under Contract No. DE-AC05-00OR22725. The authors would like to thank Stony Brook Research Computing and Cyberinfrastructure, and the Institute for Advanced Computational Science at Stony Brook University for access to the high-performance SeaWulf computing system, which was made possible by a $1.4M National Science Foundation grant (#1531492). We want to thank Jeremy Smith and Ada Sedova, from Oak Ridge National Laboratory, for providing a small sample of input sets for the Autodock-GPU experiments to help us study the application workload. We acknowledge the QMCPACK team at ORNL for discussing their code with respect to application load imbalances.

References

1. OpenMP 5.0 Reference Guide. https://www.openmp.org/wp-content/uploads/OpenMPRef-5.0-1119-01-TSK-web.pdf
2. OpenMP Verification and Validation Suite. https://github.com/SOLLVE/sollve_vv
3. Parallel Computational Pattern: Monte Carle Methods. https://patterns.eecs.berkeley.edu/?page_id=186
4. Perlmutter User Guide. https://www.nersc.gov/systems/perlmutter/
5. Summit User Guide. https://docs.olcf.ornl.gov/systems/summit_user_guide.html
6. The LLVM Compiler Infrastructure. http://llvm.org/
7. Optimizing MPI Communication on Multi-GPU Systems Using CUDA Inter-Process Communication (2012)
8. Matsumura, K., Sato, M., Boku, T., Podobas, A., Matsuoka, S.: MACC: an OpenACC transpiler for automatic multi-GPU use. In: Yokota, R., Wu, W. (eds.) SCFA 2018. LNCS, vol. 10776, pp. 109–127. Springer, Cham (2018). https://doi.org/10.1007/978-3-319-69953-0_7
9. Beyer, J., de Supinski, B.R.: IWOMP 2016 tutorial: OpenMP accelerator model (2016). http://iwomp2016.riken.jp/wp-content/uploads/2016/10/tutorial-accelerator.pdf
10. Blumofe, R.D., Joerg, C.F., Kuszmaul, B.C., Leiserson, C.E., Randall, K.H., Zhou, Y.: Cilk: an efficient multithreaded runtime system. J. Parallel Distrib. Comput. **37**(1), 55–69 (1995)
11. Bull, J.M.: Measuring synchronisation and scheduling overheads in OpenMP. In: Proceedings of First European Workshop on OpenMP, pp. 99–105, Lund, Sweden (1999)
12. Ciorba, F.M., Iwainsky, C., Buder, P.: OpenMP loop scheduling revisited: making a case for more schedules. ArXiv arxiv:1809.03188 (2018)
13. Criado, J., et al.: Optimization of condensed matter physics application with OpenMP tasking model. In: Fan, X., de Supinski, B.R., Sinnen, O., Giacaman, N. (eds.) IWOMP 2019. LNCS, vol. 11718, pp. 291–305. Springer, Cham (2019). https://doi.org/10.1007/978-3-030-28596-8_20

14. Donfack, S., Grigori, L., Gropp, W.D., Kale, V.: Hybrid static/dynamic scheduling for already optimized dense matrix factorization. In: 2012 IEEE 26th International Parallel and Distributed Processing Symposium, pp. 496–507 (2012)
15. Huey, R., Morris, G.M., Olson, A.J., Goodsell, D.S.: A semiempirical free energy force field with charge-based desolvation. J. Comput. Chem. **28**, 1145–1152 (2007)
16. Guan, J., Yan, S., Jin, J.M.: An OpenMP-CUDA implementation of multilevel fast multipole algorithm for electromagnetic simulation on multi-GPU computing systems. IEEE Trans. Antennas Propag. **61**(7), 3607–3616 (2013)
17. Kalé, L., Krishnan, S.: CHARM++: a portable concurrent object oriented system based on C++. In: Paepcke, A. (ed.) Proceedings of OOPSLA 1993, pp. 91–108. ACM Press (September 1993)
18. Kale, V., Iwainsky, C., Klemm, M., Müller Korndörfer, J.H., Ciorba, F.M.: Toward a standard interface for user-defined scheduling in OpenMP. In: Fan, X., de Supinski, B.R., Sinnen, O., Giacaman, N. (eds.) IWOMP 2019. LNCS, vol. 11718, pp. 186–200. Springer, Cham (2019). https://doi.org/10.1007/978-3-030-28596-8_13
19. Kim, J., et al.: QMCPACK: an open source ab initio quantum Monte Carlo package for the electronic structure of atoms, molecules and solids. J. Phys.: Condens. Matter **30**(19), 195901 (2018). https://doi.org/10.1088/1361-648x/aab9c3
20. Komoda, T., Miwa, S., Nakamura, H., Maruyama, N.: Integrating multi-GPU execution in an OpenACC compiler. In: 2013 42nd International Conference on Parallel Processing, pp. 260–269 (2013)
21. Leopold Grinberg, C.B., Haque, R.: Hands on with openmp4.5 and unified memory: developing applications for IBM's hybrid CPU + GPU systems (Part ii) (2017)
22. Morris, G.M., et al.: Autodock4 and AutoDockTools4: automated docking with selective receptor flexibility. J. Comput. Chem. **30**(16), 2785–2791 (2009)
23. Nakao, M., Murai, H., Iwashita, H., Tabuchi, A., Boku, T., Sato, M.: Implementing lattice QCD application with XcalableACC language on accelerated cluster, pp. 429–438 (2017)
24. Trott, O., Olson, A.J.: AutoDock Vina: improving the speed and accuracy of docking with a new scoring function, efficient optimization and multithreading. J. Comput. Chem. **31**(2), 455–461 (2010)
25. Scogland, T.R.W., Feng, W., Rountree, B., de Supinski, B.R.: CoreTSAR: adaptive worksharing for heterogeneous systems. In: Kunkel, J.M., Ludwig, T., Meuer, H.W. (eds.) ISC 2014. LNCS, vol. 8488, pp. 172–186. Springer, Cham (2014). https://doi.org/10.1007/978-3-319-07518-1_11
26. Tandon, P., Rosner, D.E.: Monte Carlo simulation of particle aggregation and simultaneous restructuring. J. Colloid Interface Sci. **213**(2), 273–286 (1999)
27. Wolfe, M.: Scaling OpenACC applications across multiple GPUs (2014)
28. Xu, R., Tian, X., Chandrasekaran, S., Chapman, B.: Multi-GPU support on single node using directive-based programming models (January 2016)

Memory

Preliminary Experience with OpenMP Memory Management Implementation

Adrien Roussel[1,2,3]([✉]), Patrick Carribault[1,3], and Julien Jaeger[1,2,3]

[1] CEA, DAM, DIF, 91297 Arpajon, France
{adrien.roussel,patrick.carribault,julien.jaeger}@cea.fr
[2] Exascale Computing Research Laboratory, Bruyères-le-Châtel, France
[3] CEA, Laboratoire en Informatique Haute Performance pour le Calcul et la simulation, Université Paris-Saclay, 91680 Bruyères-le-Châtel, France

Abstract. Because of the evolution of compute units, memory heterogeneity is becoming popular in HPC systems. But dealing with such various memory levels often requires different approaches and interfaces. For this purpose, OpenMP 5.0 defines memory-management constructs to offer application developers the ability to tackle the issue of exploiting multiple memory spaces in a portable way. This paper proposes an overview of memory-management from applications to runtimes. Thus, we describe a convenient way to tune an application to include memory management constructs. We also detail a methodology to integrate them into an OpenMP runtime supporting multiple memory types (DDR, MCDRAM and NVDIMM). We implement our design into the MPC framework, while presenting some results on a realistic benchmark.

Keywords: OpenMP 5.0 · Data allocation · Memory management

1 Introduction

For the past decades, the main trend has been to enhance the compute capabilities of processors through frequency increase, functional unit extension (*e.g.* SIMD) or core duplication. It leads to the current generation of supercomputer nodes design with several multi-core processors linked together. But this large spectrum of compute capabilities puts the stress on the memory part to keep feeding such functional units. For example, SIMD operations may require more memory bandwidth to enable issuing one instruction requiring a large number of register inputs. However, proposing a new memory type with a larger bandwidth, for the same overall cost, exposes a smaller storage. That is why various kinds of memory appeared in the HPC community. For example, Intel launched the Knights Landing many-core processor [26] which embeds a high bandwidth stacked memory named MCDRAM. The next generation of such an approach is called HBM and will be available in some processors like ARM-based Fujitsu A64FX [30]. This approach improves the throughput of bandwidth-hungry units,

© Springer Nature Switzerland AG 2020
K. Milfeld et al. (Eds.): IWOMP 2020, LNCS 12295, pp. 313–327, 2020.
https://doi.org/10.1007/978-3-030-58144-2_20

but there still is a need for a large storage with lower bandwidth but better performance than regular disks. This is why the notion of persistent memory appears in clusters like the flash memory NVDIMM technology [15].

While these new memory types may fulfill the requirements of many parallel applications (HBM/MCDRAM for compute-intensive parts, NVDIMM for I/O dedicated portions), allocating data in these target memory spaces in a portable and easy way is tedious. Thus, memory management is becoming one major concern for HPC application developers. Since version 5.0, OpenMP tackles this issue by introducing *memory management* extensions [22]. It is now possible to control data allocation and placement on specific memory spaces through OpenMP constructs. For this purpose, OpenMP defines multiple memory spaces: application developers have then to specify some parameters (traits) for a specific allocator (e.g., data alignment, pool size, ...).

This paper proposes a first experience of implementing these OpenMP memory management constructs. It makes the following contributions:

– Preliminary implementation of OpenMP memory management constructs targeting DRAM, MCDRAM and NVDIMM into the MPC framework [7][1] (a thread based MPI implementation with a OpenMP 3.0 runtime system)
– Port of a C++ mini-application with effort to support STL objects.
– Experiments on portability with various target architectures exposing different memory types.

This paper is organized as follows: Sect. 2 exposes an overview of the OpenMP specification for memory management. Section 3 presents related work in this area. Section 4 details our approach to implement these OpenMP constructs into the MPC framework and enable their support inside an application. Finally, this papers illustrates experimental results in Sect. 5 before concluding in Sect. 6.

```
1   // Initialization
    omp_memspace_handle_t mcdram = omp_high_bw_mem_space;
3   omp_alloctrait_t mcdram_traits[1] = {omp_atk_alignment, 64};
    omp_allocator_handle_t mcdram_alloc;
5   mcdram_alloc = omp_init_allocator(mcdram, 1, mcdram_traits);

7   // Allocation
    void* Allocate(size_t size, omp_allocator_handle_t allocator) {
9     return (void*)omp_alloc(size, allocator);
    }
11
    // Deallocation
13  void Release(void **ptr, omp_allocator_handle_t allocator) {
      if (*ptr != NULL) {
15        omp_free(*ptr, allocator) ;
          *ptr = NULL ;
17    }
    }
```

Listing 1.1. Functions for OpenMP Memory Management

---

[1] Available at https://mpc.hpcframework.com/.

2   Memory Management in OpenMP 5.0

OpenMP 5.0 introduces constructs and API routines to manage portable data allocation in various memory banks. Thus it defines a set of memory spaces (`omp_memspace_handle_t`) and parameters (*traits*) that can affect the way data are allocated in this target memory (`omp_alloctrait_t`). Even though each implementation can propose its own spaces and traits, OpenMP 5.0 defines default spaces (*default, large capacity, constant, high bandwidth* and *low latency*), and allocator traits (such as *alignment, pool size* and *fallback*). Thus, the user has to create an allocator handle (`omp_allocator_handle_t`) by specifying a target memory space and a set of traits. This operation is performed by calling the initialization function named `omp_init_allocator`. Listing 1.1 highlights this process at the top part.

After this setup, the application can allocate data with this new allocator. The runtime will thus be responsible for allocating data into the target memory bank with the specified trait values. There are two ways to manage data allocations with OpenMP: functions and directives. The first method is to call the functions `omp_alloc` and `omp_free`. Both take an allocator handle as input (which should be initialized first). Listing 1.1 shows this approach.

```
   float A[N], B[N];
2  #pragma omp allocate(A) allocator(omp_large_cap_mem_alloc)

4  #pragma omp parallel
   {
6    #pragma omp task allocate(omp_const_mem_alloc: B)
     {
8      /* ... */
     }
10 }
```

Listing 1.2. Directives for OpenMP Memory Management

The second method relies on the **allocate** directive and clause (see Listing 1.2). The directive takes a list of data variables to allocate through the handle specified in the **allocator** clause. This clause can be used in several constructs such as **task**, **taskloop** and **target**. Users have to specify in this clause the handle to use to allocate data, and the list of data variables. The handle allocator can be defined by the user or a predefined allocator. There is one allocator given by the OpenMP standard per memory space.

3   Related Work

This section details different approaches to deal with multiple memory levels inside an HPC compute node: dedicated allocations, portable allocations and OpenMP implementations.

Dedicated Memory Management. The first approach deals with dedicated interfaces to allocate data inside a specific target memory type. Even if some memory
kinds can be configured as a cache level to enable automatic hardware-driven
management (*e.g.* MCDRAM in Intel KNL [9,18,21]), fine-grain data allocation can lead to better performance. Thus, some research papers set up this
MCDRAM as *flat mode* meaning that a specific action is required to put data
into this target memory. This action may have a coarse-grain scope (*e.g.* relying
on the *numactl* library [8] or forcing the global memory-placement policy [19]),
or a more fine-grain approach (*e.g.* using memory allocators like *memkind* [6] to
deal with placement on a per-allocation basis [5]). Similar fine-grain initiatives
also exist for other types of memory *e.g.*, persistent [2,16,25].

Portable Memory Management. Runtime systems are already able to deal with
memory management for performance portability concerns [1,4,12]. This list is
not exhaustive as multiple approaches exist in this domain, especially focusing
on heterogeneous systems. Some other initiatives also deal with high bandwidth
memory management like MCDRAM for KNL processors. These forms of memory management have been explored within domain specific languages in [24].

High level programming interfaces are widespread in the HPC community.
Previous works such as [10,11] have to deal with memory allocation in a portable
way, but only for the GPGPU concerns now. These interfaces enable abstract
memory allocations through wrapper functions or objects.

OpenMP Memory Management. While some initiatives have been already proposed for memory management in a portable way, there is no standard way to
do it. OpenMP now provides a way to standardize memory management for a
wide system spectrum. Based on directives and functions, software developers
are able to address memory allocations in an easy way: they do not need to deal
with the actual low-level allocation method into a specific memory. As far as
we know, LLVM [20] has the most up-to-date OpenMP runtime implementation
for the support of memory management constructs. Even if this runtime system
is well advanced, the front-end part of supported compilers (Clang and Intel)
does not support the full specification. Until now, it supports allocation in standard and high bandwidth memory banks only with few traits (*e.g.* `pool_size`,
`fallback` and `alignment`). For the high bandwidth memory support, LLVM
forwards memory allocations to `hbw_malloc` from the *memkind* library.

Paper Positon: While our work is similar to the LLVM approach (design and
implementation of memory-management constructs inside an existing OpenMP
runtime), the objective of this paper is to give a preview our implementation of
multiple memory levels (DDR, MCDRAM/HBM and NVDIMM) its portability aspects. Moreover, we have experimented how to integrate those OpenMP
functions in a portable solution with a C++ application.

4   Application- and Runtime-Level OpenMP Memory Management

This section presents the main contribution of this paper: the support of multiple memory types inside an existing OpenMP implementation (Sect. 4.1) and the port of a C++ mini-app (Sect. 4.2).

4.1   Runtime System Design for Memory Management Integration

MPC [23] is a thread-based MPI implementation which proposes an OpenMP [7] runtime system. It is compliant to OpenMP 3.1 and partially supports version 4.5. As MPC integrates its own NUMA aware allocator, we have decided to design and implement the memory management constructs inside this framework. MPC is compatible with GNU and Intel compilers for OpenMP lowering and thread-based specific features. But these compilers have currently a limited support of the `allocate` directive and clause. Thus, our work focuses on providing initialization functions and allocation/deallocation calls (`omp_alloc` and `omp_free`) for multiple memory types: DDR, high bandwidth MCDRAM and large-capacity NVDIMM. For this purpose, it is necessary to enhance the existing implementation with an advanced hardware topology detection and an approach for initializing and allocating data. This section details those steps.

Automatic Memory Banks Discovery. OpenMP offers a set of predefined memory spaces with a way to fallback if the application tries to allocate in non-existing type. Thus, the first step is to discover available memory banks on the target machine. For this purpose, a hardware detection tool has to be integrated into the OpenMP runtime system to list available memory spaces on a system at execution time. Most of the runtime systems already rely on the *hwloc* library for hardware topology discovery and thread binding. Recent work [13] adds the support of heterogeneous memory types such as *high bandwidth memory* (*e.g.* MCDRAM from Intel's KNL processor) or *large capacity* memory bank like *NVDIMM* technology. On such machines, MCDRAM memory space is exposed as a no-core NUMA node with a special attribute named `MCDRAM`. Checking the presence of MCDRAM in a system is thus possible by browsing all the NUMA nodes and searching for the one which has this defined *hwloc* attribute. *Large capacity* memory spaces such as `NVDIMM` memory are viewed by *hwloc* as OS devices, and tagged with a special attribute. So, it is possible to detect such memory banks by listing all the OS devices and searching for *large capacity* memory banks.

The basic block of our design relies on the hardware detection module based on *hwloc* in the MPC framework. It is called at runtime initialization and for every runtime entry point that is not in a parallel region to detect and save available hardware components.

Memory Management Initialization. The allocation process is separated into two parts: the initialization of allocators and the data allocation (as seen in Listing 1.1).

First of all, the `omp_init_allocator` function initializes some user-defined traits in a `omp_alloctrait_t` structure, and link them into a memory space in a `omp_memspace_handle_t` structure. From a runtime point of view, it is necessary to save a dynamic collection of allocators. By default, in our implementation, this structure contains pre-defined allocators only. Its size can then be enlarged to allow users to create new allocators with some specific traits. This structure maps an allocator handle (*i.e.* `omp_alloc_handle_t`) to an allocator structure (*i.e.* `omp_alloc_t`). This collection is only accessible from each thread in a read-only access mode. Indeed, we do not ensure thread safety for this structure yet. Thus, all the allocators have to be initialized outside a parallel region. We are currently working on thread safety to enable the creation of allocators inside parallel regions. In this way, concurrent threads may benefit from allocators inside parallel regions within the `omp_alloc` function.

Various traits are proposed in the specification, such as memory alignment as illustrated in Listing 1.1. Traits have a default value, but the initialization process may set them user-defined values. The MPC framework currently supports the **alignment** and **fallback** traits. Future work is needed to support more traits in the framework.

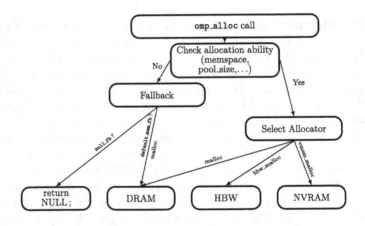

Fig. 1. `omp_alloc` call procedure

Data Allocation Process. The final step is to implement the data-allocation mechanisms. Figure 1 sketches this process. For this purpose, an allocator can be retrieved from the collection based on the handle structure. Depending on the trait values, the data allocation process is different. For example, we test the value of the fallback trait if the runtime detects that the requested memory space is unavailable. Trait checking is quite similar no matter what the selected memory space is. Once the traits values are set, we need to link a memspace to an allocation function. Depending on the desired memory space, this function differs. For example, `malloc` from *glibc* is the function used to allocate data in DRAM memory space (denoted as `omp_default_mem_space`) while `hbw_malloc` from the *memkind* library enables data allocation in the high bandwidth memory space (denoted as `omp_high_bw_mem_space`). To support all the set of the specification defined memory spaces, runtime developers may have to integrate various allocator library inside the OpenMP runtime. For example, data allocation in high bandwidth or in large capacity memory spaces are currently well supported within the *memkind* library.[2] The MPC framework comes with its own NUMA-aware allocator [28] based on kernel page reuse. For more convenience, and to avoid multiple library integrations, we link our allocator to the OpenMP runtime. Data allocations in DRAM (referred to as default memory space) and in high bandwidth memory space are thus operated by our allocator. As MCDRAM is currently detected as a no-core NUMA node, we redirect all the dynamic allocations queries to this NUMA node. We also support data allocation in large capacity devices like `NVDIMM`. For this purpose, we have integrated the `nvmem`[3] library inside the MPC framework.

The deallocation process is quite similar to the allocation one. When `omp_free` is called, we check the memory space specified in the allocator structure and then call the appropriate data free function.

```
template <typename T>
class omp_allocator
{
public:
    ...
    omp_allocator_handle_t& allocator;

    omp_allocator(omp_allocator_handle_t& alloc) : allocator(alloc) {}

    pointer allocate(size_type n, const T* hint = 0) {
        return (T*)omp_alloc(sizeof(T) * n, allocator);
    }

    void deallocate(pointer p, size_type n) {
        omp_free(p, allocator);
    }
};
    ...
    std::vector<Real_t, omp_allocator<Real_t> > m_x(N, 0., omp_allocator<Real_t>(
        allocator);
```

Listing 1.3. Custom Allocator for STL Objects

4.2 Enabling Portable Application Memory Management

After implementing partial memory management support into the runtime, it is necessary to modify the target application as presented in Listing 1.1. This

---

[2] See https://memkind.github.io/memkind for more information.
[3] Available at https://pmem.io.

section illustrates the case of LULESH [17], an hydrodynamics application from the CORAL benchmark suite. This example provides some valuable experience on how to port an existing C++ application to use OpenMP memory management functions. While porting C codes leads to additional codes as shown in Listing 1.1, many C++ applications exploit STL objects [27] (*e.g.* vector, stack, list, ...). Such objects manage allocators through a template parameter `Allocator`. We propose a custom allocator object (see Listing 1.3) that integrates the OpenMP `omp_allocator_handle_t` structure features. Thus, all the methods (e.g., constructor/destructor, `resize` or `insert`) use OpenMP allocation constructs. This example also illustrates that the new allocator has to be passed as a template parameter of the STL object and as input of the constructor (to indicate the right memory spaces to the allocator).

5   Experimental Results

This section illustrates our implementation inside the MPC framework on one benchmark allocating data in various memory banks based on the OpenMP 5.0 memory-management functions. For this purpose, we modified the LULESH benchmark (as previously explained in Sect. 4.2) by inserting calls to `omp_alloc` functions to allocate data in various memory spaces.

Experimental Environment.   On the hardware side, the target platforms cover the different memory kinds that our implementation supports. Thus we rely on 4 different systems. The first one is a compute node containing a 68-core Intel Knights Landing processor [26], 16 GB of MCDRAM and 96 GB of regular DRAM memory. This configuration will be used to evaluate the allocation inside a high bandwidth memory. To test the large storage memory, we use a compute node equipped with two NVDIMM technology storages (with a capacity of 1.5 TB each). This persistent-memory node is composed of two 24-core Intel Cascade Lake processors (Xeon Platinum 8260L), each clocked at 2.40 GHz. Finally, two systems are available to ensure portability by exposing only regular DDR: one AMD ROME node (two 32-core AMD EPYC 7502 processors at 2.50 GHz with 128 GB of DDR) and one Intel Skylake node (two 24-core Intel Xeon Platinum 8168 Skylake processor at 2.70 GHz with 96 GB of DDR). On the software side, all benchmark versions were compiled with -O3 and linked to the MPC framework (configured with standard options) for the OpenMP runtime.

5.1   Coarse-Grain OpenMP Memory Allocation

This section describes the experiments conducted on the modified LULESH benchmark targeting a single memory space. Thus, it aims at testing the ability of our implementation to allocate data in a specified memory space following the OpenMP 5 standard.

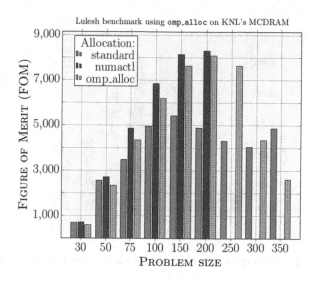

Fig. 2. Coarse-grain data allocation management in MCDRAM

High-Bandwidth Memory. The first evaluation concerns the MCDRAM memory on Intel KNL node with 64 threads. Figure 2 shows the *Figure of Merit* (FOM - number of elements solved per microsecond) according to the mesh size on different versions of LULESH (with a fixed total number of iterations: 100). The first bar (*standard*) represents the regular run (everything is allocated in DDR) while the second bar (*numactl*) is controlled by the numactl command that places all data into the MCDRAM. The third version (*omp_alloc*) is modified with OpenMP memory management constructs. All of the three executions were compiled and run within the MPC OpenMP implementation. These results show only a 5% difference in performance between the execution with numactl and the application modified to use omp_alloc, for problem sizes from 30 to 200. There are no results for problem sizes greater than 200 for the *numactl* version because all the data does not fit in MCDRAM and the application stops. From 200 to 350, however, the *omp_alloc* execution can execute even though the allocation does not fit into MCDRAM, and the performance diminishes. This is due to the cache memory mode, as data does not fit in MCDRAM, the application performance is lead the DRAM bandwidth because some data are allocated in it. Performance of the original application without the use of numactl are lower than the two previous ones. In conclusion, we are able to allocate data in the MCDRAM high bandwidth memory bank with the OpenMP memory management functions. The performance difference between omp_alloc and numactl charts is due to the fact that numactl is much more aggressive and allocates all the data in MCDRAM. In our modified implementation, we only moved data dynamically allocated such as arrays and vectors, so not all the data are moved to MCDRAM.

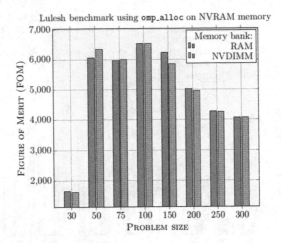

Fig. 3. Coarse-grain data allocation management in NVDIMM

Large-Capacity Memory Space. Figure 3 presents the FOM running LULESH on a dual-socket 24-core Skylake node (i.e., 48 OpenMP threads) equipped with a *NVDIMM* device. While the two versions rely on OpenMP to allocate data, the first one (*RAM*) allocates all data in regular DDR (default allocator) while the second one (*NVDIMM*) changes the OpenMP allocator to target the *large capacity* space. With minor modifications, this graphic shows the ability to perform data allocation in large capacity memory devices like *NVDIMM* technology. As explained in [14], the NVDIMM memory can be configured in two modes. Our results are similar for both selected memory spaces. We can conclude that the node is configured in a 2LM mode (*i.e.* similar to KNL cache memory mode): all the data allocation are thus directed to NVDIMM memory. Since no error message are emitted from the vmem library, we are assured all allocated memory is in NVRAM. We do not have any error message when using *vmem* library, which means that we are able to allocate memory in NVRAM.

5.2   Fine-Grain OpenMP Memory Allocation

An previous analysis [3] of the LULESH benchmark has already determined the relevant data to be placed in high bandwidth memory bank. The purpose of this work was to detect which functions are bandwidth bound. Application performance can thus be improved if data operated in these functions are placed in memory banks with a higher bandwidth. This analysis demonstrated that some functions are sensitive to bandwidth, such as *EvalEOSForElems*, *AllocateGradients* and *CalcForceNodes*. We thus placed all the data relative to these function in omp_high_bw_mem_space (*i.e.* MCDRAM here) while the other data are placed in omp_default_mem_space (*i.e.* DRAM memory).

The objective of this experiment is to illustrate the benefit of fine-grain management for data allocation: i.e., choose in which memory bank to allocate

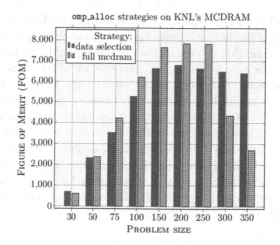

Fig. 4. Fine-grain data allocation management in MCDRAM

through the `omp_alloc` function. Figure 4 presents the results of this approach (*data selection*) compared to allocating everything inside the MCDRAM (*full mcdram*). For this experiment, we change the number of iterations performed to 250 from the previous experiment while still varying the problem size. We can observe that allocating all data in MCDRAM is generally about 10% better between problem sizes of 75 and 250. Performance is about 50% less that the data selection method beyond problem sizes of 250. Below a problem size of 75, then are about the same. Performance decreases beyond and are worse than standard allocation model. These results show that selecting MCDRAM may suffer a bit in performance at small scale, it may be significantly important at large scale, where many HPC applications run. For all the tested configurations, we observe no performance decrease. However, performance seems to be bound to 6500.

In conclusion, as previously stated in several papers like [5], we show that allocating all data in MCDRAM memory might not be the most relevant choice. Indeed, when data do not fit inside this high bandwidth memory bank, application performance is deteriorated, even more than without the use of MCDRAM. From this experiment, we aim to warn developers about data allocation. OpenMP offers ways to allocate easily, in a portable way, data in various memory banks. However, the strategy to select which data to move from one memory bank to another is still in charge of the developers. Currently, no runtime mechanism to automatically move data from memory banks exists.

5.3 Portabilty Across Hardware Platforms

The design of OpenMP memory-management constructs enables portability of applications whatever the available memory types on the target hardware. With the help of the *fallback* trait, data can be allocated in a default memory space (default_mem_fb) if the specified one does not exist. However, an application can also terminate if the fallback property is set to abort_fb. We propose here an experiment that highlights the portability of our OpenMP memory-management implementation. For this purpose, we ran the LULESH benchmark with the fine-grain data allocation strategy as sketched in the previous section (selected functions allocated in the high bandwidth memory space while the other ones target a default allocator). We executed it on several platforms, without any code modification. The selected machines are the ones composed of AMD EPYC, Intel Skylake and Intel KNL processors previously described in Sect. 5. All the runs were performed with 48 threads, and we fix the size problem to 350 for 100 iteration. We set the fallback trait to default_mem_fb to forward data allocation to DRAM memory space if high bandwidth memory is not found. Results are gathered in Table 1.

Table 1. FOM results

System	AMD ROME	Intel Skylake	Intel KNL
FOM (z/s)	4834.99	4416.18	5397.94
Time (s)	890	970	790

The execution on KNL achieve better performance than the two other machines. Indeed, as KNL platform benefits from MCDRAM, some selected data allocation are directed to high bandwidth memory based on OpenMP constructs. However, the two others do not have the MCDRAM memory type, so all data allocations are forwarded to classical DRAM memory without any application cancellation. We conclude that we are able to ensure portability with OpenMP memory management constructs. The main advantage of this approach is to achieve this result without any significant modification to the application, and maintain portability.

6   Conclusion and Future Work

This paper presents our experiences with the OpenMP memory management constructs at the application-level and the runtime-level. From the application side, developers should integrate data allocation calls with a standard like OpenMP, to provide portability. Through the LULESH benchmark, we have illustrated that these new constructs are easy to integrate. However, C++ STL objects users have to change the default allocator and implement a new one which encapsulates OpenMP function calls. We also have implemented these constructs into the OpenMP runtime of the MPC framework. While we do not support all the specification yet, we have implemented the major basic blocks into an OpenMP runtime system targeting various memory levels (DDR, MCDRAM and NVDIMM). For this purpose, we detail our implementation from hardware detection to data allocation process.

Our results show that this implementation is feasible and that there are advantages that provide performance improvements for user applications. We illustrate that it is easy to make portable applications with slight modifications. Our implementation is able to allocate data in default, high bandwidth and large capacity memory spaces. Our experiments also show that data allocations should be performed with care: the best strategy is not always to allocate all data in the fastest memory.

As a future work, we plan to support all the features provided by the specification, especially remaining traits. We also plan to work on coupling the OpenMP memory management constructs with the `affinity` clause. Since the last version of the OpenMP, 5.0, the specification introduces a new `affinity` clause in `task` directives to give some hints at scheduling time in order to enhance data locality. This clause has been already implemented and evaluated by others [29]. Information from allocators will be needed from the runtime for the affinity clause. Indeed, this information can assist the task scheduler to make smarter decisions about affinity. In addition of that, it has a low memory footprint to keep this information and can significantly improve application performance. Thus we plan to evaluate this coupling to enhance the task scheduler.

Acknowledgments. This work was performed under the Exascale Computing Research collaboration, with the support of CEA, Intel and UVSQ.

References

1. Augonnet, C., Thibault, S., Namyst, R., Wacrenier, P.A.: StarPU: a unified platform for task scheduling on heterogeneous multicore architectures. Concurr. Comput.: Pract. Exp. **23**(2), 187–198 (2011). https://hal.inria.fr/inria-00550877
2. Bhandari, K., Chakrabarti, D.R., Boehm, H.J.: Makalu: fast recoverable allocation of non-volatile memory. ACM SIGPLAN Not. **51**(10), 677–694 (2016)
3. Brunie, H., Jaeger, J., Carribault, P., Barthou, D.: Profile-guided scope-based data allocation method. In: MEMSYS 2018 - International Symposium on Memory Systems. Alexandria, United States (October 2018). https://hal.inria.fr/hal-01897917
4. Bueno, J., et al.: Productive programming of GPU clusters with OmpSs. In: 2012 IEEE 26th International Parallel and Distributed Processing Symposium, pp. 557–568 (2012)
5. Butcher, N., Olivier, S.L., Berry, J., Hammond, S.D., Kogge, P.M.: Optimizing for KNL usage modes when data doesn't fit in MCDRAM. In: Proceedings of the 47th International Conference on Parallel Processing, ICPP 2018. Association for Computing Machinery, New York (2018). https://doi.org/10.1145/3225058.3225116
6. Cantalupo, C., Venkatesan, V., Hammond, J., Czurlyo, K., Hammond, S.D.: memkind: an extensible heap memory manager for heterogeneous memory platforms and mixed memory policies. Tech. rep., Sandia National Lab (SNL-NM), Albuquerque, NM (United States) (2015)
7. Carribault, P., Pérache, M., Jourdren, H.: Enabling low-overhead hybrid MPI/OpenMP parallelism with MPC. In: Sato, M., Hanawa, T., Müller, M.S., Chapman, B.M., de Supinski, B.R. (eds.) IWOMP 2010. LNCS, vol. 6132, pp. 1–14. Springer, Heidelberg (2010). https://doi.org/10.1007/978-3-642-13217-9_1

8. Chandrasekar, K., Ni, X., Kale, L.V.: A memory heterogeneity-aware runtime system for bandwidth-sensitive HPC applications. In: 2017 IEEE International Parallel and Distributed Processing Symposium Workshops (IPDPSW), pp. 1293–1300 (May 2017)

9. Demeshko, I., Salinger, A.G., Spotz, W.F., Tezaur, I.K., Guba, O., Heroux, M.A.: Towards performance-portability of the Albany finite element analysis code using the Kokkos library of Trilinos. Tech. rep., Sandia National Lab. (SNL-NM), Albuquerque, NM (United States); Sandia (2016)

10. DeVito, Z., et al.: Liszt: a domain specific language for building portable mesh-based PDE solvers. In: Proceedings of 2011 International Conference for High Performance Computing, Networking, Storage and Analysis, SC 2011. Association for Computing Machinery, New York (2011). https://doi.org/10.1145/2063384.2063396

11. Edwards, H.C., Sunderland, D.: Kokkos array performance-portable manycore programming model. In: Proceedings of the 2012 International Workshop on Programming Models and Applications for Multicores and Manycores, PMAM 2012, pp. 1–10. Association for Computing Machinery, New York (2012). https://doi.org/10.1145/2141702.2141703

12. Gautier, T., Ferreira Lima, J.V., Maillard, N., Raffin, B.: XKaapi: a runtime system for data-flow task programming on heterogeneous architectures. In: 27th IEEE International Parallel & Distributed Processing Symposium (IPDPS), Boston, Massachusetts, United States (May 2013). https://hal.inria.fr/hal-00799904

13. Goglin, B.: Exposing the locality of heterogeneous memory architectures to HPC applications. In: Proceedings of the Second International Symposium on Memory Systems, MEMSYS 2016, p. 30–39. Association for Computing Machinery, New York (2016). https://doi.org/10.1145/2989081.2989115

14. Goglin, B., Rubio Proaño, A.: Opportunities for partitioning non-volatile memory DIMMs between co-scheduled Jobs on HPC Nodes. In: Euro-Par 2019: Parallel Processing Workshops, Göttingen, Germany (August 2019). https://hal.inria.fr/hal-02173336

15. Huang, H.F., Jiang, T.: Design and implementation of flash based NVDIMM. In: 2014 IEEE Non-Volatile Memory Systems and Applications Symposium (NVMSA), pp. 1–6. IEEE (2014)

16. Iwabuchi, K., Lebanoff, L., Gokhale, M., Pearce, R.: Metall: a persistent memory allocator enabling graph processing. In: 2019 IEEE/ACM 9th Workshop on Irregular Applications: Architectures and Algorithms (IA3), pp. 39–44. IEEE (2019)

17. Karlin, I., Keasler, J., Neely, R.: Lulesh 2.0 updates and changes. Tech. Rep. LLNL-TR-641973 (August 2013)

18. Kayraklioglu, E., Chang, W., El-Ghazawi, T.: Comparative performance and optimization of chapel in modern manycore architectures. In: 2017 IEEE International Parallel and Distributed Processing Symposium Workshops (IPDPSW), pp. 1105–1114 (May 2017)

19. Kirk, R.O., Mudalige, G.R., Reguly, I.Z., Wright, S.A., Martineau, M.J., Jarvis, S.A.: Achieving performance portability for a heat conduction solver mini-application on modern multi-core systems. In: 2017 IEEE International Conference on Cluster Computing (CLUSTER), pp. 834–841 (September 2017)

20. LLVM Foundation: LLVM Compiler Infrastructure, version 10.0.0 (2020). https://llvm.org/releases/download.html#10.0.0

21. Nagasaka, Y., Matsuoka, S., Azad, A., Buluç, A.: High-performance sparse matrix-matrix products on intel KNL and multicore architectures. In: Proceedings of the 47th International Conference on Parallel Processing Companion, ICPP 2018. Association for Computing Machinery, New York (2018). https://doi.org/10.1145/3229710.3229720

22. OpenMP Architecture Review Board: OpenMP application program interface version 5.0 (2018). https://www.openmp.org/wp-content/uploads/OpenMP-API-Specification-5.0.pdf

23. Pérache, M., Jourdren, H., Namyst, R.: MPC: a unified parallel runtime for clusters of NUMA machines. In: Luque, E., Margalef, T., Benítez, D. (eds.) Euro-Par 2008. LNCS, vol. 5168, pp. 78–88. Springer, Heidelberg (2008). https://doi.org/10.1007/978-3-540-85451-7_9

24. Reguly, I.Z., Mudalige, G.R., Giles, M.B.: Beyond 16GB: out-of-core stencil computations. In: Proceedings of the Workshop on Memory Centric Programming for HPC, MCHPC 2017, pp. 20–29. Association for Computing Machinery, New York (2017). https://doi.org/10.1145/3145617.3145619

25. Schwalb, D., Berning, T., Faust, M., Dreseler, M., Plattner, H.: nvm malloc: memory allocation for NVRAM. ADMS@ VLDB 15, 61–72 (2015)

26. Sodani, A., et al.: Knights landing: second-generation Intel Xeon phi product. IEEE Micro 36(2), 34–46 (2016)

27. Standard C++ Foundation: ISO International Standard ISO/IEC 14882:2017(E) - Programming Language C++ (2017). https://isocpp.org/std/the-standard

28. Valat, S., Pérache, M., Jalby, W.: Introducing kernel-level page reuse for high performance computing. In: Proceedings of the ACM SIGPLAN Workshop on Memory Systems Performance and Correctness, MSPC 2013. Association for Computing Machinery, New York (2013). https://doi.org/10.1145/2492408.2492414

29. Virouleau, P., Roussel, A., Broquedis, F., Gautier, T., Rastello, F., Gratien, J.-M.: Description, implementation and evaluation of an affinity clause for task directives. In: Maruyama, N., de Supinski, B.R., Wahib, M. (eds.) IWOMP 2016. LNCS, vol. 9903, pp. 61–73. Springer, Cham (2016). https://doi.org/10.1007/978-3-319-45550-1_5

30. Yoshida, T.: Fujitsu high performance CPU for the post-k computer. In: Hot Chips 30th Symposium (HCS) (August 2018)

A Study of Memory Anomalies
in OpenMP Applications

Lechen Yu[1(✉)], Joachim Protze[2], Oscar Hernandez[3], and Vivek Sarkar[1]

[1] Georgia Institute of Technology, Atlanta, GA, USA
{lechen.yu,vsarkar}@gatech.edu
[2] RWTH Aachen University, Aachen, Germany
protze@itc.rwth-aachen.de
[3] Oak Ridge National Laboratory, Oak Ridge, TN, USA
oscar@ornl.gov

Abstract. Incorrect usage of OpenMP constructs may cause different kinds of defects in OpenMP applications. Most of the existing work focuses on concurrency bugs such as data races and deadlocks, since concurrency bugs are difficult to detect and debug. In this paper, we discuss an under-examined defect in OpenMP applications: memory anomalies. These occur when the application issues illegal memory accesses that may result in a non-deterministic result or even a program crash. Based on the latest OpenMP 5.0 specification, we analyze some OpenMP usage errors that may lead to memory anomalies. Then we illustrate three kinds of memory anomalies: use of uninitialized memory (UUM), use of stale data (USD), and use after free (UAF). While all three anomalies can occur in sequential programs, their manifestations in parallel OpenMP programs can be different, and debugging such anomalies in the context of parallel programs also imposes an additional complexity relative to sequential programs. To measure the effectiveness of memory anomaly detectors on OpenMP applications, we have evaluated three state-of-the-art tools with a group of micro-benchmarks. These micro-benchmarks are either selected from the DRACC benchmark suite or constructed from our own experience. The evaluation result shows that none of these tools can currently handle all three kinds of memory anomalies.

Keywords: Memory anomalies · OpenMP · Tools

1 Introduction

OpenMP is the de facto standard for on-node parallel programming in HPC. It provides a unified execution model for parallel applications written in C/C++ and Fortran. OpenMP integrates multiple parallel paradigms in its execution model, including task parallelism, single program multiple data (SPMD), and heterogeneous parallelism. Each parallel paradigm is implemented by a set of high-level constructs, and programmers can mix these paradigms in a single

© The Author(s) 2020
K. Milfeld et al. (Eds.): IWOMP 2020, LNCS 12295, pp. 328–342, 2020.
https://doi.org/10.1007/978-3-030-58144-2_21

OpenMP application. The unified execution model can help programmers fully utilize computing resources in a single mainstream programming system.

The unified execution model brings about high expressibility, but it also increases the complexity of OpenMP. According to Fig. 1, every time a new paradigm is introduced into OpenMP, the size of the specification increases significantly, e.g., when task parallelism was added in OpenMP 3.0, and heterogeneous parallelism was added in OpenMP 4.0 and 4.5). The latest OpenMP 5.0 [20] specification is now already larger than 600 pages. Correctly understanding the semantics of OpenMP constructs becomes challenging even for experienced programmers, which makes OpenMP applications error-prone. There has been a large amount of prior work related to the correctness of OpenMP applications, including tools [3–5,7,11,16,21,24,26], benchmarks [1,9,12], and empirical studies [13,14,17]. Most of this past work focuses on concurrency bugs such as data races, deadlocks, and atomicity violations, since debugging concurrency bugs are notoriously difficult for programmers. However, other types of bugs may also be manifest at runtime, for example, memory anomalies [2]. To the best of our knowledge, there has been no comprehensive study thus far to analyze memory anomalies in OpenMP applications.

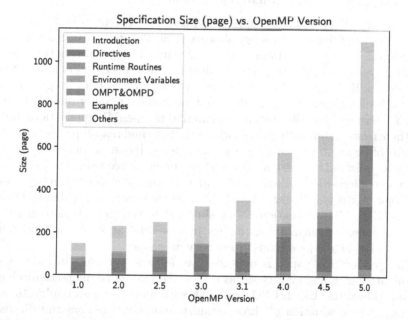

Fig. 1. A comparison among the size of OpenMP specifications: OpenMP 1.0 and 2.0 have separate documents for Fortran and C/C++, so we show the accumulated number of pages for each section. Starting from OpenMP 4.0, the *examples* appendix became a standalone document; for comparison we include the *OpenMP examples* document into the page count.

Since C/C++ delegates the responsibility of memory management to programmers, memory anomaly is a common problem in C/C++ applications. It happens when the program issues memory operations to certain memory regions that are not ready for memory access (e.g., freed or uninitialized memory locations). Memory anomalies can be further classified into sub-categories according to their runtime behavior, such as the use of uninitialized memory (UUM), use of stale data (USD), and use after free (UAF). For C/C++ applications, memory anomalies have been well-studied, and several dynamic detectors are available. Prior work refers to memory anomalies also as memory vulnerabilities and memory errors, and all these terms are used alternatively for the same group of defects.

In this paper, we investigate the impact of memory anomalies on OpenMP programs. We have conducted a study of memory anomalies in OpenMP applications, guided by the following research questions:

- **RQ1 (Bug patterns):** What are the common bug patterns of memory anomalies in OpenMP? What are the root causes of these memory anomalies?
- **RQ2 (Bugfix):** How to fix memory anomalies in an OpenMP application?
- **RQ3 (Tool effectiveness):** What is the effectiveness of state-of-art memory anomaly detectors on OpenMP applications?

To answer RQ1–RQ3, we have examined the semantics of OpenMP constructs that are related to memory allocation/deallocation. We found that memory anomalies may result from incorrect settings of the data-sharing attribute and map-type. These two properties indicate a variable's visibility among threads and devices. If these two properties are not explicitly set up by programmers, OpenMP will apply a complex rule-based mechanism to determine them at runtime. To illustrate probable memory anomalies in OpenMP applications and analyze their relationship with data-sharing attribute and map-type, we constructed a group of benchmarks with memory anomalies, based on our own experience as well as collected memory anomalies from open-source benchmarks, We leveraged these micro-benchmarks to evaluated three state-of-art memory anomaly detectors: AddressSanitizer (ASan) [22], MemorySanitizer (MSan) [23], and Valgrind [18]. The evaluation result shows that the three tools can precisely detect a subset of memory anomalies in OpenMP applications, and none of them can tackle all three kinds of memory anomalies.

The rest of this paper is organized as follows. Section 2 introduces data-sharing attributes and map-types, as well as the rule-based inference mechanism. Section 3 illustrates UUM, USD, and UAF with some buggy examples. In Sect. 4, we present an evaluation of three memory anomaly detectors and discuss the evaluation results. We summarize related work in Sect. 5, and finally, in Sect. 6, we conclude and mention possible directions for future work.

2   OpenMP's Data-Sharing Attribute and Map-Type

In this section, we outline the data-sharing attribute and map-type. These two properties are commonly used in OpenMP to specify variables' visibility. Due

to their effect on memory access, incorrect settings of data-sharing attribute
or map-type may result in unexpected behavior, which is the major source of
memory anomalies in OpenMP applications.

2.1 Semantics

According to the OpenMP specification [20], an OpenMP application starts execution on the host (CPU) and may offload computations and data to other
target devices (accelerators). Each device (host and target devices) has a group
of threads and an independent memory space, and threads are not migratable
among devices. By invoking corresponding OpenMP constructs, an OpenMP
application can utilize any supported parallel paradigm (tasking constructs for
task parallelism, parallel and worksharing constructs for SPMD, target constructs for heterogeneous parallelism). Multiple paradigms may be cooperatively
applied in a single OpenMP application, to separate the workload into available
computing resources properly.

OpenMP uses the data-sharing attribute to define the intra-device visibility
of allocated variables. The data-sharing attribute allows two types of visibility:
private and *shared*. Memory accesses to a shared variable operate on the variable's original memory region, and proper synchronization needs to be carried
out to avoid race conditions. For a private variable, each (implicit or explicit)
task creates a local instance of the variable. Memory accesses in a particular
thread are performed on the local instance, which is not visible to other threads.
In addition, there are two variants of the private visibility: *first-private* and *last-
private*. The former declares the initialization of the local instance by the original
variable. The latter denotes that the original variable is to be updated by the
last assigned value.

When it comes to heterogeneous parallelism, a variable may have multiple
storages on different devices. Since a device's memory space may not be visible
to threads on other devices, programmers need to specify data transfers through
map-types to synchronize these independent storages. For variables accessed by
target regions (code sections executing on the target device), their map-types
needs to be correctly set up to avoid potential memory anomalies. In total, there
are five available options:

- *to*: copy the variable from host to target device
- *alloc*: allocate an uninitialized storage on the target
- *from*: copy the variable from the target device to host
- *delete/release*: deallocate the storage on the target device
- *tofrom*: a combination of 'to' and 'from'.

During the execution of an OpenMP application, the underlying OpenMP runtime automatically issues necessary data transfers according to the specified
map-types. For map-type 'to' and 'alloc', the corresponding data transfer is carried out before the target region, while for map-type 'from', 'delete', and 'release',
the data transfer is inserted at the end of the target region.

2.2 Determining Data-Sharing Attribute and Map-Type

According to the OpenMP specification, specifying the data-sharing attribute for every variable is not mandatory. OpenMP defines a set of inference rules to determine the data-sharing attribute at runtime, which helps reduce the programming effort. Table 1 lists all inference rules for the data-sharing attribute. The first column describes these rules' preconditions. For a particular variable, the data-sharing attribute is determined by the variable type, enclosing construct, and the default value. The second and third columns show each rule's type and output, where PRE, EXP, and IMP stand for 'predetermined', 'explicit', and 'implicit', respectively.

For certain OpenMP constructs, the specification defines a number of predetermined rules for associated data sharing attributes. Most of these rules cannot be overwritten by programmer-specified data-sharing attributes[1]. If no predetermined rules match and the data-sharing attribute is unspecified in the program, OpenMP turns to implicit rules. The output of implicit rules depends on the default data-sharing attribute. When no `default` clauses present in an OpenMP application, OpenMP sets the default data-sharing attribute to 'shared' for a `parallel` construct, and 'first-private' for a tasking and target constructs.

The `reduction` clause is a special case in terms of data-sharing attributes. For each variable appearing in a `reduction` clause, the OpenMP implementation needs to allocate a local instance for each task. At the end of the scope, the runtime combines the original value with each local instance's final value. Therefore, the data-sharing semantics of the `reduction` clause is a combination of first-private and last-private.

OpenMP also defines inference rules for map-type. Compared to the data-sharing attribute, map-type's inference rules are much more straightforward. For a variable accessed by a target region and having no explicit map-type: a) If the variable is a scalar, then it is not mapped, and its data-sharing attribute is set to 'first-private' by the predetermined inference rule; b) Otherwise, it is mapped to the target device with map-type 'tofrom'.

3 Memory Anomalies in OpenMP Applications

To answer the three research questions proposed in Sect. 1, we have conducted a study on OpenMP to find out probable memory anomalies. By scrutinizing the semantics of OpenMP constructs, we found that incorrect OpenMP usage may lead to three kinds of memory anomalies: use of uninitialized memory (UUM), use after free (UAF), and use of stale data (USD). We devised a few buggy examples from our own experiences as well as collected defects in open-source benchmarks. In this section, we illustrate these examples and talk about our findings related to RQ1 and RQ2.

---

[1] Iteration variable is an exception. Its data-sharing attribute can be overwritten to private or last-private, according to the enclosing construct.

Table 1. Inference rules for data-sharing attributes

Precondition		Rule type	Data-sharing attribute
Declared inside a construct		PRE	private
Static class member, objects with dynamic storage duration		PRE	shared
A loop iteration variable in a `for`, `parallel for`, `task loop`, or `distribute` construct		PRE	private
A loop iteration variable in a `simd` or `loop` construct		PRE	last-private
Listed in a `reduction` clause		EXP	private
Listed in a data-sharing attribute clause (programmer-specified data-sharing attribute)		EXP	Determined by the clause
An unmapped variable in a `target` construct		IMP	first-private
`default` clause is not present	In a `parallel` construct	IMP	shared
	In a `task`, `taskloop`, `target`, `target enter data`, `target exit data`, `target update` construct	IMP	first-private
`default` clause is present	In a `parallel` and `teams` construct	IMP	Determined by `default` clause
	In a `task`, `taskloop`, `target`, `target enter data`, `target exit data`, `target update` construct	IMP	

3.1 Use of Uninitialized Memory

Programmers may specify incorrect data-sharing attributes in an OpenMP application. Typically these incorrect settings will introduce bugs. If a private variable is set to be shared, then a data race may occur. If a shared variable is set to private, then subsequent memory accesses to this variable may become UUMs.

In Fig. 2, we present a few examples of UUMs. The first UUM is in line 8, and its root cause is the incorrect data-sharing attribute set in line 5. This error can be fixed by setting the data-sharing attribute to 'shared', removing the `private` clause, or using a sum `reduction`.

Incorrect map-type is another source of UUMs. We show an example in Fig. 3. In line 10, the map-type is set to 'alloc', so that a storage for array b is allocated but not initialized on the target device. The subsequent read in line 17 is a UUM since b is uninitialized. To fix this error, b's map-type should be set to 'to' or 'tofrom'.

In some cases, OpenMP constructs are not the root cause of memory anomalies, but they make memory anomaly detection difficult, such as the two UUMs in Fig. 2 (in line 23 and 29). These two UUMs are associated with OpenMP constructs (`reduction` clause and `atomic` construct). The memory anomaly detector must take OpenMP constructs into account, and correctly model their semantics. Otherwise, the memory anomaly detector may cause false alarms or miss some bugs when examining an OpenMP application.

3.2 Use After Free

Figure 4a displays an example of UAF. The outer task spawns the inner task in line 6, and the inner task tries to access a in line 9 and 10. However, the generating task does not suspend after creating the inner task. It may terminate

```
1   int counter = 0;
2
3   // the local instance of counter in the parallel-for
4   // loop is uninitialized
5   #pragma omp parallel for private(counter)
6   for (int i=0; i<N; i++){
7       #pragma omp atomic update
8       counter++;
9   }
10
11  // sum is uninitialized
12  int sum;
13  int SIZE = 512;
14  int a[SIZE];
15
16  // initialize array a
17  for (int i = 0; i < SIZE; i++) {
18      a[i] = 1;
19  }
20
21  #pragma omp parallel for reduction(+:sum)
22  for(int i = 0; i < SIZE; i++) {
23      sum+=a[i];
24  }
25
26  #pragma omp parallel for
27  for(int i = 0; i < SIZE; i++) {
28      #pragma omp atomic
29      sum+=a[i];
30  }
```

Fig. 2. UUMs in `parallel for` constructs

before the inner task issues the two read operations. So that these two reads become UAF since a has been deallocated. To avoid such errors, programmers need to understand a variable's lifetime correctly, and pay special attention to shared variables.

3.3   Use of Stale Data

USDs are defined against the dataflow. For example, Cilk proposed a notion *serial elision* that a parallel application's dataflow needs to be consistent with its sequential version [10]. Based on the serial elision property, a USD happens when a Cilk application generates an inconsistent dataflow with the sequential version. However, in OpenMP applications, the serial elision property may not hold since the specification does not enforce it.

```
1    #define N 5000
2
3    int a[N], b[N*N], c[N];
4
5    init(a, b, c);
6
7    // b's map-type should be "to"
8    #pragma omp target            \
9       map(to:a[0:N])             \
10       map(alloc:b[0:N*N])        \
11       map(tofrom:c[0:N])
12   {
13      #pragma omp teams distribute
14      #pragma omp parallel for
15      for(int i=0; i<N; i++)
16         for(int j=0; j<N; j++)
17            c[i]+=b[j+i*N]*a[j];
18   }
```

Fig. 3. A UUM resulting from incorrect map-type

We redefine USDs in OpenMP applications with regard to the uncertainty of unified memory. An OpenMP implementation may activate unified memory when executing target regions. By the `requires(unified_shared_memory)` directive, programmers can notify the OpenMP implementation that unified memory is indispensable for the correctness of the results. Otherwise, the OpenMP implementation assumes that the application always generates correct and consistent results regardless of unified memory.

To distinguish the executions with and without unified memory, we refer to the execution with unified memory enabled as the *unified memory version*, and the execution without unified memory as the *original version*. USDs are defined against these two versions:

Definition 1 (Use of Stale Data). *For an OpenMP application without* require *directives, A USD happens if the original version has inconsistent dataflow with the unified memory version.*

Similar to UUMs, USDs may also arise from incorrect data-sharing rules and map-types. Figure 4b shows an example of USD. For the unified memory version, map clauses are optional since the effect of memory accesses are observable to any devices. So that the print statement in line 18 returns the value written by line 16. For the original version, each device's memory space is isolated. Because array a's map-type is set to 'to' in line 10, the value of array a on the target device is not copied back to the host. Thus the print statement returns the initial value of a[0], which is inconsistent with the unified memory version. To fix this USD, array a's map-type should be set to 'from' or 'tofrom'.

```
1  #pragma omp parallel
2  #pragma omp single
3  #pragma omp task
4  {
5    int a = 10;
6    #pragma omp task shared(a)
7    {
8      // a may be released
9      if (a > 0)
10       printf(a);
11   }
12 }
```

(a) UAF in a task construct

```
1  #define N 5000
2
3  int a[N], b[N];
4
5  init(a, b);
6
7  // a's map-type should be 'from'
8  // or 'tofrom'
9  #pragma omp target    \
10   map(to: a[0:N])      \
11   map(to: b[0:N])
12 {
13   #pragma omp teams distribute
14   #pragma omp parallel for
15   for (int i=0; i<N; i++)
16     a[i] = b[i] + b[i];
17 }
18 print(a[0]);
```

(b) USD in a target construct

Fig. 4. UAF and USD

4   Evaluation of Memory Anomaly Detectors

In this section, we try to answer RQ3. We present the evaluation of three state-of-the-art memory anomaly detectors. All experiments were performed on a compute node of CLAIX cluster running CentOS 7, and all benchmarks are compiled with LLVM 10.0.

4.1   Memory Anomaly Detectors and Benchmarks

We evaluated three dynamic memory anomaly detectors and compared their effectiveness. All three tools are commonly used when debugging C/C++ applications. ASan is a dynamic analysis tool developed by Google. It can detect a variety of memory anomalies related to pointer dereference (e.g., UAF, buffer overflow). MSan is another dynamic detector from Google. Is uses the same infrastructure as ASan, but is designed to detect UUMs. Valgrind is a debugging and profiling tool suite running on top of a dynamic instrumentation framework. The memcheck tool is capable of detecting memory anomalies and memory leaks. In our evaluation, we used ASan and MSan implemented in LLVM 10.0, and the memcheck tool in Valgrind 3.14.0.

To measure the effectiveness of the three detectors, we constructed a benchmark suite consisting of 22 small OpenMP applications. 15 benchmarks were chosen from DRACC [1] and each of them contains a memory anomaly caused by incorrect data transfer. The remaining seven benchmarks are created by ourselves. Since in DRACC there exist no memory anomalies resulting from the data-sharing attribute, we devised the seven benchmarks based on our experience on OpenMP to improve the benchmark suite's coverage[2].

4.2 Evaluation Result

Table 2 lists the evaluation result on the 15 DRACC benchmarks. Columns 1–2 record the benchmark name and the error type. Columns 3–5 indicate the result of memory anomaly detection. Here we apply the same group of notions used in [12] and [5], where TP denotes that the tool correctly reports the error, and FN denotes the tool misses the known error.

Out of the 15 known errors, ASan and MSan successfully reported 6 and 5 memory anomalies. ASan detected all buffer overflows and MSan pinpointed all UUMs. These results match our expectation because their detection algorithms are customized for a specific set of memory anomalies. Valgrind detected 9 out of 15 memory anomalies, which outperforms the other two detectors. However, Valgrind's bug report is quite noisy. It reported a large number of memory anomalies in system libraries, making the bug report difficult to understand. On the other hand, all three detectors missed USDs. To detect USDs, memory anomaly detectors need to model an OpenMP applications' dataflow correctly. Currently, none of the three detectors takes the dataflow into account.

Table 3 lists the evaluation result on the remaining seven benchmarks. Similar to Table 2, Valgrind outperforms ASan and MSan on the number of detected errors. In addition, ASan failed to detect a UAF, and MSan missed two UUMs in DAS_OMP_003 and DAS_OMP_005. These three memory anomalies are expected to be detected. One possible reason is that ASan and MSan handle some OpenMP constructs improperly, since both benchmarks use the `atomic` construct to protect memory accesses to an uninitialized variable.

4.3 Lesson Learned

The evaluation result indicates that none of the three tools can handle all memory anomalies. Because different kinds of memory anomalies have distinct runtime behavior, it is challenging for a single detector to capture all memory anomalies. To reduce the possibility of missing memory anomalies, programmers could apply multiple detectors simultaneously when debugging an OpenMP application.

5   Related Work

In this section, we relate our study on OpenMP to representative work in memory anomaly detection and bug studies.

---

[2] https://github.com/FuriousBerserker/MemoryAnomalyBench.

Table 2. Evaluation result on DRACC benchmarks

Benchmark	Memory anomaly	Effectiveness		
		ASan	MSan	Valgrind
DRACC_OMP_022	UUM	FN	TP	FN
DRACC_OMP_023	Buffer overflow	TP	FN	TP
DRACC_OMP_024	UUM	FN	TP	FN
DRACC_OMP_025	Buffer overflow	TP	FN	TP
DRACC_OMP_026	USD	FN	FN	FN
DRACC_OMP_027	USD	FN	FN	FN
DRACC_OMP_028	Buffer overflow	TP	FN	TP
DRACC_OMP_029	Buffer overflow	TP	FN	TP
DRACC_OMP_030	Buffer overflow	TP	FN	TP
DRACC_OMP_031	Buffer overflow	TP	FN	TP
DRACC_OMP_032	USD	FN	FN	FN
DRACC_OMP_033	USD	FN	FN	FN
DRACC_OMP_049	UUM	FN	TP	TP
DRACC_OMP_050	UUM	FN	TP	TP
DRACC_OMP_051	UUM	FN	TP	TP
Overall		6/15	5/15	9/15

Table 3. Evaluation result on additional benchmarks

Benchmark	Memory anomaly	Effectiveness		
		ASan	MSan	Valgrind
DSA_OMP_001	UUM	FN	TP	TP
DSA_OMP_002	UUM	FN	TP	TP
DSA_OMP_003	UUM	FN	FN	TP
DSA_OMP_004	UUM	FN	TP	TP
DSA_OMP_005	UUM	FN	FN	TP
DSA_OMP_006	UAF	FN	TP	FN
DSA_OMP_007	USD	FN	FN	FN
Overall		0/7	4/7	5/7

5.1   Memory Anomaly Detection

Memory anomalies in C/C++ applications have been comprehensively studied in the past decades, and a large number of memory anomaly detectors have been proposed [6,8,18,22,23]. These detectors monitor the execution of a C/C++ application, recording relevant metadata for each memory locations (e.g., status, base address, bound). When a memory location is accessed, the tools examine associated metadata to check the legality of the memory access. These detectors can pinpoint memory anomalies at runtime, with acceptable overhead to the program execution. When applied to OpenMP applications, these detectors may generate false positives and false negatives due to the misunderstanding of OpenMP constructs.

To the best of our knowledge, currently, there exists no memory anomaly detector designed for OpenMP applications. Since manually detecting memory anomalies is time-consuming, memory anomaly detectors are indispensable when testing an OpenMP application. Our study provides an overview of memory anomalies in OpenMP applications, which can serve as guidance for tool developers in future development.

5.2   Bug Studies

There have been several bug studies on OpenMP. Münchhalfen et al. conducted a study on OpenMP 4.0 and proposed a classification of OpenMP usage errors [17]. The study comprehensively scrutinized the semantics of OpenMP constructs, including tasking and target constructs, illustrating potential incorrect usages and discussing their harmful effects on the program execution. These usage errors are further categorized into *syntactic defects*, *semantic defects*, and *performance defects* according to each error's root cause and runtime behavior. However, this study only covered a subset of memory anomalies (UUM and USD on the accelerator), and did not provide any concrete examples.

By analyzing data races in real-world OpenMP applications, Liao et al. created DataRaceBench, a micro-benchmark suite designed to evaluate the effectiveness of data race detectors [12]. DataRaceBench contains more than 100 micro-benchmarks with and without data races. Through the provided evaluation script, DataRaceBench can automatically calculate the precision, recall, and accuracy of a data race detector. To further improve the OpenMP standard coverage of DataRaceBench, Liao et al. carried out a study on OpenMP 4.5. They classified OpenMP constructs and clauses into three categories, *parallel semantics*, *shared semantics*, and *synchronization semantics*. Each category is summarized as a group of semantics labels. For any uncovered label, a new micro-benchmark is added to DataRaceBench to enhance coverage.

Apart from OpenMP, there also exist bug studies targeting other programming languages. Lu et al. conducted a concurrency bug study on real-world applications [15]. They examined 105 randomly selected real-world concurrency bugs from four open-source server and client applications. Wang et al. conducted a concurrency bug study on Node.js [25]. They collected 57 real bug cases from GitHub and organized them into a benchmark suite. Nong et al. conducted a comparison of five state-of-art memory anomaly detectors [19]. They used 520 C/C++ programs to measure the effectiveness and efficiency of these detectors. The result indicates that the effectiveness of these detectors varies widely due to the applied detection technique, while the performance is similar. Although all three studies are not related to OpenMP, we picked up some analysis methods when carrying out our study.

6 Conclusion

In this paper, we presented a study of memory anomalies that can occur in OpenMP programs. Memory anomalies are common errors in C/C++ applications. For OpenMP applications, memory anomalies may arise if programmers specify erroneous data-sharing attributes or map-types. We have compared the effectiveness of three state-of-the-art memory anomaly detectors. The evaluation results indicate that no single tool can detect all memory anomalies in an OpenMP application.

For future research, we plan to compare the performance of memory anomaly detectors on OpenMP applications. We also plan to extend current tools with new detection algorithms.

Acknowledgment. This research was supported in part by the Exascale Computing Project (17-SC-20-SC), a collaborative effort of the U.S. Department of Energy Office of Science and the National Nuclear Security Administration, in particular its subproject on Scaling OpenMP with LLVM for Exascale performance and portability (SOLLVE). This work has received funding from the European Union's Horizon 2020 research and innovation programme under grant agreement 824080.

References

1. DataRaceOnAccelerator (2019). https://github.com/RWTH-HPC/DRACC
2. Kloeckner, A., Berger, M.: Shared memory and OpenMP (2012). https://cims.nyu.edu/~stadler/hpc17/material/ompLec.pdf. Accessed 15 May 2020
3. Atzeni, S., et al.: Archer: effectively spotting data races in large OpenMP applications. In: 2016 IEEE International Parallel and Distributed Processing Symposium (IPDPS), pp. 53–62. IEEE (2016)
4. Atzeni, S., Gopalakrishnan, G., Rakamaric, Z., Laguna, I., Lee, G.L., Ahn, D.H.: Sword: a bounded memory-overhead detector of OpenMP data races in production runs. In: 2018 IEEE International Parallel and Distributed Processing Symposium (IPDPS), pp. 845–854. IEEE (2018)
5. Bora, U., Das, S., Kureja, P., Joshi, S., Upadrasta, R., Rajopadhye, S.: Llov: a fast static data-race checker for OpenMP programs. arXiv preprint arXiv:1912.12189 (2019)
6. Cai, Y., et al.: Detecting concurrency memory corruption vulnerabilities. In: Proceedings of the 2019 27th ACM Joint Meeting on European Software Engineering Conference and Symposium on the Foundations of Software Engineering, pp. 706–717 (2019)
7. Chatarasi, P., Shirako, J., Kong, M., Sarkar, V.: An extended polyhedral model for SPMD programs and its use in static data race detection. In: Ding, C., Criswell, J., Wu, P. (eds.) LCPC 2016. LNCS, vol. 10136, pp. 106–120. Springer, Cham (2017). https://doi.org/10.1007/978-3-319-52709-3_10
8. Chen, Z., Yan, J., Kan, S., Qian, J., Xue, J.: Detecting memory errors at runtime with source-level instrumentation. In: Proceedings of the 28th ACM SIGSOFT International Symposium on Software Testing and Analysis, pp. 341–351 (2019)

9. Diaz, J.M., Pophale, S., Hernandez, O., Bernholdt, D.E., Chandrasekaran, S.: OpenMP 4.5 validation and verification suite for device offload. In: de Supinski, B.R., Valero-Lara, P., Martorell, X., Mateo Bellido, S., Labarta, J. (eds.) IWOMP 2018. LNCS, vol. 11128, pp. 82–95. Springer, Cham (2018). https://doi.org/10.1007/978-3-319-98521-3_6

10. Frigo, M., Leiserson, C.E., Randall, K.H.: The implementation of the Cilk-5 multithreaded language. In: Proceedings of the ACM SIGPLAN 1998 Conference on Programming Language Design and Implementation, pp. 212–223 (1998)

11. Gu, Y., Mellor-Crummey, J.: Dynamic data race detection for OpenMP programs. In: Proceedings of the International Conference for High Performance Computing, Networking, Storage, and Analysis, p. 61. IEEE Press (2018)

12. Liao, C., Lin, P.H., Asplund, J., Schordan, M., Karlin, I.: DataRaceBench: a benchmark suite for systematic evaluation of data race detection tools. In: Proceedings of the International Conference for High Performance Computing, Networking, Storage and Analysis, pp. 1–14 (2017)

13. Liao, C., Lin, P.-H., Schordan, M., Karlin, I.: A semantics-driven approach to improving DataRaceBench's OpenMP standard coverage. In: de Supinski, B.R., Valero-Lara, P., Martorell, X., Mateo Bellido, S., Labarta, J. (eds.) IWOMP 2018. LNCS, vol. 11128, pp. 189–202. Springer, Cham (2018). https://doi.org/10.1007/978-3-319-98521-3_13

14. Lin, P.H., Liao, C., Schordan, M., Karlin, I.: Exploring regression of data race detection tools using DataRaceBench. In: 2019 IEEE/ACM 3rd International Workshop on Software Correctness for HPC Applications (Correctness), pp. 11–18. IEEE (2019)

15. Lu, S., Park, S., Seo, E., Zhou, Y.: Learning from mistakes: a comprehensive study on real world concurrency bug characteristics. In: Proceedings of the 13th International Conference on Architectural Support for Programming Languages and Operating Systems, pp. 329–339 (2008)

16. Matar, H.S., Unat, D.: Runtime determinacy race detection for OpenMP tasks. In: Aldinucci, M., Padovani, L., Torquati, M. (eds.) Euro-Par 2018. LNCS, vol. 11014, pp. 31–45. Springer, Cham (2018). https://doi.org/10.1007/978-3-319-96983-1_3

17. Münchhalfen, J.F., Hilbrich, T., Protze, J., Terboven, C., Müller, M.S.: Classification of common errors in OpenMP applications. In: DeRose, L., de Supinski, B.R., Olivier, S.L., Chapman, B.M., Müller, M.S. (eds.) IWOMP 2014. LNCS, vol. 8766, pp. 58–72. Springer, Cham (2014). https://doi.org/10.1007/978-3-319-11454-5_5

18. Nethercote, N., Seward, J.: Valgrind: a framework for heavyweight dynamic binary instrumentation. ACM Sigplan Not. 42(6), 89–100 (2007)

19. Nong, Y., Cai, H.: A preliminary study on open-source memory vulnerability detectors. In: 2020 IEEE 27th International Conference on Software Analysis, Evolution and Reengineering (SANER), pp. 557–561. IEEE (2020)

20. OpenMP Architecture Review Board: OpenMP Application Programming Interface 5.0 (2018). https://www.openmp.org/wp-content/uploads/OpenMP-API-Specification-5.0.pdf. Accessed 5 Aug 2019

21. Protze, J., Hahnfeld, J., Ahn, D.H., Schulz, M., Müller, M.S.: OpenMP tools interface: synchronization information for data race detection. In: de Supinski, B.R., Olivier, S.L., Terboven, C., Chapman, B.M., Müller, M.S. (eds.) IWOMP 2017. LNCS, vol. 10468, pp. 249–265. Springer, Cham (2017). https://doi.org/10.1007/978-3-319-65578-9_17

22. Serebryany, K., Bruening, D., Potapenko, A., Vyukov, D.: Addresssanitizer: a fast address sanity checker. In: Presented as Part of the 2012 {USENIX} Annual Technical Conference ({USENIX}{ATC} 2012), pp. 309–318 (2012)

23. Stepanov, E., Serebryany, K.: MemorySanitizer: fast detector of uninitialized memory use in C++. In: 2015 IEEE/ACM International Symposium on Code Generation and Optimization (CGO), pp. 46–55. IEEE (2015)
24. Swain, B., Huang, J.: Towards incremental static race detection in OpenMP programs. In: 2018 IEEE/ACM 2nd International Workshop on Software Correctness for HPC Applications (Correctness), pp. 33–41. IEEE (2018)
25. Wang, J., et al.: A comprehensive study on real world concurrency bugs in Node.js. In: 2017 32nd IEEE/ACM International Conference on Automated Software Engineering (ASE), pp. 520–531. IEEE (2017)
26. Ye, F., Schordan, M., Liao, C., Lin, P.H., Karlin, I., Sarkar, V.: Using polyhedral analysis to verify OpenMP applications are data race free. In: 2018 IEEE/ACM 2nd International Workshop on Software Correctness for HPC Applications (Correctness), pp. 42–50. IEEE (2018)

Author Index

Printed in the United States
By Bookmasters